Virginia Woolf's

MODERNIST PATH

Her Middle Diaries & the Diaries She Read

Barbara Lounsberry

CU00793663

UNIVERSITY PRESS OF FLORIDA

Gainesville/Tallahassee/Tampa/Boca Raton

Pensacola/Orlando/Miami/Jacksonville/Ft. Myers/Sarasota

Permission information can be found on page 256.

This book may be available in an electronic edition.

First cloth printing, 2016
First paperback printing, 2019

24 23 22 21 20 19   6 5 4 3 2 1

LIBRARY OF CONGRESS CATALOGING-IN-PUBLICATION DATA
Names: Lounsberry, Barbara, author.
Title: Virginia Woolf's modernist path : her middle diaries and the diaries she
read / Barbara Lounsberry.
Description: Gainesville : University Press of Florida, 2016. | Includes
bibliographical references and index.
Identifiers: LCCN 2016027491 | ISBN 9780813062952 (cloth)
ISBN 9780813064307 (pbk.)
Subjects: LCSH: Woolf, Virginia, 1882-1941—Diaries. | Novelists,
English—20th century—Diaries.
Classification: LCC PR6045.O72 Z8119 2016 | DDC 828/.91203 [B] —dc23
LC record available at https://lccn.loc.gov/2016027491

The University Press of Florida is the scholarly publishing agency for the State
University System of Florida, comprising Florida A&M University, Florida
Atlantic University, Florida Gulf Coast University, Florida International
University, Florida State University, New College of Florida, University
of Central Florida, University of Florida, University of North Florida,
University of South Florida, and University of West Florida.

UNIVERSITY PRESS OF FLORIDA
2046 NE Waldo Road
Suite 2100
Gainesville, FL 32609
http://upress.ufl.edu

For Sam, the writer, and Madeline, the painter

Contents

Acknowledgments

First thanks go to poet Kathleen Kelly and to editor Shannon McCarthy, who named this volume and whose thoughtful questions led to this project's shape. Novelist and poet Nancy Price also lent her ear and practiced eye to the refinement and polish of the work. My gratitude goes as well to Woolf scholars Panthea Reid and Mark Hussey, who each read two drafts of the book and offered suggestions that strengthened and enriched it immeasurably.

My eternal thanks go as well to those in England directly involved with the editing and publishing of Woolf's luminous diaries. Anne Olivier Bell, the accomplished and witty editor of Woolf's 1915 to 1941 diaries, allowed me to interview her in Sussex regarding her work and graciously served me lunch on the long wood table where much of the editing unfurled. Quentin Bell, before his death, fully and promptly answered all my letter questions regarding his Aunt Virginia and her diaries.

Andrew McNeillie, assistant editor of the 1920 to 1941 diaries, took time from the 2001 Woolf Conference in Wales to recall and reflect on his work.

In England, Sybil Oldfield, the Woolf scholar, kindly gave over a whole Sunday afternoon to take me to Monk's House and to the nearby bridge over the River Ouse. I am indebted as well to Dorothy Sheridan, head of Special Collections at the University of Sussex, for allowing me to work with the Monk's House papers.

Over a score of years, the curators of the Henry W. and Albert A. Berg Collection of English and American Literature in the New York Public Library have also shared their expertise during my hours of work with Woolf's manuscripts. This access was vital. I wish also to thank the International Virginia Woolf Society, whose members are so welcoming of papers and essays.

My gratitude extends as well to many arms of the University of Northern Iowa. The Graduate College and the College of Humanities and Fine Arts provided grants and leaves that allowed this work to grow. Especial thanks go to Rosemary Meany and others in the Rod Library who helped me locate and retrieve many of the obscure diaries Woolf read.

Abbreviations

CR   *The Common Reader.* 2 vols.

D   *The Diary of Virginia Woolf.* Ed. Anne Olivier Bell. 5 vols.

E   *The Essays of Virginia Woolf.* Ed. Andrew McNeillie and Stuart N. Clarke. 6 vols.

L   *The Letters of Virginia Woolf.* Ed. Nigel Nicolson and Joanne Trautmann. 6 vols.

MOB   *Moments of Being.* Ed. Jeanne Schulkind.

PA   *A Passionate Apprentice: The Early Journals, 1897–1909.* Ed. Mitchell A. Leaska.

ROO   *A Room of One's Own*

RN   *Virginia Woolf's Reading Notebooks.* Ed. Brenda Silver.

SF   *The Complete Shorter Fiction of Virginia Woolf.* Ed. Susan Dick

TG   *Three Guineas*

Introduction

A diary is not only a text: it is . . . a way of life, of which the text is merely a trace or by-product.

So says French diary theorist Philippe Lejeune (268). By July 1918, diary-keeping has become a way of life for Virginia Woolf. She started as an early teen, trying to keep a daily journal in a small, brown, leather diary with a lock and key. The year was 1897. Thirty-seven handwritten diary books follow across her days—until four days before her suicide in March 1941. These books are the doorway to her fiction and nonfiction. They also show Woolf to be one of the world's great diarists, in fact, "the Shakespeare of the diary," as diary scholar Anna Jackson dares to suggest (*Diary Poetics* 151).

Woolf's first twelve diary books are strikingly experimental. Not one resembles another.[1] In these first dozen journals (covering ages fourteen through thirty-six), Woolf tries travel diaries, a natural history diary, diaries with titled entries and book-like tables of contents—and even an occasional life diary. This experimental first diary stage leads to the years 1917 and 1918: Woolf's most intensive years of diary-writing. She keeps *two* diaries now, a country diary and a city diary, and writes in *both* diaries on seventeen days. Has any other diarist done this?

In July 1918—as my volume opens—she brings her city diary to the country, a telling move. Within four months the country diary fuses with the city diary, creating the ideal "Country in London" state Woolf first envisioned at age twenty-one in her pivotal 1903 diary. The country, for Woolf, stands for nature, the unconscious, and the female, while the city embodies culture, the conscious mind, and the male (*PA* 177–79). These domains join. A crisis occurs in November 1918 that leads to a new audience and purpose for the diary, and with it the start of Woolf's second stage as a diarist: her mature, spare modernist period, 1918 to 1929. Woolf's own crisis mirrors what Pericles Lewis calls the crisis of *representation* (in both form and content) that defines the modernist period with its multiple, often competing, movements (xviii).

The pared number of entries most clearly marks Woolf's second (modernist) diary stage. Her experimental first diary period, from 1897 to 1918, harbors her greatest number of entries per year. Her tiny first extant diary offers 309 entries across 1897. Her first diary as a professional writer delivers 135 entries through the first five months of 1905 (before it abruptly stops). Her 1917–1918 country diary, the Asheham House natural history diary, contains 143 entries across fourteen months.

For the year 1919, however, Woolf writes just sixty-six diary entries, followed by sixty-three entries in 1920. In September 1920, she records taxing T. S. Eliot "with wilfully concealing his transitions. He said that explanation is unnecessary. If you put it in, you dilute the facts. You should feel these without explanation" (D 2: 67–68). From that date to the end of the year, Woolf toys with elision in the conversations she records. In May 1921, a year for which she writes just fifty-one diary entries, Woolf reports a talk with John Maynard Keynes during which the economist asks her about her second novel, the 1919 Night and Day. "[B]ut don't you see you must put it all in before you can leave out," she explains (D 2: 121). In 1922 she writes just forty-six diary entries; in 1923 (31 entries), 1924 (31), 1925 (32), 1926 (51), 1927 (33), 1928 (30), 1929 (35). In her second diary stage Woolf strips the *periodic diary* down—presses it about as far as it can go and still convey a life. Some might point to busy days to explain the scaled-back number of entries; however, Woolf was busy throughout her professional life. Sparse entries allow her to escape the diary's greatest traps: daily dullness and numbing repetition. Instead, she can explore the fragment, the art of concision, the rhetoric of brevity.

Beyond leanness, Woolf's middle diaries also display the modernist inward turn. Vincent Sherry calls the interior Woolf's "most readily identifiable modernist provenance" (258). In her important March 9, 1920, diary entry, Woolf writes: "In spite of some tremors, I think I shall go on with this diary for the present. I sometimes think that I have worked through the layer of style which suited it—suited the comfortable bright hour after tea; & the thing I've reached now is less pliable" (D 2: 24). Her earth (or geological) tropes—"worked through the layer of style . . . less pliable"—suggest that she now seeks to probe more deeply into herself and her world, that she is ready to address matters less pliable, "comfortable," and "bright."

She tells her September 1923 diary, "I am perhaps encouraged by Proust to search out & identify my feelings, but I have always felt this kind of thing in great

profusion, only not tried to capture it, or perhaps lacked skill & confidence"
(*D* 2: 268). She is growing in both skill and assurance and will increasingly try
to capture interior states. She tries, in fact, a month later when she describes a
night of psychic terror that descends without summons and holds her painfully
in its grip. In September 1926, she records parallel morning anguish: "[T]ossing
me up. I'm unhappy unhappy! Down—God, I wish I were dead" (*D* 3: 110). In
late July 1926, she traces in her diary "a whole nervous breakdown in miniature"
as she tries to understand the workings of "My own Brain" (*D* 3: 103).

Alongside inner feelings and "State[s] of Mind" (*D* 3: 110), Woolf's middle
diary stage exhibits her dodges and feints as she tries to net her soul. In this
book I trace Woolf's development as a diarist from 1918 to 1929 and also reveal
the importance of *others'* diaries to her creative life—something never before
shown . As will be seen, others' diaries particularly encourage Woolf to explore
her soul: Barbellion's famous *Journal of a Disappointed Man*, for instance, read
in April 1920. James Boswell's *Journal of a Tour to Corsica*, read in 1923, endorsed
exploration of the soul, and in June 1924, Woolf reviews Stendhal's early journals. Their passionate focus on the soul likely triggered her willingness that
June, and after, "to cancel that vow against soul description" and probe "the
violent moods of [her] soul" (*D* 2: 304).

As Drew Patrick Shannon notes, Woolf's "discussion of 'the soul' versus 'life'
in the diary . . . directly relates to her predicament as a professional writer: how
can 'life' and 'the soul' coexist on the page? How to keep 'life' from swamping
'the soul'?" (36). However, Jürgen Schlaeger reminds us of the value of the inner
search: "Whenever the conscious mind sets about extending its control over its
own subconscious or unconscious *hinterland*, that *hinterland* seems to compensate its losses in territory by an uncanny growth in depth and sophistication"
(22). This happens to Woolf in her second stage, her diary a key part.

Woolf's middle diaries reveal the crucial role of Vita Sackville-West in
Woolf's highly productive 1920s—the *diary* nuances now fully probed. The
diary documents in 1922 and 1924 that Vita initially rattles Woolf's aplomb.
However, at the end of 1925 Vita rescues Woolf—or Woolf seizes on Vita as
rescue (as she has done before with other women)—from what Woolf calls
her "wounded & stricken year" (*D* 3: 52). From 1926 to 1929, the diary reveals
Woolf in literary flood as she rides the "ardour & lust" of creation (*D* 3: 129).
Her favored diary figure of the early 1920s, the interior mine to be tunneled,
becomes a gushing oil well.

Formal experiment—another modernist focus—occurs alongside the taut
inward turn. Woolf never stops her play with diary form, from her first leather

diary "ever . . . scornful of stated rules!" to her final poignant push in 1940 for a meatier diary (*PA* 134; *D* 5: 255). Woolf's diary—more than any of her other works—reveals that she was always a modernist in the sense of making her work "new." Although settling in 1919 into her mature diary style, Woolf still fiddles with form. Her 1920 diary is a diary of conversations—in many styles. Her 1923 diary is distinguished by six *play* scenes. Her 1926 diary turns outward in May and June to become a diary of the General Strike and then turns inward in the fall for eleven brief *titled* "State of Mind" pensées—probes of the boundaries between sense, thought, and art. In 1927, she begins a two-and-a-half-year experiment with a loose-leaf diary meant to "snare a greater number of loose thoughts" (*D* 1: 228).

Few people keep loose-leaf diaries, according to Lejeune, who surveyed 583 diarists in 1987 and 1988. At least 90 percent of those surveyed used bound diary books rather than loose pages (176). Woolf's interest in loose-leaf diaries from late 1918 onward reveals her rare mind as well as her modernist wish to catch discontinuous, stray, or "loose thoughts." Lejeune believes the bound diary book gives most diarists what they seek: "the assurance of continuity" (176). (This will be true for Woolf, too, in 1929.) Loose-leaf diaries, in contrast, foreground detachment and accentuate the diary's inherent fragility. As Woolf prepares to "let [her]self down into [her] mind" from 1927 to 1929, to embark on a period of "lonel[iness]" and separation, to become more poetic in order to write *The Waves*, the detached leaves of her loose-leaf diary physically aid (and enact) the break (*D* 3: 219).

A diary invites its writer to explore a string of paradoxes, a fact that gives the diary its potential richness and power.[2] The diary's intrinsic oppositions, or—to use Woolf's own 1908 diary words—its "symmetry . . . of infinite discords," explain her lifelong attraction to the form (*PA* 393). Lejeune defines a diary as a *"series of dated traces"* (61). Any diary offers fragmented traces of life, yet, in sum, an accumulative approach to truth and life. Lejeune calls the diary the "art of the fragment," a phrase Woolf seems to endorse when she calls her 1920 diary a "mosaic" (325; *D* 2: 42). She rereads her previous entries—a constant behavior that allows her to make her diary artful—and then adds the important absent "pieces." As Peter Lowe notes of the fragments in Woolf's final novel *Between the Acts*, fragments "are not necessarily the alternative to harmony but rather, if we could but see or hear it, traces of that harmony itself" (12). Woolf herself writes in an essay that "the only way of getting at the truth [is] to have it broken into splinters by many mirrors and so select" (*E* 6: 238).

Fragments, additionally, resist any single, dominating narrative. Instead they offer a series of contingent states. Woolf's diary allowed her to experiment semiprivately with nonlinear narration, to search beyond accepted patterns of order and significance. This was practice for her modernist works. Diary entries, and the blank space around them, *together* form a productive opposition for both the diary writer and the diary reader. For the *writer*, each new blank page invites invention—even verbal improvisation. The disjoining of serial plot into single, vignette-like instants accentuates the writer's power to create. Each time, the blank page can offer something new.

The diary *reader* becomes engaged, too, in the creative terrain formed from the intermittent life traces. On the one hand, the date on each entry "creates a sincerity effect," Lejeune explains: "It sucks you in" (87). The date anchors the entry to a specific time (and often place), fostering reader credulity. Diary readers then begin unconsciously—they can hardly help themselves—to fill in imaginatively the vacant space between entries. What may have occurred? Work? Illness? Travel? What is suggested but not said?

Gaps in time and space invite the diary reader to think of *alternatives*—just as they do the diary writer. Additionally, while the diary dates "suck [readers] in," they create, paradoxically, a Brechtian "alienation" as well, which, as it happens, also invites thought. As Rachael Langford observes, each date draws the reader's attention to the diary as a text and, therefore, pulls the reader back from total immersion in the life, creating the distance Bertolt Brecht sought to promote thought (102).

A related fruitful paradox involves the *motion* fostered by separate, seemingly *static*, entries. As noted above, a diary's dates both draw readers in and keep them at a thoughtful distance: the dates establish both continuity and discontinuity, the reader in constant imaginative activity and flux. The entries themselves supply a further form of continuity amid discontinuity. The diary gives structure to the diarist's days. It orders life's disorder—another paradox—or at least tries to do so.

"Life needs discontinuity and renewal," Lejeune asserts (183). A diary supplies both. An entry ends, but then comes a new entry. A rhythm of discontinuity-yet-renewal occurs that reflects life's regular renewals and answers Woolf's own persistent need for movement and change. As she writes poetically in her 1925 novel *Mrs. Dalloway*: "[W]aves collect, overbalance, and fall; collect and fall; and the whole world seems to be saying 'that is all' more and more ponder-ously, until even the heart in the body which lies in the sun on the beach says too, That is all" (39).

For brief periods, Lejeune explains, the diary "sculpts life as it happens" (173). Diarists become caught up in the movement as they sculpt, "moving along with it, emphasizing certain lines and directions, transforming this inescapable drift into a dance" (182). "Writing a diary is 'progressive,'" Lejeune insists: "[I]t advances with the moving front of life. . . . [I]t is always on the very crest of time moving into unknown territory" (208).

Lejeune believes the preference for loose-leaf pages (or for the indefinite space of a computer file used by today's cyber-diarists) reveals the diarists' wish to avoid death. Such diarists "escape both the obligation of filling in and the need to stop" at a last page (190). As hinted above, Woolf's diaries—loose-leaf or bound—allowed her constant play with the paradox of *time*, another modernist preoccupation. In *Mapping Literary Modernism: Time and Development*, Ricardo J. Quinones argues that the Renaissance's creative heights grew from the productive tension between the predictive and innovative sides of time (7). The nineteenth century, in contrast, saw the "overwhelming triumph" of mechanism and prediction and the "almost total suppression" of the innovative side of time (7). Modernisms' obsessive experimentalism rose in revolt. Quinones suggests that "we can detect . . . the felt need to right the balance, to correct the damage, to revive the innovative along with the predictive aspect of time and then, when the innovative seems excessive or even menacing, to reassert the roles of reasonable intelligence and orderly occurrence" (230). Woolf's diary, and any diary, restores the balance between time as predictive and time as innovative. It serves as the ideal point of departure for her modernist art.

"The diary is a wager on the future," Lejeune insists (324). As such, diary-keeping is a life-affirming, life-*assisting* act and way of life. Although a diary is often thought to be a struggle *against* time, Lejeune suggests it is "actually based on a prior *yielding* to time (which is atomized, exploded, reduced to moments)" (170). The diary assists the diarist's personal growth across time. "I lay by provisions for a future writer, and leave traces for a future adult whom I am helping by recording his history, someone who will later help me better understand the confusion I'm experiencing," Lejeune explains. "We are helping each other across time. . . . The current identity that it is the diary's purpose to create and define will one day become part of the unforeseeable identity, one which it will have given rise to and which will judge it" (334, 324). One thinks of Woolf's "Elderly Virginia," whom she creates at the start of 1919 and her second diary stage (*D* 1: 234). Elderly Virginia not only encourages her younger diary self but also will *use* the diary for further public art.

"[L]ife is difficult for all of us," Lejeune takes as his basic premise, yet he points out that life "also provides an infinite number of outlets, passions, and imaginative behaviors" to assuage life's blows—diary-writing being only one such behavior but most often a helpful one (313). The diary acknowledges in its overall structure the relentless march of impersonal chronological time but answers it with the haphazard, personal, compressed or extended time of the disparate entries. (One thinks of the striking of Big Ben versus the unfolding scenes in *Mrs. Dalloway.*) Facing inevitable death, each diarist enacts to a greater or lesser degree the desperate drive of Holocaust ghetto diarists, whose diaries, as Langford and Russell West note, "restore substantiality to an existence officially reserved for obliteration" (9). In *A Book of One's Own*, Thomas Mallon makes the point more gently: "[T]he accumulated past makes the shrinking future more bearable" (xv).

The eighteenth-century diarist Nicolas Rétif de la Bretonne kept 366 separate diary books—one book for each day of the year, including leap year. Each book became a diary of one date over many years. This original behavior reveals many diarists' wish. "To me the future is a deep, frightening abyss that I dare not sound," Bretonne wrote. "[B]ut I am doing what people do when they are afraid of the water: throwing a stone into it. . . . I toss another stone into the future, knowing that the river of time, flowing along, will eventually leave it high and dry" (Lejeune 90).

In the end, the annual diary (as Woolf's diary becomes in her second diary stage) is "an annual life insurance," as Lejeune explains: "[B]y writing today, you prepare yourself to be able to live tomorrow, and to piece together, in a predetermined framework of writing, the story of what you will have lived. All journal writing assumes the intention to write at least one more time. . . . The diarist is protected from death by the idea that the diary will continue" (188–89).

Diary *reading* and *rereading* also propitiates time. What the diarist bets on, "if there is any bet," Lejeune suggests, "is escaping death by building up traces and hoping to be reread. . . . The diary no longer leads to the contingency of an absurd ending, but toward the transcendence of one or several future rereadings. You don't imagine it finished; rather, you see it reread (by yourself) or read (by another)" (209, 191).

Virginia Woolf regularly rereads her diary, and she voraciously devours *others'* diaries across her life. In the following pages, I trace Woolf's development as a diarist across her middle, modernist stage—something never as yet attempted in-depth. I offer close readings of each of Woolf's thirteen middle diary books, treating each (1) as a work of art in itself; (2) as it relates to her other diaries; and (3) as it intersects with her public works (letters and published essays, reviews, fiction and nonfiction). This method lays bare Woolf's development as a diarist and—a bonus—as a public writer as well. It reveals, as never before, Woolf's steady march toward diary art (and beyond) in her middle diary stage.

A last new insight this book conveys is the crucial role of *other* diaries in Woolf's creative life. In his mammoth 2014 volume *The Novel: A Biography*, Michael Schmidt calls Woolf "among the best-read writers of the twentieth century" (640). As I've noted elsewhere, she was more steeped in diary literature than any other well-known diarist before her—and likely even since. In the following pages, I examine fourteen key diaries Woolf read from 1919 to 1929 that helped shape her public prose. "[W]e return texts to their contexts in order to understand them more precisely," Michael H. Whitworth explains (10). Woolf herself understood the, perhaps unusually intense, role reading played in her work. "I ransack public libraries," she told her 1921 diary, "& find them full of sunk treasure" (*D* 2: 126). We watch as she absorbs this scattered treasure into her mind's "compost heap" and see it emerge transformed into art. The following pages thus reveal the influence of others' diaries on Woolf's modernist prose.

From her first diary book to her last, Woolf treats her diary as a living entity: as a fragile, but breathing, "life." In her second diary stage, as this volume will show, her diary becomes increasingly hardy and sure-handed—although it can also signal coming illness. Woolf sought in others' diaries the natural human voice and also suggestive life traces beyond her own that she could transform into art. Others' diaries refresh Woolf and "replenish . . . [her] cistern" (*D* 3: 33). By their very existence, they prove life beyond death.

Diary-writing becomes now a way of life for Woolf. If a diary is life insurance, Woolf's policy in her middle stage delivers high returns.

1

Crisis Calls for a New Diary Audience
and Purpose

Four events in late 1917 and 1918—moments rarely noted by Woolf's biographers—signal Virginia Woolf's transition to her second diary stage: her mature, spare modernist diaries, 1918 to 1929. Because Woolf's semiprivate diaries serve as the interface between her unconscious and her public prose, these moments must be seen as vital to her development not only as a *diarist* but also into the public writer so widely revered today.

The three Woolf diary books treated in this chapter disclose striking steps. Suddenly, in 1917, inordinate diary-writing begins—the most intensive period in Woolf's entire forty-four-year diary history. In the fall of 1917, as she emerges from a lengthy illness, Woolf begins to keep *two* diaries: a country (natural history) diary and a city diary. The second step comes in July 1918, when she brings her city diary to the country and begins to merge her two diaries. Nature and culture, the unconscious and the conscious, the female and the male join.

In August 1918, Woolf finds in Lord Byron's poem *Don Juan*, with its brief, open-ended cantos, the "method" she has long sought for her diary and other prose (*D* 1: 181). She now recognizes the rapid, spontaneous diary style she has been using as a "method" in itself, with artistic benefits. When she pens her mature diary credo in 1919, she uses the same words for her diary as she has for *Don Juan*.

In early November 1918 a crisis occurs. It turns on representation and on the female support so essential to Woolf's writing life. The word *crisis* comes from the Greek word *krinein*, meaning "to separate, to judge, to decide." Woolf's crisis comes when Hampstead, which she calls the country-in-London and "the heart of the women's republic," for the first time withdraws its support. In Chinese, the word *crisis* is composed of two characters: one represents danger and the other opportunity. At this moment of crisis, Woolf makes *in her diary* an extraordinary salvaging move. She creates a new audience and purpose for her diary, replacing her aging Hampstead female (now) detractors with Elderly Virginia. She will now parent herself. With this move, she offers her diary credo in her 1919 diary and enters her mature second diary stage. She reads Wilfrid Scawen Blunt's antiwar, anti-imperialist diaries along the way and finds there ammunition for *Three Guineas*—and also a male aristocrat whom she scorns.

Virginia Woolf's Second 1918 Hogarth House Diary: July 27–November 12

"[An] elastic shape which will hold whatever you choose to put into it. . . . Still, it doesn't seem an easy example to follow; & indeed like all free & easy things, only the skilled & mature really bring them off successfully."

(August 8, 1918; D 1: 181)

Virginia Woolf brings her London diary to the country in mid-1918. That she totes her new Hogarth diary to Asheham House on July 31, when she embarks on her nine-and-a-half-week summer holiday, suggests she no longer feels the Asheham House natural history diary adequate for the diary she now desires. Thirty-two Hogarth (city) diary entries preserve the 102 days, July 27 through November 12, along with sixty-four almost daily Asheham diary entries during the Sussex holiday, July 31 through October 6.[1] On fifteen days Woolf pens entries in *both* diaries.

We can picture her at Asheham House with the two diaries before her: the smaller Asheham diary (4 inches wide and 6 ½ inches long), its red cover adorned with waving lines of green, gray, and white; and the larger, dark-gray-covered Hogarth diary (7 inches wide and 8 ¾ inches long). Clearly, she experiments. Which diary will she choose to write in, and when she writes in both, in what order? She writes eight staccato sentences for her August 3 Asheham diary entry: "A dreary drizzling day. L[eonard, her husband]. to Lewes to fetch a parcel. I on M's walk & round the top. All butterflies clinging to grass. Found mushrooms after tea. Murry's [Katherine Mansfield and John Middleton Murry] didn't come. K. ill. Guns very loud" (*CM* 31). They appear to be a summary of her more elaborate Hogarth diary entry for that day, which begins, "There's nothing but rustic news to record, since as we expected the Murrys have put us off" (*D* 1: 177). However, which entry was written first?

Her August 7 Hogarth entry clearly is penned second, for it begins drolly, "Asheham diary drains off my meticulous observations of flowers, clouds, beetles & the price of eggs" (*D* 1: 179). Revealingly, she writes a long Hogarth diary entry on August 27, dissecting her brother's visit and her own stop at Charleston, her older sister Vanessa's nearby home, on the day she writes in her natural history diary, "Fine & windy. Nothing new" (*CM* 33).

Woolf's second Hogarth diary book of 1918 resembles her pivoting 1903 diary with its London, country, and return-to-London "chapters." In 1903, twenty-one-year-old Virginia Stephen vowed to forget London in the country and the male tradition as well—a defining turn toward nature, the unconscious, and the female repeated often in subsequent diaries. In the country fifteen years later, thirty-six-year-old Virginia Woolf finds a way to *integrate* London and the male tradition and, in so doing, adds a new dimension to her diary; indeed, she starts to fuse her two diaries.

She brings her Hogarth diary to the country, but she leaves her reading notebook behind in Richmond. Happy mistake! Its absence forces her to use her Hogarth diary more extensively as a reading notebook than in the past—to the diary's gain. "While waiting to buy a book in which to record my impressions first of Christina Rossetti, then of Byron, I had better write them here," she explains pragmatically in her fifth Hogarth diary entry, August 4, suggesting her original intent to keep literary thoughts apart. "Christina has the great distinction of being a born poet" (*D* 1: 178). And she is off, the entire entry probing Rossetti's life and art, lamenting that "she starved into austere emaciation, a very fine original gift" (*D* 1: 179). Leonard Woolf chose this entry to begin *A Writer's Diary*, the first version of Woolf's diary to reach the public.

Woolf then turns to Byron—to the male literary tradition—in her next two Hogarth entries. In her August 8 entry we learn it is not Byron's *diary* but his great poem *Don Juan* that supplies Woolf with the "method" she will apply in her diary and in more public works as well. She calls *Don Juan* "the most readable poem of its length ever written," suggesting her high regard for "readability" as a literary goal, "a quality," she asserts, "which it owes in part to the springy random haphazard galloping nature of its method":

> This method is a discovery by itself. Its[2] what one has looked for in vain—a[n] elastic shape which will hold whatever you choose to put into it. Thus he could write out his mood as it came to him; he could say whatever came into his head. He wasn't committed to be poetical; & thus escaped his evil genius of the false romantic & imaginative. When he is serious he is sincere; & he can impinge upon any subject he likes. He writes 16 canto's [*sic*] without once flogging his flanks. (*D* 1: 180–81)

Woolf has written her own diary *hab nab at a venture* from the start, since devouring Sir Walter Scott's journal before starting her own diary in her early teens: Scott, her diary father who praised Byron's diary method in *his* diary and adopted it as his own.[3] So what can this August 8 declaration mean? It marks Woolf's recognition of the rapid, spontaneous diary style she has been using as a method in itself (with artistic advantages) and her sense of the open-ended stretch of a diary—like that of endless cantos—as an "elastic shape" of great allure.

This method is a discovery by itself. These words mark this entry as one of the most important in Woolf's whole diary history. A swift pen and quick turns of subject can save Woolf from pitfalls just as they did Byron: the traps of diary preaching, rote repetition, and (especially) diurnal dullness.[4] In their place one finds the fast flight of the mind.

Woolf opens this second 1918 Hogarth diary confidently, revealing growing ease with her periodic diary. "As usual, this diary has skipped a day or two," she begins July 27 at Hogarth House. "But first one must pause to say that here a new volume starts . . . & therefore there is every appearance of a long, though intermittent life. If it survives the summer, when the evenings are unfavourable to writing, it should flourish in the winter" (*D* 1: 171–72). Once more she personifies her diary, here as a vulnerable but potentially flourishing life.

Traits of Woolf's first two Hogarth diaries persist across this third. Woolf continues to reread her previous entry before starting the next, which allows her to reply to her entries as if in deep talk. As in her first 1918 Hogarth diary, she stops an entry mid-sentence, writes a new date, and continues the sentence—linking her entries another way beyond talk—and she notes again that diary-keeping soothes her (*D* 1: 196). "Since I'm back from the [1917] Club & waiting for L.," she writes on November 4, "I had better assuage my fretfulness with pen & ink. I have a pen . . . which perhaps serves the purpose of a babies coral" (*D* 1: 214). The mothering touch of diary-writing emerges in another turn on pens nine days before: "Here I am experimenting with the parent of all pens—the black J. *the* pen, as I used to think it, along with other objects, as a child, because mother used it; & therefore all other pens were varieties & eccentricities" (*D* 1: 208). Through her diary Woolf will mother herself.

She also continues gestures to coax vivid diary prose. She denies her ability to write and, in so doing, buys time to gather force. "I'm paralyzed by the task of describing a week end at Garsington," she writes on July 29 before delivering one of her most exquisite comic scenes (*D* 1: 173). "If I weren't too lazy I think I should try to describe the country; but then I shouldn't get it right," begins one of her more elaborate psychological dances, on August 24. "I shouldn't bring back to my own eyes the look of all those old beautiful very worn carpets which are spread over the lower slopes of the hills; nor should I convey the look of clouded emerald which the downs wear, the semi-transparent look, as the sun & shadows change, & the green becomes now vivid now opaque" (*D* 1: 185). She paints here once more her modernist aesthetic: the melding shades first caught at age seventeen in her 1899 Warboys diary (*PA* 155–56).

Along with denials, she uses questions to move herself along. Some questions merely goad memory—again in conversational style. "What did we discuss?" she asks herself in her August 16 entry about a Charleston visit (*D* 1: 182). "What has happened this last week—following upon the superb success of Brighton?" she presses September 8 (*D* 1: 190). She continues to be curious about people and, increasingly, about her own feelings. "What for instance is Lytton's view of Mrs Asquith; & hers of him; & Maynard's of them both," she asks her diary on August 16; "Am I getting blasé—is the 17 Club less enthralling?" (*D* 1: 183, 208). Other questions—on literature, politics, war—are more profound.

She finds in metaphor-shifting a new way to conjure prose. "I have let the first freshness of the Webbs fade from my mirror," she laments September 18 at the start of her lively two-entry re-creation of the Webbs' visit: "[B]ut let me bethink me of another metaphor which they imposed upon me, towards the end of Sunday. I was exalted above a waste of almost waveless sea, palish grey, & dented with darker shadows for the small irregularities, the little ripples which represented character & life love & genius & happiness" (*D* 1: 193). The new trope opens a new groove that allows her to proceed.[5]

She treats her long September entry recounting the Webbs' visit as if she were a novelist setting a scene: "I must now skip a great deal of conversation & let us suppose that Sidney & Beatrice & I are sitting on the road side overlooking Telscombe, smoking cigarettes, in bright sunshine, while the Silver Queen slowly patrols above Newhaven" (*D* 1: 195). She reports Beatrice's breathtakingly illusion-free view of marriage—"I daresay an old family servant would do as well [as a husband]"—and rounds out the day with Pepys's "& so to bed" (*D* 1: 196).

Because two-thirds of this diary's days unfold in the country, topics of consuming interest in her first 1918 Hogarth diary—the 1917 Club, for instance—recede in this second 1918 journal. Women and their treatment, however, remain major subjects. In her first 1918 Hogarth diary Woolf mocks the January passage of the Suffrage Bill, which gave British women over the age of thirty the right to vote, and she does the same in October when the House of Commons passes a bill to allow women to stand for Parliament. "Yes, I can speak of myself with more confidence today as noble & profound," she cracks the next day in her October 24 Hogarth entry:

> I am capable of standing for Parliament & holding office, & becoming just like Herbert Fisher perhaps. To me the vote was as surprising as to some retired cleric in the vales of Westmorland, who will see in it the death knell of liberty, I daresay, & preach a sermon to that effect next Sunday. Then the great lady at Stocks [antisuffragist Mrs. Humphry Ward] must be feeling uncomfortable, though I am malicious enough to suppose that if by some process of selection she alone could represent Belgravia in the House of Lords, the change would not seem so devastating. (D 1: 207)

Emerging here is Woolf the witty (and wicked) diary portraitist.

Woolf looks at women in literature as well as in political affairs. Electra "lived a far more hedged in life than the women of the mid Victorian age," Woolf notes in an August Hogarth entry, "but this has no effect upon her, except in making her harsh & splendid. She could not go out for a walk alone; with us it would be a case of a maid & a hansom cab" (D 1: 185). When Woolf turns to Milton in September, she finds him "the first of the masculinists" (D 1: 193). *Paradise Lost*, she complains, provides "no help in judging life; I scarcely feel that Milton lived or knew men & women; except for the peevish personalities about marriage & the woman's duties" (D 1: 193). Thinking of Byron, she is amused at how easily she pictures his effect upon women. Had women only laughed at him instead of worshiped him, she believes, he might have escaped the "Byronic" (D 1: 179–80).

Age, as well as gender, continues to claim Woolf's mind. In fact, her view of age in this second 1918 Hogarth diary is more grim than in the first. She observes physical change closely. Katherine Cox's engagement to be married begins the diary; however, Woolf doubts that Will Arnold-Forster is worthy of his bride-to-be. This is partly because Duncan Grant reviles him for being forty-five, "& always has been," and partly because he reminds Woolf "of one of those old ladies, who have yellow hair & very pink cheeks, but you can count their years in the way the flesh is drawn tight across the bone, & crinkled with very delicate fine lines" (D 1: 182, 212). Cabinet member Herbert Fisher, her cousin, possesses "eyes with that pale frosty look which blue eyes get in age," and the resolutely unromantic Beatrice Webb, whose own diaries will offer great riches to Woolf in 1926, tells her that "[i]n old age people become of little account" (D 1: 203, 196). Sidney Webb, in turn, remarks that he and Beatrice are now sixty "& therefore may expect a stroke within the next 5 years" (D 1: 197).

However, what particularly strikes one in this diary is the crisis that occurs: the fact that Hampstead, the "country-in-London" and "the heart of the woman's republic," fails for the first time to support and succor Woolf. When woman meets age and illness in Hampstead, age and illness trump. They demoralize and demean. When she visits Katherine Mansfield in Hampstead on November 9, Woolf finds her fellow writer "husky & feeble, crawling about the room like an old woman. . . . Illness, she said, breaks down one's privacy so that one can't write"—a sober vision (*D* 1: 216).

On November 3, her earliest Hampstead supporter, her Greek teacher Janet Case, also deflates her, an act Woolf attributes largely to the disabling force of age. "I was depressed at her age, at something unstable about her," Woolf tells her diary (*D* 1: 214). The depression remains, for she writes in her next day's entry: "I've been thinking a good deal about this melancholy state of impending age. From the way Janet took certain remarks of mine about 60 as an age limit (for the Webbs) I felt that she took age to be a shameful disease that one shrank from hearing named. . . . And then it seems as if she were now always playing for safety" (*D* 1: 215). Her now elderly former teacher chills her by implying that her first novel, *The Voyage Out*, is not "up to the scratch," not "immortal," and by urging her to write biography rather than fiction (*D* 1: 213). These words freeze Woolf's writing flow.

She responds to this Hampstead crisis with a rescuing gesture in her diary. Feeling Case's "chill falling upon the last pages of [her] novel," she turns despair to affirmation: "The depression however now takes the wholesome form of feeling perfectly certain that nothing I can do matters, so that one is both content & irresponsible—I'm not sure that this isn't a happier state than the exalted state of the newly praised. . . . It proves itself so genuine that no amount of Hampstead cold water can impair it. Praise? fame? Janet's good opinion? How beside the mark they are!"[6]

These words aid her, for she begins to speak of her novel-in-progress (*Night and Day*) in the next sentence—opening a further diary layer (her own writing) that she will increasingly explore. "I keep thinking of different ways to manage my scenes," she asserts and then pictures life as "an immense opaque block of material" she will elucidate (*D* 1: 214). She now talks of her work to her *diary*, if she cannot talk of it to Case—and she will do even more in her next diary.

Her language turns poetic in the stark contrapuntal close to this diary. The diary ends with the Armistice, Woolf's first chance to chronicle a historic moment comparable to Samuel Pepys's on-site witness to the Great Fire of London or Fanny Burney's to the Battle of Waterloo. The war staggers to a close across Woolf's diary pages, and she chronicles its barbarities to the end. "Already I've half forgotten the soldier with the nickel knee plate & the metal arch to his foot, though he talked at the top of his voice, & boasted, & made me hate him," she writes on July 31—showing she has *not* forgotten him (*D* 1: 177).

In October, as hope of peace begins to stir, she reports that the Northcliffe newspapers "do all they can to insist upon the indispensability & delight of war" (*D* 1: 200). When her cousin, the cabinet member Herbert Fisher, pays her a personal call October 15 to confide in her "We've won the war today," she records his claims that "the proportion of men who have never been hurt, or even seen anything horrible is very large" and that "thousands & thousands of soldiers . . . all wanted the war conditions of life to go on 'without these bloody shells.' . . . They'll find their old lives too dull" (*D* 1: 203, 204). Here is first-hand, cabinet-level insistence on male love of war—one of the starting points of Woolf's 1938 *Three Guineas*.

Woolf seeks to understand the urge to kill and frames this urge (and war) as impulses antithetical to the diary pulse—the diary representing "life" as opposed to death. "The reason why it is easy to kill another person," she posits, "must be that one's imagination is too sluggish to conceive what his life means to him—the infinite possibilities of a succession of days which are furled in him" (*D* 1: 186). What does a diary promise, after all, but "the infinite possibilities of a succession of days"?

That she associates her diary with "life," truth, and "reality" is revealed in her October 18 entry following Fisher's call, an entry showing she knows well the central role the war has claimed. Looking back on her long account of Fisher's visit, she is almost apologetic: "My theory is that for some reason the human mind is always seeking what it conceives to be the centre of things; sometimes one may call it reality, again truth, again life—I dont know what I call it; but I distinctly visualise it as a possession rather more in H.F.'s hands than in other peoples. For the moment he makes all the rest of the world's activities appear as ramifications radiating from him" (*D* 1: 205).

Woolf herself turns to nature for sign of the Great War's end. Although Fisher proclaims victory on October 15, she locates the start of peace not then, nor on Armistice Day, November 11, but on October 17, when the night, "beautiful, cloudless, still & moonlit, was to my thinking the first of peace, since one went to bed fairly positive that never again in all our lives need we dread the moonlight" (*D* 1: 205–06). If only this had proved true.

Woolf draws once more on nature to portray Armistice Day in London. In the diary's final contrapuntal entries, the vulgarity of men and women caught in what Woolf will call in 1938 nationalism's "unreal loyalty" is set off in high relief against nature's somber grief. "Twentyfive minutes ago the guns went off, announcing peace," Woolf begins (with irony) her November 11 Armistice Day entry: "A siren hooted on the river. They are hooting still. . . . The rooks wheeled round, & were [wore] for a moment, the symbolic look of creatures performing some ceremony, partly of thanksgiving, partly of valediction over the grave. A very cloudy still day, the smoke toppling over heavily towards the east; & that too wearing for a moment a look of something floating, waving, drooping" (*D* 1: 216).

But all changes the next day in the diary's closing entry. Nature disapproves of, but cannot stop, the coarse human acts. "We should have done well, I think, to be satisfied with the aspect of peace," she begins, "how the rooks flew slowly in circles, & the smoke drooped; but I had to go to Harrison [her dentist], & I think we were both conscious of a restlessness which made it seem natural to be going up to London. Disillusionment began after 10 minutes in the train" (*D* 1: 216). She sees a woman in black velvet and feathers shaking hands with two soldiers:

> "Its thanks to you boys &c &c." She was half drunk already, & soon pro-
> duced a large bottle of beer which she made them drink of; & then she
> kissed them, & the last we saw of her was as she ran alongside the train
> waving her hand to the two stolid soldiers. But she & her like possessed
> London, & alone celebrated peace in their sordid way, staggering up the
> muddy pavements in the rain, decked with flags themselves, & voluble
> at sight of other people's flags. The Heavens disapproved & did their ut-
> most to extinguish, but only succeeded in making feathers flop & flags
> languish. (*D* 1: 216–17)

Woolf's second 1918 Hogarth diary marks the start of her mature diary style. Her Asheham House natural history diary merges into her Hogarth city diary during this time frame, creating her ideal "Country in London" state. She identifies Byron's "random haphazard galloping" in *Don Juan* as the method she seeks for both her semiprivate diary and her public prose, and she begins to write in her diary of others' works and of her own works as well (*D* 1: 181). The November Hampstead crisis—involving women's support—will lead, as next will be shown, to a new audience and a more public purpose for her diary.

Virginia Woolf's Third 1918 Hogarth House Diary: November 15, 1918–January 24, 1919

> *"If Virginia Woolf at the age of 50, when she sits down to build her memoirs out of these books is unable to make a phrase as it should be made, I can only condole with her & remind her of the existence of the fireplace, where she has my leave to burn these pages to so many black films with red eyes in them. But how I envy her the task I am preparing for her! There is none I should like better."*

(January 20, 1919; *D* 1: 234)

A vision of flourishing diary books—a series of them—opens the third 1918 Hogarth diary on November 15. However, Woolf lacks funds for writing books, and the war's paper shortage further thwarts diary-keeping. "I've no money to buy another book," Woolf begins this diary forthrightly; "besides by waiting the paper question may once more take its place in the scale of my pleasures; good books, cheap books, books that make one wish to finish them in order to have the pleasure of buying another" (*D* 1: 217). She pictures the joys of diary-keeping in the years of peace to come. But the practical problem remains: she needs a new diary book, so she turns to her 1918 *reading notebook*—the book practically a twin in appearance to her first 1918 Hogarth diary—and turns it upside down and continues her 1918 Hogarth diary there. Diary and literary criticism now literally conjoin.[7]

Eleven entries—in purple ink on white unlined paper—capture the seventy-one days from November 15, 1918, to January 24, 1919. Woolf tracks the progress of peace in her opening entry, linking this new diary to the last diary's close. If life, truth, and reality all converged on Herbert Fisher's war in her second 1918 Hogarth diary, that focal point bursts. "Peace is rapidly dissolving into the light of common day," Woolf observes in her first entry, alluding to Wordsworth and noting nature's renewed sway: "You can go to London without meeting more than two drunk soldiers; only an occasional crowd blocks the street. . . . But mentally the change is marked too. Instead of feeling all day . . . that the whole people, willing or not, were concentrated on a single point, one feels now that the whole bunch has burst asunder & flown off with the utmost vigour in different directions. We are once more a nation of individuals" (*D* 1: 217). Movement and difference return, and the unnatural ends. "The first effect of peace on our circle is to set Desmond loose" from the Navy, Woolf explains (*D* 1: 218).

Woolf finishes her second novel, *Night and Day*, on November 21. A change of great import then comes to her diary in December and January. She thinks of diary experiments and rereads her previous diaries. In her important November 4 rebound from Janet Case's "chill" in her second 1918 Hogarth diary, she writes: "I keep thinking of different ways to manage my scenes; conceiving endless possibilities; seeing life, as . . . an immense opaque block of material" (*D* 1: 214). Forty-three days later, she thinks of her diary as this "block" of life and imagines another form for it: "Suppose I buy a block, with detachable leaves, I think I shall snare a greater number of loose thoughts. No doubt this is pure fancy, but then so much of one's mental affairs are controlled by fancy" (*D* 1: 228). She seeks a diary form to capture more "life" (and the fanciful unconscious mind): the "block" or loose-leaf diary. The loose pages will make the block of life less "opaque."

She rereads her previous diaries, and she also thinks of Thomas Carlyle in early December and of fame.[8] She spends a December weekend with Roger Fry in Guildford and reports favorably of *his* old age. She then parents her sister's sons for more than two weeks across the holidays while Vanessa gives birth to her daughter. However, a toothache shadows this kindly act, followed by headache, swift removal of the boys, rationed work, and recovery in bed. What happens, then, between those early December diary entries and her resumption of her diary on January 20, 1919, after a thirty-three-day gap? Diary rereading and thoughts of a new diary form. Thoughts of fame and posterity. The happy stay with Roger. Whatever served as catalyst, Woolf comes to terms a bit with old age—from which she recoils across her 1918 diaries—and in so doing refocuses her diary in her first entry of 1919, providing it a new audience and purpose.

That she knows the importance of this moment is telegraphed in the fact that she recopies her last three entries (January 20, 22, and 24) into her new diary book (when she buys it), expanding and polishing the entries as she recopies—an unusual act for her. "I mean to copy this out when I can buy a book, so I omit the flourishes proper to the New Year," she begins briskly on January 20, 1919, after the long diary gap (*D* 1: 325). "I have just re-read my years diary," she continues, "& am much struck by the rapid haphazard gallop at which it swings along, sometimes indeed jerking almost intolerably over the cobbles" (*D* 1: 325). She uses here the key words from her August 1918 praise of Byron: his "springy random haphazard galloping" in *Don Juan*'s open-ended cantos (*D* 1: 181).

And she further probes this "method," consoling herself with the fact that if her diary "were not written rather faster than the fastest typewriting, it would never be written at all; & the advantage of the method is that [it] sweeps up accidentally several stray matters that I should exclude if I took thought; & it is these accidents that are the diamonds in the rubbish heap" (*D* 1: 325). When she recopies the entry into her new 1919 diary, she expands the description and changes "rubbish" to the more alliterative "dust": "Still if it were not written rather faster than the fastest typewriting, *if I stopped & took thought*, it would never be written at all; & the advantage of the method is that *it* sweeps up accidentally several stray matters which I should exclude *if I hesitated*, but which are the diamonds of the *dust*heap" (*D* 1: 233–34; revisions in italics).

And then a new persona, Elderly Virginia, enters the diary, an appreciative future reader and working writer. Woolf envisions herself at age fifty, "build[ing]" her memoirs from her diaries. "Already," she writes, "my 37th birthday next Saturday is robbed of some of its terrors" (*D* 1: 325). How different this January 20, 1919, entry is from the January 24 entry of the year before: Woolf trembling before the shadow of age thirty-six. Elderly Virginia, one might say, takes the role of Woolf's elderly (but now declining) Hampstead teacher, Janet Case. Case did not affirm her fiction, but Elderly Virginia may. Hampstead's Katherine Mansfield may now be too enfeebled to make a "public of two," so Woolf replaces *her* with a hardier collaborator.

Like her diary mother, Fanny Burney, at age sixteen, at thirty-six Woolf pictures herself reading, enjoying, and making use of her diaries as "an old tabby." The coming years lose their terror as Woolf stakes a claim for posterity through her projected diary-memoirs. Vanessa mothered a daughter, so Virginia births her own nurturing mother figure.[9] Her vision of "Virginia Woolf, at the age of 50" might also be viewed as yet another lowering of the psychological bar, for Woolf imagines incapacity and gives herself permission to destroy her diary if it cannot serve. Diarizing is not "writing," she tells herself, allowing it to be a subterranean aide (*D* 1: 325).

Elderly Virginia becomes a new reader—a future reader—for the diary (besides Woolf's current self and Leonard). Woolf's vow to use her journal for Elderly Virginia's memoirs provides new purpose for the diary as well.[10] "Partly for [the] benefit of this elderly lady," Woolf continues, "(no subterfuge will then be possible: 50 is elderly, though, I agree, not old) partly to give the year a solid foundation I intend to spend the evenings of this week of captivity in making out an account of my friendships & their present condition, with some account of my friends characters; & to add an estimate of their work, & a forecast of their future works. The lady of fifty will be able to say how near to the truth I come" (*D* 1: 325).

Woolf's 1915 diary portraits were brief sketches, the likeness allowed to accrue across time. Influenced by the Goncourt brothers' palpitatingly alive

Journal portraits (read in late 1917), Woolf's Hogarth diary portraits become more elaborate in 1917 and 1918, with character emerging in lively dialogue and scenes. With this important January 20, 1919, entry, Woolf takes an even larger canvas and a more formal approach to her diary portraits.

After listing all her friends in her next entry, January 22, she begins her "memoir portraits" with Lytton Strachey. That she seeks a formal portrait is seen in her use of that word: "All the unpleasantness that I wish to introduce into my portrait of Lytton is contained in [three words] as if in deep wells" (*D* 1: 327). When she recopies this entry into her new 1919 diary book, she sharpens the line to the even more precise and painterly "I shall only need *one drop of this gall* for his portrait, but I fancy *a tinge* of the kind is perceptible in him too."[11] Toward the end she critiques her portrait: "Written down these words are too emphatic; one does not get them tempered & combined with all those charming subtle & brilliant qualities which make him as he is in the flesh" (*D* 1: 327). In recopying, she again expands and sharpens her words into the image she hopes to see: "Written down these words are too emphatic *& linear; one should see them* tempered & combined with all those charming, subtle & brilliant qualities which *compose his being* in the flesh" (*D* 1: 236; revisions in italics). She wishes here the melding shades and lights of her modernist aesthetic.

Brief as it is, the eleven-entry third 1918 Hogarth diary, hidden away in a reading notebook, becomes one of the most consequential in Woolf's long diary history. Her first entry introduces T. S. Eliot and captures him acutely, and by her next-to-last entry, January 22, she lists him among the friends who will receive a "memoir portrait" for Elderly Virginia. Knife-bearing Harry Stephen and plaintive Miss Louise Matthaei continue to haunt the diary, diamonds to be mined for *Mrs. Dalloway*.[12]

Of greatest moment, however, are the further probe of her "haphazard galloping" diary method and its virtues and the introduction of Elderly Virginia as a brilliant counter to declining years and female support. Woolf's transformation of the destructive specter of old age and literary chill into the constructive persona of Elderly Virginia "building" her memoirs represents a remarkable rescuing move—and it occurs in the diary. Roger Fry's vitality appears crucial to Woolf's revision of advancing age, for she adds a final paragraph to her January 20, 1919, entry: "I admit I don't like thinking of the lady of 50. Courage however. Roger is past that age, & still capable of feeling & enjoying & playing a very considerable part in life" (*D* 1: 325). These words recall the close of her first diary at age fifteen: "courage & plod on" (*PA* 134).

Female spirits have blessed and authorized Woolf's diaries in the past: "pagan" (and pregnant) Lady Katherine Cromer in 1903; her mother's ghostly spirit in 1905 Cornwall; Jane Carlyle haunting Carlyle House in 1909; and Fanny Burney channeled through Walter Lamb in 1915. Elderly Virginia joins this empowering female line in January 1919. Woolf will now parent herself. Elderly Virginia signifies a new—and potentially public—audience for Woolf's diary prose and gives the diary new purpose and scope.

Virginia Woolf's 1919 Diary

> *"I believe that during the past year I can trace some increase of ease in my profes-sional writing which I attribute to my casual half hours after tea. Moreover there looms ahead of me the shadow of some kind of form which a diary might attain to. I might in the course of time learn what it is that one can make of this loose, drifting material of life; finding another use for it than the use I put it to, so much more consciously & scrupulously, in fiction."*

(Easter Sunday, April 20, 1919; D 1: 266)

Great care is lavished on this long-anticipated diary. We picture Woolf shop-ping in London. She chooses a large diary book—10 ¾ inches long and 8 ½ inches wide—with a dark gray paper cover, the same color as her second 1918 Hogarth diary, which praises Byron's elastic form. Back home in Richmond, she prepares the book's white unlined pages as if each is a canvas. She draws a red vertical line one inch from the left edge of each page. To the line's left she will write her diary date in front of a right-facing angle bracket: Mon. Jan 20th 1919>. The larger rectangle to the right frames the entry.[13] She writes "1919" in big numbers at the top of the first page, underlines it twice, and then bothers to recopy her January 20, 22, and 24 entries from her reading notebook turned 1918–1919 diary, expanding and polishing these entries as she recopies them. The 1919 diary begins, therefore, with a new diary *audience* (Elderly Virginia) and a new diary *purpose* (material for Elderly Virginia's memoirs).

Woolf continues her formal portraits for her future memoir-writing self. She daubs further at her Lytton Strachey portrait (January 31 and February 4), then turns to Desmond MacCarthy (February 4 and 18), and attempts Saxon Sydney-Turner and Katherine Mansfield on February 18 as well. Her Saxon sketch displays her now teeming metaphorical mind. One metaphor begets another and, therefore, continually refreshed views. "But Saxon's fidelity is al-most that of the senile colly, or broken down ass," she writes, "—the pensioner who can draw upon a memory of the past for a seat at one's table in perpetuity.

His present condition makes him appear almost exclusively in the character of almoner" (D 1: 242). She often views people in terms of nature, finding inexhaustible range there:

> However, poor Saxon's life is now in the uncomfortable & unbecoming season which is so painfully well reproduced out of doors. Sleet, & mud & chill, & nothing growing; no warmth, no brilliancy, not even a modest domestic glow. . . . But faithful—there is something worth having in Saxon's fidelity; something that makes his most meagre visitation not altogether fruitless. One is aware, even after two hours of tepid & almost entire silence, that he is strictly true, genuine, unalloyed. . . . Granted that he is not richly supplied with the gifts one might need, still I come to think in my weary age that safety—a modest competence—a truth as flawless as diamond or crystal—is not negligible, nor without its curious flashes of high remote beauty. (D 1: 242)

Senile colly to flawless crystal. She offers in these seven sentences at least eight different images of Sydney-Turner, capturing through the shifting prism of metaphor the lights and shades and subtle truths of character.

She can unpack tropes in her portraits—yet always in fresh and subtle ways—as in the above image of Sydney-Turner as an earth stone, or in this sketch of Lady Ottoline Morrell as first tree, then colorful bird: "She has the slim swaying figure of a Lombardy poplar . . . & a feeble mincing step on the street, like that of a cockatoo with bad claws. She has an indomitable spirit—plucking life out with those same gouty claws as if she were young & had illusions by the score. She had swooped down upon the land agents wife, & upon Rosa Allatini—for no reason save that the land agents wife writes novels, & Rosa Allatini has had her novel burnt by the hangman" (D 1: 246).

Writing swiftly, Woolf will correct an imprecise trope. E. M. Forster strikes her in July as "fantastic & very sensitive; an attractive character to me, though from his very qualities it takes as long to know him as it used to take to put one's gallipot over a humming bird moth. More truly, he resembles a vaguely rambling butterfly; since there is no intensity or rapidity about him" (D 1: 295).

Edward L. Bishop's fine insights in his article "Metaphor and the Subversive Process of Virginia Woolf's Essays" apply to Woolf's diary tropes as well. He suggests that in her essays Woolf "provides a shower of images, in part to capture the complexity of the thing under consideration, but also to provide a number of possible points of connection, a number of blueprints, we might say, except that one need only apprehend one image fully for the others then to become instantly intelligible as well" (584). Furthermore, her "figures enlist the reader as an active partner in this delicate and difficult business of communication" (584). Metaphor, he points out, is also an "instrument of inquiry" (573). The profusion of Woolf's diary metaphors in 1919 links to the profusion of her diary questions. "Now is life very solid, or very shifting?" Woolf asks her diary, while her tropes, Bishop observes, capture "this irreconcilable conjunction" (*D* 3: 218; 581). Noting that Paul Ricoeur argues that metaphor represents the conjunction of mimesis and poiesis, Bishop suggests that "for any writer the descriptive and the poetic functions of language are not ultimately separable, but for Woolf they were practically indistinguishable" (581).

The brilliantly shifting portraits for Elderly Virginia's memoirs represent only one ornament of Woolf's mature, modernist diary style. Two other features distinguish the 1919 diary and Woolf's seasoned diary form. As noted above, the diary teems with questions. Woolf's curiosity is rife. She begins as well to address her *own* writing—adding a further strand to the diary tapestry. In her 1915 diary, she spoke only once—and with trepidation—of her forthcoming first novel, *The Voyage Out*. Olivier Bell believes her publication anxiety hastened her illness and the end of the 1915 diary after only six weeks (*D* 1: 3). Four years later, the diary (with its Elderly Virginia) becomes a trusted writing confidante.

One or all of the following may account for Woolf's willingness now to address the subject closest to her identity: her "precious art" (as she calls it on March 22). She begins to write in-depth of others' writing—Byron's, Christina Rossetti's—with her August 1918 diary. This might lead naturally to turning the same lens on herself. The loss of Hampstead's female support on November 3, 1918, seems particularly important, for Janet Case's "chill" on the final pages of *Night and Day* prompts Woolf to divert immediately *to her diary* the writer's talk denied. Elderly Virginia replaces Case. And as she pens portraits of her friends for Elderly Virginia's memoirs, surely (she may have thought) those memoirs would also welcome accounts of her own writerly griefs and joys.

Finally (and happily), 1919 unfolds as a continually encouraging year for Woolf's prose, enabling her to report to her diary one triumph after another. On April 2, she takes *Night and Day* to Gerald Duckworth, who says he is quite sure he will publish this second novel.[14] On May 12, the Hogarth Press issues three works: poems by T. S. Eliot, a long poem by John Middleton Murry, and Woolf's story experiment "Kew Gardens." Critical contempt greets the two poets, while Woolf's story, buoyed by a positive review, enters a second edition.[15] "But how success showered during those days!" Woolf exclaims in her June 10 entry. "Gratuitously, too, I had a letter from Macmillan in New York, so much impressed by The Voyage Out that they want to read Night and Day" (D 1: 280). "I felt gorged & florid with my comparative success," she writes on June 14, following a visit to the Murrys (D 1: 281).

Night and Day is published to praise on October 20, enabling Woolf to tell her November 28 entry that "its on the cards . . . that N & D is a marked success; I expect a letter every day from someone or other, & now I can write with the sense of many people willing to read."[16] In truth, she has charted her pre- and postpublication temperature so thoroughly in her diary that she exclaims in her November 6 entry: "But what a bore I'm becoming! Yes, even old Virginia will skip a good [deal] of this" (D 1: 310).

Woolf's March 27 entry, reporting Leonard's first response to *Night and Day*, suggests a link between the explosion of questions and the diary's emergence now as a highly personal writer's diary. Woolf uses *questions* to probe and extend her art:

> Shall I own that I attribute some of [Leonard's pessimism] . . . to Night & Day which L. has spent the past 2 mornings & evenings in reading? I own that his verdict . . . gives me immense pleasure: how far one should discount it, I don't know. . . . L. finds the philosophy very melancholy. . . . Yet, if one is to deal with people on a large scale & say what one thinks, how can one avoid melancholy? I don't admit to being hopeless though—only the spectacle is a profoundly strange one; & as the current answers don't do, one has to grope for a new one; & the process of discarding the old, when one is by no means certain what to put in their place, is a sad one. Still, if you think of it, what answers do Arnold Bennett or Thackeray, for instance, suggest? Happy ones—satisfactory solutions—answers one would accept, if one had the least respect for one's soul? (D 1: 259)

Questions here light the way.

If her own writing becomes a rich new thread in the mature diary's fabric, Monk's House arrives as a new figure as well. Country house-hunting (as well as her fiction's fate) supplies dramatic tension across the 1919 diary, just as the search for Hogarth House excites the 1915 diary book. The country continues to aid Woolf. On June 9 she tells her diary that at Asheham House she counts upon "becoming clearer & more concentrated, & reading print as if through a magnifying glass" (D 1: 278).

That this Sussex country provides an essential foundation—did not her current diary begin with the 1917 Asheham diary?—explains the rush to replace

Asheham House with a dwelling close by. "To give up every foothold in that region seemed unthinkable," Woolf continues, the foothold trope particularly revealing (*D* 1: 278). London remains a "temptation," the nexus of Bloomsbury where "the presence of these very brightly lit brains makes things go swiftly, & without padding" (*D* 1: 304, 261). However, London also remains tied to the (predominantly male) literary tradition. Secure in the country, she writes from Monk's House in late September: "I've reviewed Hope [Mirrlees]; [Sir Edmund] Gosse & [Frank] Swinnerton, all in the past 10 days so that the great autumn downpour [of newly published books] is beginning. It crosses my mind now & then that Night & Day will be one drop of it: but that seems to belong to London—not here" (*D* 1: 302).

Sadly, Hampstead persists in the 1919 diary as a site of female chill. "[W]e approach the heights of Hampstead—the immaculate & moral heights of Hampstead," Woolf writes scornfully in her November 15 entry and follows these words with a now-familiar diary gesture—confessed inability to write: "Had I the energy left I would write that scene of revelation & explanation with Margaret [Llewelyn Davies]. . . . Tentatively she began it—how Janet & she felt that perhaps—they might be wrong, but still in their view—in short my article on Charlotte Brontë was so much more to their liking than my novels. Something in my feeling for human beings—some narrowness—some lack of emotion—here I blazed up & let fly."[17]

Some issues, in short, persist in this 1919 diary. Woolf strives to write a diary of public history as well as one of personal and artistic life. "In public affairs, I see I've forgotten to say that peace was signed," she writes on July 12. "I've forgotten the account I was going to write out of the gradual disappearance of things from shop windows; & the gradual, but still only partial reappearance of things. Sugar cakes, currant buns, & mounds of sweets. The effect of the war would be worth describing" (*D* 1: 291). A week later she declares, "One ought to say something about Peace day, I suppose, though whether its worth taking a new nib for that purpose I dont know" (*D* 1: 292).

Her September 30 entry begins: "This is opened to record the Strike bulletin," and as she follows the railway strike and its effect on Sussex signal man Thomas Pargiter (whose last name she will borrow for *The Years*), she considers how to write of labor politics, just as she pondered how to render the effects of war (*D* 1: 302). "Still, what's to be read in the papers is hardly fit for my private page," she judges in her October 7 entry. "I wonder if I could expound the railway strike? What they asked, & what they got?" (*D* 1: 304). In 1926, she will write a more elaborate strike diary.

Sixty-six entries preserve the 333 days from January 20 through December 28, 1919. Missed days are noted but accepted with equanimity. When the move from Asheham House to Monk's House causes a forty-three-day diary gap, Woolf opens a new Monk's House diary on September 7 with "I suppose this is the first day upon which I could easily sit down & write in my long suffering & by this time I hope tolerant diary."[18] By December, she declares of a six-day gap: "Another of these skips, but I think the book draws its breath steadily if with deliberation" (*D* 1: 315). Woolf sees across this diary even more roles her diary serves. Diary strokes still soothe her. Her diary still "marks their place" and stores impressions. "Life piles up so fast that I have no time to write out the equally fast rising mound of reflections, which I always mark down as they rise to be inserted here," she begins her March 19 entry. "I meant to write about the Barnetts, & the peculiar repulsiveness of those who dabble their fingers self approvingly in the stuff of others' souls."[19]

As the above hints, the "mound of reflections" includes seeds for future works. "I must note for future use, the superb possibilities of Freshwater, for a comedy," she closes her January 30 entry. "Old Cameron dressed in a blue dressing gown & not going beyond his garden for 12 years, suddenly borrows his son's coat, & walks down to the sea. Then they decide to proceed to Ceylon, taking their coffins with them, & the last sight of Aunt Julia [Cameron] is on board ship, presenting porters with large photographs of Sir Henry Taylor & the Madonna in default of small change" (*D* 1: 237). On March 30, she confesses: "I open this book today merely to note that Miss *Eleanor Ormerod*, destroyer of insects, promises well for Murry: should he take kindly to my first" article (on Lady Hester Stanhope, whose brilliant talk and exploits are recorded in Dr. Charles Meryon's diaries, which Woolf read in 1909 and 1910) (*D* 1: 260).

On October 7, Woolf begins to reread (yet again) her 1917 and 1918 Hogarth House diaries. She does so with a critical eye and identifies for the first time a further function of her diary—to stay time: "I began reading the first volume of my [Hogarth] diary; & see that its second anniversary is now reached. I dont think the first volume makes such good reading as the last; a proof that all writing, even this unpremeditated scribbling, has its form, which one learns. Is it worth going on with? . . . I wonder why I do it. Partly, I think, from my old sense of the race of time 'Time's winged chariot hurrying near'—Does it stay it?" (*D* 1: 304).

The 1919 diary must ever take its place as the diary that offers Woolf's fullest expression of her mature diary goals. The diary that expands in its opening entry to become a private preserve of portraits for Elderly Virginia's memoirs enlarges even more by April, when Woolf imagines the whole diary as a work of art. On Easter Sunday, April 20, she notes, "I got out this diary, & read as one always does read one's own writing, with a kind of guilty intensity" (*D* 1: 266). She then thinks of Elderly Virginia, and of posterity as well: "I confess that the rough & random style of it, often so ungrammatical, & crying for a word altered, afflicted me somewhat. I am trying to tell whichever self it is that reads this hereafter that I can write very much better; & take no time over this; & forbid her to let the eyes of man behold it" (*D* 1: 266).

Having noted her diary's defects (and protected it from men), she can then see its promise:

> And now I may add my little compliment to the effect that it has a slap-dash & vigour, & sometimes hits an unexpected bulls eye. But what is more to the point is my belief that the habit of writing thus for my own eye only is good practise. It loosens the ligaments. Never mind the misses & the stumbles. Going at such a pace as I do I must make the most direct & instant shots at my object, & thus have to lay hands on words, choose them, & shoot them with no more pause than is needed to put my pen in the ink. . . . Moreover there looms ahead of me the shadow of some kind of form which a diary might attain to. (*D* 1: 266)

Woolf seems to envision here an ideal (Platonic) diary form—or at least a personal diary art—she might reach. She then spurs herself with a question: "What sort of diary should I like mine to be?" And answers: "Something loose knit, & yet not slovenly, so elastic that it will embrace any thing, solemn, slight or beautiful that comes into my mind" (*D* 1: 266). She carries forward here the watchwords of Byron's "method" in *Don Juan* across eight months from her August 8, 1918, diary entry: "random" thoughts in an "elastic" form, a blank open-ended space that can be filled with the loose, drifting material of life (*D* 1: 181).

Then she imagines her diary a creative receptacle. "I should like it to resemble some deep old desk, or capacious hold-all, in which one flings a mass of odds & ends without looking them through," she writes. "I should like to come back, after a year or two, & find that the collection had sorted itself & refined itself & coalesced, as such deposits so mysteriously do, into a mould, transparent enough to reflect the light of our life, & yet steady, tranquil[,] composed with the aloofness of a work of art" (*D* 1: 266). Woolf appears here to invite her creative unconscious to work upon her diary. She has asked her unconscious to work for her before. In her 1906 Blo' Norton diary she lists all the elements of the Norfolk country scene, then declares: "Compose these all somehow into a picture; I am too lazy to do it" (*PA* 315). In her diary's portrait of Desmond MacCarthy just two months before this April 1919 "deep old desk, or capacious hold-all" trope, Woolf imagines herself creating a publishable book from Mac-Carthy's desk, a book that "shall appear as a proof to the younger generation that Desmond was the most gifted of us all" (*D* 1: 241–42).

Woolf ends her diary credo with advice to herself on how to achieve the "loose knit" yet not "slovenly" form and style she seeks. Her answer is *greater* freedom—and trust in the unconscious: "The main requisite, I think on re-reading my old volumes, is not to play the part of censor, but to write as the mood comes or of anything whatever; since I was curious to find how I went for things put in haphazard, & found the significance to lie where I never saw it at the time" (*D* 1: 266).

Woolf's diary credo unites conflicting states. What at first is so "slovenly" that the diarist bids "whichever self it is that reads this" to keep it from "the eye of man" by entry's end holds out the promise of achieving "the aloofness of a work of art." In perhaps her most empowering diary gesture, Woolf once more confesses artistic failure in order to free herself to try.

The 1919 diary offers the full flowering of Woolf's mature diary style. All the blooms have opened: portraits; scenes; public history and private life; a common reader's diary and uncommon writer's love for her art—all animated with morphing metaphors and with questions, questions, questions pressing and enlarging it all.[20] The flowering does not occur overnight; rather, it represents the steady unfolding of possibilities latent in her 1915 diary.

How did Woolf achieve the range, depth, and richness of her 1919 seasoned diary style? Three behaviors stand out. The sheer attention she directs to diary-keeping from the start of her Asheham House natural history diary in August 1917 reveals the importance of diary-writing to her at this time. The Asheham House diary begets the Hogarth House diary. I know of no other diarist who writes in two different diaries—country and city diaries—on the same day. This intensive diary *writing* occurs in concert with persistent, one might almost say, obsessive, diary *rereading*. Many diarists never reread their entries. Woolf enriches her diary because she constantly rereads it with a critical and curious eye. Finally, from 1916 through 1919 she also reads (and writes of) others' diaries: Mary (Seton) Berry's, the Goncourt brothers' collaborative *Journals*, Stopford Brooke's innovative diaries, Henry Crabb Robinson's ebullient *Diary*, and Wilfrid Scawen Blunt's *Diaries*.[21] In light of this formidable focus, the diary now blooms.

Wilfrid Scawen Blunt's *Diaries*

"I've rambled very painfully over the diaries of Wilfrid Blunt," Virginia Woolf writes to Saxon Sydney-Turner on September 12, 1919: "I have a great prejudice against Blunt, though he hates the British Empire, but then he reads his poems to Mrs Asquith, and they have parties where they make speeches, and they're all so rich and distinguished, and their writing is so much admired, and it is so pretty and smart compared with middle class writing. But I have no room to develop this very important argument" (*L* #1081, 2: 389).

Wilfrid Scawen Blunt (as he signed his diaries, poems, and political prose) was born in 1840 at Crabbet Park, a four-thousand-acre Sussex domain bordering the Shelleys' estates. His father was Lord Byron's Harrow schoolmate (and "fag"), and Blunt himself marries Byron's granddaughter, Lady Annabella Noel. Before this distinguished match, however, he is orphaned at twelve, taught by the Jesuits, but absolved of university days when, at eighteen, he is placed in the English diplomatic corps at Athens. His subsequent transfers to the courts at Frankfort, Constantinople, Paris, Buenos Aires, Portugal, and Spain (where he was remembered as a handsome matador) whet his taste for political affairs.

However, Blunt dabbles in the arts as well and writes his first poems at age twenty-four. He quits the diplomatic corps after his marriage and, after a series of romantic horseback trips with his wife in Spain, Algeria, and Asia Minor (beginning in 1875), he starts to focus his pen on English imperialism. He writes on the Irish Home Rule movement and particularly on the national drive for self-government in Egypt, but also in India and Islamic lands. In 1888, Blunt becomes the first Englishman jailed for supporting Irish independence, a two-month jail stay he never forgets. He publishes *The Land War in Ireland*; *The Future of Islam*; *Secret History of the English Occupation of Egypt*; *Gordon at Khartoum*; and *India under Ripon: A Private Diary*.

All of these are described in *My Diaries: Being a Personal Narrative of Events, 1888–1914*, the work Woolf "ramble[s] very painfully" over in 1919, three years before Blunt dies, at age eighty-one. As Lady Gregory, Blunt's friend of forty years, observes in the preface to the American edition of *My Diaries*, Blunt's home-rule, anti-imperialist, and antiwar writings represent "[a]n unusual and gallant record for a Sussex gentleman of many acres, of inherited wealth and ease" (1: xiv).

Woolf might have been kinder to Wilfrid Scawen Blunt. He was a committee member of the Peace and Arbitration Society,[22] and his *Diaries* strikingly document British treatment of war as sport. Readers may wonder where Woolf derived this *Three Guineas* view. One answer: from diaries such as Blunt's. Three months after the Boer War begins, Blunt's December 13, 1899, diary entry reports a visit from Walter Gaisford. The soldier laments, Blunt records, that "the Khalifa and his dervishes had all been killed, so that there would be nobody left to shoot, he complained, even in the Soudan. 'There is hope, however, that, when the Boers are polished off, we may go on to a war with Abyssinia when more sport will be to be had.' This is the way our young fellows look at war ('a high old rabbit shoot')" (1: 341).

On January 16, 1909, the centenary of his father's wound at the Battle of Corunna in Spain, Blunt reflects on his father's tales of that war: "The campaign . . . must have been carried on in a curiously amateur way. My father, like the rest of the officers, was allowed to take with him his fowling-piece and a brace of pointers for sport on the campaign. . . . The pointers were left behind while fording a river which they could not swim, and thus put an end to the sport" (2: 229).

Woolf might have taken more to Blunt's *Diaries*. In many respects he resembled Lady Hester Stanhope, immortalized in physician Charles Meryon's six diary volumes and recently celebrated by Woolf herself in a 1919 essay. Like Lady Hester, Blunt builds himself a hermitage in the Levant (in the desert outside of Cairo) and cultivates his own garden, attacking British imperialism all the while. Like Lady Hester, he takes to wearing Arab dress, and he adventures regularly into the desert at some peril while working out his own highly personal religious views. However, unlike Lady Hester, Blunt never cuts the English cord. While Lady Hester's isolated, outsider role increased across her days, Blunt never more than winters in his Egyptian enclave, and he spends the final decade of his life in Sussex, leading (he tells us) "the life there of a country squire to which I was born, and which is naturally mine."[23]

In the end, Blunt could afford to be less committed to the East than could Lady Hester Stanhope. Perhaps this crucial difference joined other sore points to make Woolf's 1919 "ramble" through Blunt's *Diaries* "very painful." Blunt, after all, calls G. F. Watts "on the whole the greatest [painter] in England since [Joshua] Reynolds," and he describes the 1910 Post-Impressionist Art Exhibition as "an extremely bad joke or a swindle. . . . a pornographic show"—although he admires Roger Fry's art criticism and knows Desmond MacCarthy (2: 103, 329, 330).

His views of women remained similarly retrograde. In 1909, when his friend and former "Soul" mate, Margot Asquith, and her Prime Minister husband face both threat and attack from the Suffragettes, Blunt advises her to "cease the war" with the women and particularly to stop imprisoning them for their views, a punishment he well knew (2: 235). However, his March 12, 1909, diary entry reveals his true colors, for he describes his most recent letter to Margot Asquith:

> I am answering: "You must not be angry with me for what I said in favour of the Suffragettes. I have no brief for them, nor do I take much interest one way or another in their cause. I should be against them if I thought there was the smallest chance of woman rule in England, but there is none, no more than there is danger of 'the Yellow Peril' in Europe, or the 'Negro Peril' in America. Women have never ruled men anywhere and never will except indirectly by being better and kinder and less selfish than we are. You are one of these. . . . The whole woman's movement is not worth a curl of your brown head. (2: 237)

Ten months later, Blunt offers Woolf a scene of turf restriction that she will reprise in her 1929 *A Room of One's Own*. Henry Cust was at Lympne with Herbert Asquith when "the suffragettes assaulted Asquith, striking him on the face with their fists, or rather with their wrists (he gave a demonstration). He, Harry, was Secretary of the Golf Club and intervened, telling the women that whatever their dispute with the Prime Minister might be it was impossible they should be allowed to walk on the grass, as it was against the regulations of the Club" (2: 275). Although Blunt admired some woman writers, including Elizabeth Barrett Browning as a *poet*, his scorn of her letters as "poor literature" in his 1900 diary might have spurred Woolf to read them (1: 373).

In the end, Blunt's greatest sin, for Woolf, may have been to offer a preaching political diary. She had read diaries published in defense of women: Dr. Meryon's diaries recounting Lady Hester Stanhope's extraordinary days and Lady Charlotte Bury's *Diary of a Lady-in-Waiting* defending herself and Princess Caroline of Wales. However, here was a diary in defense of *political* views; in fact, an I-told-you-so diary from start to end.

Nevertheless, *My Diaries: Being a Personal Narrative of Events 1888–1914* manages, like many diaries, to fascinate. By the end of volume one the reader is fully immersed in Blunt's life and crusades.

Blunt himself had some sense of his diary's value. He writes at age seventy-eight in the foreword to *My Diaries*, "[T]he truth of history needs to be told, and not only in Blue Books, where the essential facts are travestied, but by individual testimony such as mine, recording the words of statesmen in out of office hours, when they have spoken their naked thought to me in very different language" (1: xv).

Earlier, in a 1913 entry expressing "black melancholy" at his failure in life, Blunt laments: "My poetry, my Eastern politics, my Arab horse breeding, were strings to my bow and they have one after another snapped, and to-day looking through my memoirs I perceive how slackly they are written and how unworthy they are of survival. Yet the diaries are full of things too important for me to destroy" (2: 409). He closes *My Diaries* a year later, "reserving my Diary of the War itself for a posthumous occasion, if it should seem worth transcribing to those I may name literary executors of my last Will and Testament" (2: 431). He hoped, then, his last diaries would reach us as well.[24]

The online Diary Junction calls Blunt's *Diaries* "spicy." Biographer Elizabeth Longford suggests that "as a social diarist [Blunt] is on a par with Charles Greville"—a high compliment (4). *My Diaries* may have been sent to Leonard Woolf to review.[25] Alternatively, Lytton Strachey may have recommended them to the Woolfs. Blunt wrote *Gordon in Khartoum*, after all, and he speaks often in his *Diaries* of Bill Gordon, Gordon's military nephew. Blunt brings Crabbet roses to Cardinal Manning for his birthday in 1891, details the theft of Manning's diaries, and reports the Cardinal's lonely death. Queen Victoria appears in the *Diaries* as a virulent British imperialist.[26] Strachey likely found Blunt's *Diaries* useful for *Eminent Victorians* and *Queen Victoria*.

For Woolf, however, Wilfrid Blunt was the kind of man who built a hunting lodge in the New Forest—a site she rejects in her 1906 diary. He was the kind of man who called Wells Cathedral "the most perfect in England"—a site she rejects in her 1908 diary (1: 237). He was the kind invited to join the Pembrokes' Wilton Club, who viewed Wilton—and even the British politics he loathed— from *inside* the walls.[27] Virginia never reviewed *My Diaries*; nevertheless they gave her indelible views of war as male sport, as well as a scene of turf restriction that will start her 1929 *A Room of One's Own*. "I read Wilfrid Blunt (diaries) at breakfast," she writes to Lytton Strachey on September 14, 1919. "I don't like aristocratic writing, do you?" (*L* #1082, 2: 390).

2

New Diary Realms

Talk, the Soul, and Literature

Virginia Woolf begins to reach out with her 1920 diary. Using one of her most helpful diary feints, she names barriers only to begin to traverse them. In January, she wonders how far she should allow herself to report indiscretion in her diary. In March, she ponders something more profound: whether she can write a "diary of the soul" (D 2: 26). She fully endorses the soul's reality. In a December 1918 review, she had declared that the soul "alone is important; that living core which suffers and toils is what we all have in common" (E 2: 343).

The soul entwines with its expression in literature. In April, Woolf considers whether her diary can "trench upon literature" (D 2: 28). On her thirty-eighth birthday, January 25, 1920, she had conceived of "a new form for a new novel"—her first modernist novel, Jacob's Room (D 2: 13). Declaring that she could "think [herself] a novelist" if she could record Mrs. Clifford's "talk," Woolf experiments across her 1920 diary with different ways to render conversations (D 2: 12). She practices, in short, for her public prose.

Her 1920 diary thus takes steps toward literature. It certainly meets Cyril Connolly's dictum that literature is "something that will be read twice." Her diary also begins to reflect H. L. Mencken's belief that "[a] great literature is chiefly the product of inquiring minds in revolt against the immovable certainties of the nation."

In April 1920, Woolf is sent the literary traces of another inquiring mind in revolt: W.N.P. Barbellion's famous Journal of a Disappointed Man. It incites her exploration of the soul, offers her much of the Septimus Smith plot for Mrs. Dalloway, and provides visions of two trips to a lighthouse. In October, she publishes a lengthy commemorative essay on John Evelyn's diary, probing the diary's power.

Virginia Woolf's 1920 Diary

"By the way, Morgan keeps a diary, & in his diary Morgan writes conversations— word for word, when the humour takes him."

(April 10, 1920; *D* 2: 27)

Talk—in different formats—filters through Virginia Woolf's 1920 diary, a lovely large diary with an oriental cover.[1] Tiny aquamarine pagodas, bridges, and leafy-branched trees repeat across the cover, and Woolf takes nearly as much care with this book's interior as with her 1919 diary's. She prepares its white un- ruled pages in advance, ruling a vertical line in blue ink one-and-a-half inches from the left-hand edge. However, she makes no effort to recopy and polish her opening January entry, as she did in her first 1919 diary offerings; rather, she tears the pages from the end of the 1919 diary and pastes them into the new book, touting her diary's rebellion. "To begin the year on the last pages of my old book . . . is all upside-down of course," she acknowledges, "but of a part with the character of the work" (*D* 2: 3). These words at age thirty-seven echo the close of her first surviving diary at age fifteen: "I write this morning what would more fitly have been written last night. But my diary has ever been scornful of stated rules!" (*PA* 134).

Shunning rules frees Woolf to further her diary art. In her March 9, 1920, entry, she vows to probe more deeply into herself and her world, to face mat- ters less "pliable," "comfortable," and "bright" (*D* 2: 24). She calls on Elderly Virginia for support: "I fancy old Virginia, putting on her spectacles to read of March 1920 will decidedly wish me to continue. Greetings! my dear ghost; & take heed that *I* dont think 50 a very great age. Several good books can be writ- ten still; & here's the bricks for a fine one" (*D* 2: 24). "Elderly Virginia" becomes now "old Virginia," but her diary role persists. She will not only relish but also *use* Woolf's diary prose. In fact, this projected older self spurs the diarist on.

In January, Woolf ponders the value of scandal for her diary. "I might fill this page & the succeeding ones with the Shoves' gossip, but I have never deter- mined how far it is permitted to go here in indiscretion," she writes. "I should have to write at length to retail this specimen properly which is the conclusive reason against it" (*D* 2: 7). However, she then manages to register Philip Mor- rell's infidelities and illegitimate children.

New realms—shallow and deep—thus start to open in this 1920 diary: in- discretion, the soul, and that "shadow of some kind of form" of literature she has glimpsed in her Easter 1919 diary credo (*D* 1: 266). Woolf's April 10 report that E. M. Forster also keeps a diary in which he records talk "word for word" appears in the paragraph just before she considers "trench[ing] upon literature" in her diary (*D* 2: 27, 28). She has captured scenes and dialogue in earlier diaries, of course, but now, perhaps fired by Forster's example, she formally experiments across her 1920 diary with different ways to render talk—as if practicing for *Jacob's Room*. And she starts on the path to elision as well. Even before learning of Forster's diary practice, Woolf tells her diary after her January 24 visit with writer Lucy Clifford, "[I]f I could reproduce her talk of money, royalties, editions, & reviews, I should think myself a novelist" (*D* 2: 12).

Ten days later, she catches her French dressmaker's accent in this seamless substitutionary narration (with its opening nod to Samuel Pepys): "To Madame Gravé's this afternoon—& found her in her great new house. Maman is getting very trying poor dear. You set her on the stool & she does nothing. Then she wants the stool again—But you've just been there & done nothing maman! Then she calls me cruel—very trying. And when she sleeps her mouth hangs down, as though she were dead. She's getting senile. All this simply, tenderly even, as we wander about the house, looking at the furniture" (*D* 2: 17).

In the entry immediately *after* her note of Forster's diary talk, Woolf tries two-voiced conversation: "Hanny came up. 'Mrs Woolf?' Yes—but who—? We met years ago at the Squires—Hannay. Ah, you do art criticism now? Tell me what I ought to think of the carvings. And these Peruvian bowls—" (*D* 2: 30). She then critiques her effort in parentheses: "(I don't think this expresses him, though. A man who spaces his words with long silences—...)" (*D* 2: 30).

Nine days later, when Forster himself spends the night, she writes "I wish I could write his talk down" and then tries, abandoning quotation marks and placing voices now on separate lines. Forster begins:

> I must now write a postcard. Yes, I must really catch the first post if possible. I'll take it myself—Is there time still—I'll tell you what it is. The seat is being painted. The boy is so stupid he'll paint it after its been rained upon. Then it will be ruined.
> Nonsense said L. it wont hurt it.
> But are you sure? (*D* 2: 33)

This try pleases her more. "This is very like Morgan," she declares, "so too his reliance on Leonard. 'Where d'you get your boots? Are Waterman pens the best'" (*D* 2: 33).

Woolf's May 31 entry conveys her intimate duet with Katherine Mansfield within the trio formed from John Middleton Murry's intrusions (*D* 2: 43–45), and the diary closes with a rash of dialogue trials. Three of the last four entries offer talk variants and, in fact, experiment with elision. Woolf tries out dashes to telegraph her rapid verbal flights with Lytton Strachey on December 12: "At once we plunge, even on the cold pavement, into literature. Eliot's book— 'serious' far far better than the journalists—disgraceful review by Lynd. . . .— Shall Lytton write to the Nation? What about Vic? So we pace to Nessa's door. And Ralph [Partridge]? Well, I wdn't marry Ralph—A despot. True. But whats to happen to C[arrington]. She can't live indefinitely with me—Perhaps with him? Door opens, in I go" (*D* 2: 79).

Her final entry in 1920 reprises a visit to the Case sisters in escalating stream-of-consciousness: "Miss Leonard calling. 'A name you don't often hear. But theres a bootmaker in Oxford called Leonard. My brother had a pair of boots made there. His wife didn't quite like it oh eh ha ho!' (little laughs like notes of a flute)" (*D* 2: 82).

Sixty-three entries preserve the 361 days from January 7, 1920, to January 2, 1921—three fewer than in the 1919 diary. Alongside its drive to capture talk, the 1920 diary offers Woolf's first full record of a work's composition: from initial glimpse through the peaks and precipices of creation. Following the November 1918 Hampstead crisis, Woolf begins to address her own writing in her diary. Her 1919 diary, in consequence, charts every vibration before and after the October release of her second novel, *Night and Day*. She records in her November 15, 1919, entry "one of those slight distastes [for writing] which betokens a change of style," and her January 26, 1920, entry defines that change as a new form for long fiction (*D* 1: 311). The new modernist form she describes mirrors her diary's traits: "looseness & lightness . . . & speed" (*D* 2: 13). Questions in this January entry serve as probes of her new novel form, and she speaks of her wish to be "sufficiently mistress of [her] dialogue" in the novel (*D* 2: 13).

Few diaries capture the creative process as fully as Woolf's diary now will do. "I'm planning to begin Jacob's Room next week with luck. (That's the first time I've written that)," she notes in that rich April 10 entry, which ponders "trench[ing] on literature" (*D* 2: 28). However, invention can halt, and she confesses in her next entry, April 15, that criticism—even when just—can retard her. Arthur Walkley has attacked her article on Henry James. "This slightly checks me from beginning *Jacob's room*," she notes.[2] However, owning and mulling the critique in her diary allows her to proceed, for she ends this entry begun in the chill of criticism: "My notion is to write this [*Jacob's Room*] in chapters straight off; not beginning one unless I can count on so many days clear for finishing it" (*D* 2: 31). And two days later she can assure herself, "The pain from Walkley is dying out, since I've begun Jacob's Room" (*D* 2: 31).

On May 11 she reports, "It is worth mentioning, for future reference, that the creative power which bubbles so pleasantly on beginning a new book quiets down after a time, & one goes on more steadily. Doubts creep in. Then one becomes resigned. Determination not to give in, & the sense of an impending shape keep one at it more than anything" (*D* 2: 35). In August, she ponders creation. "How shifting & vacillating one's mind is! Yesterday broody & drowsy all day long, writing easily, & yet without strict consciousness, as though fluent under drugs: today apparently clear headed, yet unable to put one sentence after another—sat for an hour, scratching out, putting in, scratching out" (*D* 2: 59). And when she coins her image of life as "a little strip of pavement over an abyss" in her October 25 entry, she broods on it and writes on November 23: "[S]o my strip of pavement (I bag that phrase for Jacob) widens" (*D* 2: 72, 75).

Woolf continues to attend to women in this 1920 diary and turns from private observations to thoughts of public prose. Arnold Bennett's September book, which declares that "intellectually and creatively man is the superior of woman," leads Woolf to think of "making up a paper upon Women" as a retort—the first diary sign in the 1920s of the 1929 *A Room of One's Own* (*D* 2: 69; n12). And as she comes to know their new Hogarth Press partner, Ralph Partridge, whom she will soon call a "despot," she records his November tale of his visit to a London brothel: "Girls paraded before him—that was what pleased him—the sense of power" (*D* 2: 79, 75).

Although "old Virginia" tenders support and helps her view old age in a constructive light, Woolf still observes age across this diary and vacillates in her view. The literal shrinkage brought by age repeatedly strikes her. In January, Roger Fry, whose vitality inspired the creation of "Elderly Virginia" in the January 1919 diary, now appears to her "slightly shrunken, aged?" (*D* 2: 10). When she asks herself in her memorable October 25 entry why life is so tragic, "so like a little strip of pavement over an abyss," age figures in her reply: "Its having no children, living away from friends, failing to write well, spending too much on food, growing old—" (*D* 2: 72). Earlier, when Lilian Harris faces blindness, Woolf exclaims, "What courage can make one, at 50, look down the remaining years, with that calamity to darken them!" (*D* 2: 13). All in all she still prefers "the nondescript anonymous days of youth" (*D* 2: 78).

A similar hesitation lingers regarding London as a productive site. Hampstead continues to vanish in 1920 as a supportive "republic of women." "[N]ot very agreeable," Woolf tells her diary of a June tea with Janet Case.[3] Luckily,

Monk's House compensates. It continues to enchant. By this point, it does not surprise us to see Woolf wish to keep nature and the country a private, unconscious domain. "I dont like these civic interruptions into rural life," she writes in her August 17 entry of Lady Cecil's impending call (D 2: 57). When John Squire and Siegfried Sassoon descend on her on August 31, she confesses, "Somehow that the downs should be seen by cultivated eyes, self conscious eyes, spoils them to me" (D 2: 62).

Woolf seems nourished not only by unspoiled nature itself but also by the regularity of country life attuned to nature. "[E]veryone does the same thing at the same hour," she declares on October 1. "Everyone is in his, or their garden; lamps are lit, but people like the last daylight. . . . What I mean is that we are a community."[4] Her ambivalence toward London registers. "London yesterday I hated," she writes on August 17 from the country. "More truly it was not London but a certain yard of the line between Richmond & Mortlake where we stopped for an hour & a half. . . . But as the train swung out into open country[,] life seemed fresher, sweeter, saner" (D 2: 57–58).

However, Vanessa returns to Gordon Square in the autumn, greatly increasing London's pull. When Woolf spends the night at Gordon Square in August—sleeping in Maynard Keynes's empty bed—she declares: "The ease & rapidity of life in London a good deal impressed me—everything near at hand, to be compassed between lunch & tea, without setting out & making a job of it. Roger, Duncan, Nessa, Clive, & so on; I seeing it all much composed & in perspective owing to my outsider's vision" (D 2: 55). In the arresting October 25 entry she identifies as the "first day of winter time," Woolf attributes some of her sense of life's tragedy, her view of life as "a little strip of pavement over an abyss," to her suburban isolation: "Here I sit at Richmond, & like a lantern stood in the middle of a field my light goes up in darkness. . . . Its having no children, living away from friends. . . . Nessa's children grow up, & I cant have them in to tea, or go to the Zoo" (D 2: 72).

This wish for London, and a kind of city community to complement her country commune, will mount and mount across diaries to come. In November she writes, "Ralph [Partridge] hints at a plan of sharing a London house with us—which tempts me, on some days" (D 2: 73). But on other 1920 days she recoils. When she feels "muzzled" in the Bloomsbury Group on December 19, she seeks independence: "Indeed, Nessa wouldn't have me living next door for something. Indeed, my retort is, I wouldn't live there. I see myself now taking my own line apart from theirs. One of these days I shan't know Clive if I meet him. I want to know all sorts of other people—retaining only Nessa & Duncan,

I think" (*D* 2: 81). And two days later, the last diary words of 1920 are framed as this probe: "We should be dining with Nessa &c: but have been put off; & oh dear, I'm glad to sit over the fire—& how could I if I lived in London?"[5]

Nevertheless, though *all* of Bloomsbury fails to draw her, something in London itself does. During a June trip to the city, Woolf catches sight of an old, blind beggar woman singing and holding a brown mongrel dog, an image of defiant London she will preserve in her diary—and then in *Jacob's Room*: "There was a recklessness about her; much in the spirit of London. Defiant—almost gay..." (*D* 2: 47). And then questions pour forth in Woolf's most characteristic diary rhythm: "How many Junes has she sat there, in the heart of London? How she came to be there, what scenes she can go through, I can't imagine. O damn it all, I say, why cant I know all that too?" (*D* 2: 47). This defiant, singing, old beggar woman may be another version of old Virginia: a female blind Homer performing her art.

In the diary entry just before, Woolf offers her first intuition of what she will call in her 1923 diary her "turn & turn about method" (*D* 2: 247). Tellingly, nature inspires the insight that will undergird Woolf's country-and-London rhythm as well as her writing turns. Woolf begins her June 5 entry: "Here we are in the prime of the year which I've thought of so often in January & December, always with pleasure.... What I believe is that one brings out the taste of the month one's in by opposing to it another" (*D* 2: 45). Here are the suggestive "discords" of her 1908 diary aesthetic (*PA* 393). Like the seasons, the country and city also bring out the "tastes" in each other. So, too, different styles of prose.

The 1920 diary opens with a vivid evocation of the country: their Monk's House life as a specimen day. It closes in artful full circle with a scene of Rodmell social life. The country thus encloses the 1920 diary, which takes some steps toward literary art. Woolf's second entry, in fact, foreshadows the rich range of life to come. "Ah, that's all very well," she remarks wryly of her evocative specimen day, "but a fate conspires against a solemn opening ceremony. True, I've taken a new nib; but I'm perched high in bug [*sic*] chair ... waiting for Lotty to bring in tin tacks, with which to mend my aged broken down eared arm chair" (*D* 2: 5). The 1920 diary moves from "solemn" and "beautiful" to homely comedy. However, as Olivier Bell notes, Woolf treats it all with ease and familiarity (*D* 2: viii). "[A]s I think this diary records," she writes January 14, "I have warmed to [Marjorie Strachey] these past years" (*D* 2: 7). Woolf flies to her diary "for refuge" in the middle of Monk's House baking on August 2. "Poor wretched book! Thats the way I treat you!—Thats the drudge you are!"

she exclaims affectionately. "Still, take comfort from the thought that I brought you all the way from London, to save scribbling on half sheets which get lost" (*D* 2: 53). The country and London merge once more.

In early 1918, Woolf sought to extend individual diary entries to embrace other days, to allow few days to slip through her hands. By 1920, having worked through this expansive method, she inclines to compress and elide. "I must skip over forgotten days & alight at Ottoline's last night," she writes briskly on February 13 (*D* 2: 19). This long entry ends: "Last week end at the Arnold Forsters I've entirely left out" (*D* 2: 20). On March 9 she writes, "Monday at the [1917] Club, which I see I've ceased to describe" (*D* 2: 25). Her May 26 entry moves equally swiftly, treating her diary as a work of art (as she imagined in her 1919 diary credo): "Running through this I see I've left out one or two important pieces in the mosaic" (*D* 2: 42). She then supplies them. Her September diary portrait of T. S. Eliot, composed "as if one were making out a scientific observation," reveals her "tax[ing] him with wilfully concealing his transitions" (*D* 2: 67). Her subsequent diary conversations elide and elide.

As these December conversations begin to unfold, Woolf reverts to her suggestive "deep old desk, or capacious hold-all" figure from her Easter 1919 diary credo in order to sum up the year (*D* 1: 266). What does she want to tell her diary, she asks herself December 5: "How hard we work—thats what impresses me this winter: every compartment stuffed tight, chiefly owing to the press. Whether we can keep it up, I don't know" (*D* 2: 78). Two weeks later, the figure remains: "I ought to say how happy I am. . . . My only guess is that it has something to do with working steadily; writing things out of my head; & never having a compartment empty" (*D* 2: 80).

In an August double entry on *Don Quixote*, Woolf describes again the style she favors in both her fiction and her diary. *Quixote* has "the loose, far scattered vitality of the great books," she declares (*D* 2: 57). Within its own loose, far-scattered vitality, Woolf's 1920 diary moves toward new depths of subject (the soul) and style (literature). The diary's most striking figure—life as "a little strip of pavement over an abyss"—depicts this diary's role. The 1920 diary experiments with ways to retail talk. "I've had my dive into their heads & come out again, I think," Woolf declares April 20 (*D* 2: 32). In May, she writes of Samuel Koteliansky, who brings the soulful Russians to the Hogarth Press: "He always speaks the truth, & gropes after it in psychology—rather a queer thing to do. . . . We are publishing Gorki, & perhaps this marks some step over a precipice—I don't know" (*D* 2: 34). If the soul and human psychology are "the abyss"— along with death—Woolf now starts to take her dive. Her more expansive 1918 diary style matched the more fully sketched *Night and Day*. As her fiction style changes in 1920, her diary prose, too, begins to refine and elide.

W.N.P. Barbellion's *Journal of a Disappointed Man*

Virginia Woolf's haunting figure of life as a "little strip of pavement over an abyss" may have come from W.N.P. Barbellion's *Journal of a Disappointed Man*, sent her in April 1920 (*D* 2: 72, 32). This *Journal* caused a sensation when published in March 1919. In fact, toward the close of her Easter 1919 entry that offers her diary credo, Woolf describes herself in her bath at Monk's House overhearing Desmond MacCarthy's "disquisition" to Leonard "upon the authenticity of Barbellion's diary" (*D* 1: 267).

Barbellion primed the mystery his diaries exude. He never names the "creeping paralysis" that dooms his "brilliant career," although he knows by 1915 it is multiple sclerosis (274, 62). H. G. Wells wrote the *Journal's* introduction, framing *The Journal of a Disappointed Man* as proof of Britain's shameful neglect of its young scientists. This caused some reviewers to claim Wells faked the *Journal* to make his point. These rumors grew when readers learned there was no "W.N.P. Barbellion." Barbellion was the pointedly chosen pen name of a twenty-nine-year-old dying natural historian afflicted not only with multiple sclerosis but also with the more ordinary name of Bruce Frederick Cummings.

Cummings took the initials "W.N.P." from the names of those he thought the world's greatest failures: Wilhelm (the German Kaiser), Nero, and Pilate. "Barbellion," a word he thought "appropriately inflated," came from a Bond Street confectioner's shop (ii). The final turn of the screw came from the last words of *The Journal of a Disappointed Man*, the bracketed whisper "Barbellion died on December 31 [1917]," for it soon came to light that Cummings/Barbellion did not die on that date. Rather, he was still around in 1919 to read the reviews of *The Journal of a Disappointed Man* and to prepare his 1918 and 1919 diaries for genuinely posthumous publication in 1920 as *A Last Diary*.

"I possess the qualifications of an artistic liar," Cummings confesses to his *Journal* as early as age twenty-two, and at twenty-three, more than two years before he knows what preys on him, he anticipates his *Journal's* close: "As an artist in life I *ought* to die; it is the only artistic ending—and I ought to die now or the Third Act will fizzle out in a long doctor's bill" (*JDM* 53, 88). Barbellion's *Journal* is an artful text. "1917. I am now editing my own Journal—bowdlerising my own book!" Cummings exclaims in a footnote he appends to a 1915 entry (180). The spare *Journal of a Disappointed Man* he crafts for publication—only 535 entries to cover fifteen years—opens with an epigraph, the famous words from Ecclesiastes, "The race is not to the swift, nor the battle to the strong, neither yet bread to the wise, nor yet riches to men of understanding, nor yet favour to men of skill; but time and chance happeneth to them all." The diary ends with two one-word entries—"Miserable." "Self-disgust."—and the announcement of the diarist's death. Disappointment indeed.

In between, Cummings draws the reader into the life of a promising young natural historian (and writer) with this first charming entry at age thirteen: "Am writing an essay on the life-history of insects and have abandoned the idea of writing on 'How Cats Spend their Time'" (1). He divides his *Journal* into three parts, and within these he chooses to title occasional entries, just as Woolf does in her 1899, 1903, and 1905 to 1909 diaries and will do again in 1925, 1926, and 1927. The *Journal's* untitled part 1 covers Cummings' life in the western country of North Devon from ages thirteen to twenty-one, where he is forced to subordinate his passion for natural history to assist his ailing newspaper editor father. Part 2, titled "In London," chronicles the completely self-taught zoologist's euphoria when he wins a place at the Natural History Museum in South Kensington through a competitive examination; and part 3, titled "Marriage," follows his life from his 1915 marriage to his distant cousin, the fashion designer Eleanor Benger, through his painful physical decline when he chooses to halt the diary and announce his death.

Like Woolf, Cummings read voraciously, taught himself ancient and modern languages, and knew well the pages of other diarists. He appends to a 1913 entry, for instance, this quotation on the "soul" from the *Journal of Eugénie de Guérin*: "The life of the Soul is different; there is nothing more changing, more varied, more restless . . . to describe the incidents of one hour would require an eternity" (*JDM* 95n). This passage may have quickened Woolf's own interest in the soul. Cummings calls Marie Bashkirtseff, the Russian art student and diarist who died of consumption in Paris in 1884, his diary "mother" and wonders whether transmigration of souls occurs (*JDM* 238, 139). He worries that his diary repeats hers: "She feels as I feel. We have the same self-absorption, the same vanity and corroding ambition. She is impressionable, volatile, passionate—ill! So am I. Her journal is my journal. All mine is stale reading now. She has written down all my thoughts and forestalled me!" (*JDM* 139).

Cummings harbored the grandest ambitions. He thought of himself as a Keats or a Hamlet (or a Bashkirtseff) struck down tragically before his time. Despite its desperate fabrications, *The Journal of a Disappointed Man* remains one of the great diaries of illness. Cummings' skill as a scientific observer and knowledge of anatomy—honed through years of dissecting and collecting—make his accruing record of his bodily changes of value, both for those with multiple sclerosis and those seeking to understand and treat the disease. His *Journal* records sight problems in one eye at age twenty-three and "numb feeling on one side of my face, and my right arm . . . less mobile," and continues recording through "locomotor ataxy," retracting tendons, and locked legs at age twenty-nine (93, 80, 361).

The Journal of a Disappointed Man describes depression and its effects. This June 1913 entry titled "Depression" may have struck a chord with thirty-eight-year-old Woolf:

> The melancholy fit fell very suddenly. All the colour went out of my life, the world was dirty gray. On the way back to my hotel caught sight of H____, jumping into a cab. . . . But the sight of him aroused no desire in me to shout or wave. . . . The sea-coast here is magnificent, the town is pretty—I know that, of course. But all looked dreary and cheerless. . . . There perhaps on the other side of the street was my own brother. But I was not even faintly interested and told the cabman to drive on. (*JDM* 89)

A month later, back at work in the Kensington Museum after a two-month sick leave, suicidal impulses rise in the twenty-three-year-old. "Thoughts of suicide—a pistol," he tells his July 1913 diary (*JDM* 93). Six days later he writes: "Several times I have gone to bed and hoped I should never wake up. Life grows daily more impossible" (*JDM* 93). On February 20, 1914, he confesses, "The idea of a pistol and the end of it grows on me day by day," and by January 20, 1917, with "millions of bacteria . . . gnawing away [his] precious spinal chord," he declares: "I grow tired of my own dismal life just as one does of a suit of dirty clothes" (*JDM* 110, 274, 275). Cummings re-creates hauntingly in his *Journal* the February 1917 scene in a London chemist's shop when he asks for morphia tabloids only to be denied by a "smiling youth" who says their sale violates the new Defence of the Realm Act (280).

Cummings' March 1, 1917, plea to control his own fate rings powerfully to-day—and may have done so for Woolf in 1920. "I am too ill for any scientific work so I write labels and put things away," he explains:

> My life has been all isolation and restriction. And it now appears even my death is to be hedged around with prohibitions. Drugs for example—how beneficent a little laudanum at times in a case like mine! and how happy I could be if I knew that in my waistcoat pocket I carried a kindly,

easy means of shuffling off this coil when the time comes as come it must. It horrifies me to consider how I might break the life of E[leanor] clean in two, and sap her courage by a lingering, dawdling dying. But there is the Defence of the Realm Act. (*JDM* 282, 283)

A week later, he continues the theme in an entry titled "Death":

[F]or all practical purposes, I have done with life, and my own existence is often a burden to me and is like to become a burden also to others. I wish I possessed the wherewithal to end it at my will. With two or three tabloids in my waistcoat pocket, and my secret locked in my heart, how serenely I would move about among my friends and fellows, conscious that at some specially selected moment—at midnight or high noon— just when the spirit moved me, I could quietly slip out to sea on this Great Adventure. (*JDM* 286)

At least four facets of Cummings' *Journal of a Disappointed Man* may have influenced Woolf in 1920. First is his preoccupation with his soul. Second, he writes in a March 1917 entry, "I am simply marking time on the edge of a precipice awaiting the order, 'Forward,'" offering Woolf the "precipice" trope she employs in her own May 5, 1920, diary entry ("this marks some step over a precipice") and then transforms into her striking (but slightly more hopeful) figure of life as a "strip of pavement over an abyss" in October.[6]

More than this, however, Cummings' *Journal* saga of trials with Harley Street doctors, and the tale that emerges of a suicidal young man and his loving designer wife in the grips of arrogant physicians, may have supplied a model for suicidal Septimus Smith and his hat-making wife, Rezia, in Woolf's next novel, *Mrs. Dalloway*. "Doctor's Consulting Rooms—my life has been spent in them!" Cummings exclaims at age twenty-five. "Medical specialists—Harley Street men—I have seen four and all to no purpose" (*JDM* 134). At twenty-seven, he tells his *Journal*, "I could write a book on the Doctors I have known and the blunders they have made about me," and we learn that Cummings' two-faced primary physician not only fails to tell the young scientist his disease is multiple sclerosis but also urges Cummings to marry—"If you enjoy only twelve months' happiness, it is worth while"—while at the same time advising his fiancé *not* to marry him (260, 209).

That Eleanor Benger disregards the doctor's counsel and not only marries Cummings but also gives birth to their daughter showed Woolf a young couple battling valiantly both medical and legal restraints. Like Woolf, Cummings marries in the London Register's Office. Only through accident does he learn he has multiple sclerosis. Like Leonard Woolf, Cummings is called for an Army physical exam, and, like Leonard, he carries a sealed letter from his physician. The Army doctor never opens Cummings' letter, for he rejects him the second he places his stethoscope to Cummings' erratic heart. When Cummings idly opens the envelope on the train home, he feels more than the death knell of his fatal disease; he burns with guilt at marrying two months before, given his certain death. Eleanor, as it happens, has kept the doctor's secret, and only a year later, in November 1916, is Cummings' guilt assuaged when she tells him she has known all along of his illness.

Cummings does not fight literally in the Great War as does Septimus Smith. Nevertheless he falls victim to the war, for a month after his marriage he forces Eleanor to move from their London flat to the country outside the Zeppelin zone.[7] The Zeppelins terrify Cummings—mostly for fear they will destroy his journals, his last hope for recognition.

A more poetic, but equally suggestive, scenario emerges from Cummings' earliest diaries. As a fourteen-year-old he tells of cycling "to the Lighthouse at _____" and finding on the way a dying curlew that he holds in his arms (*JDM* 4–5). Cummings abandons his bicycle and continues but must hand the bird to his friend when he begins to sink in the water. This friend lets the bird go; the "tide swept it upstream, and the poor bird, I fear, perished by drowning" (5). We perish each alone. Four years later, Cummings records another journey "to the Lighthouse," a day of incredible collector's luck (*JDM* 14).

Cummings' diaries—both the famous *Journal of a Disappointed Man* and posthumous *A Last Diary*—are works of a complex, sophisticated diarist. Cummings shared many of Woolf's motives for diary-keeping and added several more of his own. "For to me self-expression is a necessity of life," he tells his *Journal* in 1915, and as his body fails, the journals come more and more to hold his "real self" (*JDM* 169, 170). He believed early on that "bald confession in this Journal is sweet for the soul and strengthens it," and he views his journal as so much his "faithful friend" and confidant that he worries that continuing it after his marriage would constitute "infidelity" to his new wife (*JDM* 137, 211). He decides finally to share his diary with Eleanor.

"My Journal keeps open house to every kind of happening in my soul," he claims at age twenty-five, stirring Woolf perhaps to make her diary do the same, and in an essay-entry titled "The Graph of Temperament" at age twenty-seven, he declares: "In this Journal, my pen is a delicate needle point, tracing out a graph of temperament so as to show its daily fluctuations: grave and gay, up and down, lamentation and revelry, self-love and self-disgust. You get here all my thoughts and opinions, always irresponsible and often contradictory or mutually exclusive, all my moods and vapours, all the varying reactions to environment of this jelly which is I" (*JDM* 211, 287). Woolf will rework Cummings' "graph of temperament" figure into her own "temperature chart of a book" image in her 1925 diary. More publicly, his description above of "fluctuations" of thoughts and moods will be enacted in her novels to come.

Like Woolf's diary, Cummings' journal served as a receptacle for the "irresistible overflow" of his mind and thus gave "relief" that could not be refused.[8] However, while Woolf enjoyed many publishing outlets, Cummings saw his diary as his sole audience. "In default of others, I am myself my own spectator and self-appreciator—critical, discerning, vigilant, fond!—my own stupid Boswell, shrewd if silly," he writes at age twenty-five (*JDM* 180). Unlike Woolf, Cummings sees his diaries as his revenge for the world's misprision. He writes in his *Last Diary* that he regards publication of *The Journal of a Disappointed Man* as "a *revanche*" and a "dagger": "The world has always gagged and suppressed me—now I turn and hit it in the belly."[9]

Cummings' diaries record literary ambition thwarted by ill health. "For a long time past my hope has simply been to last long enough to convince others of what I might have done—had I lived," he explains in *The Journal of a Disappointed Man* (134). Woolf knew herself that illness could thwart a soul. In 1920, Barbellion's *Journal of a Disappointed Man* pressed her toward the soul. It gave her much of the Septimus Smith plot in *Mrs. Dalloway* soon to come, a vision of two journeys "to the lighthouse," and the image of that yawning precipice.

John Evelyn's Diary

"Should you wish to make sure that your birthday will be celebrated three hundred years hence, your best course is, undoubtedly, to keep a diary," Virginia Woolf begins her October 28, 1920, *Times* tribute to "John Evelyn" (*E* 3: 259). Only one person in a generation, she imagines, "has the courage to lock his genius in a private book and the humour to gloat over a fame which will be his only in the grave" (*E* 3: 259). Most people, she notes, prefer to trust in their published novels, histories, plays, or poems for fame to enjoy in life. She, like Evelyn (we can hardly fail to notice), stakes *both* claims.

Evelyn was born in 1620, and his famous diary chronicles the seventeenth century through his death in 1706 at age eighty-five. He visits fellow diarist Samuel Pepys in the Tower of London in 1676 and later sits for a portrait at Pepys's request that Pepys hangs in his library. Evelyn, in turn, persuades Pepys to carry his precious tennis-ball-size kidney stone to Evelyn's brother, to convince the brother to submit to the knife.

Evelyn is godfather to Christopher Wren's son. In fact, he gives architectural advice to Wren in Oxford and, in 1666, joins with him in recommending "a noble cupola" for St. Paul's Church in London, "a form of church-building not as yet known in England, but of wonderful grace" (Bray 1: 377; 2: 20). Evelyn conducts Margaret, Duchess of Newcastle, to the Royal Society in 1667 to view firsthand several experiments. He even writes of a Peter Walsh, a Catholic priest who would not acknowledge the Pope's infallibility, and he describes the Russian ambassador's grand entrance into London replete with furs, Persian carpets, Persian horses, hawks, bows and arrows, and other presents—a lavish scene that might have influenced Woolf's 1928 *Orlando* (Bray 2: 247; 1: 366–67).

Woolf seeks to understand in her lengthy commemorative essay how this seventeenth-century diarist differs from his 1920 descendants. She likely saw personal continuities. Evelyn begins his diary at age eleven in imitation of his father.[10] He loses his beloved mother, who "inclined to a religious melancholy, or pious sadness," when he is fourteen, causing him to write later in his diary: "Thus ended that prudent and pious woman, in the flower of her age, to the inconsolable affliction of her husband, irreparable loss of her children, and universal regret of all that knew her" (Bray 1: 2, 8). Evelyn's father dies six years later, leaving the twenty-year-old with (in Woolf's 1903 diary words) "No father, no mother, no work" (*PA* 212). In short, Woolf might easily have pictured a child sent to school in Lewes, Sussex, who (like her) played bowls on the green. She had followed his footsteps to Wilton and to Stonehenge—although we have no sign she counted the Stonehenge pillars, or took a hammer to them, as Evelyn did (Bray 1: 290–92). Evelyn possessed greater material wealth than Woolf. His father was the last High Sheriff for Sussex and Surrey counties combined, and when this father dies, John is sent abroad with a large purse (and with his own painter to copy artworks) to begin the observing and collecting that will mark all his days.[11]

Like Woolf, Evelyn wrote throughout his life and, like her, he attended to the natural world. She locates an advantage for Evelyn in seventeenth-century ignorance. In collecting his Tables of Veins and Arteries, his Venetian glass, his transparent beehive and lead diving bell, Evelyn could be "justly confident that with his own hands he might advance not merely his private knowledge but the knowledge of mankind," she explains (*E* 3: 260).[12] That Evelyn "used his eyes" Woolf also admires, for she believes in 1920 "[t]he visible world has receded so far from us" that Evelyn's extensive talk of buildings and gardens, paintings and "prospects," strikes readers as strange—even dull (*E* 3: 261). Woolf admires the fact that "[w]herever there was a picture to be seen by Julio Romano, Polydore, Guido, Raphael, or Tintoretto, a finely built house, a prospect, or a garden nobly designed, Evelyn stopped his coach to look at it, and opened his diary to record his opinion" (*E* 3: 262).

Woolf's praise of the seventeenth-century diarist is not, however, unalloyed. She quotes Pepys amusingly on Evelyn's "little conceitedness"—though it was largely warranted—and suspects herself that he may have been "something of a bore" (*E* 3: 263). As with Wilfrid Blunt, she cannot help but notice that "though he deplored the vices of his age, he could never keep away from the centre of them" (*E* 3: 263). Furthermore, he and his diary lack the mystery she always craves. "His writing is opaque rather than transparent," she complains. "We see no depths through it, nor any very secret movements of mind and heart" (*E* 3: 263–64). This, of course, is what *she* now seeks.

In truth, Evelyn's diary *method* was not hers, and she likely saw the method's failings. Evelyn kept memoranda of his daily affairs. At two disparate points in his life he took time to assemble (and revise) these memoranda into his memoir/diary. At age forty he wrote up his first thirty-five years, from birth through his visit to Rome in 1655; the period from 1655 to 1684 he re-created between 1680 and 1684. Thus only in the final twenty-two years is Evelyn's diary a contemporary (rather than retrospective) diary. Such a diary invited the scorn of readers like Thomas De Quincey, who complained when Evelyn's diary first appeared in 1818 that he omitted the conversation of the notable men he knew. This absence Woolf likely also noticed in 1920 as she experimented in her own diary with ways to preserve talk. Richard Garnett defended Evelyn from De Quincey's scorn: "[H]e does not consider that the Diary in its present shape is a digest of memoranda made long previously, and that time failed at one period and memory at the other" (Bray 1: xiii).

In fine, Evelyn was "no genius"—as Woolf bluntly acknowledges in her tribute (*E* 3: 263). We must consider his diary "the uninspired work of a good man," she declares, a common view today of Evelyn's diary—although his vivid on-the-scene reports of the plague, the Great Fire, the entrance of Charles II into London, and Whitehall twenty-five years later on the eve of Charles' death are justly prized (*E* 3: 259). In seeking to understand this diary's longevity, Woolf finds herself lauding the diary form. "But even as we drowse" over his diary, she writes, "somehow or other the bygone gentleman sets up, through three centuries, a perceptible tingle of communication, so that without laying stress upon anything in particular we are taking notice all the time" (*E* 3: 264). A diary's very accumulative schema harnesses untold force, she implies. Evelyn was "not an artist, perhaps," she writes; "yet as an artistic method this of going on with the day's story circumstantially, bringing in people who will never be mentioned again, leading up to crises which never take place, has an undoubted merit."[13]

Furthermore, diaries appeal to our unfailing interest in our fellow creatures. Woolf suggests that we can:

> only vaguely and falteringly explain that, whether alive or dead, good or bad, human beings have a hold upon our sympathies. . . . That is enough for us. . . . First we have the oddity of [Evelyn's life]; then the difference; then as the years go by the sense of coming to know the man better and better. When that is established, the circle in which he moves becomes plain; we see his friends and their doings; so that by degrees it is not one person but a whole society of people whom we watch at their concerns. (*E* 3: 265–66)

This is true of Woolf's diary as well—and she will use Evelyn's "artistic method" of "going on with the day's story circumstantially" in her modernist novels.

3

Jealousy, Illness, and Diary Rescue

Can a diary help heal and restore? Emphatically. Virginia Woolf's 1921 diary reveals—more explicitly than any of her other diary books—her use of her diary (when necessary) as a treatment center for literary distress of several sorts. In this diary Woolf meets two foes. The first is physical and mental exhaustion, a danger that will rise periodically across her days as these pages will show. In 1921, Hogarth Press work takes the time previously given to her diary—to her peril. Woolf knows that diary-writing refreshes her. However, in early January she gives over her "casual half hours after tea" to Russian lessons for Press translations of Chekhov, Gorky, the Tolstoys, and more (*D* 1: 266). The Woolfs also devote the year to printing Bloomsbury works, making the months ripe for rivalry—for literary envy of several shades.

Dante called jealousy a "fatal spark." Onasander called it "a pain of mind," while John Dryden saw it as "the jaundice of the soul." Proverbs asks, "Who is able to stand before envy?" (27:4). Woolf's 1921 diary proves that she can. She uses her diary to "medicine" herself. She turns to her diary for the psychological sense of catharsis: "the relief of tension and anxiety by bringing repressed feelings and fears to consciousness." The diary becomes an anodyne, "a comforter" or "reliever of pain." During this time, Woolf also links arms with (and salutes) another literary doctor: Anton Chekhov and *his* notebooks.

Virginia Woolf's 1921 Diary

> "*I am not satisfied that this book is in a healthy way.*"
> (March 1, 1921; *D* 2: 94)

Subtle changes in style—and premonition of ill health—distinguish Virginia Woolf's 1921 diary. Her wish to capture talk persists; in fact, she re-creates twenty-eight different conversations within the diary's fifty-one entries. However, while her 1920 diary experiments with different ways to render talk—almost no two conversation styles the same—Woolf alights immediately in her 1921 diary upon a smooth, compressed, rather novelistic style that she sustains across the diary. Her opening entry (on her birthday, January 25) illustrates the scenic blend of description and talk:

> Then, if I had time, I could write a new chapter in Clive's life. Spring has miraculously renewed herself. Pink almond blossoms are in bud. Callow birds crow. In short, he's out of love & in love, & contemplated eloping with a Spaniard in a motor car. "But after all, I said to myself as I walked back, I like to think of my book & my armchair. It's terrible, terrible. I can't give up my old friends after all." The dusky one lives in Chelsea, has a car, no husband, children, & is beautiful as the Southern night. No one has ever seen her, & she, to her credit, has never heard of Maynard Keynes. (D 2: 87)

This witty Bloomsbury scene launches the 1921 diary.[1]

Woolf then swings into a completely different, although similarly compressed and integrated, narrative—this chapter on Sydney Waterlow:

> Then we're just over the crest of a Sydney swell: such a solemn heaving one; the poor man's bosom all clouded & turgid owing to [John Middleton] Murry; who sits at Hampstead promulgating doctrines, & caring not at all that S. seriously thinks of leaving wife & children. "I have no solid core. I am unlike everyone else, & probably more unhappy." Indeed his bloodhound eyes drooped & almost spilt tears. We talked sense into him, & the inflated tumour burst. He came down happier to breakfast; & a little less certain of the worth of Murry's goodness. (D 2: 87)

Woolf's third entry, February 5, re-creates Keynes's Memoir Club paper on "Dr Melchior," capturing three separate voices in brief snippets of talk like those above, while her fourth entry (February 16) preserves T. S. Eliot's words during their stroll along the Strand; Murry's confession of adultery with Elizabeth Bibesco; and Lytton Strachey's disgust with Clive (D 2: 89–92). The diary appears now fully at ease with indiscretion.

"A great deal to say, I suppose: a great many portraits to sketch; conversations to write down; & reflections to work in—had I time; which I have not," Woolf begins her April 29 entry foregrounding her integrative method (D 2: 114). Here, too, is her habitual cry of lack of means before delivering her long talk with Lytton Strachey where they ponder their place among writers and also their writing styles: "And he said he could always recognise my writing though I wrote so many different styles, 'which is the result of hard work' I insisted."[2] Woolf's interest in elision persists. When she re-creates her talk with Bertrand Russell in her December 3 entry, she writes: "[W]e struck out like swimmers who knew their waters. One is old enough to cut the trimmings & get to the point" (D 2: 146–47).

The profusion of compact scenes sprinkled with lively talk makes the 1921 diary as colorful as its cover: another oriental print.[3] "If I had time," "had I time," she laments in many of her 1921 entries—just as she cried lack of space in her tiny first (1897) diary (D 2: 87, 114). The Hogarth Press now commands so much of her day that she cannot give her 1921 diary the "solemn" launch she desires (D 2: 86). In her fourth entry, February 16, she again laments the Press's tug: "Russian [for Press translation] is snatching all the time spared for this book. I can only keep up with L. by running as hard as I can. . . . Russian from 12.15 to 12.45 & from 5:30 to 6. from 9.30 to 10, & on the way to Waterloo & back again must have some result. So far the chief one is as I say that I don't write here" (D 2: 90). As late as November, the Press continues to displace the diary. "My apology for not writing is quite truthfully, the Hogarth Press," she tells her diary. "Roger's woodcuts, 150 copies, have been gulped down in 2 days. I have just finished stitching the last copies—all but six" (D 2: 144).

Along with Chekhov's *Note-book*, the Woolfs spend the year printing Bloomsbury works: Virginia's *Monday or Tuesday*, Leonard's *Stories of the East*, Clive Bell's *Poems*, and Roger Fry's *Twelve Original Woodcuts*.[4] Add to this Lytton Strachey's April launch of *Queen Victoria* and the year is rife for friendly rivalry; in fact, for literary envy of many sorts. Woolf's struggle with this disabling phantom becomes the overarching theme (and crisis) of the 1921 diary. *Queen Victoria* appears at the same moment as *Monday or Tuesday*; however, Ralph Partridge botches Virginia's publication notice, resulting in an obscurely placed "quite unintelligent" *Times* review (D 2: 106).

The diary becomes both sounding board and curative for Woolf's anguish. Morning diary-writing on April 8 signals her distress. As usual she declares the worst at the outset—her failure—and once more projecting the worst allows her to step back, reflect, and move ahead:

10 minutes to eleven a.m. And I ought to be writing Jacob's Room;—I can't, & instead I shall write down the reason why I can't—this diary being a kindly blank faced old confidante. Well, you see, I'm a failure as a writer. I'm out of fashion; old; shan't do any better; have no head piece;[5]

the spring is everywhere; my book out (prematurely) & nipped, a damp firework. . . . I mean by that they don't see that I'm after something interesting. So that makes me suspect that I'm not. And thus I can't get on with Jacob. Oh & Lytton's book is out & takes up three columns: praise, I suppose. I do not trouble to sketch this in order; or how my temper sank & sank till for half an hour I was as depressed as I ever am. I mean I thought of never writing any more—save reviews. To rub this in we had a festival party at 41 [Gordon Square]: to congratulate Lytton; which was all as it should be. (*D* 2: 106)

We see how serious this is, how readers' understanding buoys her confidence, and its absence stalls her. As with the November 1918 rebound from Hampstead rebuke that brought forth supportive "old Virginia" (that "kindly blank faced old confidante") and her April 1920 emergence from Walkley's attack, probing in her diary the causes of her depression allows Woolf to address them and rescue herself:

Well, this question of praise & fame must be faced. (I forgot to say that Doran has refused the book [*Monday or Tuesday*] in America). How much difference does popularity make? . . . One wants, as Roger said very truly yesterday, to be kept up to the mark; that people should be interested, & watch one's work. What depresses me is the thought that I have ceased to interest people—at the very moment when, by the help of the press, I thought I was becoming more myself. . . . As I write, there rises somewhere in my head that queer, & very pleasant sense, of something which I want to write; my own point of view. (*D* 2: 106–7)

These words echo those of her Easter 1919 diary credo: "Moreover there looms ahead of me the shadow of some kind of form which a diary might attain to" (*D* 1: 266). The diary unleashes vision.

The severity of Woolf's creative crisis can be gauged from the fact that she frames her hypersensitivity to criticism as an illness to be treated in ensuing diary entries.[6] "I must hurriedly note more symptoms of the disease, so that I can turn back here & medicine myself next time," she begins her April 12 entry, underscoring her diary's salutary role (*D* 2: 108). She records Strachey's praise of her short story "The String Quartet" and Roger Fry's belief that she is "on the track of real discoveries, and certainly not a fake" (*D* 2: 109). However, she also carefully notes Lytton's five thousand copies sold in a week compared to her three hundred, *his* second edition, his Max Beerbohm caricature, and the presents he receives, including a bust of Prince Albert and photograph of Queen Victoria (*D* 2: 110). She records these tributes partly from her sense of fairness due his success and partly to write her envy to defang it.

Strachey's triumph, however, is not the only success this diary traces. On May 26, Woolf reports that Keynes earns £120 for his articles—a rate quite out distancing hers.[7] Even Leonard arouses envy. Her wish to keep up with him has mired her in Russian study, and she knows it. She asks her diary in her second entry, January 31, "And now, am I to learn Russian with [Leonard] and Kot? If he can read it & solace his age with it I shall be furious" (*D* 2: 88). In her next entry (February 5) she confesses: "Jealousy or ambition has won the day, & I've just had my first Russian lesson & mortgaged my time to the extent of doing three lessons weekly" (*D* 2: 89). As we have seen, this immediately becomes three lessons a *day* (*D* 2: 90).

And it is not only Leonard's language skill she seeks to equal; she marks his stories' success as well. After noting the further "symptoms" of her publication dis-ease in her April 10 entry, she asks herself, "And suppose every one (that is to say the 6 people who matter) praise Leonard, shall I be jealous" (*D* 2: 108). She evades direct answer by asserting all will be forgotten in six weeks. However, twenty-three days later, when Hamilton Fyfe declares in the *Daily Mail* that Leonard's "Pigs and Swine" ranks among the world's great short stories, she asks again in her diary:

> Am I jealous? Only momentarily. But the odd thing is—the idiotic thing—
> is that I immediately think myself a failure—imagine myself peculiarly
> lacking in the qualities L. has. I feel fine drawn, misty, attenuated, inhu-
> man, bloodless & niggling out trifles that don't move people. "Limbo" is
> my sphere; so they say in the Daily News. Then Romer Wilson has brought
> out a novel—to which Squire will certainly give the Hawthornden prize,
> thus robbing Katherine [Mansfield] of it: so I have some cause for plea-
> sure. I write this purposely, to shame it out of me. A full stop in Jacob, ow-
> ing partly to depression. But I must pull together & finish it off. (*D* 2: 116)

These last words, written May 3, reprise those of her first entry, January 25: "I must pull myself together to bring it off" (*D* 2: 86).

A gap caused by illness darkens the 1921 diary for two months. The diary hints that the disabling blend of Press work with literary anxiety-and-envy contributes to the break. "How hard we work. . . . Whether we can keep it up, I don't know," she had noted in her December 5, 1920, entry (*D* 2: 78). She asks if *she* can "keep up" in her February 5 and 16, 1921, entries, and on March 1 she declares, "I am not satisfied that this book is in a healthy way" (*D* 2: 89, 90, 94). If the diary serves as Woolf's literary interface, these passages disclose some apprehension of physical and creative flag.

The last words of Woolf's June 7 diary entry before a gulf of sixty-four days reveal the forces at war within her. She reprises a long talk with Eliot, then exclaims: "And Eliot astounded me by praising Monday & Tuesday! This really delighted me. . . . It pleases me to think I could discuss my writing openly with him. . . . Ulysses he says is prodigious" (*D* 2: 125). Despite Eliot's gratifying praise, Joyce's prodigious novel seems to cast such a shadow that she enters creative chill. Furthermore, had not Russian lessons displaced her diary on many days, the diary might have refreshed her and tempered the shade.

No diary entries are made from June 8 through August 7. Olivier Bell reports that on June 10 Woolf attended a concert and that night could not sleep. Headache arrived the next day, followed by two months of ill health (*D* 2: 125). As with the longer bout that halted the 1915 diary, Woolf writes her way back into the world through her diary: "[T]wo whole months rubbed out—These, this morning, the first words I have written—to call writing—for 60 days; & those days spent in wearisome headache, jumping pulse, aching back, frets, fidgets, lying awake, sleeping draughts, sedatives, digitalis, going for a little walk, & plunging back into bed again—all the horrors of the dark cupboard of illness once more displayed for my diversion" (*D* 2: 125).

The "dark cupboard of illness" offers a new and fuller vision of Woolf's "deep old desk, or capacious hold-all" from which her writing springs. Her "hold-all" now harbors dark cupboards as well as sifting and compositing bins. In this August 8 entry, Woolf names her symptoms and treatments (for future reference perhaps) but then also lists benefits from the plunge into the abyss: "Let me make a vow that this shall never, never, happen again; & *then* confess that there are some compensations. To be tired & authorized to lie in bed is pleasant. . . . I feel that I can take stock of things in a leisurely way. Then the dark underworld has its fascinations as well as its terrors" (*D* 2: 125–26).

Despite such consolations, Woolf acknowledges in her August 11 entry that she thought of making her will for the first time during her illness, and she states, "Sometimes it seems to me that I shall never write out all the books I have in my head, because of the strain" (*D* 2: 129). Happily, her August 17 entry reports with pleasure: "Really I think my scribbling is coming back" (*D* 2: 131). Reader support remains vital to that recovery, for her next words are: "Here I have spent the whole day, off & on, making up an article—for Squire perhaps, because he wants a story, & because Mrs Hawkesford has told Mrs Thomsett that I am one of the, if not the, cleverest women in England. It's not nerve power so much as praise that has lacked, perhaps" (*D* 2: 131). In her June 5 entry, five days before her illness, Woolf projects the same deprivation upon Murry, who has attacked Chekhov's *Note-book* in the *Nation*. "In my theory," she writes, "he's all parched for praise—run mad for lack of it" (*D* 2: 123).

Woolf's reemergence as a writer brings renewed reverence for her gift. On September 10 she writes from the country: "I have done with fidgets long ago.... I recovered. ... Much more important (to me) than anything else, was my recovery of the pen; & thus the hidden stream was given exit, & I felt reborn" (*D* 2: 134). The country retains its nurturing role. In her important March 1 entry in which she worries her diary is not "in a healthy way," she identifies Russian lessons and the Press at Richmond as interfering with her deeper art: "[H]alf the time I learn Russian I look in the fire & think what I shall write tomorrow. Mrs Flanders is in the orchard [in *Jacob's Room*]. If I were at Rodmell I should have thought it all out walking on the flats. I should be in fine writing trim. As it is Ralph Carrington & Brett have this moment gone; I'm dissipated; we dine & go out to the Guild. I cant settle as I should to think of Mrs Flanders in the orchard" (*D* 2: 94).

Recalling Rodmell as "all gold & sunshine," she worries again that London consciousness will mar her retreat (*D* 2: 95). Of Edward Shanks, the prize-winning poet, she despairs: "This surly poet, so we judged him (and his poetry is Squire's poetry) proposes to live in the [Rodmell] village. We shall meet him. He will look in. Oh dear—no more dreaming & rambling for me—" (*D* 2: 95). The words "He will look in" followed by "Oh dear" form a suggestive construction, recalling George Duckworth's trespass in her youth. In Woolf's diary, "Oh dear" always precedes heartfelt worry.

Rambling appears vital to country nurture, for in her August 18 entry Woolf equates herself with suffering Prometheus in her no-work house-bound state:

Nothing to record; only an intolerable fit of the fidgets to write away. Here I am chained to my rock: forced to do nothing; doomed to let every worry, spite, irritation & obsession scratch & claw & come again. This is to say that I may not walk, & must not work. ... No one in the whole of Sussex is so miserable as I am.... [W]hat wouldn't I give to be coming through Firle woods, dusty & hot, with my nose turned home, every muscle tired, & the brain laid up in sweet lavender, so sane & cool, & ripe for the morrows task. How I should notice everything— the phrase for it coming the moment after & fitting like a glove; & then on the dusty road, as I ground my pedals, so my story would begin telling itself. (*D* 2: 132–33)

Fortunately, in March she could escape to another country of the mind: Cornwall, which represents not only untrammeled nature but also her own treasured youth. "Why am I so incredibly & incurably romantic about Cornwall?" she asks herself in her March 22 entry. "One's past, I suppose.... I shall go down to Treveal & look at the sea—old waves that have been breaking precisely so these thousand years. But I see I shall never get this said" (*D* 2: 103). Of course we know she *does* get it said, in *To the Lighthouse*, and within only six years—and with *The Waves* to follow.

If the country continues to nourish her while Richmond dissipates her force, London looms loud and unnatural in the 1921 diary—largely because Vanessa spends most of the year in France. Gordon Square in 1921 means Clive Bell and his amorous sallies. Woolf writes in her fourth entry, February 16: "I find 46 [Gordon Square] a little blaring & brazen always, & didn't much mind catching the last train home. Lytton slipped out with us & whispered his horror & repulsion in the hall.... For the truth is no one can speak in their natural voice" (*D* 2: 92).

If London is unnatural, Hampstead now is moribund and antipathetic. In this diary it is Miss Minna Green, Leonard's assistant, who marches with "that regiment of the wage earning women's republic" (*D* 2: 140). "Poor Lilian [Harris]—poor Margaret [Llewelyn Davies]. They sit beside the corpse of the Women's Guild [in Hampstead]; the blinds are drawn; they are sad & white, brave, tearless, but infinitely mournful," Woolf writes on November 15 (*D* 2: 142). Revealingly, she links their plight both to age sixty and to loss of work. "I see what has happened," she writes. "When one leaves a life work at 60, one dies. Death, at least, must seem to be there, visible, expectant. One ought to work—never to take one's eyes from one's work; & then if death should interrupt, well, it is merely that one must get up & leave one's stitching" (*D* 2: 142).

The Hampstead women meet a fate they scarcely deserve, Woolf asserts. Male voices override this former female stronghold—male voices scornful of women. Hampstead now means Murry and his "hypnotised rabbits": Koteliansky, Sydney Waterlow, John Sullivan (Murry's assistant editor at the *Athenaeum*), and the painters Mark Gertler and Dorothy Brett (*D* 2: 88). "Kot dined here," Woolf tells her diary on December 11, and then asks herself, "Why did I go to bed with the gooseflesh after hearing discourse of Sullivan Gertler & Sydney Waterlow? They have grease in their texture. And they despise women"

(*D* 2: 149). A week later, she notes that even Gertler is shocked by Waterlow: "Sydney says [to Gertler] 'Now what do you do about women's society? Do you copulate with your models?'" (*D* 2: 150).

But Woolf is too pressed in 1921 to give much diary space to women. She fears for Dora Carrington's independence and tries to help her on May 15 before she casts her fate with the "ogre & tyrant" Ralph Partridge (*D* 2: 118). Eight days later, Woolf praises the independence of working women. She derides herself for condescending to "very plain poor serviceable women" like Miss Green who "bob up as happy as grigs & twice as able as I am" (*D* 2: 120).

Old age remains a specter—like literary envy—to be eyed and propitiated across the diary. Woolf sees midlife comforts as traps to be skirted. She records others' ages besides her own and in December takes time to quote Bertrand Russell's sobering confession to her: "My brain is not what it was. I'm past my best. . . . The brain becomes rigid at 50" (*D* 2: 147–48). Given the uncertainties of old age, Woolf intensifies her drive to make it salutary. Her diary-displacing Russian lessons exist for this end. She will be furious, she declares in her second diary entry, if Leonard "can read [Russian] & solace his age with it" (*D* 2: 88). On March 13, she imagines unearthing great treasures of undiscovered Russian literature. "Anyhow this is provision for old age," she declares (*D* 2: 99). In August, she happily imagines "reading Greek when I'm old; old as the woman at the cottage door, whose hair might be a wig in a play, its so white, so thick" (*D* 2: 134). And of course "old Virginia" serves as perpetual solace as her future writer self. Woolf thus sagely provisions for the years to come.

Roger Fry returns in 1921 (alongside "old Virginia") as a fortifying elder spirit. "Still old Roger has a quality of imagination which attracts me—loose & warm & genuine," Woolf writes on February 21 (*D* 2: 94). On December 18, she calls their greater intimacy "one of the good effects of middle age" (*D* 2: 150). Lady Cromer, the "Pagan" authorizing Woolf's 1903 diary, returns as well in 1921 to serve once more (with Fry and Old Virginia) as an older spirit empowering the diary. When Woolf goes for tea with Lady Cromer on May 9, she first thinks she has grown now too "exacting" to think Lady Katherine "somehow celestial"; however, when Lady Cromer returns the visit on November 16, Woolf writes, "She spoke with that old mellow worldly benignancy, as if all her thoughts were easy & shabby & loose, which I find so charming" (*D* 2: 117, 144). It is Fry's and Lady Cromer's "easy" and "loose" style that Woolf seeks for her diary and other prose.

Woolf introduces a fourth spiritual support August 13 as she recovers from her illness. She varies her diary style by copying two paragraphs of Leigh Hunt's memoirs into her diary, in case she "should want to cook this up again some-where" (*D* 2: 130). She describes Hunt as "our spiritual grandfather, a free man," and declares that "[t]hese free, vigorous spirits advance the world, & when one lights on them in the strange waste of the past one says Ah you're my sort—a great compliment.... Then I like his inquisitive human sympathies" (*D* 2: 130). All these traits, of course, are her own.

A secondhand Minerva treadle printing press arrives on November 3, and the next day Woolf finishes *Jacob's Room*. She has pulled herself together. Completion of this first novel in her new modernist style unleashes a torrent of writing plans, and on November 15 we see Woolf use her diary as a "planner":

> I am struggling with Henry James' ghost stories for The Times.... Then
> I must do Hardy; then I want to write a life of [Sir George] Newnes;
> then I shall have to furbish up Jacob; & one of these days, if only I could
> find energy to tackle the Paston letters, I must start Reading [*The Com-
> mon Reader*]: directly I've started Reading I shall think of another novel,
> I daresay. So that the only question appears to be—will my fingers stand
> so much scribbling? (*D* 2: 142)

True. Woolf settles into a lively compact scenic style—laced with talk—in her 1921 diary and expands her diary style to include a lengthy passage from Leigh Hunt's memoirs and a letter from Clive Bell. She grapples with literary envy and her need for public and private support, and by year's end emerges, if not with victory, at least with greater knowledge of this "disease" and with her generosity intact. The 1921 diary, begun in jealousy at Leonard's Russian, ends with plea-sure at his latest "trophies": the League of Nations Union request to reprint his *International Government*; the Webbs' wish for his editing skills; and his *Village in the Jungle* sold among other rare first editions (*D* 2: 152). "All very good," are the last words of the 1921 diary. But does she protest too much?[8]

Woolf struggles in "the dark cupboard of illness" in 1921 but uses her diary to "medicine" and thus rescue herself. She emerges to finish *Jacob's Room* and to envision a stream of writing projects. In her next-to-last entry, December 18, she lists with great pleasure hers and Leonard's turn of fortune: "With luck we may have £400 instead of £250; & we might buy a motor car, & we might buy the meadow; & we might run up another lodge, & we might take in a new strip of garden. & so on & so on" (*D* 2: 151). Three of her four desires involve the country—and the fourth, the motorcar, would take her there.

But the year has brought its trials and has called for determination. "I want to push on" becomes the diary's mantra. On April 17, in the midst of her pain over

Monday or Tuesday, Leonard describes the plan for *his* new book, a revised version of the Wandering Jew. Virginia responds as co-owner of the Hogarth Press. "[L]ike a good business man, I pressed him to promise it for the press," she tells her diary. "Its true that sales & reviews flag, & I much doubt if M[onday]. & T[uesday]. will sell 500, or cover expenses. But I want to push on with it nevertheless; & a solid big book like L's is essential" (*D* 2: 111–12).

Woolf might have closed her 1921 diary on the high note of their turn in fortune (and possible country additions); however, she adds a "postscript" the next day to record further challenge to her prose. And once more, she vows to press forward. *Times* editor Bruce Richmond objects to her use of the word *lewd* in her Henry James piece. She delivers the whole pressuring conversation in a stark scene, and then asks: "But what is one to do about it? He made it sufficiently clear not only that he wouldn't stand 'lewd,' but that he didn't much like anything else. I feel that this becomes more often the case, & I wonder whether to break off, with an explanation, or to pander, or to go on writing against the current. This last is probably right" (*D* 2: 152). She ends her 1921 diary determined to write "against the current," to give her "hidden stream" its exit; that is, to be even more—herself.[9]

Anton Chekhov's Diary and Notebooks

Monday or Tuesday, the title of the only short story collection Virginia Woolf ever published, derives from (and salutes) Anton Chekhov's *Note-book*, published the same month by the Hogarth Press. "There is no Monday which will not give its place to Tuesday," Chekhov wrote as one of sixty-seven "Themes, Thoughts, Notes, and Fragments" in the *Note-book* (140). Samuel Koteliansky, Katherine Mansfield's Russian émigré friend, brought Chekhov's manuscripts to the Woolfs. Like Virginia, Chekhov kept several kinds of diaries and notebooks across his too-short life. These works might have seemed ideal for persons yearning to learn Russian, for entries consist of tiny kernels of life compressed into a sentence or two, at most a short paragraph. Leonard Woolf, who translated the diaries and notebooks with Koteliansky, could work his way through these nuggets as if each were a separate translation exercise.[10]

The Hogarth Press's English version of Chekhov's *Note-book* offers three separate Chekhov texts. It opens with forty-nine diary entries penned from 1896 to 1903. Certainly periodic, these entries are so widely spaced and spare—twenty brief entries for 1896; twenty-three for 1897; three for 1898; two for 1901; and one for 1903—that they stretch our good will toward the periodic diary as we long for greater glimpse of the writer's life. The brief records fascinate, and they may have spurred Woolf toward a sparer diary herself.

Chekhov shows brutal honesty regarding his work. "Performance of my 'Seagull' at the Alexandrinsky Theatre. It was not a success," he reports October 17, 1896 (5). He treats his diary as a potentially public (as well as private) book, for he uses it to correct the historical record. He takes time to record on December 4, 1896: "For the performance on the 17th October see 'Theatral,' No. 95, page 75. It is true that I fled from the theatre, but only when the play was over" (5). He also refers to Leo Tolstoy regularly in his diary. Chekhov finds the older writer irritated, making "stinging remarks about the *décadents*," during his February 1896 visit (2). When Tolstoy returns the call on March 28, 1897, the two speak of immortality (9). Chekhov's only two diary entries for 1901 report a September 12 visit to Tolstoy and their December 7 telephone call (12).

Had Chekhov kept only this diary, the Woolfs would have had next to nothing to print. However he also kept "Note-books" from 1892 to 1904 that contained 583 notations, along with a separate work titled "Themes, Thoughts, Notes, and Fragments" that offered 67 more notes. It contains not only the line "There is no Monday which will not give its place to Tuesday" but also fourteen passages that found their way into a draft of *The Three Sisters* and a passage that became part of Chekhov's short story "Whitehead."

Chekhov's notebooks—and his minimalist diaries—differ exceedingly from Woolf's diary. His "Note-books" and "Themes, Thoughts, Notes, and Fragments" solely collect matter to be transmuted into art. They are Woolf's "deep old desk, or capacious hold-all" open for our inspection. As Leonard and Koteliansky explain in their foreword to the *Note-book*: "This volume consists of notes, themes, and sketches for works which Anton Chekhov intended to write, and are characteristic of the methods of his artistic production. . . . If he used any material, he used to strike it out in the note-book" (i). Chekhov jotted down names that might be useful. "For a farce: Kapiton Ivanovitch Boil" is one of his "Note-book" entries (42). Narrative kernels or miniscule play plots also abound, like that of a squire who plants cherry trees, or: "In Act I, X., a respectable man, borrows a hundred roubles from N., and in the course of all four acts he does not pay it back" (58–59, 66).

The notebooks preserve haunting aphorisms: "The more refined the more unhappy" (26); "Viciousness is a bag with which man is born" (33); "People love talking of their diseases, although they are the most uninteresting things in their lives" (28); "Man is what he believes" (101). To say these are Chekhov's views, however, would be dangerous, for Koteliansky explains that many items in the notebooks are "something which C. either personally or indirectly heard someone say" (101n). Thus we wonder if Chekhov or another playwright voiced this complaint: "Everybody goes to the theatre to see my play, to learn something instantly from it, to make some sort of profit, and I tell you: I have not the time to bother about that canaille" (103). We wonder—and perhaps Virginia Woolf wondered—if Chekhov or another posed this question: "Why did Hamlet trouble about ghosts after death, when life itself is haunted by ghosts so much more terrible?"[11]

The notebooks teem with views on women. However, are these Chekhov's thoughts or those of others deemed sufficiently serviceable to record? At a minimum, Chekhov's "Note-books" offered Woolf a window on Russian thoughts on women. Several passages deride them. "To me all women are alike" appears to be an overheard remark or potential line of dialogue (119). The separate "Themes, Thoughts, Notes, and Fragments" contains the sneer, "What a lot of idiots there are among ladies. People get so used to it that they do not notice it" (142). An exclamation recalling Dr. Johnson also appears in the "Note-books": "What empty words these discussions about the rights of women! If a dog writes a work of talent, they will even accept the dog" (115).

However, the notebooks also preserve statements defending women. "When a woman destroys things like a man, people think it natural and everybody understands it," unfolds one of the 583 notebook entries; "but when like a man, she wishes or tries to create, people think it unnatural and cannot reconcile themselves to it" (119). Similarly, at least one notebook entry asks for equality in love: "To demand that the woman one loves should be pure is egotistical: to look for that in a woman which I have not got myself is not love, but worship, since one ought to love one's equals" (20).

We rest on safest ground to say that Chekhov eyed gender difference, just as Woolf was carefully doing in England. One item muses, "Suppose I had to marry a woman and live in her house, I would run away in two days, but a woman gets used so quickly to her husband's house, as though she had been born there" (96). Another entry focuses on age: "The difference between man and woman: a woman, as she grows old gives herself up more and more to female affairs; a man, as he grows old, withdraws himself more and more from female affairs" (19). The following notebook observation may have influenced Woolf's famous words in *Three Guineas* on women and national pride: "Russians abroad: the men love Russia passionately, but the women don't like her and soon forget her" (33). Uniforms are disdained in a December 1896 diary entry (6).

Woolf links arms with Chekhov and honors his notebooks by naming her short-story volume *Monday or Tuesday*. She had admired him even before she read his *Note-book*. In her May 16, 1918, *Times Literary Supplement* review of three Chekhov short-story collections, she called the Russian "one of the nebulous, undefined writers"—traits always attractive to her—and also "more on a level with ourselves" than other authors (*E* 2: 244, 245). This last she said a month earlier of Pepys's diary: that it made him one of ourselves (*E* 2: 235).

Her April 10, 1919, description of Chekhov's short story "Gusev" helps us see the similarity between his short fictions and Woolf's emerging *diary* scenes: "We are given scraps of their talk; a few of their thoughts. . . . But it is impossible to say that this is humourous or that tragic, or even that it is proper to call the whole a short story, since the writer seems careless of brevity and intensity, and leaves us with the suggestion that the strange chords he has struck sound on and on" (*E* 3: 35).

Four months later, in an August 14, 1919, review titled "The Russian Background," Woolf declares, "We are by this time alive to the fact that inconclusive stories are legitimate. . . . [L]ife 'of itself' is so terrible and marvellous that no fantastic colouring is necessary" (*E* 3: 84, 85). When she revises this review for her 1925 *Common Reader* essay "The Russian Point of View," she uses words that echo (at the start) her 1920 tribute to John Evelyn's diary. Chekhov's "method which at first seemed so casual, inconclusive, and occupied with trifles, now appears the result of an exquisitely original and fastidious taste, choosing boldly, arranging infallibly, and controlled by an honesty for which we can find no match save among the Russians themselves" (*CR* 1: 177). Chekhov's "Notebooks," when Woolf came to read them, revealed how very fastidious Chekhov's mind and method were.

Woolf's 1921 salute to Chekhov in *Monday or Tuesday* adds to our growing sense of Chekhov's strong impact on British modernism, along with that of other Russian writers. As Roberta Rubenstein writes in her fine *Virginia Woolf and the Russian Point of View*, Chekhov's works encouraged Woolf to break from tradition; his "focus on unremarkable characters engaged in inconsequential actions in stories without plots paradoxically enlarged the possibilities of the art of fiction" (60). He offered artistic freedom.[12] He showed her that short stories and plays—works, in short, in various forms and lengths—could be vehicles for exploring many of the diary's fundamental traits: discontinuity yet continuity; the self as fragile and fragmented yet part of larger whole; in fact, "life as an inescapable ensemble," as Michael Levenson suggests (197). Woolf "almost out-Chekhov[ed] Chekhov," Claire Davidson-Pegon notes—not only in her short stories but also in *Jacob's Room* and *To the Lighthouse* (157).[13]

Chekhov's diary and notebooks illustrated for Woolf extreme brevity and compression, the path she increasingly follows in her second, modernist diary stage. Omission, she finds, paradoxically creates more reader involvement and more reader freedom, as readers reformulate the text in their own ways. In linking her own work with Chekhov's, Woolf seconds his intimation that daily life—that very life caught in a diary—offers all we need, and all there is, of heartbreak and hope.

4

Voice and Motion

"The voice is a wild thing. It can't be bred in captivity," Willa Cather wrote in *The Song of the Lark* (258). Virginia Woolf moves toward her distinctive voice and finds her rhythmic movement in her 1922 and 1923 diary books, which are explored in this chapter.

Her 1922 diary stands out as one of her most resilient journals. Across the year, she turns from male voices repeatedly—and with assurance. In fact, she *replaces* "unsympathetic" male voices, male sites, and male works with female. She feels she is striking closer to her own voice. She also activates the "quick change" movement envisioned in her 1921 diary.

She moves on many levels in her 1923 diary book. She writes six (surface) play scenes in this diary while also pursuing her soul and the rush of "extraordinary emotions" she begins to feel (*D* 2: 246). With *Mrs. Dalloway* in "full talk" in January 1923, and *The Common Reader* "on its feet" in March, Woolf tells her diary on March 6: "I want to make life fuller & fuller" (*D* 2: 225, 237). She seeks greater freedom and movement and sets her eyes on London once more.

In 1922, Woolf reads Alie Badenhorst's Boer War *Diary*, a powerful antiwar document and important addition to her understanding of women and war. In July 1923, she receives James Boswell's *Journal of a Tour to Corsica*. She finds there a journal bold in experiment, rich in voice and movement—and baring of the soul.

Virginia Woolf's 1922 Diary

> *"There's no doubt in my mind that I have found out how to begin (at 40) to say something in my own voice; & that interests me so that I feel I can go ahead without praise."*
>
> (July 26, 1922; *D* 2: 186)

Resilience radiates from Virginia Woolf's 1922 diary. Her vigor particularly impresses for it stands in the face of influenza, heart and lung anomalies, and a stream of doctors who dog her days and narrow her life across most of 1922. Influenza arrives with the new year, causing an eighteen-day gap between Woolf's first diary entry (January 3) and her second (January 22). Not quite vanquished, the dangerous malady returns, and with it a twelve-day gap between her second and third entries. When it goes, the influenza leaves behind a worrisome elevated temperature and also an irregular heartbeat, the persistence of which causes Woolf's doctor in early March to forbid their long-planned trip to Italy.

In May, illness returns causing a forty-four-day diary gap as well as the extraction of three teeth to thwart pneumonia germs and normalize the elevated temperature. (This fails.) In July, a specialist finds that Woolf's lungs differ in size and diagnoses tuberculosis. In fact, doctors tell Leonard his wife soon may die (*L* 2: 498). And yet. And yet. None of these physical irregularities seems to ruffle Woolf. Instead, she draws on the lessons of her 1921 diary and "medicines" herself: she fortifies herself with the praise and support she needs. To this end she activates the "quick change" tack envisioned in her 1921 diary and turns once more from male voices as she moves toward her own.

Surely some of Woolf's buoyancy comes from the fact that despite her erratic heartbeat and temperature, she does not *feel* particularly ill. She flouts, in fact, her doctors' orders. She writes in her second entry, January 22: "No work for 2 or 3 weeks, [Dr Fergusson] says. But I fancy I shall finish Hardy tomorrow" (*D* 2: 158). In her first entry she declares her intent to turn from her editor's prescriptions: "No more reviewing for me, now that [Bruce] Richmond re-writes my sentences to suit the mealy mouths of Belgravia (an exaggeration, I admit) . . . [I]t is odd how stiffly one sets pen to paper when one is uncertain of editorial approval" (*D* 2: 155). Shunning stiffness and disapproval, she writes only five reviews in 1922, replacing this journalism with her own more fluid and far-reaching literary criticism. "Reviews seem to me more & more frivolous," she notes in her February 18 entry. "Criticism on the other hand absorbs me more & more" (*D* 2: 169). If male voices disapprove, she will write and publish her own *Common Reader* criticism.

Woolf begins, in fact, this year her "quick change" tactic to elude the stall and stiffening of dispraise. In her April 8 entry the year before, amid her anguish at the "unintelligent" response to *Monday or Tuesday*, she decided to divert her mind to other interests should her writing fail to please. "I think the only prescription for me is to have a thousand interests," she writes in 1921: "[I]f one is damaged, to be able instantly to let my energy flow into Russian, or Greek, or the press, or the garden, or people, or some activity disconnected with my own writing" (*D* 2: 107). She discovers in 1922 that she can apply this "quick change theory" to her *writing* too (*D* 2: 189). She begins the maneuver even before she names it. Her June 23, 1922, entry reports:

Jacob, as I say, is being typed by Miss Green, & crosses the Atlantic on July 14th. Then will begin my season of doubts & ups & downs. I am guarding myself in this way. I am going to be well on with a story for Eliot, lives for Squire, & Reading [*The Common Reader*], so that I can vary the side of the pillow as fortune inclines. . . . If they say your fiction is impossible, I shall say what about Miss Ormerod, a fantasy. If they say, You can't make us care a damn for any of your figures—I shall say, read my criticism then. (*D* 2: 178–79)

In July, she recommends a similar tack to Lytton Strachey who is "depressed; blocked by the play he can't write—& never will be able to write, say I; [but] if he lubricated himself with journalism, he might reel off some history or biography, & so pass by the play unmoved; & this is his line, & a good one, too, I say" (*D* 2: 185).

In September, she reports the strategy's success in her own life. It has made the summer of 1922 infinitely more productive than the summer of 1921, which was spent in the "dark cupboard of illness": "The new plan of rotating my crops is working well so far: I am always in a fizz & a stew, either to get my views on Chaucer clear, or on the Odyssey, or to sketch my next chapter [of Mrs. Dalloway's story]" (*D* 2: 198). On October 4, noting that *Jacob's Room* will be published on October 27, she can boast with some confidence: "It is I think true, soberly & not artificially for the public, that I shall go on unconcernedly whatever people say. At last, I like reading my own writing. It seems to me to fit me closer than it did before. . . . So evidently my plan of the two books running side by side is practicable. . . . At forty I am beginning to learn the mechanism of my own brain—how to get the greatest amount of pleasure & work out of it" (*D* 2: 205, 206). Two days after *Jacob's Room* appears she can further exalt to her diary: "We have bitten off a large piece of life—but why not? Did I not make out a philosophy some time ago which comes to this—that one must always be on the move?" (*D* 2: 210).

Woolf's 1922 resilience springs from this "quick change" movement and also from her sense that she is striking now closer to her own voice as a writer, as she says above. In February, she treats the *Dial*'s negative review of *Monday or Tuesday* as medicine she can swallow: "I've just had my dose of phenacetin—that is to say a mildly unfavourable review of Monday or Tuesday. . . . Yet, I'm glad to find, I have acquired a little philosophy. It amounts to a sense of freedom. I write what I like writing & there's an end on it" (*D* 2: 166). In her next entry, she locates her strength in her "queer individuality," a quality she highly regards: "People with this gift go on sounding long after the melodious vigorous music is banal" (*D* 2: 168). Thus when Leonard reads and admires *Jacob's Room* on July 26, she can write: "I am on the whole pleased. Neither of us knows what the public will think. There's no doubt in my mind that I have found out how to begin (at 40) to say something in my own voice; & that interests me so that I feel I can go ahead without praise" (*D* 2: 186).

Perhaps. However, she tracks praise carefully across the 1922 diary and manages to fortify herself with a good deal of it. Woolf's ability to create the support she needs to further her art is one mark of her genius. Her diary serves as one supportive beam; it also documents her maneuvers. In it we see that nature and women furnish further support. The country still fosters creative movement. After a forty-four-day diary gap, Woolf writes on June 11 of the "acute" depression she feels at leaving the country: "One lives in the brain there—I slip easily from writing to reading with spaces between of walking. . . . Perfection is such that it becomes like a normal state."[1] On August 3, she writes from Rodmell that Ted Hunter, the London solicitor, "remains quiescent" regarding his plans to build a cottage on their north green—a phrase that recalls George Duckworth's trespass. She wishes that "the Woolves be left by themselves in chastity & glory" (*D* 2: 188).

In her important August 22 country entry seeking to understand what suddenly blocks her work on "Mrs Dalloway," she again names male trespass—and male criticism—as cause: "I am once more writing off the fidgets. Ah, but how divinely happy we were until 12.30 on Thursday when Clive boarded the enchanted island with news from the world of Mary & Colefax! Never have I been so happy in my life. The day was like a perfect piece of cabinet making—beautifully fitted with beautiful compartments. . . . But I shall walk to Asheham & try to start the machine again. . . . leave me, leave me, is all I say: to work my brain" (*D* 2: 191–92). The "dark cupboard of illness" of the 1921 diary has become the "perfect piece of cabinet making—beautifully fitted with beautiful compartments" by the 1922 diary, hinting at Woolf's ideal writing trim.

Four days later, when she tries hard to value culture over nature, she cannot sustain the regard: "After all, one must respect civilization. This thought came to me standing in a Brighton street the other day from which one sees the downs. Mankind was fuming & fretting & shouldering each other about; the down was smoothly sublime. But I thought this street frenzy is really the better of the two—the more courageous. . . . But I daresay this thought was forced upon me: I much prefer the downs myself" (*D* 2: 195).

Clive Bell invades the downs in August and stops the hum within the perfect cabinet. Hampstead does the same. In the 1922 diary, the male voices of Hampstead become so degrading that, as with her doctors and her editor, Woolf turns firmly away. As early as her second entry, January 22, Woolf writes that Sydney Waterlow "lives in the pigsty—by which I mean the Murrys & the Sullivans & the Gertlers" (*D* 2: 158). When Waterlow visits Rodmell in August, Woolf finds him reproducing "in his heavy lifeless voice exactly the phrases in which Murry dismisses my writing 'merely silly—one simply doesn't read it—you're a back number.' . . . it becomes, I don't know why, curiously enervating, humiliating & depressing" (*D* 2: 190, 191). This sends her, of course, into creative chill. However, once more, she explores her depression in her diary and restarts the stalled machine. "Slowly the cloud withdraws," she writes:

> Not that I can put pen to paper at this moment; but the waters, which that great grampus dislodged, meet together again. I am once more washed by the flood, warm, embracing, fertilising, of my own thoughts. I am too feeble to analyse the psychology, which I guess to be interesting. Its as if some foreign body had dispersed reality for the moment; the foreign body being of some gross material, inimical to thought. And if I can only protect this for the present, I shall be able to write. So the question for me is, how far to withdraw from unsympathetic society in the future? Is this cowardly, or merely good sense? For instance, here is Brett already inviting us into the heart of the enemies camp—Hampstead Thursday evenings. If I go I shall be rasped all over, or any rate dulled & blunted, by the presence of Sullivan, Kot & Sydney. If I don't go shall I soften & rot in the too mild atmosphere of my own familiars? Perhaps the best plan would be to live in a neutral territory—neither friend nor foe, & by this means sink the exacting claims of egoism. Is there such a society possible though?[2]

Woolf seeks now the ideal place for prose.

If Hampstead's male voices comprise an "unsympathetic society" Woolf rejects in the 1922 diary—seeks to *replace*, in fact, with a neutral territory of her mind—she replaces the unsympathetic male voice in the Hogarth Press with a female voice as well. The question of Ralph Partridge arises as early as Woolf's third entry, February 4. From the earliest days of the partnership, she has called Partridge a "despot" (*D* 2: 79). Among his failings in 1922, one cannot help but notice, is his inability to praise, and thus to support. An incident that leaves Leonard to clean the type "crystallised all our grumblings of the past," Woolf tells her diary. "They are to the effect that he is lazy, undependable, now industrious, now slack, unadventurous, all corroded by Lytton, can't praise, yet has no view of his own . . . rather a serious detraction from his merits, as a partner in an enterprise. Should the enterprise be modified? Should we part company? Should we hire a woman drudge?" (D 2: 160). Questions, as usual, lead the way and show Woolf already on the path to female replacement.

Woolf re-creates in her June 23 entry her shouting match with Partridge over his and Dora Carrington's infidelities. "We have had a mad bull in the house— a normal Englishman in love; & deceived. My comments could fill a book, & perhaps *will* fill a book," she writes prophetically, for Partridge's fate and the identity of the Press will take up much of the remaining 1922 diary.[3] "I should have left you if you had treated me like that," she reports shouting that day at Partridge (D 2: 177). On July 28, she writes again of the degrading atmosphere: "I'm afraid its a sordid business, as C[arrington]. said. . . . P's conduct is that of the village Don Juan. Again, he behaves like a bull in a garden. And with it he is malicious. He is a male bully, as L. says. I am reminded of the tantrums of Adrian & Clive. There is something maniacal in masculine vanity."[4]

Like the Woolfs' own separate reputations, the Hogarth Press list continues to grow and to become more distinguished across 1922. They accept Eliot's "The Waste Land," and in publishing (although not printing) Virginia's *Jacob's Room*, they take on their largest project to date. The Press has supported Virginia's reach toward her own individuality, just as she imagined in her 1921 diary. To that degree, the Press *is* her identity. No wonder Partridge's belligerence and inability to praise rattle the supportive structure Woolf seeks to create.[5] She says as much in a November 10 letter to him: "After all we have given the press whatever character it may have, and if you're going to tell me that you care more about it than I do, or know better what's good for it, I must reply that you're a donkey" (L #1317, 2: 583).

The "enterprise" must be modified. After a "stormy week end at Tidmarsh," Woolf writes in her November 7 entry: "I'm afraid I have concluded that Ralph must go. . . . Suppose one could get a young man or woman of wits who would work violently & rashly" (D 2: 211).

In the weeks that follow Woolf does more than just imagine a "woman of wits"; she actively recruits one for the Press. At the 1917 Club, she overhears the then unknown Marjorie Joad declare her intent to become a printer. Woolf follows Joad into the writing room, "pluck[s] her out," and invites her to Hogarth

House (*D* 2: 213). By her December 15 entry, the "final parting" with Partridge is fixed and Joad tapped as his successor. Woolf pictures Partridge "rigid & ossified in middle age"—and this (projected) stiffness she, of course, rejects.[6]

In the 1922 diary, Marjorie Joad replaces bullish Ralph Partridge, *Mrs. Dalloway* replaces that "he-goat" James Joyce's *Ulysses* (read and rejected during the year), and Woolf's own *Common Reader* criticism supplants Bruce Richmond's *Times* book reviews (*D* 2: 202). Throughout this diary, Woolf moves with assurance toward her own voice and subjects, assembling sympathetic females as aids. Although Bruce Richmond has risen up stiff and restrictive, on February 14 Woolf finds his wife, Elena, just the support she likes. "She keeps her mystery. . . . I find her sympathetic—so maternal, quiet, kindly; & liking literature as a lady does; & saying such unexpected things about it, as a lady does. . . . Would have like[d] a country life . . . best of all; & hates London, where she has had however her great successes. Like my father, I am attracted by the simple & affectionate & womanly," Woolf explains.[7]

Two days later, she offers an admiring portrait of another affirming older woman, Violet Dickinson: "I feel her somehow to be the sketch for a woman of genius. All the fluid gifts have gone in; but not the boney ones" (*D* 2: 166). Here is the movement, the fluidity Woolf seeks. "Old Virginia" never appears in the 1922 diary. Perhaps her encouragement is less needed in 1922 than in 1919, 1920, and 1921; or is her presence now simply assumed? Perhaps sympathetic Elena Richmond and Violet Dickinson suffice.

Another sympathetic woman makes her first appearance in the 1922 diary (along with Marjorie Joad). Vita Sackville-West endears herself with words of praise. "Mrs Nicolson thinks me the best woman writer—& I have almost got used to Mrs Nicolson's having heard of me. But it gives me some pleasure," Woolf notes on August 3 as an instance of her growing fame (*D* 2: 187). Clive Bell has passed along Vita's high praise, and when the two writers finally meet in December at Gordon Square, Woolf's diary registers the tremor. This next-to-last entry shows Woolf rather reeling. She starts this December 15 entry meaning to write down the "terrific Hogarth Press discussion ending in the final parting with Ralph," but then Lottie distracts her and she confesses: "I am too muzzy headed to make out anything. This is partly the result of dining to meet the lovely gifted aristocratic Sackville West last night at Clive's" (*D* 2: 216). Woolf's portrait of Sackville-West leads to thoughts of her own youth: "I keep thinking of sounds I heard as a child—at St Ives mostly" (*D* 2: 217). Her thoughts then return to Vita, and she starts a new paragraph abruptly: "The aristocratic manner is something like the actresses—no false shyness or modesty . . . makes me feel virgin, shy, & schoolgirlish. Yet after dinner I rapped out opinions. She is a grenadier; hard; handsome, manly" (*D* 2: 217). What a praising, manly motherly figure this is! She will become more than a support-ing brace; rather, a great fertilizing force. Yet Woolf does not know it at this moment.

Forty-six diary entries etch the 365 days from January 3, 1922, through Janu-ary 2, 1923. Equal in size to the large 1919 through 1921 diaries (8 ¼ inches wide and 10 ⅝ inches long), the 1922 diary book first saw use for drafts of *Jacob's Room*. Those completed in November 1921, parsimonious Woolf turns the book over and uses the vacant pages for her 1922 diary.[8] Her diary and modernist fic-tion now unite.

She concludes this diary following the pattern of her 1921 diary close; that is, she writes an exalting, rather euphoric closing entry but then tempers it with a more somber end. In 1921, her "cheerful" thoughts of their rising fortune and possible purchase of a motorcar, meadow, lodge, or garden are chastened by her next day's "postscript" reporting Bruce Richmond's rejection of her word *lewd* and her vow "to go on writing against the current" (*D* 2: 151, 152). In the 1922 diary, she treats the Hogarth Press as a begetter of life—and herself as birth mother—in her closing December entries, only to add a final entry on January 2, 1923, that rejects the trope for sober unfigured truth.

"I should be at Aeschylus. . . . But these are historic days. The Hogarth Press is in travail," she opens the first of her December entries, December 3 (*D* 2: 215). "To be in the labors of childbirth," is one meaning of *travail*. The Woolfs, in truth, sought to beget a new organizational scheme. Woolf's next entry—the final diary entry in 1922—offers her "muzzy headed" musings on Vita Sackville-West and closes with further images of the Hogarth Press as procreator. "And though I would give a good deal to combine with Lytton in producing litera-ture," she writes (suggestively) of Partridge's proposed new Press partnership involving Lytton, she then adds self-confidently, "there is little to be got from [Lytton] save his own works. I mean, I think by our own merits now we attract all the young" (*D* 2: 217).

"[W]e attract all the young" would have made an exultant close to the 1922 diary. However, Woolf appends to this December 15 entry a more severe Janu-ary 2, 1923, entry almost as reprimand. "If I were a dissembler I should date this the last day of 1922. So it is to all intents," she opens this entry, which returns to motherhood and comes full circle to Vanessa. Woolf's third 1922 entry de-scribed her "painful" meetings with her traveling sister (*D* 2: 159). "I set out to prove that being childless I was less normal than she," Woolf wrote on February

4. "As we had only 2 hours together, & she left for Paris next morning, & perhaps I shant see her till May, anyhow not continuously, I felt a sort of discontent, as the door closed behind her. My life, I suppose, did not very vigorously rush in" (*D* 2: 159). By December 1922, Woolf portrays herself as no longer childless—rather as in travail, if books be life, and, in fact, as perhaps "producing literature" with Lytton.[9] However, metaphor will not do. She returns again to Vanessa and to motherhood:

> We came back from Rodmell yesterday, & I am in one of my moods, as the nurses used to call it, today. And what is it & why? A desire for children, I suppose; for Nessa's life; for the sense of flowers breaking all round me involuntarily. Here's Angelica—here's Quentin & Julian. . . . They make my life seem a little bare sometimes. . . . Let me have one confessional where I need not boast. Years & years ago, after the Lytton affair, I said to myself . . . never pretend that the things you haven't got are not worth having; good advice I think. At least it often comes back to me. Never pretend that children, for instance, can be replaced by other things. (*D* 2: 221)

She seeks then to "like things for themselves" and closes her 1922 diary not with the lure of Vita Sackville-West or of a more womanly press "attract[ing] all the young" but with a more severe—and characteristic—reflection: "I will leave it here [her sense of childlessness], unfinished, a note of interrogation—signifying some mood that recurs, but is not often expressed. One's life is made up, superficially, of such moods; but they cross a solid substance, which too I am not going to hack my way into now. So this is the end of 1922" (*D* 2: 221, 222).

The 1922 diary stands forth as one of Woolf's most poised and confident diaries. She has grown a philosophy, as she notes in her February 17 entry, and launches her "quick change" tactic to escape the stall and stiffness of dispraise. Self-assurance grows as well as she strikes closer and closer to her own "queer individuality" as a writer, a feat assisted by repeated turns from the male. In fact, she replaces the male with the female.[10] Her voice and motion begin to align.

Alie Badenhorst's Boer War Diary

"Please let the Boer woman send us her book," Virginia Woolf writes to Katherine Arnold-Forster on August 23, 1922, "though we are rather overwhelmed at present" (*L* #1276, 2: 549). The book was *Tant' Alie of Transvaal: Her Diary, 1880–1902*, translated by Emily Hobhouse, herself a diarist. The Woolfs chose not to publish this diary; instead, it came out from Allen & Unwin in 1923. Beyond the inopportune timing—the Hogarth Press was "overwhelmed" with submissions and in organizational "travail"—Alida Badenhorst's diary was long: 319 printed pages. The Hogarth Press's largest project to that date, *Jacob's Room*, reached only 176.

Nevertheless *Tant' Alie of Transvaal: Her Diary, 1880–1902* is a stirring antiwar text that likely fed into *Mrs. Dalloway*, then in an early stage of composition. Woolf might easily have identified with the South African diarist. Alie de Wet (her maiden name) grew up with a half-brother in a blended family. At age eight she begins nursing her invalid father. Only marriage to F. J. (Frikkie) Badenhorst at age nineteen frees her from this role. Alie is close to her two sisters, one of whom marries Frikkie's brother. The three sisters come to live in separate homes but on the same large Transvaal farm.

Alie shares Woolf's love of nature and also the diagnosis of tuberculosis. In 1899, when she is thirty-two, Alie reports a "consumptive cough" (103). She has a tooth drawn, but as with Woolf in 1922, this offers no relief. Another doctor diagnoses jaundice. Throughout her diary, Alie's skepticism regarding doctors echoes Woolf's in 1922. "Dr. Russell came and sent for the other doctor and together they examined me and found lungs, heart, liver all bad," Alie writes in July 1901. "I took their stuff but it did not help much" (230). Three months later, when her six-year-old son, Wessels, nearly dies of the "wasting sickness" in the Klerksdorp concentration camp, Alie defies her doctors' orders not to give her son food. "Many a time I said to myself: Doctors!—a doctor is a murderer and no more," she exclaims (262). These words would fortify Woolf's thoughts for *Mrs. Dalloway*.

Badenhorst's *Diary* provides an on-site woman's view of the Boer War. Alie's farmer husband, Frikkie, departs for military service in November 1899. She will not see him again for more than two-and-a-half years. She copies into her diary the few censored letters she receives from him, first from the battlefield, then as a prisoner of war, and they paint a harsh picture. His December 29, 1899, letter describes the British use of the poisonous gas lyddite, which emits green smoke and turns the grass yellow, and the British troops' deliberate targeting of horses (102, 95). "The burghers complain of the horrible stench at the trenches on account of dead horses and men," Frikkie writes. "There are so many that the vultures cannot devour all. . . . on one spot lie one thousand and eleven horses" (102).

In January 1900, the British begin to seize noncombatants in their homes, and as the year and war advance, English treatment of the Boers anticipates that of the Germans of the Jews in the 1930s. By May 1900, Alie must surrender her farm's 110 oxen "as all commando property now belonged to the English Government" (149). In June, the English take her horses, and in July she must send a list of her possessions: "We had to get a permit to keep anything, and everyone [*sic*] of our Kaffir servants must have a pass. . . . It was proclamation after proclamation and regulation after regulation; sometimes I felt in despair and as if I could stand no more. . . . Anyone seeking news was put in prison as well as he who gave it" (151, 152). By March 1901, Frikkie asks her in a letter, "Who could have thought that such times could have come to us, we, who lived at peace with our children" and she learns he has "been given a number, which was always written after his name like a convict" (213, 215).

The British use women and children as pawns in the war, as leverage to pressure Boer surrender. On April 15, 1901, Alie and her three boys (ages three, six, and twelve) are taken from their home and placed in a women's concentration camp in Klerksdorp, joining more than three thousand others (273n1). "I had read books about war and how farms were laid waste, but never had I dreamed I should see and suffer it," she writes (208). "I [was] driven forth from my home. . . . My children cried; the two youngest boys were pale as death and held me fast; the little one kept crying for his chickens" (210).

The women's concentration camp shields the British stronghold, for it is strategically placed to front the near Boer forces. "I saw at once that if there were fighting that night the first to be shot must be we women and children," Alie reports (210). "[T]here was thorny wire round the camp with four or five gates in it, and at each gate was a policeman, so that we could not go past them into the town without a pass. Nothing could have been harder or more trying for a Boer woman. We had always loved our freedom, and just the thought that there was a fence round us made us feel ill" (224).

And then the starving begins. From May 1901 to its close in 1902, Badenhorst's *Diary* calls to mind Samuel Pepys's and John Evelyn's diary entries on the London plague of 1665, for she makes monthly tolls of the mounting dead. "[O]ur food was so bad; meat that one could not make soup of; if one held a joint of ribs against the light one could see through it; the sight thereof turned one sick," she notes. "The sickness in camp grew more deadly; every day burials were held. There was a large tent, and therein the bodies were placed; one morning the pigs began eating the corpses; they ate a child's poor little hand" (242).

Badenhorst's *Diary* underscores the importance of individual morality. From April to December 1901, old men, women, and children starve to death under the cruel British camp superintendent Howard Bass, who withholds available food.[11] When Bass himself dies in December, his kinder replacement increases provisions. From that point, the monthly death figures fall. However, both Alie and editor Hobhouse shock us with the fact that women and children suffer most in the Boer War. "There have died in the camps over twenty-thousand women and children innocent sheep led to the slaughter," Alie writes when peace arrives in June 1902, but Hobhouse emends her in a footnote with the documented figures: 26,251 women and children died in the camps—along with 1,676 "men and lads" over sixteen, more than four times the 6,189 Boer fighting men who died (315).

The Kaffirs suffer as well. In February 1902, when her Kaffir housemaid of sixteen years dies, Alie writes: "I wept over her death as if she had been my sister and felt more than ever cast down. How terrible it was for them. We had many Kaffirs on our farms, and nearly all had been driven forth by the enemy, and they, too, died by heaps. Nearly all the Natives I knew were dead; more than thirty-one from our farm alone" (287). Promises made in the peace accord fall short and finally falter. "It is true that the peace was made with the promise of three million pounds that should be given to us [the Boers], but we are all ruined, and what shall the share be for each?" Alie asks her diary. "We now possess nothing, no cattle, no oxen, no horse, no wagon, no plough. How then can we begin!" (313–14).

Alie Badenhorst's *Diary* exists both as a product and a casualty of war. After April 21, 1900, when she hears nothing (for a year) from captured Frikkie, Alie becomes a diarist. "Striving to forget this weary time of sorrow I began to write this book," she explains, "for being no longer able to write to him I felt that I must give utterance to my thoughts and sufferings" (142). In November 1900, finding she has less to do than in peacetime, for she can obtain no thread for sewing, cotton for crocheting, or wool for knitting, she decides to enlarge her diary with an account of her early life. "So I thought I would write a book. . . . I . . . said to myself that first I must go back to show what my life had been, and now I have done so, and told you all that has past [*sic*] in my life up to this evening and I shall take up the thread of my tale from this moment. . . . I have written it all down now and again as I have found time and leisure" (180).

Five months later, however, when her home is destroyed and she and her children sent to the concentration camp, "The English did not even give me time to run back for my diary, or rather history-book, which I had written, to bring it with me; and I have had to begin it again" (212). We lament the loss of the original—likely even more detailed—diary, and better understand the imprecision in the reconstructed diary's dates. Furthermore, editor Hobhouse reminds us that another war intervened to delay the release of even this reconstructed diary. Hobhouse had completed her translation by 1914; however, as it was "the eve of the European War, [it] had of necessity to be laid aside" (8).

Like her original diary, Alie Badenhorst, too, became a casualty of war. She lives only six years beyond the return of peace. When she dies in 1908 at age forty, she leaves behind her children, ages ten, thirteen, and nineteen. Her *Diary* also lives on, in fact, cries out with questions and exclamations that still resound powerfully today. "Many times have I asked: 'Is it right that another nation, already a large country and possessing other lands, should come here in order to take away our country which is all that we have?" she asks in 1900 (175–76). In 1901, she records a Hollander woman's question: "[W]hat would great nations like Germany or America say if they could see what Great Britain does to poor women and children" (220).

In 1923, editor Hobhouse frames Badenhorst's *Diary* as a response to British Prime Minister Lloyd George's call to Britons to "strip War remorselessly of its glamour, and reveal its real hideousness to the eyes of the new generation" (5). This, of course, is what Woolf will do in *Mrs. Dalloway*. Fellow diarist Emily Hobhouse describes a dream in her preface to Badenhorst's *Diary* that might have resonated strongly with Woolf. "It has long been my dream to see issued a range of . . . books from all lands stretching back to all ages, recording war from the standpoint of women and children: those passive but heroic figures massed obscurely in the background of every war, but ultimately bearers of its worst and most long-enduring burdens" (7).

The Boer word *tante* means "aunt," but it is also a title of respect for any elderly person known or unknown (16, 15). In his foreword, Alie's husband summarizes the Boer War's legacy. "The weariness and struggles, the sorrows, losses and privations of that devastating war were too much for her," Frikkie Badenhorst explains. "When at last I came back after two long years as prisoner of war, she was suffering from the heart. She never recovered from the shocks the war had brought her, but passed quietly away at an early age" (11). *Mrs. Dalloway*'s Septimus Smith also cannot recover from the shocks of war, and Woolf gives him a less quiet end. In the bleak month of September 1901, a month in which 142 die in the Klerksdorp camp, Alie Badenhorst writes in her *Diary*, "But now, here, all was dark for us, and we felt as if we hardly cared ever to look at the sky" (256). Eighteen months before, only three months into the war, she declared: "I was worn out with anxiety and strain and more than once dreaded I should go mad" (130).

Virginia Woolf's 1923 Diary

"My soul peeped out. For it is the soul I fancy that comments on visitors & reports their comments, & sometimes sets up such a to-do in the central departments of my machinery that the whole globe of me dwindles to a button head. . . . Soul, you see, is framing all these judgments, and saying as she sits by the fire, this is not to my liking, this is second rate, this vulgar; this nice, sincere, & so on. And how should my soul know?"

(February 19, 1923; D 2: 235, 236)

The soul peeps out—and the play's the thing—across Virginia Woolf's 1923 diary. This diary will be remembered as the volume that offers six play scenes, including one involving the Woolfs and the T. S. Eliots. The diary begins on January 7 in full dramatic dress. "Let the scene open on the doorstep of number 50 Gordon Square," Woolf proclaims, and then describes Maynard Keynes's Twelfth Night Party for which they donned oriental costumes, painted their faces, and brandished Leonard's Ceylonese sword (D 2: 222). "Sh[akespear]e I thought would have liked us all tonight," she writes (D 2: 223).

A play-reading craze infects Bloomsbury, propelled by Keynes and Lydia Lopokova at 46 Gordon Square. "[W]e now read plays at 46," Woolf tells her diary on March 17. "46 is become a centre" (D 2: 238–39). This rash of drama causes Woolf to erupt in July with her own play, *Freshwater*, the "superb possibilities" of which she envisioned in her 1919 diary (D 1: 237). Her zest for drama spills over into the four play scenes she writes simultaneously in her July diary entries—as well as into brief scenes in August and November.[12]

Her first entry signals her focus. After her opening dramatic flourish, Woolf ends her long first entry with a "work list": "I shall write at Mrs Dalloway till, next Monday, perhaps, bringing her into full talk, I hope" (D 2: 225). "Full talk" becomes an aim for *The Common Reader* essays she writes in tandem. She seizes upon "talk" as a way to make her literary criticism more artful and also afloat in "a current of life" (D 2: 261). Since "full talk" and its delivery are goals for both her fiction and nonfiction in progress, should we be surprised that the 1923 diary (like the 1920 diary) becomes a practice ground for talk? A mere thirty-one entries preserve the 347 days between January 7 and December 19, 1923—and more than twenty of them reproduce talk.[13]

Portraits, of course, surround the conversations—more than thirty portraits in the thirty-one entries, making this 1923 volume another talking portrait gallery. Eliot emerges as Prufrockian in Woolf's sixth entry, February 19—a vivid illustration of how her reading permeates her prose: "I . . . could wish that poor dear Tom had more spunk in him, less need to let drop by drop of his agonised perplexities fall ever so finely through pure cambric. . . . He is like a person about to break down—infinitely scrupulous, tautologous, & cautious" (*D* 2: 236). Her December 19 entry, the last of the year, admits how compressed her diary has now become yet manages a final portrait of Eliot drunk. "How elliptical this book becomes!" she exclaims. "I dont respect events any more" (*D* 2: 278).

In 1923, Woolf sees her diary as apt space for the voice and the soul, if not for events. Her third entry, January 28, reveals her genuine regard for human character. "I have seen quantities of people—having them here, as my invalid ways induced, bright pictures, tunes on the gramophone," she notes, letting her metaphors run, "—but I must not insult the human soul for which I have really so much respect" (*D* 2: 228). Her own soul enters this 1923 diary more fully than in any previous volume. It "peep[s] out," as she declares on February 19. The soul's presence would signify a "real diary," she asserts, and as this entry progresses she appears to see that her soul has been present all along, that her soul "is framing all these [diary] judgments . . . as she sits by the fire" (*D* 2: 234, 236).[14] "As to the soul," she resumes in March, "I've been snubbed by Squire," suggesting her soul harbors her "precious art" and her feelings about it (*D* 2: 239). In June, her own hypocrisy and Lady Ottoline Morrell's following a "defiling" weekend at Garsington make her wish to capture "the slipperiness of the soul" with her pen.[15]

Her next entry, June 13, reports a wave of "extraordinary emotions" that has recently engulfed her (*D* 2: 246). Interestingly, these mysterious feelings arise within her wish for "full talk" in a garden with thick hedges, like the Escallonia hedge that figures so prominently in the novel that will follow *Mrs. Dalloway*: the autobiographical *To the Lighthouse*. "Often now I have to control my excitement—as if I were pushing through a screen; or as if something beat fiercely close to me," she notes. "What this portends I don't know. It is a general sense of the poetry of existence that overcomes me. Often it is connected with the sea & St Ives" (*D* 2: 246). Her December 15, 1922, diary entry first recorded "shocks" from childhood, recurring "sounds I heard as a child—at St Ives mostly"—that return and appear to increase in 1923 (*D* 2: 217).

In her next entry, June 19, she moves from soul and feelings in her *life* to their presence in her literature. "One must write from deep feeling, said Dostoevsky. And do I? Or do I fabricate with words, loving them as I do?" she asks, and then answers: "No I think not" (*D* 2: 248). She concludes this extended interrogation of her writing by declaring that "[h]aving made this very inadequate confession about the soul, I may turn now to the body" (*D* 2: 249). Once more she gives a glimpse of her soul, which is linked to her art.

Woolf reads Marcel Proust's *Remembrance of Things Past* during this remembering summer, and his work, too, turns her thoughts inward: toward the soul and her emotional life. "I have always felt this kind of thing in great profusion, only not tried to capture it, or perhaps lacked skill & confidence," she admits on September 11 (*D* 2: 268). With her diary's aid, she is growing in art and assurance and will increasingly try the inward probe. She tries a month later when she seeks "to capture" a night of psychic terror that holds her painfully in its grip:[16]

> I meant to record for psychological purposes that strange night when I went to meet Leonard. . . . What an intensity of feeling was pressed into those hours! It was a wet windy night; & as I walked back across the field I said Now I am meeting it; now the old devil has once more got his spine through the waves. (but I cannot re-capture really). And such was the strength of my feeling that I became physically rigid. Reality, so I thought, was unveiled. . . . I had a satisfaction in being matched with powerful things, like wind & dark. I battled. . . . Saw men & women walking together; thought, you're safe & happy I'm an outcast; . . . & then, turning the corner of the station stairs, saw Leonard, coming along. . . . He was rather cold & angry (as, perhaps was natural). And then, not to show my feelings, I went outside & did something to my bicycle. . . . All the way back we talked about a row (about reviewers) at the office; & all the time I was feeling My God, thats over. I'm out of that. Its over. Really, it was a physical feeling, of lightness & relief & safety. & yet there was too something terrible behind it—the fact of this pain, I suppose; which continued for several days—I think I should feel it again if I went over that road at night. (*D* 2: 270, 271)

Woolf has been accused of emotional reserve in her diary, yet she here provides one of the fullest views of psychic terror we know.

In her next-to-last entry, December 3, she confesses another black night of the soul, "Adrian's catastrophe," as she calls the surprise news of her brother's marital separation. "I am too shaky to write," she tells her diary. "[H]e stayed here & I felt come over me the old despair; the crouching servile feeling which is my lowest & worst; . . . & the old futile comparisons between his respect for Nessa & his disrespect for me came over me, that made me so wretched at Fitzroy Sqre" (*D* 2: 277).

The soul thus opens while the surface play unfolds. These diary *expansions* rest, however, on a core of continued interests. As noted, Woolf's pursuit of "verbatim conversations" reappears from the 1920 diary, and her 1920 longing for London resurfaces as well. The capital blared and seemed unnatural in Woolf's 1921 and 1922 diaries. Clive Bell dominated Gordon Square (with his amorous liaisons) while Vanessa traveled abroad. But the atmosphere changes in 1923, becomes more literary, even Shakespearean, with the Keynes's Twelfth Night Party in early January and the play-reading center at 46 Gordon Square. With *Mrs. Dalloway* in "full talk" in January and *The Common Reader* "on its feet" in March, Woolf tells her diary on March 6: "I must take the social side into my own hands" (*D* 2: 237). She seeks greater freedom and movement.

Vanessa returns to London, and Woolf's report of her arrival occurs in the same June 13 entry that confesses the rush of "extraordinary emotions" (*D* 2: 246). Her June 28 entry reveals that she links London to *movement* as well as to a unity of art: "I might go & hear a tune, or have a look at a picture, or find out something at the British Museum, or go adventuring among human beings. Sometimes I should merely walk down Cheapside. But now I'm tied, imprisoned, inhibited" (*D* 2: 250). We have heard this plaintive cry before, not only in her 1920 diary when she first mentions the move to London but also in her Prometheus-bound tableau when she is forbidden to walk at Rodmell in August 1921 (*D* 2: 55, 72, 132–33).

And the cry matters. It signals starvation: artistic, intellectual, social, and more. She then whispers in parenthesis to Old Virginia or some other future reader, "(I'm letting my pen fling itself on paper like a leopard starved for blood . . . so do not, in years to come, look too harshly upon this first outcry, the expression of many yet unheard)" (*D* 2: 250). Although not her *first* outcry, she predicts the future well: she will often in the coming entries declare her wish for London—and her resolve to make the move. This entire long June 28 entry declares that her work requires "freer intercourse, wider intercourse"— freedom, the very trait named in her 1919 diary credo to turn her diary into art (*D* 2: 251).

Woolf's focus on her novel (*Mrs. Dalloway*) and her *Common Reader* essays in progress may explain the mere thirty-one diary entries in 1923—fifteen fewer than her 1922 diary and twenty fewer than 1921. She may also be experimenting with a leaner diary form. Others' diaries fill in and refresh her across the year. Her moving tribute to Katherine Mansfield in two January entries includes the lament: "She said she would send me her diary to read, & would write always" (*D* 2: 227). Diaries here mean life to Woolf and commune preserved.[17] Her July

17 play scene closes with Augustine Birrell's gift to her of James Boswell's *Journal of a Tour to Corsica* (with *its* energetic movement and talk of the soul).

Most moving, however, is Woolf's February recall of her Aunt Katherine Stephen's diaries. After exclaiming that it would interest her if her own diary were "ever to become a real diary," Woolf thinks of her visit to "old Kate, in the dining room at 4 Rosary Gardens; & how she opened the cabinet . . . & there in a row on a shelf were her diaries from Jan 1 1877. Some were brown; others red; all the same to a t. And I made her read an entry; one of many thousand days, like pebbles on a beach" (*D* 2: 234). As she writes her novel across 1923, Woolf twice gives herself permission to burn "The Hours" [*Mrs. Dalloway*] if it fails to please (*D* 2: 251, 260). She imagines a similar act in this February diary entry: "And said Kate[,] I intend to live to 1944 when I shall be 84. And on her last day she will say to the charwoman who attends her, Bring me the diaries which you will find in the cabinet; & now, put them on the fire" (*D* 2: 235).

Fortunately, both "The Hours" and Woolf's diaries prove too serviceable for this fate. The 1923 diary records another year of surface and interior stretch—a year of both voice and movement. On February 10 Woolf introduces her horse trope when she asks herself if "this next lap will be influenced by Proust?" (*D* 2: 234). In March she admires Vanessa "astride her fine Arab, life I mean," (*D* 2: 239), and in May she confesses that she stayed in Paris without Leonard at the close of their Spanish holiday "by way of facing life. Yes, I clap the spurs to my flanks & see myself taking fences gallantly" (*D* 2: 241). In June, she uses the same figure for Margot Asquith: "She rides life, if you like; & has picked up a thing or two, which I should like to plunder & never shall" (*D* 2: 244). On July 28, she again claims the horse for herself as she embraces the year's challenges: "I've taken my fences, as I say, & got some good gallops for my trouble. I have also to remind myself that risks imply falls" (*D* 2: 258–59). In fact, she is riding "a great horse, in a spirited & independent way," as she declares a few sentences later—the horse trope always an allusion to her diary mother, Fanny Burney, who lived in London and begged her father to let her write plays and leap the pales of fiction (*D* 2: 259).[18] "Never settle, is my principle in life," Woolf proclaims, trying to explain the "something stirring us to live more stormily than last year" (*D* 2: 259).

James Boswell's *Journal of a Tour to Corsica*

James Boswell appears in 1923 to refresh Virginia Woolf and propel her on. Augustine Birrell's mid-July gift of Boswell's *Journal of a Tour to Corsica; & Mem-*

oirs of Pascal Paoli may have reinforced Woolf's July 8 resolve "to record con-versations verbatim" (*D* 2: 251). His *Journal* also endorsed explorations of the soul and offered impressive illustration of a private diary's use for published *Memoirs.*

Despite her twenty-year admiration for Boswell (begun with her 1903 diary praise of his 1785 *Journal of a Tour to the Hebrides with Samuel Johnson, LL.D*), Woolf may not have read Boswell's earlier *Journal of a Tour to Corsica.* Pub-lished in February 1768, this artful *Journal* saw a second edition in June 1768 and a third (with corrections and a congratulatory letter from Lord Lyttelton) in 1769. However, as S. C. Roberts, the editor of the new 1923 edition, reports in his "introduction," after this auspicious start, the Corsican *Journal* was only reprinted in 1879 "in company with, and somewhat under the shadow of, the *Letters between Erskine and Boswell.*"[19]

Boswell launched *his* life diary in 1758 at age eighteen. At twenty-three he embarks for Utrecht to study law, famously accompanied to Harwich by his new friend Samuel Johnson. The young Scotsman soon tires of Holland and his studies, however, and early shows his drive to know great men in his suc-cessful continental pursuit of Voltaire and Rousseau. "[T]hese two men are to me greater objects than most statues or pictures," he writes home from Berlin (ix). Rousseau gives Boswell letters of introduction to Corsica and its famous General Pascal Paoli.

Woolf saw Boswell's diary method: "From my first setting out on this tour, I wrote down every night what I had observed during the day, throwing together a great deal, that I might afterwards make a selection at leisure."[20] It took him two years to shape his 1765 Corsican journal into publishable form; in so doing he dispensed with diary dates to offer a single continuous narrative. "In writing this Journal, I shall not tire my readers, with relating the occurrences of each particular day," he politely explains. "It will be much more agreeable to them, to have a free and continued account of what I saw or heard, most worthy of observation" (14–15).

Editor Roberts rightly reminds us that it was Paoli—not Samuel Johnson—who inspired Boswell's first literary achievement (ix). If Woolf had not read this Corsican *Journal* before, she discovers in 1923 that it exhibited all the traits she admired in her 1909 "Genius of Boswell" essay. The Scotsman's vast curios-ity—so like her own—propels the Corsican *Journal.* Boswell stops in the city of Corte on his way to Paoli in order "to see every thing about the capital of Corsica" (19). At the Franciscan convent where he lodges, he "look[s] about with great attention" for inscriptions and then visits the rooms of the university in Corte (19, 20). "As I wished to see all things in Corsica, I desired to see even the unhappy criminals," he declares in his happy fashion and swiftly describes the three he sees, and also the hangman of Corsica, "a great curiosity" (21, 22). Roberts astutely praises the "unaffected good humour which made Boswell irresistible to his own, as to later, generations" (xiii).

The poet Thomas Gray wrote that Boswell's Corsican tour showed that "any fool may write a most valuable book by chance, if he will only tell us what he heard and saw with veracity" (xiii). However, as editor Roberts observes, this hardly credits Boswell's deft selection and composition of the mass. The Corsican *Journal* is a more fully achieved work of art than the later Hebrides *Journal*. Boswell structures his *Journal* in dramatic yet symmetrical fashion. In the first quarter of his book—27 of 109 pages—he introduces his trip and recounts his early sights in Corsica, building suspense all the while as he crosses not only the sea but also the mountains of Corsica on his way to the gallant Paoli. He then pauses and increases our anticipation by recounting his own anxiety: "I had the strongest desire to see so exalted a character; but I feared that I should be unable to give a proper account why I had presumed to trouble him with a visit, and that I should sink to nothing before him. I almost wished yet to go back without seeing him"(27). The next fifty-five pages—fully half the book—are given over to Paoli, who fulfills the anxious Boswell's every hope. Then Boswell takes us down the mountain and away from Corsica in the *Journal*'s final quarter.

In his very choice of Corsica and Paoli, Boswell reveals his drive to stand out with something new. "I wished for something more than just the common course of what is called the tour of Europe," he declares in his *Journal*'s confident second sentence; "and Corsica occurred to me as a place which no body else had seen, and where I should find what was to be seen no where else, a people actually fighting for liberty, and forming themselves from a poor inconsiderable oppressed nation, into a flourishing and independent state" (1). The place itself, in Boswell's hands, embodies a stirring lesson (and a private psychodrama as well). At this time, greater freedom and independent movement are sought by Woolf as well.

Woolf praised not only Boswell's curiosity in her 1909 "Genius of Boswell" essay but also his powers of observation. In the Corsican *Journal* one finds everywhere what Roberts aptly describes as the young man's "exquisite sensitiveness to his surroundings which is one of his most engaging qualities" (xiii). Boswell revels in sensory language and depicts everything in the glow of his own vitality. "The prospect of the mountains covered with vines and olives, was extremely agreeable; and the odour of the myrtle and other aromatick shrubs and flowers that grew all around me, was very refreshing," he writes (10). His descriptions are models of clarity and concision. The three "unhappy criminals" are these: "a man for the murder of his wife; a married lady who had hired one of her servants to strangle a woman of whom she was jealous; and the servant who had actually perpetrated this barbarous action" (21). The servant was tortured "by having lighted matches held between his fingers. . . . His hands were so miserably scorched, that he was a piteous object" (21). Boswell offers a fuller portrait of the lonely Corsican hangman, yet it exudes the same simple clarity—and human sympathy:

> Being held in the utmost detestation, he durst not live like another inhabitant of the island. He was obliged to take refuge in the castle, and there he was kept in a little corner turret, where he had just room for a miserable bed, and a little bit of fire to dress such victuals for himself as were sufficient to keep him alive; for nobody would have any intercourse with him, but all turned their backs upon him. I went up and looked at him. And a more dirty rueful spectacle I never beheld. He seemed sensible of his situation, and held down his head like an abhorred outcast. (22)

Far from abhorred, of course, is Pascal Paoli, whose vast portrait is just as skillfully drawn. Forty-year-old Paoli had been Corsica's general and political leader for ten years in 1765, when Boswell appeared at his door. The Corsicans sought their freedom from the nearby Republic of Genoa. Soon after assuming charge of the Corsican army, Paoli drove the Genoese to the remotest corners of the isle. The Italians responded with a treaty with the French, who garrisoned troops in Corsican towns. Thus, as Boswell correctly saw—and Woolf would have appreciated—Corsica (like England, another island nation) sought freedom from foreign tyrants.

Modeling the increasing intimacy with (and admiration for) Paoli he hopes his readers will share, Boswell shows himself losing his "timidity" (30). "Every day I felt myself happier. . . . I enjoyed a sort of luxury of noble sentiment. . . . I forgot the great distance between us" (31, 32). The Paoli traits likely most to engage Woolf were his "most perfect ease of behaviour. . . . a mark of a real great character," his incessant walking and parallel "vivacity of . . . mind" (74, 64).

Beyond this striking blend of ease and movement, Paoli emerges in Boswell's portrait as an ancient hero set down in Corsica. Boswell begins to construct his classical context through a reference to Seneca even before Paoli appears. Simultaneously, he dismisses myths regarding the Corsican's barbarity.

"[A]lthough I knew I was to see a great man," he dares to confess to Paoli, "I expected to find a rude character, an Attila king of the Goths, or a Luitprand king of the Lombards" (37). Instead, Paoli speaks of Epicurus, which allows Boswell to recall Lucan's famous lines on the golden mean and nature's laws and to "die with pleasure in his country's cause."[21] Paoli also sends Boswell to 1 Maccabees, which Boswell retells at length as "it very well applies to Great Britain and Corsica" (56).

In fact, Paoli has a memory like Themistocles, Boswell declares: "His memory as a man of learning, is no less uncommon. He has the best part of the classicks by heart, and he has a happy talent in applying them with propriety, which is rarely to be found."[22] Boswell then links Paoli to Virgil in his allusion to the Roman custom of tossing walnuts at weddings—and to Homer in respect to Paoli's Telemachan ring of dogs. "Having dogs for his attendants, is another circumstance about Paoli similar to the heroes of antiquity," Boswell pointedly declares (76). Earlier, Boswell regrets his inability to capture the "fire" with which Paoli describes the ancients. "He just lives in the times of antiquity," Boswell insists (65). By the end, Boswell's portrait fulfills the claim of his *Journal*'s last sentence, that Paoli "is one of those men who are no longer to be found but in the lives of Plutarch" (110).

The great man's exalted portrait stands out in high relief against the endearing, lowly (but aspiring) Everyman that Boswell makes of himself in this *Journal*. Boswell's drive to become one with his surroundings—and to try on roles—permeates this volume. He takes an oar and helps row the boat for several hours on his way from Leghorn to Corsica, "which gave [him] great spirits" (9). On the island, he again gets down and walks with his "hearty" guides, "doing just what I saw them do" (24). When he makes his first convent stay at Canari, he admits that "[i]t appeared a little odd at first. But I soon learnt to repair to my dormitory as naturally as if I had been a friar for seven years" (15).

In this way he becomes "a great favourite" among the Corsicans, he does not fail to tell us (52); in fact, he orders made for himself the dress of a Corsican chief, replete with feathered cap and snake's head pike. A drawing of Boswell thus arrayed serves as frontispiece for the *Journal*'s 1923 edition. Boswell's greatest moment of emulation comes, however, when he rides "mounted on Paoli's own horse, with rich furniture of crimson velvet, with broad gold lace, and had my guards marching along with me. I allowed myself to indulge a momentary pride in this parade, as I was curious to experience what could really be the pleasure of state and distinction with which mankind are so strangely intoxicated" (31).

Boswell appears deliberately to stress his own failings in the *Journal*, not only to highlight Paoli's perfections but also to model the transforming power of classical greatness that is his theme. "Never was I so thoroughly sensible of my own defects as while I was in Corsica," he confesses. "I felt how small were my abilities, and how little I knew" (81). He ventures "to reason like a libertine" with Paoli "that I might be confirmed in virtuous principles by so illustrious a Preceptour" (66).

In a passage that might have particularly arrested Woolf, Boswell bares his soul to Paoli. Boswell confesses that his "mind naturally inclined to melancholy" and describes the psychic paralysis that has gripped him and "exhausted all the sweets of his being" (60–61). (Three months after reading Boswell's *Journal*, Woolf will describe in *her* diary her own night of physical paralysis and psychic pain.) Paoli then discusses the materiality and immateriality of the soul and concludes: "I hold always firm one great object. I never feel a moment of despondency."[23] Boswell takes this as a lesson: "The contemplation of such a character really existing, was of more service to me than all I had been able to draw from books, from conversation, or from the exertions of my own mind. I had often enough formed the idea of a man continually such, as I could conceive in my best moments. . . . But I saw my highest idea realized in Paoli" (61–62). He repeats this sentiment later in the *Journal*: "From having known intimately so exalted a character, my sentiments of human nature were raised, while, by a sort of contagion, I felt an honest ardour to distinguish myself, and be useful, as far as my situation and abilities would allow" (82–83).

Boswell's Corsican *Journal* is thus an artful journey to mental and moral heights. Samuel Johnson saw the *Journal*'s merit. In a September 1769 letter to Boswell he admired the *Journal* of Corsica above Boswell's history of the place, and this may have impressed Woolf in 1923. "Your History is like other histories, but your Journal is in a very high degree curious and delightful," Johnson declared. "Your History was copied from books; your Journal rose out of your own experience and observation. You express images which operated strongly upon yourself, and you have impressed them with great force upon your readers. I know not whether I could name any narrative by which curiosity is better excited, or better gratified" (vii–viii).

Boswell hoped for political as well as literary triumph for his Corsican *Journal*.[24] The Italians thought he bore a commission from the English court to negotiate a treaty with the Corsicans—an error that, of course, delighted Boswell and that he sought to make true. Beyond exalting Paoli as a classical hero, Boswell took pains to show him as a friend of Great Britain well versed in

England's history, language, parliamentary debates, and magazines—even able to offer "very judicious and ingenious criticism on . . . Swift's works" (35). Back in England, Boswell worked tirelessly for Corsica's freedom. He supervised the publication of *British Essays in behalf of the Brave Corsicans*. He raised funds in Scotland and extolled the Corsican freedom fighters in Ireland. He even turned up dressed in his Corsican chief garb at the 1769 Shakespeare festival in Stratford-on-Avon—and chronicled the moment in *London Magazine*.

Roberts believes that Boswell's *Journal* "was no mean instrument in fanning the flame of enthusiasm for Paoli and his compatriots" (xi). Horace Walpole, David Garrick, and historian Catharine Macaulay wrote "noble letters" to Boswell regarding his *Journal*. Anna Barbauld (whom Woolf knew from Henry Crabb Robinson's diary) wrote a poem on Corsica that celebrated "the working thoughts which swelled the breast / Of generous Boswell"; and Gray declared Paoli a man born two thousand years after his time (xi–xii).

Time, however, trumped Boswell's moves. In 1769, Corsica fell under French control, and England took no steps to intervene. Paoli resisted as long as he could but eventually escaped to England where, thanks to Boswell, he became a welcomed figure in Johnson's circle. Art is long; politics short, Woolf might have observed of Boswell's enduring *Journal*—an artful journal rich in voice, movement, and bearing of the soul. How delightful, too, to encounter another Lord Holland (from her 1908 diary reading) in Roberts' introduction, explaining England's silence as Corsica fell. "Foolish as we are," Lord Holland declared, "we cannot be so foolish as to go to war because Mr Boswell has been to Corsica" (xii).

5

Spare, Modernist Perfection

Virginia Woolf appears in consummate command in her 1924 diary. She consciously curbs the number of her diary entries and brakes as well her previous need for praise. She adds a calendar to her diary cover and sets out a writing "programme" for *Mrs. Dalloway* and *The Common Reader* that she follows to a T. She moves with such confident command in 1924 that she views old age, that formerly frightening specter, now as an amiable, even elevated, state.

Change and the *movement* to London invigorate her. London supplies the motion she craves. By October, she declares her new home "perfect": "The studio the best study I've ever had" (*D* 2: 317). As London expands for Woolf, so does her focus on women—perhaps due to her growing interest in Vita Sackville-West. Woolf allows her feelings and her soul to dilate in this diary. In the fall, she links her soul to the country and to poetry—and all three to expansion: as her natural roots bursting forth.

As she finishes her novel and her essays across this diary, she sends out shoots of other works as well. The diaries she reads assist her. *The Letters & Journals of Anne Chalmers*, a precocious Scottish teenager, which Woolf reviews in February 1924, were edited by Chalmers' daughter. They recall and preserve a dead mother. They describe summer holidays at the Scottish seaside with "a large and clever family" and even offer the name Mrs. Ramsay (24). During the summer, Woolf reads *The Diary of the Lady Anne Clifford with an Introduction by Vita Sackville-West*, another case of a daughter thinking back through, and immortalizing, a dead (fore)mother. Lady Clifford's Renaissance diary also offers women's history. It supplies grist for Woolf's *Common Reader* essays "The Elizabethan Lumber Room" and "Donne after Three Centuries." Even more importantly, its tale of a ferocious fight over a daughter's inheritance inspires the plot of *Orlando* (1928).

In July, Woolf reviews the early journals of Stendhal, the father of the psychological novel. She finds that Stendhal uses a diary even more than she does to cultivate public prose. Stendhal's early journals direct Woolf's mind (yet again) to the soul, to the many nuances and contradictions of character—in short, even deeper into the psychological novel.

Virginia Woolf's 1924 Diary

> *"It strikes me that in this book I practise writing; do my scales; yes & work at certain effects. I daresay I practiced Jacob here,—& Mrs D. & shall invent my next book here; for here I write merely in the spirit—great fun it is too, & old V. of 1940 will see something in it too. She will be a woman who can see, old V.: everything— more than I can I think."*

(October 17, 1924; D 2: 319–20)

A sure hand pilots the 1924 diary. A mere thirty-one entries log the 440 days from January 3, 1924, to March 18, 1925—the same number as in the 1923 diary with its 347 days. One feels the diarist's calibrations throughout, starting with a three-month calendar she draws after the opening page.[1] Woolf launches this diary expectantly—"This year is almost certainly bound to be the most eventful in the whole of our (recorded) career"—and in the flush of immediate house-hunting success she writes five diary entries in January, a pace that, had she maintained it, would have yielded sixty entries for 1924.[2] However, she brakes herself with her ninth entry, March 4: "Really I'm writing too much here. The twelve months at this rate will overflow" (D 2: 295). From this moment she appears consciously to curtail herself, to ration her diary-writing: March (2 entries), April (2), May (2), June (2), July (2), August (3); September (3), October (1), November (2), and December (2).

Similar command shows in her May 26 entry given over, in part, to writing plans. "But my mind is full of The Hours [*Mrs. Dalloway*]," she declares. "I am now saying that I will write at it for 4 months, June, July, August & September, & then it will be done, & I shall put it away for three months, during which I shall finish my essays [*The Common Reader*]; & then that will be—October, November, December–January: & I shall revise it January February March April; & in April my essays will come out; & in May my novel. Such is my programme" (D 2: 301). She adheres precisely to this scheme, *The Common Reader* published April 23, 1925, and *Mrs. Dalloway* three weeks later, on May 14.

With almost equal skill she handles her previous yen for praise. Just as on March 4 she curbs her *number* of diary entries, at the close of her first entry she checks her urge to treasure (and measure) success: "Oh dear, oh dear, no boasting, aloud, in 1924. I didn't boast at Charleston" (*D* 2: 282). The inserted qualifier "aloud" implies she may boast silently to herself, or in her diary; however, "aloud" may also mean she thinks her diary a separate hearing "self," even as potential public prose. In the event, few accolades feather the 1924 diary. On March 12, Woolf notes of the farewell party for writer Edmund Blunden: "We were all toothless insignificant amiable nonentities—we distinguished writers—Not a fig would I give for anyone's praise or curse" (*D* 2: 297). In September, trying to "keep the quality of a sketch in a finished & composed work"—her novel *Mrs. Dalloway*—she asserts that "none can help & none can hinder me any more" (*D* 2: 312).

In fact, she disdains in this diary those *needing* praise. In a May 26 portrait of "sinister & pedagogic" T. S. Eliot, she observes: "There's something . . . biting in the back, suspicious, elaborate, uneasy, about him: much would be liberated by a douche of pure praise, which he can scarcely hope to get" (*D* 2: 302). Tellingly, on December 13 she lists Dadie Ryland's "love of praise" as one of several traits that keeps her from seeing him as a "permanent partner" in the Hogarth Press (*D* 2: 323). Among the flaws of Ryland's predecessor, Ralph Partridge, had been his *withholding* of praise.

Alongside boasts and diary entries to hold them, much else is held in check as Woolf steers this volume. In her opening entry we see her carefully gauge her time: "Now it is six, my boundary, & I must read Montaigne, & cut short those other reflections about, I think, reading & writing which were to fill up the page. I ought to describe the walk from Charleston too; but can't defraud Montaigne any longer" (*D* 2: 282). We glimpse here how this diary is "cut short." Topics now suffice for their elaboration. "I have said nothing of my speech at the London group, which drew tears; or of a host of matters," she admits April 15. "Indeed most of life escapes, now I come to think of it: the texture of the ordinary day" (*D* 2: 300, 298). On May 26 she acknowledges, "I have left the whole of society unrecorded," and on July 3 she observes, "But I have let Garsington languish like a decaying wreath on my pen" (*D* 2: 302, 305).

Given her narrowed time for diary-keeping, we see her discipline herself. In her second entry, January 9, that hails her purchase of 52 Tavistock Square, she disdains giving "auctioneers particulars" and chooses instead to preserve the serendipitous talk that led to the London home (*D* 2: 283). On February 9, she banishes worries regarding the house: "Is it noisy? No need to go into my broodings over that point" (*D* 2: 291). In contrast, in August she employs "I dont now describe" as a mantra to release this striking country scene:

I dont often trouble now to describe cornfields & groups of harvesting women in loose blues & reds & little staring yellow frocked girls. But thats not my eyes' fault: coming back the other evening from Charleston, again all my nerves stood upright, flushed, electrified (whats the word?) with the sheer beauty—beauty abounding & superabounding, so that one almost resents it, not being capable of catching it all, & holding it all at the moment. . . . And I dont describe encounters with herds of Alderneys anymore—though this would have been necessary some years ago— how they barked and belled like stags round Grizzle; & how I waved my stick & stood at bay; & thought of Homer as they came flourishing & trampling towards me: some mimic battle. (*D* 2: 311)

But of course she does describe it—and evocatively so. One might say she makes literature of it.

Portraits and talk undergo similar retrenchment. For at least a third of her portraits, Woolf settles for swift likenesses in the rapid-fire style of poet-diarist William Allingham, whose diary she reviewed in 1907. On March 12, for instance, she writes: "Jack Squire, fat, & consequential; Eddie [Marsh] grown grey & fatherly" (*D* 2: 297). On July 3, she stacks up adjectives, "Good prim priggish bright eyed Peter [Lucas]," as she does in August with the "little staring yellow frocked girls" (*D* 2: 305, 311). That month, looking forward to reading Shakespeare's plays, she declares: "It is poetry that I want now—long poems. . . . I want the concentration & the romance, & the words all glued together, fused, glowing . . ." (*D* 2: 310). So she fuses them in her diary. Equally swift (yet bridled) is talk, a major focus of the 1923 diary with its six play scenes. Only in her December 21 entry does Woolf declare, "I wish I could write conversations" (*D* 2: 326).

Woolf moves with such sure command in 1924 that she views that formerly frightening, then ambiguous, phantom, old age as now a welcome, even elevated, state. The *change* and the *move* to London energize her. "Already I feel ten years younger," she declares in her opening entry (*D* 2: 281). "Youth is a matter of forging ahead. . . . I'm pleased to find [how] volatile our temperaments still are . . . at the ages of 42 & 43—for 42 comes tripping towards me, the momentous year" (*D* 2: 282). She describes their age as "full summer" in her third entry, January 12, and in August, when a slight depression descends on her at Rodmell "as if we were old & near the end of all things," she again turns to her diary to talk herself round. "Nevertheless, in spite of the grumbling with which this began, honestly I don't feel old," she concludes, "& its a question of getting up my steam again in writing" (*D* 2: 285, 307, 308).

When she seizes her diary on October 17 to herald her completion of *Mrs. Dalloway*, it is to foresee inventing her next book within her diary's pages and to envision "old V[irginia]. of 1940" admiring her diary books. And a formidable projected self Old Virginia is: "a woman who can see . . . everything—more than I can I think" (*D* 2: 320). In the important August 2 entry that rejects depression with its sense of failure and old age, Woolf also transforms her stark 1920 precipice trope—life as "tragic . . . a little strip of pavement over an abyss"—into a more vigorous scene (*D* 2: 72). "And if we didn't live venturously, plucking the wild goat by the beard, & trembling over precipices," she declares, "we should never be depressed, I've no doubt; but already should be faded, fatalistic & aged" (*D* 2: 308–9). "Trembling" could easily be "tumbling" over precipices, but both are now part of a shared Attic romp.

Woolf thus reframes some elements of her diary and restrains others. At the same time other facets expand. London, of course, means multifold expansion: a basement billiard room that becomes her studio; the rooftop rock garden; the painted panels commissioned from Vanessa and Duncan Grant. Beyond this, London represents for Woolf "something central & inexplicable" as she writes in her second entry, waxing poetic as she records her purchase of 52 Tavistock Square: "London thou art a jewel of jewels, & jasper of jocunditie—music, talk, friendship, city views, books, publishing, something central & inexplicable, all this is now within my reach, as it hasn't been since August 1913, when we left Cliffords Inn, for a series of catastrophes which very nearly ended my life, & would, I'm vain enough to think, have ruined Leonard's" (*D* 2: 283). "So I shall have a room of my own to sit down in, after almost 10 years, in London," she exalts February 3, framing that soon-to-be-memorable phrase (*D* 2: 291).

And just as she found Bloomsbury more lovely than Kensington in her 1905 diary, she now finds London surpassing Richmond. On May 26, she calls London "enchanting" and must again tally its charms: "I step out upon a tawny coloured magic carpet, it seems, & get carried into beauty without raising a finger. . . . And people pop in & out, lightly, divertingly like rabbits. . . . One of these days I will write about London, & how it takes up the private life & carries it on, without any effort" (*D* 2: 301). Again we see that London supplies needed *movement* for Woolf—a fact to recall when London is denied her in 1940 and 1941. In her next sentence she contrasts London's *motion* with the still concentration of the country: "Faces passing lift up my mind; prevent it from settling, as it does in the stillness at Rodmell" (*D* 2: 301). Clearly, *both* states are required.[3] By October, she declares her new home "perfect" (*D* 2: 317).

London now opens and the Hogarth Press expands. So, too, does Woolf's interest in women across this year. In January she pays tribute to active mothers. "I love the distracted busy ways of these mothers—" she writes of Molly MacCarthy and Karin Stephen, "no parsimony of life, as there is with the childless—always something that must be decided, or done" (*D* 2: 286). Again *action* impresses her, not necessarily nurture, for she complains of Old Mrs. MacCarthy, "Really I fancy these old ladies, without occupation, the most trying in the world" (*D* 2: 286).

She describes in her February 3 entry her first meeting with her longtime adversary Arnold Bennett and takes time to preserve two sentences of his talk: "'I dont understand women—' This said as a schoolboy might say it. Everyone laughs. Then 'No woman is as sensitive as I am—no woman could be . . . '" (*D* 2: 290). One suspects *she* laughs at neither line. And after announcing her completion of *Mrs. Dalloway* on October 17, she looks around and describes the Campbell sedition case filling the press and sees "school boy" antics once more. "[W]e are now condemned to a dose of lies every morning: the usual yearly schoolboys wrangle has begun. If I were still a feminist, I should make capital out of the wrangle. But I have travelled on—as K[atherine]. M[ansfield]. said to me, she saw me as a ship far out at sea" (*D* 2: 318).

Woolf may have traveled on, but her sights remain on women. Mocking praise in one of the few moments in this diary she allows herself to measure fame, she does so as a probe of male and female difference: "So very likely this time next year I shall be one of those people who are, so father said, in the little circle of London Society which represents the Apostles, I think, on a larger scale. Or does this no longer exist? To know everyone worth knowing. I can just see what he meant; just imagine being in that position—if women can be. Lytton is: Maynard; Ld Balfour; not perhaps Hardy" (*D* 2: 319). *If women can be.*

In her final diary entry of 1924, her mind moves again to women's treatment as she projects the fate of novelist, critic, and poet Richard Aldington: "[He is] a bluff, powerful, rather greasy eyed, nice downright man, who will make his way in the world, which I dont much like people to do. All young men do it. No young women; or in women it is trounced; in men forgiven. Its these reflections I want to enmesh, in writing; or these are among them" (*D* 2: 326).

She is inventing *A Room of One's Own* in this diary, just as her October 17 entry foretells.[4] In her November 1 entry, Woolf writes of Mary Hutchinson's party: "If one could be friendly with women, what a pleasure—the relationship so secret & private compared with relations with men. Why not write about it? truthfully?" (*D* 2: 320). Her next words suggest she believes diary-writing furthers this goal. Why not write about women's friendship? truthfully? she asks. "As I think, this diary writing has greatly helped my style; loosened the ligatures" (*D* 2: 320).

Woolf's warming friendship with Vita Sackville-West across 1924 likely fuels her interest in women. She calls Vita "dense" in January and "unshaded" and "rigid" in July—the latter two traits serious flaws in Woolf's aesthetic. But in July, Woolf also admires Vita's perfect body and easy aristocratic manner: "[N]o inhibitions, no false reserves; anything can be said; but as usual, that fatal simplicity or rigidity of mind which makes it seem all a little unshaded, & empty. More mind, my God—(I'm too jangled even to quote correctly)" (*D* 2: 287, 306–7). She means to quote "more brain, O Lord, more brain!," from George Meredith's poem "Modern Love," but again Vita "jangles" her aplomb.

But Vita's status rises in September when Woolf reads her long story *Seducers in Ecuador*: "I see my own face in it, its true. But she has shed the old verbiage, & come to terms with some sort of glimmer of art; so I think; & indeed, I rather marvel at her skill, & sensibility; for is she not mother, wife, great lady, hostess, as well as scribbling?" (*D* 2: 313). Directing her own life and art with a sure and vigorous hand, Woolf admires similar prowess in Sackville-West: "Vita was here for Sunday, gliding down the village in her large new blue Austin car, which she manages consummately," she writes on September 15. By this entry's end, one of Woolf's typical mixed portraits tips toward interested approval: "Oh yes, I like her; could tack her on to my equipage for all time; & suppose if life allowed, this might be a friendship of a sort" (*D* 2: 313).

As her interest in women expands, Woolf allows her feelings and soul to dilate. In this diary she speaks openly of her previous mental illness, describing herself in January as "creeping about, like a rat struck on the head" during her years in Richmond, admitting "a series of catastrophes" that nearly ended her life in 1913, even daring to own her "madness," hearing the voices of the dead (*D* 2: 283). In her dramatic April 15 entry that recounts, "for the psychology of it," her five-year-old niece Angelica's terrifying brush with death, Woolf turns neither from her own nor from others' feelings (*D* 2: 298). She describes Vanessa as she waits for the surgeon:

> I saw again that extraordinary look of anguish, dumb, not complaining, which I saw in Greece, I think, when she was ill. The feelings of the people who don't talk express themselves thus. My feeling was "a pane of glass shelters me. I'm only allowed to look on at this." at which I was half envious, half grieved. . . . What I felt was, not sorrow or pity for Angelica, but

that now Nessa would be an old woman; & this would be an indelible mark; & that death & tragedy had once more put down his paw, after letting us run a few paces. People never get over their early impressions of death I think. I always feel pursued. (*D* 2: 299)

In her next entry, May 5, she recalls her mother's death twenty-nine years before and does not shrink from owning what some might call unfilial response. She starts a subtle set piece on September 15 by recalling the one-year anniversary of her psychic terror—and again does not shy from mentioning it or recalling the pain. "Here I am waiting for L. to come back from London," she writes in the country, "& at this hour, having been wounded last year when he was late, I always feel the old wound twingeing" (*D* 2: 313). A month later, "brooding over" Leonard's invitation to India, she admits that his desire to go "a little hurt me. But I said to myself this is a side of life I've not lain on. I must face that too. Still nothing has been heard, though I still a little dread the mornings post, but this is concealed from L." (*D* 2: 318). But not from her diary.[5]

Along with inner feelings, the soul opens further in this diary. Perhaps E. M. Forster encourages her when he tells her in February that she had "got further into the soul" in *Jacob's Room* than any other novelist (*D* 2: 292). Stendhal's early journals, read in June, encourage her as well. In her June 21 entry, she once more cries her unfitness as prelude to this potent declaration: "If I weren't so sleepy, I would write about the soul. . . . about the violent moods of my soul. . . . I think I grow more & more poetic. Perhaps I restrained it, & now, like a plant in a pot, it begins to crack the earthenware. Often I feel the different aspects of life bursting my mind asunder" (*D* 2: 304). This bursting plant trope recalls (and refines) the figure Woolf offered for her coalescing 1918 diary volume: "[T]his book is now a natural growth of mine—a rather dishevelled, rambling plant, running a yard of green stalk for every flower" (*D* 1: 150). By 1924, the diary is less gangly. Potted now and more carefully pruned, it bursts quickly into bloom.

In August, Woolf once more finds the *country* apt terrain for her soul. "The country is like a convent," she declares, interestingly. "The soul swims to the top. . . . But oh the delicacy & complexity of the soul—for, haven't I begun to tap her & listen to her breathing after all?" (*D* 2: 308). In her 1903 diary, Woolf ended her essay-entry titled "Life in the Fields" with the words: "If you lie on the earth somewhere you hear a sound like a vast breath, as though it were the very inspiration of earth herself, & all the living things on her" (*PA* 203).

Woolf links her soul with the country and with poetry, and all three with expansion: as her natural roots bursting forth. Among its thirty-one entries the 1924 diary offers two set pieces—as if the diary moves toward art (just as Woolf envisioned in her 1919 diary credo). Woolf's July 5 entry captures her first visit to Knole, Vita's ancestral estate. In this largely condemning piece, Woolf depicts Vita's father, Lord Sackville-West, as the dead center of life's great shell. "His lordship lives in the kernel of a vast nut," she begins (*D* 2: 306). One must pass "miles of galleries," "endless treasures—chairs that Shakespeare might have sat on," to find "one solitary peer . . . lunching by himself in the centre" (*D* 2: 306). Woolf finds "the inward parts [of Knole] . . . gone dead. Ropes fence off half the rooms; the chairs & the pictures look preserved; life has left them" (*D* 2: 306). She ends this piece that skewers wealth and class: "There is Knole, capable of housing all the desperate poor of Judd Street, & with only that one solitary earl in the kernel" (*D* 2: 307).

Vita inspires another full-circle set piece on September 15. Waiting for Leonard to return from London, Woolf recalls the previous year's "wound" his present lateness revives. She then records Vita's return visit to Rodmell and the "glimmer of art" her *Seduction of Ecuador* emits (*D* 2: 313). Woolf then pauses again to think of Leonard. She thinks how hard Leonard works and prides herself that the Rodmell postman has stopped to ask "so honestly & sincerely" if Leonard would address the International Labor Party at Lewes about the League of Nations. "This sort of thing counts," she declares, naming her values: "I like their trust & admiration; & the swing from Knole & Lord Sackville's invitation . . . to postmen getting up the local meetings, which suddenly seem to me, matters of the highest importance. All this confirms me in thinking that we're splinters & mosaics; not, as they used to hold, immaculate, monolithic, consistent wholes" (*D* 2: 314). She reveals her values here, but also the modernist aesthetic: evocative "discords" and "shivering fragments" (splinters & mosaics) rather than "monolithic, consistent wholes" (*PA* 393). She closes this entry-of-contrasts full circle (and with affirmation of her marriage): "Now to the house, waiting for L." (*D* 2: 314).

Beyond these artfully shaped entries, Woolf sends out shoots of other writing in this diary as well. As she finishes her novel and her essays across the year, she begins to feel her way to her next works. On October 17, announcing the last words of *Mrs. Dalloway*, she immediately sees *To the Lighthouse*. "I see already The Old Man," she writes (*D* 2: 317). And as the year closes she twice declares her wish to write truthfully of women (*D* 2: 320, 326).

Woolf's 1924 diary treats the year as the start of a new era: the London era; the 52 Tavistock Square era; an era of sink or swim for the Hogarth Press and of poetic branching of her prose. If in her 1903 diary she turned deliberately from London and the male literary tradition, and repeated this turn again and again in later diaries, she now returns to London exultant—and on her own terms. The 1924 diary offers the best counter to the temptation to assume illness—to imagine the worst—at diary gaps. The thirty-one entries across 440 days mean inordinate action elsewhere—at the Press and with *Mrs. Dalloway* and *The Common Reader*—rather than illness of any sort.[6] They reveal as well deliberate paring and compression of her modernist style.

Woolf's spurred-horse trope persists across this diary. "But I like myself for taking my fences," she tells her diary on January 12 (*D* 2: 285). Thinking on February 23 of the many tasks before her, she observes: "My mind sits in front of a fence & pours out clouds of ideas; I have to stick spurs in sharp to make it jump" (*D* 2: 292). This scene offers a telling view of her mind. In June she reports with some confidence, "I am writing, writing, & see my way clear to the end [of *Mrs. Dalloway*] now, & so shall gallop to it, somehow or other" (*D* 2: 305), and her September 7 entry reveals not only that she continues to reread her previous entries but also that her fiction and diary prose merge. "It is a disgrace that I write nothing [in my diary]," she writes after a twenty-two-day diary gap, "or if I write, write sloppily, using nothing but present participles. I find them very useful in my last lap of Mrs D" (*D* 2: 312). Her December 13 entry reports her "galloping over Mrs Dalloway, re-typing it entirely from the start," and in her final entry of 1924, she asserts with confidence, "Only I do feel fairly sure that I am grazing as near as I can to my own ideas, & getting a tolerable shape for them. I think there is less & less wastage" (*D* 2: 323, 325).

True. The closely pruned yet still branching and artful 1924 diary—branching, perhaps, *because* so finely trimmed—is a diary of "invincible optimism" charting a "momentous year" (*D* 2: 283, 282). With the spare, modernist perfection of this 1924 diary, Woolf presses the periodic diary to its furthest reach.

Anne Chalmers' *Journals*

In the glow of her impending move to London, Virginia Woolf takes time to offer a paragraph of praise for the *Letters & Journals of Anne Chalmers* in the February 23, 1924, *Nation & Athenaeum*. Edited by Chalmers' daughter, the volume was a filial act, a daughter's resurrection of a dead mother.[7] Furthermore, as Woolf reveals in her review's opening sentence, "The greater part of [the] book consists of the journal of a tour through England" Chalmers took at age seventeen with her mother and celebrated father (*E* 3: 398).

Much in Chalmers' life (and teenage writing) might have engaged Virginia Woolf. Chalmers lived from 1813 to 1891 and was the oldest of six daughters of Grace Pratt and the soon-to-be-famous Disrupting preacher, professor, and social reformer Dr. Thomas Chalmers. "Daughters were welcome in that household," Anne's daughter reports. "On the birth of each, their father said, 'The better article' or 'Another of the best'" (17). Anne's health was "somewhat feeble" (20). To counter this, her parents sent her to visit friends at Fairlie for a week or two during several summers—an experience parallel to (if briefer than) Woolf's cherished Cornwall holidays. "[E]vidently the sea shore, the fishing, the romantic scenery, and the life of a large and clever family, appealed very strongly to her imagination," Anne's granddaughter explains in a further opening note—perhaps firing Woolf's own imagination as well (24). Anne even has tea with a Mrs. Ramsay and receives "a very handsome necklace" as a gift from her daughter (39, 42).

An imaginative Scottish teenager, Anne tries on a new name for herself in her diary—Hannah (the French form of Anne)—but soon drops it, just as fifteen-year-old Virginia abandoned her diary's "Miss Jan." Also like teenage Virginia (and teenage Fanny Burney, who called herself "Nobody" in her diary), Anne was pressed into service to entertain her famous father's friends—and similarly rebels. (The diaries of these three seventeen-year-olds might be tellingly compared.)[8] "[T]here are a number of students coming to-night, whom I suppose I must entertain at least with tea & shortbread. You cannot think how tiresome they are," Anne writes. "Mrs McLellan is here but I have to make tea and sit at the head of the table though I hope she will take that duty" (56). Chalmers' "lapses from conventionality were much commented upon" during her life, her granddaughter explains (26–27). Anne "dressed very badly" and cared nothing for her personal appearance (20). When she becomes a mother, she clothes her daughter in bright orange so she can find her in the street.

At her marriage, Anne's Edinburgh home, looking out on Castle Rock, becomes the center of a literary circle that includes Thomas Carlyle. As a girl of eight Anne sees Woolf's diary father, Sir Walter Scott, "walking somewhat lame" in the street while a band plays "Highland Laddie" (180). At age seventeen, she meets the Scottish writer Joanna Baillie during her English tour; visits William Wilberforce and admires his and Thomas Macaulay's oratory, but finds Samuel Taylor Coleridge the "most striking person" she meets in her travels (129). She confesses to her diary that she could "give no idea of the beauty and sublimity of his conversation. It resembles the loveliness of a song. . . . I burst into tears when it stopped" (128, 185).

Anne Chalmers "very often took an unusual view of the questions of the day, and certainly never was swayed by the conventional view," her granddaughter explains (26). The seventeen-year-old dares to call men "ridiculous" in her diary (159), and when she visits the House of Lords in 1830, she notices most the male dress. In a passage that might have stuck in Woolf's mind for *Three Guineas*, she writes: "They and the Chancellor were robed and wigged, and a man's air and manner look very odd in a gown. They sat down opposite the Chancellor, and certainly the three coarse ugly-looking men with the slight swagger in their manners presented a curious spectacle" (123).

In her review, Woolf admires Chalmers as a "sprightly girl" with a "freedom of spirit" whose diary observations are "full of fun" (*E* 3: 398–99). In truth, Anne recalls Elizabeth Bennet of *Pride and Prejudice*, particularly in the following diary portrait of a party bore, himself named Bennet. "[W]e expected to have some interesting information from Mr. Bennet, who had circumnavigated the world," Anne begins: "But about three-quarters of an hour before supper was announced, Mr. Bennet commenced a detail of what each inhabitant of the Sandwich Islands said to him, upon landing, and as they all said the same thing, the interest of variety was wanting. . . . [J]ust at this juncture, supper was announced, which broke in upon the story, and I ran to my own room to indulge in the heartiest fit of laughing I had enjoyed since I left Scotia" (126–27).

The Letters & Journals of Anne Chalmers clearly amused Woolf—and also may have touched her. They recall and immortalize a dead mother. They evoke summer holidays at the sea with a large and clever family and even offer the name Mrs. Ramsay. They reveal "a freedom of spirit." Much to our regret—and perhaps to Woolf's—this volume only unveils the teenage letters and journal.

Stendhal's Early Journals

"[L]ive for your genius, form it, cultivate it, correct it," Marie-Henri Beyle tells his 1804 diary at age twenty-one (Sage 61). Across his fourteen years of diaries, this outsider, this Frenchman who came to write under the pen name Stendhal, does just that. Virginia Woolf, who is steering her own life and art expertly in 1924, notes Beyle's skill in her July 5, 1824, *Nation and Athenaeum* review of the first volume of his journals, which covered the years 1801 to 1805. "Stendhal was set from the first upon mastering the art of life," she observes (*E* 3: 417). Beyle's journals, with their intense focus on the "soul," likely triggered Woolf's willingness in June 1924 (and after) "to cancel that vow against soul description" and probe "the violent moods of [her] soul" (*D* 2: 304).

She had read Stendhal's novel *The Red and the Black* at least as early as 1907, and she possessed several life ties to this man called the father of the modern psychological novel.[9] Born in Grenoble, France, on January 23, 1783, Beyle loses his adored mother at age seven, causing what diary translator Robert Sage calls "his everlasting pursuit of elusive womanhood" (ix). To compensate, Beyle forms a close bond with his sister, Pauline. He writes in his 1805 journal: "I'm obliged to go to Grenoble for a few months, and even this obligation is a pleasure, since I'll see my dear Pauline there again. I think there aren't many brothers like me, who have the good fortune to be *amico riamato* of a girl with genius and the loftiest kind of a soul" (Sage 169).

Beyle spurns university training, preferring self-education through books. Like Woolf, he admires Montaigne ("the style with the most brilliancy in France") and Shakespeare (Sage 78). "THOU ARE THE GREATEST BARD IN THE WORLD!" he exclaims in English of Shakespeare within his diary written in French (Sage 111). In his fervent, run-together diary fashion, the twenty-two-year-old writes that Shakespeare's poetry "is almost prose for me. Consequently, it's possible to be a poet in prose. . . . I must follow Shakespeare's example; how he flows on like a river that floods over its banks and sweeps all before it, what a river is his verse, how broad is his manner of painting, it is all nature!" (Sage 111, 113). This passage may have prompted Woolf toward her own fused diary words and sense that she, too, could be "a poet in prose." Diagnosed as melancholic at age eighteen, Beyle nevertheless is able to move, again like Woolf, through a variety of forms across his fifty-nine years: journalism, essays, biographies, short stories, and novels. In his first diaries he aspires to be the new Molière.

Woolf could hardly help but notice that Beyle's is a writer's diary, one even more intent than hers on cultivating and correcting genius. Like her, he uses initials across his diary. He also revels in change. In his first extant diary at age eighteen, he speaks of "the multitude of characters or passions that form my continual subject of study" (Sage 12). A month later he notes, "Even the man with the best mind is changeable," and a week later he cautions himself: "I'll nearly always be mistaken if I think that a man has only a single character" (Sage 14). Four years later, he sees even more: "For I understand the extreme of variation in myself. . . . With senses and inner faculties so variable and sensitive, it is quite possible that I shall become insane" (Sage 103).

His diary serves as his sanitarium. There he can study and shape—if not fully control—his variable "faculties." He launches his first extant journal in Milan on April 18, 1801, with a steely sense of his task: "I'm undertaking to write the history of my life day by day. I don't know whether I'll have the fortitude to carry out this plan, which I already started in Paris. There's a mistake in French already; there will be a lot more, because I'm making it a rule not to stand on ceremony and never to erase" (Sage 6).

Beyle grows into his diary across the five years Woolf reads. In July 1801 he tells himself, "I must acquire worldly experience," and in August, "a trip ought to be a sort of critique of the various things you encounter" (Sage 12, 14). His diary falters in 1802 and 1803 when he leaves Italy for Grenoble; however, his drive to know the human heart through deep scrutiny of himself intensifies at age twenty-one with his 1804 return to Paris. Diary entries grow longer and the diary itself more experimental.

Throughout his diary Beyle makes drawings—of his Paris apartment or of a country field—to add visual settings for the entries. He also rereads his diary and adds margin notes—practices Woolf follows as well. In 1804 he allows his friend Louis Crozet to write portions of his diary, and in early 1805 the two collaborate on character sketches of their friends, which Beyle calls "the most useful work that I could do" (Sage 118). These mirror the formal portraits Woolf makes of *her* friends in her 1919 diary as she enters her second, modernist, diary stage.

Beyle's 1804 and 1805 journals record his literary growth. Reading Carlo Goldoni's plays in June 1804, he identifies "naturalness" as "one of the principle parts of Art" and begins to work toward a natural style (Sage 61). In July, he tells his diary, "I must correct myself of pedantry. . . . [O]f all writers, I should be the one who offends the vanity of my readers the least, I should appear completely natural to them without their noticing it" (Sage 63). The same month he determines to "study the manners and morals of my contemporaries—what appears to them to be just, unjust, honorable, dishonorable, good breeding, ill breeding, ridiculous, agreeable, etc. That's the sort of thing that changes every half century" (Sage 66).

His confidence grows and by November he feels capable of "character portrayal": "I seem to realize that any subject would be a good one in my hands. I'm no longer afraid of running out of subjects" (Sage 78). Eleven days later, he decides he must "fathom the principle of the minor talent of the epigram and acquire it" (Sage 80). By June 1805, he decides to write about nothing but society and that in the form of anecdotes (Sage 184).

Beyle studies rigorously both society and himself—a task made more difficult by his unusual temperament, which mixes hot emotion with cold intellect. Woolf writes of Beyle's "personal fascination" in her review (*E* 3: 417). His journals offer her the suggestive "discords" she defined in her 1908 diary as her own artistic goal (*PA* 393). Unresolved tension surges through Beyle's journals between heart and head, feeling and analysis. Beyle feels he needs experience in order to write; however, he is shy, maladroit, and homely and struggles to keep his enthusiasms—both emotional and intellectual—from overwhelming any social scene. The conflict, he notes in a February 1805 entry, affects his prose as well: "It's a good thing to have these states of the *maximum* of passion, for without that it would be impossible to portray them. . . . [but] . . . Frequently, I can't write because of my ardor. . . . If I don't change my ways, I shall have been THE GREATEST BARD for myself alone, and, never having shown myself to others, I shall pass on WITHOUT FAME" (Sage 113; capitalized words in English).

Across 1805 Beyle wails that he is "up to [his] neck in sentiment": "My heart has far more experience than my head; I have loved much and judged very little" (Sage 174, 151). However, the journals show him thinking and judging himself into paralysis. Thus he writes in March 1805 of Mélanie Guilbert, the actress he pursues at this time and the only woman with whom he ever lives: "I paused too long over the enjoyment of what I was feeling, I didn't venture to kiss her, maybe I was wrong. I'm so familiar with the game of love that I have to hold myself in like the devil in order not to be suspicious, and I'm never sure of anything for the reason that I see all the possibilities" (Sage 148). Sad for romance yet happy for his art, Beyle thinks too much (like Prufrock). He savors what he feels and thinks more than the actual kiss. Through his journals he seeks ways to bridge this divide.

Related tension ripples through the journals between what scholar Ralph Schoolcraft calls Beyle's "conflicting projects of self-knowledge and self-transformation" (259). How can one ever know a morphing self? Schoolcraft has classified the more than three hundred pseudonyms Beyle used in his work—*Stendhal* only the most famous—and argues persuasively that pseudonyms helped the writer resolve his personal and literary needs. In February 1805, Beyle adopts diary pseudonyms for three of his friends: "Crozet SHALL BE CALLED Percevant; Ed. Mounier = Esprit; Mante = Grispoli" (Sage 118n2). Schoolcraft calls these journal pseudonyms (and later ones Beyle uses for himself) "organizing points" for the writer's thoughts (253). Individuals move toward character *types* and thus toward literature. Schoolcraft points out that this is a use of the pseudonym previously unknown in literature—a purely private use (253).

Woolf saw only the start of this transmutation. The fascination of what Schoolcraft calls Beyle's "idiosyncratic daily journals" rests precisely in the fact that they offer "a fractured, an undetermined, and a continuingly evolving authorial self" (260). Beyle's diaries, Schoolcraft notes, "display a self receding ever further" through pronouns and pseudonyms at the same time that Beyle "struggles to make [the self] present or form it in words" (261).

In January 1806, Beyle rereads his 1804 diary and writes: "[I]t seems to have filled its purpose well enough" (Sage 68). Two months later, he declares: "I believe I haven't found myself yet, I don't yet know what my character will be" (Sage 214). Woolf captures Beyle's rare "pungency" in her review: "He is that dry, scientific, amorous, complex, and strangely fascinating man who even in scraps tastes differently from other people, who even in this first volume [of journals] forces us to try to fit the pieces of his puzzle together" (E 3: 417, 416). She foregrounds traits that she shares with him: "Again and again he turns to examine the problems of literature. . . . Then life is taken up and turned round between his fingers. . . . By degrees the familiar features of his character begin to emerge: his ambition; his fastidiousness . . . his passionate, yet scientific, research into the nature of love; his indefatigable curiosity as to the constituents of the human soul" (E 3: 417).

Not all can be admired in this elusive Frenchman. Focused on himself as his major source of truth, Beyle seems to care only fleetingly for the natural world. He bluntly writes, "[T]hose physical details, which have no effect on the emotions, don't interest me" (Sage 186). He also shows little empathy for *others'* feelings—or even awareness of them. Woolf may have stored his dismissive words on women. His 1804 journal repeats the Arnold Bennett view Woolf quotes in her February 1924 diary. "I talked with M. Salmon about his system concerning women; I urged him to publish it," Beyle writes. "He believes that woman's whole character consists of *an insatiable desire to please,* and that it's consequently impossible to overpraise them. . . . He believes that men are more sensitive than women" (Sage 51, 52).

The next year, the bookish Beyle twice feels the veil of illusion ripped from his eyes. "One of Arsinoé's lines in *Nicomède* was a revelation to me on the subject of women, and made me see that the majority of them have petty characters which would be incapable of doing anything for my happiness," he tells his diary in January 1805. "The characters that I attribute to Portia, Pauline and Victorine are rare. The discovery of this truth will remove my bashfulness in the presence of women" (Sage 98). In May, he repeats: "What has spoiled me up to now is the false opinion I've had of them. I believed them to be Julies, and they're merely the *Parisiennes* of Dancourt" (Sage 176).

Such a naive, earnest young soul. Yet his genius was to fasten on it. Beyle's early journals show a writer turning a philosophical and a scientific eye on the soul and its relation to the senses, memory, heart, and mind. "[T]he division of man into soul and mind enlightens me more and more," he writes in April 1804 (Sage 54). Switching to English for the capitalized words, he judges in February 1805: "I may not have THE MOST UNDERSTANDING SOUL, but I at least have a soul that is all passion. If a man is to talk well, he must be in possession of himself; if he is to write well, he must perhaps be *in possession of his soul* and have one that is UNDERSTANDING for a desired passion" (Sage 110–11). That month he wishes to find a woman who shares his soul. "What I need is a poetic soul, a soul like my own, a Sappho," he tells his diary, "and I have given up trying to find it; but if I should happen to find it we'd experience a happiness that is superhuman" (Sage 116).

Sage, who translated Beyle's journals into English in 1954, suggests that a diary offered "an ideal form of self-expression" for the apprentice writer (ix).[10] In them he formed his "highly individual style" and laid his philosophical foundations (xi, 46). The same can be said of Woolf. In 2005, Schoolcraft calls Beyle's diaries his "literary workshop" and "the best means for tracing Beyle's initial attitudes toward writing as they develop, notebook by notebook" (248). When he comes (at last) to write his novels, Beyle draws on his diary observations of himself and others. Sage believes, however, that he "never attained the same degree of naked sincerity in his other writings, most of which—whether they be classified as fiction, essays, criticism, travel, or autobiography—are little more than a disguised continuation of his youthful diary, but no longer destined for himself alone" (ix–x).

On the last day of 1804, Beyle tells his diary: "I might compose a work which would please no one but myself, and which would be recognized as beautiful in the year 2000" (Sage 95). Woolf quotes this vow in her review. In the twenty-first century, Schoolcraft notes, Beyle's journals are seen "as some of the most unusual documents in French literature" (248). Sage points out that Beyle's fourteen-year diary possesses "more form" than most of the books he wrote for publication: "It has a definite beginning, middle, and end; it has unity and infinite variety; it is quite capable of standing by itself as a work of literature" (xii). In this light, *The Private Diaries of Stendhal*, Sage's fine one-volume English translation, necessarily expurgated, does not now seem enough. The time seems ripe for the full diaries in English.

In 1924, Stendhal's early journals incite Virginia Woolf further toward the soul, toward even greater nuances of character change and complexity—in short, even deeper into the psychological novel. His journals show her the many sides and shades of love and present men's and women's inner lives as volatile and fraught with conflict. In his penetrating, often scientific, view of his own thought processes and those of others, he modeled as well an objectivity she could apply with her own modernist characters.

Beyle's early journals show Woolf that a work could englobe warring qualities. In 1840, Honoré de Balzac described Beyle as one of those "all-embracing spirits," those "Janus-faced intellects, [who] encompass everything, accept both lyricism and action, drama and ode, in the belief that perfection requires a view of things as one whole" (vii). The semiprivate diary—for Beyle as well as for Woolf—offered, through its intrinsic oppositions, an ideal form for this exploration and synthesis. Beyle also declared that it was "possible to be a poet in prose."

Lady Anne Clifford's *Diary*

Diary *reading* mingles with Virginia Woolf's diary writing in 1924. Her reading notebook at the time begins with three pages of notes for her July review of Stendhal's *Journal*, followed by a page of notes on James Woodforde's *Diary of a Country Parson* (*RN* 102–3). Her notebook's next entry consists of two pages on *The Diary of the Lady Anne Clifford with an Introductory Note by V. Sackville-West*.

Woolf's reading of Lady Clifford's *Diary* offers a further sign of her growing interest in Vita Sackville-West across 1924. Woolf may have seen the Knole manuscript of Lady Clifford's diary during her first visit to Knole in July.[11] Perhaps Vita gave Woolf her 1923 published edition of this ancestral diary.[12] Lady Clifford's seventeenth-century diary held interest for Woolf beyond Vita's tie, for, as Brenda Silver notes, Woolf was steeping herself in the Elizabethans in order to write her *Common Reader* essay "An Elizabethan Lumber Room" (*RN* 8). What better timber for this room than an Elizabethan diary? As it happened, Lady Clifford's *Diary* delivered more than a window on Elizabethan life; it supplied important foundation for *Orlando* (1928) and for *A Room of One's Own* (1929) as well.

Sackville-West's edition of her forebear's *Diary* answered a plea from Maurice Hewlett, who wrote to the publisher Heinemann in November 1922: "What I really want of Miss Sackville West [*sic*] . . . is an edition of Lady Anne Clifford's Diary. That certainly ought to be published. . . . We are awfully behind the French in seventeenth-century memoirs. You will be doing a service to your country" (lxiii). Hewlett then importuned Vita directly, asking her to publish Lady Clifford's diary "with good, accurate, and lively notes" (lxiii). Vita more than complied. Her forty-eight-page introductory note—which constitutes almost a third of the 1923 volume—is lushly detailed and astute. Vita shows no great reverence for her ancestors. "[O]ne does not know whether to be more appalled by the fecundity or the mortality of the families," she observes (xlviii). She calls Sir Richard Sackville, Lady Anne's first husband, "the first wastrel of a family which was to become notorious for its prodigality" (xxxii).[13]

She also shows herself attuned to women's social constraints. Reporting that Lady Clifford always speaks of her husband "with affection and tolerance," she then adds: "[T]hough whether such sentiments were genuine or whether convention prompted them, we have no means of judging; but perhaps it is as well to remember that in an age when the outward courtesies must always be observed, it is doubtful whether even a mind so bold as Lady Anne's would depart from convention to the extent of criticising her lord" (xxxii–xxxiii).

The very partial nature of the diary she had to share required Vita's lengthy introduction. She acknowledges, on the one hand, Lady Anne's "voluminous writings" (xxiii). Born in 1590, Lady Anne kept a (mostly lost) Day-by-Day book up to the day before her death (lv); wrote surviving summaries of each year from 1650 to 1675 (ages sixty to eighty-five); and supervised (likely even dictated parts of) a three-volume family history—separate volumes on her mother, father, and self ("a true memorial of the life of me"). However, the Knole manuscript Vita possessed covered only four of Lady Clifford's eighty-six years. Furthermore, the manuscript is an eighteenth-century transcript of the seventeenth-century diary. Vita asserts that "[t]he original was probably destroyed, for its whereabouts have never been discovered, in spite of all efforts to unearth it" (lxiv).

The *Diary* Woolf reads in 1924 is penned in two styles and covers two distinct periods in Lady Anne's life.[14] Her 1603 chronicle at age thirteen is written as a continuous narrative, a reminiscence without date headings—and clearly after the fact. "A little after this," the young diarist writes (4). "About this time. . . . Some week or fortnight after" (6, 15). Nevertheless, this opening is important, for the *Diary* begins in the reign of Queen Elizabeth I, with thirteen-year-old Anne's declaration that, had not the Queen become ill, she might have become her attendant, "for at that time there was as much hope and expectation of me as of any other young lady whatsoever" (3). The diary next reports the Queen's death; however, we know from Vita's introduction that young Anne will herself come to rule over northern realms by the final third of her life.

Lady Anne's 1603 chronicle reveals her, at thirteen, regularly measuring herself against others—much as fifteen-year-old Virginia Stephen does in her first diary of 1897. Lady Anne reports that her mother is one of the lords and ladies who sits up all night with the Queen's corpse, but she, Anne, is "held too young" for this charge (5). When Elizabeth's body travels from Whitehall to Westminster Abby, the lords and ladies attending it on foot as mourners, Anne again is kept from service: "I was not high enough, which did much trouble me then" (5).

No diary survives from 1604 through 1615. When the *Diary* opens again it is 1616 and Lady Anne is twenty-five, seven years married to Richard Sackville, and the mother of a two-year-old daughter, Margaret, whom she calls the "Child" in the diary. Lady Anne's diaries for 1616, 1617, and 1619—1618 is missing—are organized by month ("January 1616," "February 1616," etc.) and proceed by days within each month ("Upon New Year's day . . . ," "Upon the 8th . . . ,"). This stage of the extant diary appears to exist primarily to document the monumental battle between Lady Anne and her husband over her vast northern estates. One can understand why Lady Clifford felt the need to keep this diary. It may have helped fortify her to resist her husband's harsh and heartless pressures to transfer her property to him. More practically, her diary helped her keep track of all the maneuvers in this cat-and-mouse battle of wits and wills that came to involve the entire court. Finally, Lady Anne may have wished to record her side of the story for historical vindication, for her success from 1616 to 1619 was far from secure.

When Lady Anne was fifteen, her mostly absent, seafaring and buccaneering father (the third Earl of Cumberland) died, leaving a will that underwent the kind of protracted litigation Charles Dickens depicts two centuries later in *Bleak House*. Vita describes the dispute succinctly in her introductory note, and as it parallels her own struggle to retain Knole as a sole inheriting daughter, a loss Woolf restores in the fictional *Orlando*, her description is of special interest.[15] Anne's father "bequeaths to his brother, Sir Francis Clifford, the new Earl of Cumberland, his northern estates, with reversion to Lady Anne in the event of the failure of heirs male. But in so doing he was ignoring the fact that according to a deed executed as far back as the reign of Edward II, the estates were already entailed upon *his child*, irrespective of sex, and since Lady Anne was his only surviving child, she was the natural inheritor of the enormous property" (xxix).

Lady Anne's husband, Richard Sackville, a lavish spender as well as cock fighter, gambler, and philanderer, marshals not only Lady Anne's own relatives against her but also the Archbishop of Canterbury and finally even the King, across the months chronicled in this diary.[16] He even takes Lady Anne's men and horses from her when she refuses to sign over her lands to him, and then her two-year-old daughter, refusing to let her see Margaret for more than six months. He consigns Lady Anne to the north and forbids her to come to London, all the while dispatching person after person to upbraid her and pressure her to sign over her lands, himself writing her letters "between kindness and unkindness" (72).[17]

The *Diary* marks Lady Anne's shrewd counters to his every move. She tells him she can do nothing until she confers with her mother. She then conveniently leaves the legal papers behind at her mother's estate. At each point she does only the minimum to forestall him. When he insists on June 8, 1616, that she pass her rights to the lands of Westmoreland "to him and my Child," she agrees on June 20 to pass "the inheritance of *Westmoreland* to my Lord if I had no heirs of my own body" (34, 35). Since she does have an heir, this preserves the estates for her daughter. And during it all, her letters flow steadily to Sackville's relatives: "I being desirous to win the love of my Lord's kindred by all the fair means I could" (69).[18]

Beyond such tactical savvy, Lady Clifford shows extraordinary courage and self-possession in refusing to bow to this massive pressure. Seeking to end her nuanced shilly-shallying, in November 1616 Sackville calls in his friend King James I "to make an agreement himself between us" (42). On January 18, 1617, Lady Clifford kneels with her husband beside King James's throne: "[H]e persuaded us both to peace and to put the whole matter wholly into his hands, which my Lord consented to, but I beseech'd His Majesty to pardon me for that I would never part from *Westmoreland* while I lived upon any condition whatsoever" (48). Bold subject. There it was—and so succinct and clear. Yet on January 20, 1617, she must repeat herself. A more formal meeting takes place with the King, now with lawyers and other nobles at hand. "The King asked us all if we would submit to his judgment in this case. My Uncle *Cumberland*, my Coz. *Clifford*, and my Lord answered they would, but I would never agree to it without *Westmoreland* at which the King grew in a great chaff" (50).

Queen Anne's role in aiding Lady Clifford deserves proper credit. Lady Clifford's *Diary* portrays a high stakes conflict at the highest levels of British government as an exercise in covert female flanking. Surely Lady Anne's poise in declaring to the King on January 18 that she "would never part from *Westmoreland* while I lived upon any condition whatsoever" was aided by her visit alone with Queen Anne immediately before and by the information she adds beside this entry: "The Queen gave me warning not to trust my matters absolutely to the King lest he should deceive me" (49).

From this point, Lady Anne never fails of letters and gifts to her Queen. On June 19, 1617, Anne writes a letter "of thankfulness for the favours she has done" (71). In November 1617, she sends the Queen "the skirts of a white satin gown all pearled and embroidered with colours which cost [her] four-score pounds without the satin" (80). A January 1619 entry reports her sending the Queen "a New Year's gift, a cloth of silver cushion embroidered richly with the King of Denmark's arms, and all one with stripes of tent stitch" (83–84). But Queen Anne, her ally, dies on March 2, 1619, and Lady Anne, now twenty-nine, finds herself reprising her mother's role. "I was one of the mourners at the Queen's funeral," she writes on May 13, 1619. "I attended the corpse from *Somerset House* to the Abbey at *Westminster*" (100).

Queen Anne had stepped in to aid Lady Clifford after she lost her foremost ally, her mother, in May 1616. The Countess of Cumberland had been the strongest advocate of her daughter's property rights, and when she dies, Anne calls it "the greatest and most lamentable cross that could have befallen me"—language that might have recalled to Woolf her own 1907 words regarding *her* mother's death: "[H]er death was the greatest disaster that could happen" (32, *MOB* 40). "I am like an owl in the desert," Lady Anne writes (28).

Vita's publishing of her foremother's *Diary* was a filial act like that of the daughter of Anne Chalmers, the nineteenth-century Scottish diarist whose diary Woolf reviewed in February 1924. Both works recall and preserve a dead mother, and Lady Clifford's *Diary two* such forebears.[19] *The Diary of Lady Anne Clifford*, therefore, offered another illustration in 1924 of "think[ing] back through our mothers if we are women," Woolf's memorable phrase-to-come from *A Room of One's Own* (76). When the Duchess of Cumberland dies, Lady Anne arranges for her body to be conveyed to Northumberland and plans to build a chapel there in her honor. She erects a pillar on the spot she parted for the last time with her mother and dies herself in the very room her beloved mother died. *The Diary of Lady Anne Clifford* thus offered Woolf a rich slice of women's history—a further theme of *A Room of One's Own*.

To Vita fell the joy of completing the triumphant "her-story." Almost our last view in the *Diary* is of Lady Anne "quick with child" in October 1619, taking to her bedchamber at Knole and not stirring forth till March 23, 1620 (107n; 109). The *Diary*'s last words on the northern estates, on December 15, 1619, do not augur well: "After supper my Lord and I had a great falling out, he saying that, if ever my land came to me I should assure it as he would have me" (112). However, Richard Sackville dies alone in London five years later at the young age of thirty-five.

Nineteen long years after, in 1643, Lady Clifford's uncle, that very Earl of Cumberland named in her father's will, also dies—and his only son and heir dies two years later, leaving Lady Anne finally the natural and now undisputed heir to her northern realms. At age fifty-five Lady Clifford comes into her northern territories and embarks immediately on their restoration, repairing from one castle to the next. Lady Anne's patience, courage, and acuity therefore reap their due reward. Thirty-one years remain for her to enjoy her northern lands and the seventeen grandchildren and nineteen great-grandchildren she lives to see. And she preserves Knole in the south as well.

Lady Clifford's tie to Wilton and the Pembrokes might also have captivated Woolf, who wrote of them so dismissively in her own 1903 diary. Six years after Richard Sackville's death, when she is forty, Lady Clifford, "to the astonishment of her friends and relations," marries Philip Herbert, Earl of Pembroke (xl). She thus becomes Duchess of Pembroke and mistress of Wilton, along with everything else. However, she was no happier inside the Wilton walls than at Knole, Vita reports, for she wrote of her two southern homes: "[T]he marble pillars of Knole in Kent and Wilton in Wiltshire were to me oftentimes but the gay arbours of anguish" (xxxix).

Nevertheless, "she turned and steered the whole course of her affairs," Bishop Edward Rainbow declared at Lady Clifford's funeral, words that might have fortified Woolf, who is steering her own affairs rather consummately at this point as well (liv). Woolf took a great deal from Vita's edition of *The Diary of the Lady Anne Clifford*. In her 1925 *Common Reader* essay "The Elizabethan Lumber Room," Woolf wittily refigures Vita's description of Lady Clifford's father nearly perishing from thirst "in the angry Irish seas"—a crisis that led to his (and his men) sucking bullets to slake their thirst (xvi). Woolf offers the even more imaginative: "The Earl of Cumberland's men, hung up by adverse winds off the coast of Cornwall for a fortnight, licked the muddy water off the deck in agony" (*CR* 1: 40).

More importantly, the *Diary* also gave Woolf a portrait of a Renaissance woman, a vision of a girl who learns to sing and play on the bass viol at age thirteen; of a young mother of twenty-six who makes rosemary cakes and pancakes and sews Irish stitch cushions; of a tireless scribbler who reads Montaigne during her northern banishment and Chaucer and Ovid's *Metamorphoses* at Knole (41, 66, 104). John Donne even pays a call on Lady Anne at Knole amid her troubles, for she becomes his patron. In the *Diary* Lady Anne's husband gives her a *Book of the Supplication of the Saints*, while she reads my *Lady's Book of Praise of a solitary life* (91, 90).

Lady Anne Clifford becomes a midlife addition to the select circle of Walter Scott and Fanny Burney, Samuel Pepys and James Boswell—that is, she becomes a diarist Woolf returns to repeatedly across her days. After *Orlando* appears in 1928 with its reprise of the inheritance battle, Woolf thinks of treating Lady Clifford to her own essay. However *The Waves* intervenes. Woolf writes to Helen McAfee of *The Yale Review* on April 15, 1930: "I am sorry not to have done the Lady Clifford; but I am sure you will understand how difficult it is to stop one piece of work and turn aside to another" (*L* #2166, 4: 157–58). More than a year later, on July 2, 1931, Lady Clifford's *Diary* remains on Woolf's mind. She writes once more to McAfee that she "may at last go into the Lady Clifford Diaries which have been on my shelves for more than a year" (*L* #2399, 4: 352). Two months later, arranging a lunch at Long Barn, Woolf writes to Vita, "I've had a divine week of doing nothing and seeing no one, and am now deep in Lady Clifford. Headaches cured I think" (*L* #2430, 4: 376).

Woolf's 1931 reimmersion in Lady Clifford's diaries surfaces in her essay "Donne After Three Centuries" for the *Second Common Reader*, published in 1932. Here Woolf gives over a long paragraph to Lady Clifford as one of the "noble ladies who brought so strange an element into Donne's poetry" (25). Lady Clifford's diary permits us to view Donne's female patrons "more closely and less romantically" than we might in the diary's absence, Woolf declares, and then she records Lady Anne's deprivations and achievements:

> Lady Anne Clifford . . . though active and practical and little educated— she was not allowed "to learn any language because her father would not permit it"—felt, we can gather from the bald statements of her diary, a duty towards literature and to the makers of it as her mother, the patroness of the poet Daniel, had done before her. A great heiress, infected with all the passion of her age for lands and houses, busied with all the cares of wealth and property, she still read good English books as naturally as she ate good beef and mutton. . . . Donne preached before her at Knole. It was she who paid for the first monument to Spenser in Westminster Abbey, and if, when she raised a tomb to her old tutor, she dwelt largely upon her own virtues and titles, she still acknowledged that even so great a lady as herself owed gratitude to the makers of books. (*CR* 2: 25–26)

Lady Clifford and her *Diary* return again to Woolf at the end of her life. Silver reports that on September 18, 1940, Woolf "began to outline a work that would begin with English literature before the Elizabethans and end with a chapter on the future. . . . Her working notes end with an entry on Lady Anne Clifford's

Diary" (*RN* 92). And in a final letter reference, hinting at the war's devastation, Woolf appeals again to Vita on February 4, 1941: "I'm going to London tomorrow to walk among the ruins. Did I tell you all my books are to bits?—so, if you have Lady Ann [*sic*] Clifford or any other Elizabethan biographer—dear me—I'm asking another favour; but could you bring them?" (*L* #3689, 6: 470).

Silver calls Woolf's three sets of reading notes on Lady Clifford's *Diary*—notes in the 1920s, 1930s, and 1940—"a good example of Woolf's developing sense not only of women's exclusion from culture but of their contributions and their history" (*RN* 8). Lisa M. Klein, in a fine 2001 article on "Lady Anne Clifford as Mother and Matriarch," points out that readers' failure to value diaries—and women's diaries in particular, even through the twentieth century—led to the long misdating of the birth and death of Lady Clifford's first son. Noting that historians' eyes are often "trained to overlook the personal and domestic as insignificant," she corrects the record, citing the clear evidence of Lady Clifford's 1619 diary: "Ironically, it is not the public data but the personal writings of a mother recording her fears, feelings, and memories in gestation and in old age that corrects the historical record and deepens our understanding of Clifford . . ." (26).

For Woolf, Lady Clifford's *Diary* brought immediate matter for *Orlando* and for two *Common Reader* essays and inspiration for *A Room of One's Own*. In *Desiring Women: The Partnership of Virginia Woolf and Vita Sackville-West*, Karyn Z. Sproles suggests that from 1922 to 1929, Woolf and Sackville-West were engaged in a joint project of expanding traditional biography and of portraying women's desire—including their desire to speak their minds. Vita's journal,[20] Woolf's diary, and Lady Clifford's diary play vital roles in this project. Lady Clifford's *Diary* might also have recalled to Woolf her own fictional Joan Martyn of 1906. Like fifteenth-century Joan Martyn, Lady Anne Clifford kept a diary and was remembered and never ever ceased to love her land.

6

Rush, Urgency, Wound, and Rescue

"[S]uspense is indigenous to the diary form and gives any diary a quality of tension not unlike the suspense in reading a novel or play," writes diary historian Harriet Blodgett (*Centuries* 8). Virginia Woolf's 1925 diary repeats—with variations—the alarming scenario of her 1921 diary. Her mind this year seems rife with fiction. "I have never felt this rush & urgency before," she tells her April diary. "I believe I can write much more quickly: if writing it is . . ." (*D* 3: 12). In May, she is "now all on the strain with desire to . . . get on to *To the Lighthouse*," but she—mistakenly—refrains (*D* 3: 18).

Perhaps the unprecedented "rush and urgency" makes it impossible for her to retain the sure command of her 1924 diary (*D* 3: 12). Her high trotting of 1924 leads to the fall of 1925. She makes the same mistake as in 1921. In January and February 1925, she gives over her *diary* time—twixt tea and dinner—to ready *The Common Reader* and *Mrs. Dalloway* for the Press. She substitutes work for diary refreshment, just as in 1921 she replaced her diary with Russian lessons before her summer collapse. Each time she does not fully reckon the physical toll and mental strain of her unrelieved work.

In 1925, Woolf also seems to underestimate the drain of her new London social life. Her diary, however, signals the danger. She begins to express disgust for her fellow creatures. The result? What was meant to be the glorious fall start of *To the Lighthouse* becomes collapse and months of headache, causing Woolf to call 1925 "this wounded & stricken year" (*D* 3: 52). Yet, as in November 1918, Woolf makes *in her diary* a remarkable rescue (involving a woman).

Across 1925, Woolf struggles against exhaustion and deaths, as well as against "a tussle of emotions" (*D* 3: 39). In June she finds that Jonathan Swift's *Journal to Stella* addresses uncannily several of her own current trials. It does more, therefore, than "replenish . . . [her] cistern," as she writes; it fortifies her as well (*D* 3: 33). In her 1928 novel-biography *Orlando*, she will let Orlando meet the prickly Irishman of the *Journal to Stella*. Swift's *Journal* will offer fuel for *A Room of One's Own* as well.

Virginia Woolf's 1925 Diary

"This is the temperature chart of a book."

(May 4, 1925; D 3: 16)

Teal blue is the (now faded) cover of Woolf's 1925 diary, a single shade suited to the book's narrowed scope. Like her small 1905 diary marking her first trials as a published writer, Woolf's prose progress fills her (much larger) 1925 diary book.[1] And why shouldn't it? The year brings the first test of her turn-and-turn-about tack conceived in her 1922 diary: never before has she offered nonfiction (*The Common Reader*) and fiction (*Mrs. Dalloway*) to her readers almost in one breath. Furthermore, *To the Lighthouse*, her next novel, presses itself persistently—even erotically—upon her and must be started. The 1925 diary becomes not just "the temperature chart of a book," but of *books*—and, ominously, of their author's threatened health as well.

Thirty-two entries chart the 308 days from March 18, 1925, through January 19, 1926—only one more entry than in the 440-day 1924 diary. Vibrant London, apotheosized repeatedly across the 1924 diary, now finds itself ignored. Only two references to London—that "jewel of jewels, & jasper of jocunditie"—enter the 1925 diary, and neither celebrates the city. Woolf's second entry, April 8, renders another haunting scene of female death in London: "a woman crying Oh oh oh faintly, pinned against the railings with a motor car on top of her."[2] Woolf cannot rid herself of the horror. "All day I have heard that voice," she continues. "A great sense of the brutality & wildness of the world remains with me" (D 3: 6).

Twelve days later, Woolf praises London only to wish to leave it through the success of her books. "I like this London life in early summer—the street sauntering & square haunting," she tells her diary on April 20, "& then if my books . . . were to be a success; if we could begin building at Monks, & put up wireless for Nelly, & get the Skeats to live at Shanks' cottage—if—if—if. . . . But really what I should like would be to have £3 to buy a pair of rubber soled boots, & go for country walks on Sundays" (D 3: 11). Here is one more version of the country in London—her ideal state.

The country appears in this diary almost too identified with fiction. On July 20, Woolf postpones her start on *To the Lighthouse* in order to launch it in the country. In fact, she places, at this moment, magical faith in the country's powers. Finishing her essay on Jonathan Swift's *Journal to Stella* in the morning, she takes up her own journal to plan: "I think a little story, perhaps a review, this fortnight; having a superstitious wish to begin To the Lighthouse the first day at Monks House. I now think I shall finish it in the two months there. . . . These 8 weeks at Rodmell always seem capable of holding an infinite amount" (D 3: 36, 37). Ten days later, she again declares from London: "I have not forced my brain at its fences; but shall, at Rodmell" (D 3: 38).

Books are to be started in the country, and the 1925 diary reveals its focus on Woolf's books in its opening words, on March 18. Woolf joins her 1924 and 1925 diaries with entries on that date in *each* book.[3] After a fifty-five-day gap from her January 6, 1925, entry, Woolf closes her 1924 diary with a short paragraph on March 18, 1925: "[H]aving sent off the last [*Common Reader*] proofs today, I have got my new diary made, & shall close this, with a thousand apologies, & some ominous forebodings at the sight of all the blank pages."[4]

Both her closing and her opening diary words fill us, too, with "ominous forebodings," particularly when compared to the sure and expectant opening of the 1924 diary: "This year is almost certainly bound to be the most eventful in the whole of our (recorded) career" (D 2: 281). Woolf starts her 1925 diary with the words "disgrace" and "distaste": "This disgrace [the delayed diary start] has been already explained—I think: two books to see through the press, mainly between tea & dinner; influenza, & a distaste for the pen" (D 3: 5). Back in 1919, diary-writing suited nicely those "casual half hours after tea" (D 1: 266), but in early 1925 that time must go to ready *The Common Reader* and *Mrs. Dalloway* for publication.

But Woolf retains some of her command from the sure-handed 1924 diary. In her third entry, April 19, she declares her intent "to make £300 this summer by writing, & build a bath & hot water range at Rodmell"—a vow she repeats the next day (D 3: 9). As in 1924, she achieves her dream by year's end—although *this* year at some cost. Woolf's mind in 1925 seems awash with fiction. In her first entry, a glimpse of Julian Bell manicuring a tennis court at school suggests a story that mirrors Chekhov's *Note-book* kernels. Woolf thinks of writing "a story about a man whose ambition it was to buy a field; this kept him alive; when he bought it, he died" (D 3: 5).

In her third entry, April 19, noting that *The Common Reader* and *Mrs. Dalloway* "tremble on the verge of coming out," she expresses her wish "to dig deep down into my new stories" without worry about readers' response (D 3: 9). The next day, she transforms her "mine" metaphor into an oil well, a trope more suited to her present creative gush: "One thing in considering my state of mind now, seems to me beyond dispute, that I have at last, bored down into my oil well, & can't scribble fast enough to bring it all to the surface. I have now at least

6 stories welling up in me, & feel, at last, that I can coin all my thoughts into words. Not but what an infinite number of problems remain; but I have never felt this rush & urgency before" (*D* 3: 12). As if pockets remain of her novel *Mrs. Dalloway*—now ready to emerge on May 14—Woolf writes this summer eight short stories centered on an evening party at the Dalloways.'

However, she also must track her books' fates. A noteworthy difference in 1925 from her diary's anxious watch over *Night and Day* in 1919 and *Jacob's Room* in 1922 is her comparative distance and calm. *The Common Reader* comes from the Hogarth Press on April 23 and *Mrs. Dalloway* on May 14. Woolf admits in her April 29 entry to being "a little fidgety" about *The Common Reader* (*D* 3: 15). "But this is quite recognisably superficial," she immediately adds, "beneath my fidgets being considerable stability" (*D* 3: 15).

Woolf now charts her books' progress more like a doctor (or a memoirist) noting data for use than as a patient whose very writing life hangs in the balance. "This is a note for future reference as they say," she opens her next entry, on May 1:

> The Common Reader came out 8 days ago, & so far not a single review has appeared, & no body has written to me or spoken to me about it or in any way acknowledged the fact of its existence; save Maynard, Lydia, & Duncan. . . . all signs which point to a dull chill depressing reception; & complete failure. I have just come through the hoping fearing stage, & now see my disappointment floating like an old bottle in my wake & am off on fresh adventures. (*D* 3: 15–16)

She literally here dissociates her disappointment from herself, casts it off, and moves forward—a healthy move. "This is the temperature chart of a book," she begins her next entry in the same vein (*D* 3: 16).

As it happened, the jettisoned bottle of disappointment was not needed. Woolf's May 9 entry records Goldsworthy Dickinson's enthusiastic praise of *The Common Reader* and "2 columns sober & sensible praise" in the *Times Literary Supplement* (*D* 3: 17). On June 1 she hears that Thomas Hardy reads *The Common Reader* with "great pleasure," and on June 14, she learns the book makes money (*D* 3: 25). By June 27, Woolf is telling her diary that *The Common Reader* is "too highly praised now," its "first fruit" an invitation to write for the *Atlantic Monthly* (*D* 3: 33).

Mrs. Dalloway's diary chart follows the same trajectory—although the applause mounts more swiftly. Woolf insists again on May 17 that her chart has general value beyond individual import. "But this is not all vanity; I'm recording for curiosity: the fate of a book," she declares (*D* 3: 22). Is she thinking here of her memoirs? By June 1, however, even this motive starts to pale. "To record my books fates slightly bores me," she admits (*D* 3: 25). Nevertheless, she tracks her books' progress throughout the year like a canny publisher (as well as doctor and memoirist). She tallies the number of copies each book sells (by week, in total, and in America) as if trying to gauge whether she's made the £300 she dreamed of in April to build a bathroom in her country home.

She may be slightly bored with *The Common Reader* and *Mrs. Dalloway* because *To the Lighthouse* has fully materialized. As early as December 1922, Woolf had noted "shocks from [her] childhood" passing through her (*D* 2: 217), which increase in 1923. Her 1924 diary notes an emerging story of "The Old Man"— Mr. Ramsay, the figure of her father in *To the Lighthouse* (*D* 2: 317). On *Mrs. Dalloway*'s publication day, May 14, 1925, Woolf can tell her diary:

> [H]onestly I am scarcely a shade nervous about Mrs D. . . . The truth is that writing is the profound pleasure & being read the superficial. I'm now all on the strain with desire to stop journalism & get on to *To the Lighthouse*. This is going to be fairly short: to have father's character done complete in it; & mothers; & St Ives; & childhood; & all the usual things I try to put in—life, death &c. But the centre is father's character, sitting in a boat, reciting We perished, each alone, while he crushes a dying mackerel—However, I must refrain. I must write a few little stories first, & let the Lighthouse simmer, adding to it between tea & dinner till it is complete for writing out. (*D* 3: 18–19)

The novel's title already has come by May 14 as well as a major scene and general setting. Significantly (and perhaps ominously), Woolf plans to give over her former *diary* time—between tea and dinner—to nurture the novel. Her diary, when she can seize time to write in it, actually aids her. She ends her June 27 diary portrait of Jack Hills with the parenthetical confession: "But while I try to write, I am making up 'To the Lighthouse'—the sea is to be heard all through it."[5] By July 20 she envisions even more of the novel in her diary and worries her theme might be too sentimental: "father & mother & child in the garden: the death; the sail to the lighthouse. . . . & then this impersonal thing, which I'm dared to do by my friends, the flight of time, & the consequent break of unity in my design. That passage (I conceive the book in 3 parts: 1. at the drawing room window; 2. seven years passed; 3. the voyage:) interests me very much" (*D* 3: 36). On finishing *Mrs. Dalloway* on October 17, 1924, Woolf declared she would invent her next book in her diary—and now she has.

Woolf arrives in the country on August 5, but something goes wrong. Her previous sure command falters. Does she start *To the Lighthouse* on August 6 as she planned, having held it back to simmer in London? We know she now possesses her novel rather in full. She pens no diary entries in August or in the first four days of September. Instead, on August 19 she faints at Charleston during Quentin's fifteenth birthday party and must be driven home and put to bed. A succession of headaches follows.[6]

What prevents Woolf from conforming to her projected course as she did so unswervingly with *Mrs. Dalloway* and *The Common Reader* the year before? Perhaps the ghosts from her past churn up unexpected emotions—anxieties too great to restrain. Her first diary entry following her August 19 collapse, however, reveals no emotional freeze. She boasts to her diary on September 5: "I have made a very quick & flourishing attack on To the Lighthouse. . . . I am still crawling & easily enfeebled, but if I could once get up steam again, I believe I could spin it off with infinite relish" (*D* 3: 39). Her confidence seems high.

However, as in 1921, she does not fully fathom the physical drain and mental strain of her previous hard work. Her diary presents warning signs of collapse, just as it did in 1921 and 1915. "[W]hy couldn't I see or feel that all this time I was getting a little used up & riding on a flat tire?" she asks herself at the start of her entry on September 5 (*D* 3: 38). In January and February she had given over her diary time to ready *The Common Reader* and *Mrs. Dalloway* for the Press. In July, Maynard Keynes brings them a pamphlet called "The Economic Consequences of Mr Churchill" requiring an edition of seven thousand. "Well; business has been brisk," she writes in her July 30 entry—her last before her August 19 collapse. "All Monday Murphy & I worked like slaves till 6 when I was stiff as a coal heaver" (*D* 3: 38).

She seems also to underestimate the toll of her London social life. At moments across her carefully steered 1924 diary, she worried that her new London life (or the Hogarth Press) would mean the death of her diary (*D* 2: 301, 323, 324). Tavistock Square was fresh, however, in 1924. On May 26, 1924, she exalted to her diary that in her new London home, "people pop in & out, lightly, divertingly like rabbits" (*D* 2: 301). However, on July 20, 1925, the Morrells "settle on us like a cloud of crows, once a week now" (*D* 3: 37). "A happy summer, very busy"; she tells her diary the day before, but then adds the ominous, "rather overpowered by the need of seeing so many people. I never ask a soul here; but they accumulate. . . . I run out after tea as if pursued. I mean to regulate this better in future" (*D* 3: 35–36). But the damage is done. In her final entry before the country, July 30, she writes again, also rather alarmingly: "Heaven knows we have had enough visitors. Sometimes I sit still & wonder how many people will tumble on me."[7]

Woolf's "cloud of crows" image—not to mention her vision of herself pursued and squashed—links to a motif seen also in her 1915 diary before her serious mental collapse. I refer to a distaste for human beings at odds with her usual zest for human life. Her 1925 diary begins with her confession of "a distaste for the pen," likely caused either by a coming shift in style (as before) or by her final push to deliver *The Common Reader* and *Mrs. Dalloway* to the Press (*D* 3: 5). Or to both. "And I do not love my kind," she declares of Roger Fry's garden party on June 27, echoing her 1915 diary. "I detest them. I pass them by. I let them break on me like dirty rain drops" (*D* 3: 33). This image of defilement ("dirty rain drops") anticipates her July 30 figure of *people* tumbling on her.

In fact, in late June 1925 she recognizes her fatigue, for she continues, "No longer can I summon up that energy which when it sees one of these dry little sponges floating past, or rather stuck on the rock, sweeps round them, steeps them, infuses them, nerves them, & so finally fills them & creates them" (*D* 3: 33). To escape humanity's dirty raindrops, she wishes to slip "tranquilly off into the deep water of my own thoughts navigating the underworld" (*D* 3: 33).

Her distaste spills over to her diary portraits. Although Woolf boasts to her diary on June 1, "I like everyone, I said at 46 the other night; & Duncan said I liked everyone, & thought everyone quite new each time," her late June diary words, as well as her diary portraits, belie this claim (*D* 3: 26). On June 5, she rails at length against Margot Asquith's daughter, Elizabeth Bibesco, whose visit forces her to sacrifice a Mozart quintet, which would have delivered "gallons of pure pleasure instead of the breakfast cup of rather impure delight" (*D* 3: 27).

Women who have fortified her in other diaries with their sympathetic strokes now only disappoint. After Bibesco's "impure delight," Woolf devotes her entire next entry, June 8, to her disappointment at Irene Noel-Baker, whom she had visited in 1906 in Greece. "Needless to say, I had some waves of ancient emotion, chiefly at the sound of her voice & sight of her hands—hands expressing motherhood, perhaps; but mostly felt very flat, unable to pump up anything, & thus uncomfortable" (*D* 3: 29).

When she returns to her diary on September 5 after a thirty-six-day absence, it is to offer a portrait titled "Disillusionment" regarding her *Times Literary Supplement* editor, Bruce Richmond, and his formerly richly sympathetic wife, Elena:

I have never had any illusion so completely burnt out of me as my illusion about the Richmonds. . . . Elena has no beauty, no charm, no very marked niceness even! . . . Even her voice & movements which used to be adorable, her distinction, her kindly charm—all have vanished; she is a thick, dowdy, obliterated woman, who has no feelings, no sympathies, prominences & angles are all completely razed bare. . . . oh the colourlessness, drabness, & coldness of her personality—she whom I used to think arch & womanly & comforting! . . . They took the colour, the sting, the individuality out of everything. . . . But E[lena]. is the great disillusionment. Partly on Thoby's account, partly through my own susceptibility to certain shades of female charm, I had still some glow at the thought of her. Now that glow is replaced by a solid tallow candle. And I feel, this morning, having pitched into bed exhausted, physically worn out, mentally bankrupt, scraped; whitewashed, cleaned. An illusion gone. (*D* 3: 39–40)

Woolf projects here on Elena Richmond her own "obliterated. . . . physically worn out, mentally bankrupt" state.

In her 1924 diary, she offered the figure of "a rat struck on the head" for her 1915–1917 illness at Richmond (*D* 2: 283). The rat reappears (ominously) in the 1925 diary. The country collapse extends to the city. When she renews her diary on November 27, Woolf attributes the fifty-six-day gap to "a good deal of rat-gnawing at the back of my head; one or two terrors; then the tiredness of the body—it lay like a workman's coat. Sometimes I felt old, & spent."[8] In her next entry, December 7, written also (tellingly) in the morning, she uses her diary once more to "run [the rats] to earth" (*D* 3: 49). She has not heard from Vita, and she misses her:

That old rat [Vita's absence] chased to his hole, there is Tom [Eliot]'s postcard about *On Being Ill*—an article which I, & Leonard too, thought one of my best: to him characteristic &c: I mean he is not enthusiastic; so, reading the proof just now, I saw wordiness, feebleness, & all the vices in it. This increases my distaste for my own writing, & dejection at the thought of beginning another novel. What theme have I? Shan't I be held up for personal reasons? It will be too like father, or mother: &, oddly, I know so little of my own powers. Here is another rat run to earth. (*D* 3: 49)

The rats gnaw and darken her view of old age too. What seemed Attic and exalted in the high-spirited 1924 diary—as life lived "venturously, plucking the wild goat by the beard, & trembling over precipices"—now seems blighted and defiled (*D* 2: 308). "Old Virginia" never appears by name in this narrowed—even stricken—1925 diary.[9] Only Edith Sitwell offers a refreshing portrait of age, Sitwell who, like Woolf, has moved to London "& is trying to get a little emotion into her poetry" (*D* 3: 24). Otherwise, Woolf sees age in this diary as loss and corruption. On May 14, her portrait of "dear old Desmond" Mac-Carthy depicts him "rather worn & aged; . . . 5 boxes of dusty articles are rather raggy & rotten for 45 years" (*D* 3: 19, 20). And in December, even that formerly vigorous, authorizing "Pagan," Lady Katherine Cromer, is "a sort of framework of discarded beauty hung on a battered shape now. With the firmness of the flesh, & the blue of the eye, the formidable manner has gone" (*D* 3: 51).

In truth, death hangs over this 1925 diary. Woolf's second entry, April 8, reports the senseless brutal London accident and the dying woman's haunting "Oh oh oh" and then the death of Jacques Raverat, the French painter and valued correspondent. Woolf's response is defiant—and courageous. "Nevertheless, I do not any longer feel inclined to doff the cap to death. I like to go out of the room talking, with an unfinished casual sentence on my lips. That is the effect it [Raverat's death] had on me—no leavetakings, no submission—but someone stepping out into the darkness. . . . More & more do I repeat my own version of Montaigne 'Its life that matters'" (*D* 3: 7, 8).

However, in early May, Woolf learns of her cousin Katherine Stephen's death, she of the red and brown diaries who meant to live till 1944. And by November 27, when Woolf must tell her diary that Madge Vaughan has died—Madge whose diaries Woolf thought promising in 1906—she can hardly summon a response. "Madge died. Rustling among my emotions, I found nothing better than dead leaves," she declares with great honesty. "Oh detestable time, that thus eats out the heart & lets the body go on. They buried a faggot of twigs at Highgate, as far as I am concerned" (*D* 3: 46). But Woolf is ill herself when she writes this and worries about her own life in her next entry, December 7. Imagining the book of criticism she might next like to write, she despairs: "But I do not know. My brain may not last me out. I cannot think closely enough. . . . And death—as I always feel—hurrying near. 43: how many more books?" (*D* 3: 50, 51).

Woolf's 1925 diary thus offers a "temperature chart" of her health (physical, mental, and spiritual) as well as of her books. In her editor's preface to Woolf's *Diary*, volume three, covering the years 1925 to 1930, Olivier Bell suggests a unity to these six years. "It is the period," she writes, in which Woolf "attained full maturity as an artist and at the same time achieved a secure and respected position in the world of letters. As a corollary, she became financially more stable and socially more adventurous. These are perhaps the most fruitful and satisfying years of her life" (*D* 3: vii). The last sentence may be true of the period as a whole, but it does not adequately define 1925 and the 1925 diary, a diary Woolf herself described in her next-to-last entry, December 21, as recording "this wounded & stricken year" (*D* 3: 52).

One senses in the 1925 diary a regression to childhood—as if Woolf's artistic return to her youth in *To the Lighthouse* colors her whole life. After the sure-handed confidence of the 1924 diary, the 1925 diary surprises, for it seems to take a step back in assurance. In her fourth entry, April 20, reflecting on the likely response to *Mrs. Dalloway*, Woolf ends her entry with the surprising words: "Oddly, for all my vanity, I have not until now had much faith in my novels, or thought them my own expression" (*D* 3: 12). This statement contradicts several previous diary assertions (from 1921 through 1924) that she is "grazing" closer and closer to her own individuality as an artist, that she is finding her own voice (*D* 2: 107, 186, 205, 261, 325). On December 7, Woolf uses the same word, "oddly," for *To the Lighthouse*: "&, oddly, I know so little of my own powers. Here is another rat run to earth" (*D* 3: 49). In her previous entry, November 27, she declares, "And I can only think of all my faults as a novelist & wonder why I do it" (*D* 3: 47).

Woolf falls into a childish state at times across this diary's pages. Bernadette Murphy takes over as Hogarth Press secretary on February 5 at Marjorie Joad's departure; however, although Woolf declares to her diary as early as April 19 that Murphy's temper and charmless Bohemian ways make her "not destined for a long life here," she appears glad in her June 14 entry to leave the crisis to Leonard: "I salute Leonard with unstinted, indeed childlike, adoration. Somehow he will gently & firmly decide the whole thing, while Angus & I wobble & prevaricate. But then I have a child's trust in Leonard" (*D* 3: 10, 29).

Two weeks before, Woolf suggests that "a placid powerful professional woman is precisely what we want to pull us together."[10] A similar child's desire for a powerful adult, for a powerful woman "to pull us together," animates Woolf's December 7 artful diary set piece. "I want to lie down like a tired child & weep away this life of care—& my diary shall receive me on its downy pillow," this entry begins. "Most children do not know what they cry for; nor do I altogether" (*D* 3: 48). She then lists her cares, starting with no letter or visit from "that devil Vita," then Eliot's lack of enthusiasm for "On Being Ill," then other thoughts brought full circle to a close, "Now, having cried my cry, & the sun coming out, to write a list of Christmas presents. . . . But no Vita" (*D* 3: 48–51).

Vita Sackville-West rescues Woolf at the close of "this wounded & stricken year"—or Woolf seizes on Vita as rescue, as she seized on Marjorie Joad at the close of 1922 and on "Elderly Virginia" at the end of 1918. Vita visits Woolf twice during her fall illness.[11] In her November 27 entry, Woolf reports that this powerful woman "is doomed to go to Persia; & I minded the thought so much (thinking to lose sight of her for 5 years) that I conclude I am genuinely fond of her. . . . Shall I stay with her?" (*D* 3: 47). But when ten days pass with no visit, no letter, Woolf uses her diary "to lie down like a tired child & weep" (*D* 3: 48). But she struggles mightily to run her rats to earth, and when Leonard tells her to contact Vita, she is able to connect her weeping December 7 entry that ends "But no Vita" with the exclamatory opening of her next entry, December 21: "But no Vita! But Vita for 3 days at Long Barn, from which L. & I returned yesterday" (*D* 3: 51).

Nigel Nicolson, Vita's son, believes this visit was "the beginning of their love-affair" (*L* 3: 223). The visit certainly invigorates Woolf's 1925 diary, for Woolf declares that because of Long Barn she "wound up this wounded & stricken year in great style" (*D* 3: 52). Her former "glow at the thought" of Elena Richmond, replaced on September 5 "by a solid tallow candle," rekindles in December in Vita Sackville-West (*D* 3: 40). "I like her & being with her, & the splendour—," Woolf continues her entry, "she shines in the grocers shop in Sevenoaks with a candle lit radiance" (*D* 3: 52). Woolf then probes her new feelings:

> What is the effect of all this on me? Very mixed. There is her maturity & full breastedness: her being so much in full sail on the high tides, where I am coasting down backwaters; her capacity I mean to take the floor in any company, to represent her country, to visit Chatsworth, to control silver, servants, chow dogs; her motherhood (but she is a little cold & offhand with her boys) her being in short (what I have never been) a real woman. . . . In brain & insight she is not as highly organised as I am. But then she is aware of this, & so lavishes on me the maternal protection which, for some reason, is what I have always most wished from everyone. What L. gives me, & Nessa gives me, & Vita, in her more clumsy external way, tries to give me. For of course, mingled with all this glamour, grape clusters & pearl necklaces, there is something loose fitting. How much, for example, shall I really miss her when she is motoring across the desert? I will make a note on that next year. (*D* 3: 52)

The 1925 diary charts the success of Woolf's quick-change motion. Essays and fiction triumph, yet as Woolf carefully marks their course we also feel the diary sour and struggle. A tension builds as Woolf tries to govern her bursting fiction, the unprecedented "rush & urgency" mounting since as early as 1923 (*D* 2: 246, 304; *D* 3: 12). Perhaps she should not have held back *To the Lighthouse* in May 1925. Perhaps it was a mistake to dally with the Dalloway party reserve.[12] We see Woolf's restraint in her July 20 entry: "But enough, enough—I coin this little catchword to control my tendency to flower into phrase after phrase. Some are good though" (*D* 3: 37). Lamentably, Robert Trevelyan tells her that her "speed is terrific, & destructive" (*D* 3: 37).

Whatever forces were at play, Woolf's sure command in 1924 precedes the stumble of 1925.[13] "Never be unseated by the shying of that undependable brute, life, hag ridden as she is by my own queer, difficult nervous system," Woolf encourages herself on September 5, employing her spurred-horse trope from Fanny Burney yet again. "Even at 43 I dont know its workings, for I was saying to myself, all the summer, 'I'm quite adamant now. I can go through a tussle of emotions peaceably that two years ago even, would have raked me raw.'"[14]

Woolf struggles against exhaustion, deaths, and "a tussle of emotions" across the year, and—in part of her mind—seeks the refreshment of diaries in the battle. In her second entry, April 8, she writes, "[T]he truth is, I must try to set aside half an hour in some part of my day, & consecrate it to diary writing. Give it a name & a place, & then perhaps, such is the human mind, I shall come to think it a duty, & disregard other duties for it" (*D* 3: 6). In her next entry, April 19, she confesses she has not achieved her "sacred half hour yet. But think—in time to come I would rather read something here than reflect that I did polish off Mr Ring Lardner successfully" (*D* 3: 9). She thus values her diary-writing over her journalism, even seeks to hallow it here.

When she learns of Katherine Stephen's death on May 4, her thoughts immediately turn from her death to the life preserved in her (possibly) surviving diaries. And at the close of June, she finds rescue in diaries from distaste for her kind, from her sense of human beings as "dry little sponges": "[N]ow I luxuriate most in a whole day alone; a day of easy natural poses, a little printing, slipping tranquilly off into the deep water of my own thoughts navigating the underworld; & then replenishing my cistern at night with Swift. I am going to write about Stella & Swift for [Bruce] Richmond. . . . It is a great stand by—this power to make large sums by formulating views on Stendhal & Swift" (*D* 3: 33).

Once more we see that diaries—others' diaries as well as her own—"replenish" Woolf's well. When she writes "On Being Ill" amid her own illness, her mind turns again to fellow diarists, for she envisions in this essay Pepys in heaven and Boswell among the great (*E* 4: 323, 325). And at Christmas, her own diary restores both community and the past. Vanessa writes to Duncan Grant that they spent a fascinating evening reading from Virginia's 1905 diary (*D* 3: 53).

In her 1919 diary, Woolf created "Old Virginia," a sympathetic and productive future self to urge her on. Her 1925 diary starts another "Old V": "Old Vita," as another strong, motherly figure to reinvigorate her prose. In her first mention of her new novel's title, *To the Lighthouse*, on May 14, Woolf describes the new work in terms of repressed erotic desire: "I'm now all on the strain with desire to stop journalism & get on to *To the Lighthouse*" (*D* 3: 18). Perhaps her repression of this desire leads to her August 19 collapse. She also has overworked herself, oversocialized, and stifled too much her own diary as refreshing outlet. What-ever the cause of Woolf's "stricken" 1925 year, love for Vita appears to release Woolf's desire and make the dry[15] and besmirched abundant once more. Woolf says all this in her final diary entry, January 19, 1926, replacing the "disgrace" and "distaste" of her opening 1925 entry with fountains and lush fruit:

> Vita having this moment . . . left me, what are my feelings? Of a dim No-vember fog; the lights dulled & damped. I walked towards the sound of a barrel organ in Marchmont Street. But this will disperse; then I shall want her, clearly & distinctly. Then not—& so on. This is the normal hu-man feeling, I think. One wants to finish sentences. One wants that atmo-sphere—to me so rosy & calm. She is not clever; but abundant & fruitful; truthful too. She taps so many sources of life: repose & variety, was her own expression, sitting on the floor this evening in the gaslight. . . . Oh & mixed up with this is the invigoration of again beginning my novel, in the Studio, for the first time this morning. All these fountains play on my being & intermingle. (*D* 3: 57)

Jonathan Swift's *Journal to Stella*

The spell of Jonathan Swift's beguiling *Journal to Stella* seeps into Virginia Woolf's July 20, 1925, diary entry—and she knows it. She reports E. M. Forster bursting in to drag them to lunch—just as Joseph Addison did with Swift—and she whispers: "([T]his is in the classic style of journalists). It comes of Swift perhaps, the last words of which I have just written" (*D* 3: 36). She refers to her *Times Literary Supplement* essay "Swift's 'Journal to Stella,'" which appears on September 24. She had told her June 27 diary that reading Swift's *Journal* would replenish her "cistern"—an apt description of her own diary-keeping as well (*D* 3: 33).

Swift's 1710 to 1713 *Journal to Stella* addressed uncannily several matters that Woolf faced herself in 1925 and, therefore, likely not only replenished but also fortified her—although it may have challenged her as well. In September 1710, at the fall of the Whig government, Swift returned to London on a mission for the Irish Bishops. His goal: to secure the "First Fruits" of Irish benefices from Queen Anne and her new ministers. These taxes, earmarked for the clergy, had gone to the Pope before the Reformation; since then, the English Crown claimed them, although the Irish Bishops wished to retain these monies to support poor Irish clerical livings.

From September 2, 1710, through June 6, 1713, Swift wrote sixty-five journal-letters to his beloved Esther Johnson (the "Stella" of the *Journal*) and her companion, Rebecca Dingley, back in Ireland. Woolf, of course, had seen journal-letters before, most notably those of her diary mother, Fanny Burney. And she had read Irish Catherine Wilmot's travel diary-letters to her brother.[16] However, Swift's journal-letters more closely resembled a daily diary than either Burney's or Wilmot's periodic journal-letters. For twenty-four of his thirty-three months in London, Swift wrote daily journal entries that he mailed every fortnight—or as soon as he came to the end of the page. Some 760 journal entries preserve this crucial turning point in Swift's career. Woolf could appreciate intense diary-keeping—on many days Swift pens *two* journal entries, one when he rises, t'other (as he would say) before he goes to sleep—for had she not herself on some days in 1917 and 1918 written entries in both her city and country diaries? Had she not written two March 18, 1925, entries this very year?

Swift's *Journal to Stella* reinforces many of our strongest, intuitive beliefs about diaries. One can hardly find a sharper illustration of our sense that diaries humanize people by revealing the "true" private self behind the public facade. Without the *Journal*, who would have guessed that formidable and touchy Dr. Swift, potent pen of the Tory ministers, skewerer of Lord Godolphin with "The Virtues of Sid Hamet's Rod," spends each morning and night chatting in his "little language" to Stella and Dingley back home? Swift himself seems to distinguish in the *Journal* between his public and private "selves." "But let me alone, sirrahs," he begs in August 1711, "for Pdfr [Poor dear foolish rogue] is going to be very busy; not Pdfr, but t'other I."[17]

Swift's *Journal* also illustrates a surer diary rule: that the most compelling diaries rise to meet the most compelling needs. Young Anne Frank needed a "friend," and her diary became it. Dying Barbellion's *Journal of a Disappointed Man* was a desperate cri de coeur and final bid for the world's regard. Like Woolf, Swift was a complex artist and person: the richness of his *Journal* (like hers) stems from the fact that he contrives it to meet many needs. One senses that the *Journal* serves as an anchor for Swift at this time of political and professional upheaval. Ill-used before by the Whigs, surrounded by enemies, Swift knew not what to expect from the new Tory leaders. However, as he ventured forth each day to seek the "First Fruits" for the Bishops and preferment for himself from the Queen—not to mention literary renown and status among the wits—even to hunt up dinners for himself (this itself often a strain), he could take heart knowing that whatever happened in the wider world, he would start and end the day in intimate talk with those who rightly prized him. "Let me go study, naughty girls, and do not keep me at the bottom of the paper," Swift chides in a December 1710 entry, but then adds, "O faith, if you knew what lies on my hands constantly, you would wonder to see how I could write such long letters; but we will talk of that some other time."[18] "Lele, lele, lele. O Lord, I am saying lele, lele [there, there], to myself in all our little keys," he writes again in February 1711 (2: 183). What steady assurance he contrives to give himself through his *Journal* at this most unsteady of times.

Woolf, who prized "conversation" in her own diary and public prose, underscored in her essay the value of Swift's *Journal* talk. "In any highly civilised society disguise plays so large a part, politeness is so essential, that to throw off the ceremonies and conventions and talk a 'little language' for one or two to understand, is as much a necessity as a breath of air in a hot room," she begins her essay, and we think of her own dolphin-mongoose-potto talk.[19] Swift recognizes this himself when he sets up his journal in his second letter, September 9, 1710: "Henceforth I will write something every day to MD [my dears], and make it a sort of journal: and when it is full, I will send it whether MD writes or not: and so that will be pretty: and I shall always be in conversation with MD, and MD with Pdfr" (2: 11).

"I want some little conversation with MD, and to know what they are doing just now. I am sick of politics," he writes in January 1712 (3: 18). In fact, his conversational style allows the *Journal* to unfold. "Yes faith, and when I write to MD, I am happy too; it is just as if methinks you were here and I prating to you, and telling you where I have been: Well, says you, Pdfr, come, where have you been to-day? come, let's hear now," he writes in January 1711. "And so then I answer; Ford and I were visiting Mr Lewis, and Mr Prior, and Prior has given me a fine Plautus . . ." (2: 149).

Swift re-creates his Irish world through his *Journal*—a sort of country in London. While his daily journal serves him in this comforting fashion, it also allows him to project himself before his absent love, to make it nigh impossible for Stella to forget him. The journal thus also becomes London in the country, for he is gone almost three years. Swift's *Journal* allows Stella (and us) to picture his exertions on almost every day. His morning and evening journal talk fulfills the most romantic of fantasies: that we are in our lover's thoughts, our private language on his lips, when he rises and when he goes to bed. One could hardly wish for greater devotion.

Woolf, who is "now all on the strain with desire" herself to write *To the Lighthouse* (*D* 3: 18), might have sensed what is so transparent to us today: that Swift's journal serves as an acceptable outlet for *his* suppressed erotic desire. The Dr. increases his intimacy with Stella by privileging her letters. His opening letter directs that mail be sent to Richard Steele at his Office at the Cockpitt, near Whitehall, "But not MD. I will pay for their Letters at St. James's Coffee house, that I may have them the sooner" (Ryland 4). Swift often writes his journal in his nightgown in bed, aligning Stella's letter next to his when he answers it. Within his journal, he holds off replying to her letters—to delay gratification for both himself and for her. "Let me go, will you? and I will come again to-night in a fine clean sheet of paper," he promises her in January 1711 (2: 135). A month later, when MD's tenth letter arrives, he writes: "O, but [I] will not answer it now, no, noooooh, I will keep it between the two sheets; here it is, just under: O, I lifted up the sheet and saw it there: lie still, you shall not be answered yet, little letter; for I must go to bed, and take care of my head" (2: 163). Two days later, February 5, 1711, he confesses that "it is still terribly cold. I wish my cold hand was in the warmest place about you, young woman, I would give ten guineas upon that account with all my heart, faith; oh, it starves my thigh; so I'll rise, and bid you good morrow. Come stand away, let me rise" (2: 164). Here is journal-letter as sexual fetish.

The complexity of it all staggers, involving as it does the most exquisite control. When he can control so little of his professional "preferment," he tries to control through his journal and its bantering conversations what else remains. This (artist's) need to control explains much of Swift's *Journal* (and other) behavior: his obsessive numbering of his journal-letters (and insistence that Stella do the same); his ritual placement of MD's letters in his cabinet. "Method is good in all things. Order governs the world. The Devil is the author of confusion," he explains to her as he puts up her last letter (2: 60). And he would not be confused. He corrects MD's spelling. His curiosity joins with his obsessive need to order and measure, for on December 23, 1710, he counts and reports the number of lines in his journal letter—199—for he "had a curiosity to reckon" (2: 117).

He forever worries out the space of his current journal-letter in progress. "Pray, young women, if I write so much as this every day, how will this paper hold a fortnight's work, and answer one of yours into the bargain?" he begins a December 1710 entry. "You never think of this, but let me go on like a simpleton" (2: 120). In February 1711, he writes, "I am in furious haste to finish mine, for fear of having two of MD's to answer in one of Pdfr's, which would be such a disgrace, never saw the like" (2: 172–73). In this way he elevates (and dramatizes and makes amusing) the entire *Journal* play.[20] Furthermore, in a final exquisite turn of the screw, Swift seeks to control what he tells "Stella" about "Vanessa," his new London love.

The *Journal* also allows Swift to control—and supply—another pressing need, one Woolf has been struggling with herself in her 1924 and 1925 diaries: the need for praise, for the confidence crucial to create. Swift's journal-letters allow him to record praise as *news* for Stella and Dingley; they permit regular doses of self-praise. And Dr. Swift medicines himself ably and amply in his *Journal*, just as Woolf does in hers. Swift talks of his works to "Stella," just as Woolf does to "Old Virginia." More than 100 references to Swift's writings appear within the 760 journal entries. (In this respect, as in others, the *Journal* is a priceless historical record.) He assumes Stella's interest in his every "project to bite the town" (2: 337). And he doesn't shy from reporting success. "My lampoon [of Lord Godolphin, "The Rod of Sid Hamet"] is cried up to the skies," he crows October 14, 1710, soon after he comes to London (2: 47). "Mr Harley bobbed me at every line to take notice of the beauties," he reports the next day (2: 48).

Swift regularly asks Stella for her opinion of his work—and how his works fare in Ireland—honest requests, but ones that invite further praise. When he follows "The Rod of Sid Hamet" with his London poem "The Shower," he reports on October 17, 1710: "This day came out the Tatler, made up wholly of my Shower, and a preface to it. They say it is the best thing I ever writ, and I think so too. I suppose the bishop of Clogher will shew it you. Pray tell me how you like it" (2: 50–51). Ten days later, he cannot resist telling Stella of poets Matthew Prior and Nicholas Rowe, who "both fell commending my Shower beyond any thing that has been written of the kind: there never was such a Shower since Danae's, &c. You must tell me how it is liked among you" (2: 61). This "&c." is found in Woolf's swift handling of praise in her 1925 diary.

And Swift further anticipates Woolf's 1925 diary in charting the temperature of more than one work in his *Journal*. On January 28, 1712, as he marks the "sixth edition of three thousand" of "The Conduct of the Allies," he adds that his "bite" of the Whig's October Club does not fare as well: "The little two-penny Letter . . . does not sell; I know not the reason; for it is finely written, I assure you" (3: 27). Fortunately, like Woolf with *The Common Reader*, he is able to report four days later, "The pamphlet of Advice to the October Club begins now to sell . . . 'tis finely written I assure you" (3: 30). Woolf thus found in Swift's *Journal to Stella* an enactment of her own careful counting of editions and of copies sold and might have found this reassuring.

As should now be clear, her diary touches several chords in Swift's *Journal to Stella*. Swift and Woolf both keep journals in tandem with published prose, and both exhibit at key moments of their careers intensive diary-writing. Both relish the conversational mode in their journals—although Swift uses it much more playfully than Woolf—and both use their journals to fortify themselves with praise. Swift shares a touch of Woolf's vast curiosity, although he propels his journal with talk; she, with questions. He measures the penknife used in the near assassination of Tory minister Robert Harley and reports that "if it had gone but half the breadth of my thumb nail lower," it would have killed Harley, his foremost ally (2: 249). "I was so curious to ask him what were his thoughts while they were carrying him home in the chair," Swift continues on to Stella. "He said, he concluded himself a dead man" (2: 249).

Like Woolf, Swift also possessed a "genial love of little ordinary human things," as she writes in her essay (*CR* 2: 61). And so alongside the Harley assassination plot, the peace with France, and the murder of Lord Hamilton, we find Swift's new periwig costing three guineas (2: 147), his drunken servant's bird, and the snows and showers of London.

Like Woolf, Swift discovers his journal's potential as his months of diary-keeping unfold. He recognizes certain capacities more swiftly than she; however, he is forty-three when he starts his *Journal to Stella* (exactly Woolf's age in 1925 when she reads him), not fourteen. By his third journal-letter, he sees how to treat news in his journal format. "[N]ow we expect every moment the parliament will be dissolved," he writes on September 15, 1710, but then adds, "but I forgot that this letter will not go in three or four days, and that my news will be stale, which I should therefore put in the last paragraph" (2: 16). By October 13, 1710, he has fathomed, "These letters of mine are a sort of journal, where matters open by degrees; and, as I tell true or false, you will find by the event whether my intelligence be good; but I do not care two-pence whether it be or no" (2: 43). By April 6, 1711, he sees the rich randomness of his diary. "[Y]ou must take the days as they happen, some dry, some wet, some barren, some fruitful, some merry, some insipid, some, etc.," he tells Stella. "I will write you word exactly the first day I see young gooseberries, and pray observe how much later you are" (2: 222).

He slowly senses his journal's value as history. In October 1710 he anticipates Fanny Burney (as well as Woolf) when he reflects, "I know it is neither wit nor diversion to tell you every day where I dine, neither do I write it to fill my letter; but I fancy I shall, some time or other, have the curiosity of seeing some particulars how I passed my life when I was absent from MD this time" (2: 56). His last entry of letter thirty-six, December 15, 1711, declares: "This will be a memorable letter, and I shall sigh to see it some years hence. Here are the first steps toward the ruin of an excellent ministry; for I look upon them as certainly ruined; and God knows what may be the consequences" (2: 434).

Toward the close of his eventful stay, he understood this even more. "My letters would be good memoirs, if I durst venture to say a thousand things that pass; but I hear so much of letters opening at your post office, that I am fearful, &c" (3: 184). They are good memoirs even so, for as Stephen D. Powell observed in 1999, "The value of the *Journal to Stella* as a historical artefact [sic] has never been questioned" (342). In fact, Harold Williams declares in his 1948 edition of the *Journal*, that Swift's journal-letters "are now of greater human and historical interest than the formal tracts in which he narrated the events of the four last years of Queen Anne's reign" (1: x). In 2014, Michael Schmidt calls Stella the subject of some of Swift's best writing (95).

Swift did not have enough time to become the major diary portraitist Woolf becomes: his *Journal to Stella* does not last even three years. Even so, he sees the possibilities. When he offers a fine portrait of Secretary of State Henry St John in November 1711, he ends it, "This is his character; and I believe you will be diverted by knowing it" (2: 395). In February 1712, he regrets he hasn't pursued portraits more. "I am sorry when I came first acquainted with this ministry, that I did not send you their names and characters," he confesses, "and then you would have relished what I would have writ, especially if I had let you into the particulars of affairs: but enough of this" (3: 47).

In her lively essay "Swift's 'Journal to Stella,'" Woolf captures in her first paragraphs Swift's complexities and contradictions. She notes his great pride, his reluctance to be obliged to anyone, which causes him to take offense when Lord Harley gives him £50 and to turn in fury on St John. Swift writes to Stella that he warned St John "never to appear cold" to him:

[F]or I would not be treated like a schoolboy; that I had felt too much of that in my life already, (meaning Sir William Temple,) that I expected every great minister, who honoured me with his acquaintance, if he heard or saw any thing to my disadvantage, would let me know in plain words, and not put me in pain to guess by the change or coldness of his countenance or behaviour; for it was what I would hardly bear from a crowned head, and I thought no subject's favour was worth it. (2: 215)

Such pride, joined to Swift's severe sense of honor and truth, kept him from entering Lady Giffard's house or from sitting down to dine with Sir John Walter, since neither had "begged [his] pardon" for previous slights (2: 78, 3: 149).[21] When St John seeks "to make up matters" by inviting Swift to dine, Swift seems perplexed by his own refusal: "[B]ut I would not. I don't know, but I would not"—an incident and words Woolf quotes (2: 216; CR 2: 60).

She notes Swift's "instinct to rend and tear his own emotions" (CR 2: 61). In truth, Swift's worldview seems embattled from the *Journal*'s start, for he writes en route to London, "Joe will give you an account of me till I got into the boat, after which the rogues made a new bargain, and forced me to give them two crowns, and talked as if we should not be able to overtake any ship" (2: 7). He must battle the rogues and puppies from the start. Woolf catches as well the many tensions of Swift's *Journal* (and character): his great ambition and wish to serve the common good and his pleasure when admired, joined, however, to the repeated belief that all will come to naught; his constant grumbling at requests to use his high connections to secure favors, followed almost invariably by his kind-hearted fulfillment of them all; the exquisite (literary) control of his *Journal* at the same time he gives the impression of its spontaneous free language play; the related tension of what he tells and what he conceals; and finally, the tension between public and private life (and public and private selves) that A. B. England suggests "becomes the central theme of the *Journal*" (138).

Death, as I have noted, hovers over Woolf's 1925 diary. Swift faced the same specter across his *Journal to Stella*. During his London stay a significant rise in mortality occurred in England (Powell 343). In August 1711, Swift remarks, almost dazed, to Stella: "I never remembered so many people of quality to have died in so short a time" (2: 334). He reports death after death—nearly fifty deaths—across his thirty-three months, just as Woolf does on a milder scale across 1925 (Powell 341). And his *Journal* words, stripped of cant, struck her, for she repeats them in her essay.

Did it move her that his words of heartfelt sorrow rise for Lady Ashburn-ham, who dies in childbirth in January 1713? "I hardly knew a more valuable person on all accounts," Swift declares. "She was naturally very healthy; I fear has been thrown away for want of care. . . . I hate life, when I think it exposed to such accidents; and to see so many thousand wretches burdening the earth, while such as her die, makes me think God did never intend life for a blessing" (3: 142; *CR* 2: 61). Had not Woolf seen another "such accident" on April 8, 1925, and told her diary of "the brutality & wildness of the world" (*D* 3: 6)?

Swift's severe later words regarding the family's mourning may have stayed with Woolf when she writes of Madge Vaughan's death in November 1925—and even of Thomas Hardy's funeral three years later. "There is something of farce in all these mournings, let them be ever so serious," Swift writes in January 1713. "People will pretend to grieve more than they really do, and that takes off from their true grief" (3: 150). Woolf quotes the last sentence in her essay, and, of course, Prue Ramsay in *To the Lighthouse* dies of some illness related to child-birth—as does Judith Shakespeare in *A Room of One's Own* (*CR* 2: 61).

Woolf's journey to her essay "Swift's 'Journal to Stella'" was itself a complex one in late June and July 1925. As was not unusual in preparing a review or essay, Woolf read beyond the *Journal to Stella*. At this time, when she is simmering her portrait of "The Old Man" (her father) for *To the Lighthouse*, she comes to Swift by thinking back through her father(s). Her reading notebooks reveal that she took six pages of notes on her father's 1882 volume *Swift*, followed by two pages of notes on Walter Scott's 1814 *Memoirs of Jonathan Swift*, and another page from several other volumes of Scott's *The Works of Jonathan Swift* (*RN* 51).

Woolf understood Swift well, and she may have identified in some respects with this diarist forebear, whom she calls the "mad parson" in her essay.[22] Two years later in her 1928 *Orlando*, she has Orlando meet Swift and declare: "But stop, stop your iron pelt of words, lest you flay us all alive, and yourself too! Nothing can be plainer than that violent man. He is so coarse and yet so clean; so brutal, yet so kind; scorns the whole world, yet talks baby language to a girl, and will die, can we doubt it, in a madhouse" (138). She knew, of course, that Swift faced dementia at the end. She notes in her essay Swift's "fierce spasms of disgust at society," spasms she felt herself at this time (*CR* 2: 63).

Tellingly, however, although she approaches her essay by reading back through her "fathers" (Sir Leslie Stephen and Sir Walter Scott[23]), she turns the essay itself from a savvy portrait of Swift into a study of the less heralded women of his life, "Stella" and "Vanessa." In so doing, Woolf forces us to regard equally the voiceless Stella, in her intelligence and patience, and the more impetuous

Vanessa. This illustrates Anne E. Fernald's point in *Virginia Woolf: Feminism and the Reader* that Woolf insisted on the feminist possibilities contained within male-authored texts.

The influence of Swift's *Journal* shows not only in the imitative opening of Woolf's July 25, 1925, diary entry but also in her witty transformation of his religious "First Fruits" into her own secular benefices. "I am going to write about Stella & Swift . . . as a sign of grace, after sweeping guineas off the Vogue counter," she writes gaily in her June 27, 1925, diary entry, naming Stella first. She continues: "The first fruit of the C[ommon]. R[eader]. . . . is a request to write for the Atlantic Monthly" (*D* 3: 33). Swift's *Journal* "replenishes" Woolf's "cistern" when she feels dry and besmirched and gives her matter for *To the Lighthouse* and *Orlando*. Her vision of Shakespeare's sister in her 1929 *A Room of One's Own* may be shaped not only by Lady Ashburnham's death in childbirth but also by Swift's casual *Journal* praise of Joseph Addison's sister. "Addison's sister is a sort of wit, very like him," Swift declares (2: 57).

7

Renewed Diary Experiment

The Reach for Literature and Beyond

Virginia Woolf expands her diary in 1926. She extends her diary further toward literature—and beyond. In February she begins "a new convention" for her diary. She will start each entry on a new page, her "habit in writing serious literature" (*D* 3: 62). Can there be clearer sign of her recommitment to her diary as art? In May and June, she expands outward toward public history with a diary of the General Strike. She then turns inward in the country for eleven titled "State of Mind" entries—probes of the boundaries between sense, thought, and art.

Her mind thus stretches this year toward worlds that "exist" *beyond* herself and her art. At the end of October, she imagines "an endeavour at something mystic, spiritual; the thing that exists when we aren't there" (*D* 3: 114). The diaries she reads propel her toward this place. Across the year Woolf returns again and again to Beatrice Webb's memoir *My Apprenticeship*, which is woven around diary extracts. This is unusual behavior for Woolf. Of all the diaries Woolf reads across her second, modernist stage, the diary excerpts in *My Apprenticeship* most shape her thought. They supply notions for *To the Lighthouse*, *The Waves*, *Flush: A Biography*, and *Three Guineas*—and especially for *A Room of One's Own* and "Professions for Women."

In September, Woolf reviews a handsome two-volume edition of the *Journals* of Thomas Cobden-Sanderson, the artist of *The Book Beautiful*. They offer a male complement to the potent diary extracts in *My Apprenticeship*. Like Webb and Woolf, Cobden-Sanderson faced bouts of depression throughout his life that led to thoughts of suicide. Like them, he sought relief in his diary and through his own form of mystical belief. Cobden-Sanderson's questing *Journals* likely encouraged Woolf's search in September 1926 (and after) for "the mystical side of this solitude," she writes (*D* 3: 113)—or what Webb calls the great Unknown.

Soon after, Woolf reviews a new reprint of the *Life of Benjamin Robert Haydon, Historical Painter, from his Autobiography and Journals*. Haydon and Woolf share the same January 25 birthday. She finds in his *Journals* her diary father (Sir Walter Scott), her diary mother (Fanny Burney), and many old diary friends. More than this, Haydon's *Journals* offer her a memorable moment for *To the Lighthouse*, matter for *A Room of One's Own*, and figures for *Flush*.

Virginia Woolf's 1926 Diary

> *"I think I shall initiate a new convention for this book—beginning each day on a new page—my habit in writing serious literature."*
>
> (February 27, 1926; *D* 3: 62)

In 1926, Woolf chooses to enlarge her diary. Fifty-one entries turn first outward and then inward in the 335 days from February 8, 1926, through January 23, 1927, an increase from the thirty-two entries of her previous diary.[1] The epigraph above, declaring her plan to treat her diary as she does her "serious literature," signals her renewed interest in her diary as art. Several entries that follow open as *scenes*.

On May 2, the Trades Union Congress declares a General Strike in Britain in support of the mine workers who struck May 1. "An exact diary of the Strike would be interesting," Woolf opens her May 5 diary entry (*D* 3: 77). Ten entries follow: an eye-witness account of the acts and atmosphere of a strike. Woolf notes deprivations. "Everyone is bicycling; motor cars are huddled up with extra people. There are no buses. No placards. no newspapers," she records in that first entry, May 5 (*D* 3: 77). Then the lights go out. The next day taxies appear and skeleton newspapers are sold, but the shops, though open, are empty.

Woolf preserves more, however, than merely the face of the crisis. Her Strike Diary registers—often through vivid similes—the emotional and spiritual currents of a strike, and in this respect it stands out. "It is all tedious & depressing, rather like waiting in a train outside a station," she writes in that first, May 5, entry (*D* 3: 77). "It is a little like the early hours of the morning (this state of things) when one has been up all night," she declares the next day. "[I]ndeed, more than anything it is like a house where someone is dangerously ill; & friends drop in to enquire, & one has to wait for doctor's news" (*D* 3: 78–79).

Her Strike Diary captures the tales that fly and the uncertainty that reigns. "Rumours are passed round—that the gas wd. be cut off at 1—false of course. One does not know what to do," she notes in her first entry (*D* 3: 77). "One believes nothing," she adds the next day: "Clive dines in Mayfair, & everyone is pro-men; I go to Harrison [her dentist], & he shouts me down with 'Its red rag versus Union Jack, Mrs Woolf.' . . . Bob [Trevelyan] drops in & says Churchill is for peace, but Baldwin wont budge. Clive says Churchill is for tear gas bombs, fight to the death, & is at the bottom of it all. So we go on, turning in our cage. I notice how frequently we break of[f] with 'Well I don't know'" (D 3: 78).

Woolf finds in the 1926 General Strike the same narrowing of voice and range she decried in her 1917–1918 World War I diaries. "A voice, rather commonplace & official, yet the only common voice left, wishes us good morning at 10," she writes in her first entry, describing the radio broadcast. "This is the voice of Britain, to wh. we can make no reply" (D 3: 77). On May 9 she observes, "Impressive as it is to hear the very voice of the Prime Minister, descendant of Pitt & Chatham, still I can't heat up my reverence to the right pitch. I picture the stalwart oppressed man, bearing the world on his shoulders. And suddenly his self assertiveness becomes a little ridiculous. He becomes megalomaniac. No I dont trust him: I don't trust any human being, however loud they bellow & roll their rs" (D 3: 81). In short, "[o]ver it all is some odd pale unnatural atmosphere," she writes, "great activity but no normal life" (D 3: 78).

On the personal plain, the strike makes the Woolfs quarrel. She responds by asserting herself. She refuses to join Leonard for lunch at the Phil Bakers. Tellingly, she reverts to her diary for support. To provide some pleasure for herself to match the renounced lunch, she declares, "I can only think of writing this [her diary], & going round the Square [walking]. . . . But the Virginia who refuses is a very instinctive & therefore powerful person" (D 3: 81). And she can declare in her May 11 entry that although to argue with Jack Squire at noon about the Archbishop of Canterbury "seems now normal," it is not, "how often do I repeat—nearly as exciting as writing To the Lighthouse or about de Q[uincey]" (D 3: 83).

Although the "solemn broadcaster" announces the formal end of the strike on May 12, Woolf's Strike Diary records its ongoing tremors: the bickering and backbiting, the trains slow and scarce into June (D 3: 84, 85, 89). She poses her pen against unnatural politics. The day before the announced settlement, she asserts: "I believe it is false psychology to think that in after years these details will be interesting. . . . But one never knows: & waiting about, writing serves to liberate the mind from the fret & itch of these innumerable details" (D 3: 83). Earlier she explains: "I will write it all out later—my feelings about the Strike; but I am now writing to test my theory that there is consolation in expression" (D 3: 81). Her pen (and diary) liberate and offer the natural human voice. She sees an ominous sight in the hours before the strike's end "officially" sounds: "5 or 6 armoured cars slowly going along Oxford Street; on each two soldiers sat in tin helmets, & one stood with his hand at the gun which was pointed straight ahead ready to fire. . . . Such sights I dare say I shall never see again; & dont in the least wish to" (*D* 3: 85). If only her wish had come true.

Woolf thus captures, and rejects, unnatural politics, as she had done almost a decade before with the war. She asks again what are "real things" and finds them in her prose. Having reached outward toward public history with her London Strike Diary in May and early June, she turns inward in the country at the end of July and enlarges her diary in a different way: with a series of eleven *titled* entries, the closest her diary ever comes to brief pensées. The build-up to these (mostly dateless) country probes is complex, involving (again) ordinary life, great men, and Woolf's art. On April 9, Woolf records a tea with Charlotte Leaf, the sister of Madge Vaughan, who kept a diary but had died in November 1925. This tea, which includes Charlotte's husband and two children, causes Woolf to ponder "natural happiness," an inquiry she pursues across the 1926 diary. "I am exiled from this profound natural happiness," she declares of the Leafs' family life:

> That is what I always feel; or often feel now—natural happiness is what I lack, in profusion. I have intense happiness—not that. . . . Writers do not live like that perhaps. . . . Also I keep thinking "They pity me. They wonder what I find in life." Then I sink a little silent, & rouse myself to talk to Kitty [the daughter]. Also I know that nothing Leonard or I have done—not our books or the Press or anything means anything to Lotta & Walter & Charles & very little to Kitty. (*D* 3: 73)

She continues this probe in her next entry, April 11:

> I wanted to go on about the Leafs. . . . Perhaps my life, writing imagining, is unusually conscious: very vivid to me: & then, going to tea with the Leafs destroys it . . . because my life is saying to itself "This is life—the only life." But when I enter a complete world of its own; where Walter cracks a joke, I realize that this is existing whether I exist or not; & so get bowled over. Violent as they are, these impressions go quickly; leaving a sediment of ideas which I shall discuss with L. . . . [a]bout natural happiness: how it is destroyed by our way of life. (*D* 3: 74)

The country offers Woolf her closest purchase on "natural happiness" of her particular sort. On March 3, she compares writing a novel in London to "[n]ailing a flag to a mast in a gale" (D 3: 64). On May 25, London becomes even more unsettling: "The heat has come, bringing with it the inexplicably disagreeable memories of parties, & George Duckworth; a fear haunts me even now, as I drive past Park Lane on top of a bus, & think of Lady Arthur Russell & so on" (D 3: 87). As she did in 1925, Woolf looks toward the country as a haven for prose. On July 22 she reports she will "put The Lighthouse aside till Rodmell. There all virtue, all good, is in retreat. Here [London] nothing but odds & ends" (D 3: 95).

This inordinate faith in the country's powers emerged in 1925 before her country collapse. In 1926, she puts off To the Lighthouse in her first country days. In its place, she tenders a new diary form: eleven probes, the first titled, suggestively, "Rodmell. 1926," a place linked in earlier diaries to nature, women, the unconscious, and the soul and its art. She declares high expectations for this new diary form. "As I am not going to milk my brains for a week," she explains, "I shall here write the first pages of the greatest book in the world. This is what the book would be that was made entirely solely & with integrity of one's thoughts. Suppose one could catch them before they became 'works of art'? Catch them hot & sudden as they rise in the mind—walking up Asheham hill for instance. Of course one cannot; for the process of language is slow & deluding. One must stop to find a word; then, there is the form of the sentence, soliciting one to fill it" (D 3: 102). Nevertheless, she seeks to catch such "rising" thoughts here.

Her next pensée, four sentences titled "Art & Thought," continues the query: "What I thought was this: if art is based on thought, what is the transmuting process?" (D 3: 102). Her mind then turns to great men. "I was telling myself the story of our visit to the Hardys. & I began to compose it: that is to say to dwell on Mrs Hardy leaning on the table, looking out, apathetically, vaguely; & so would soon bring everything into harmony with that as the dominant theme. But the actual event was different" (D 3: 102). As with Stella and Swift the year before, as she transmutes thought to art Woolf brings the obscure woman forward and rebalances the great man's portrait. However, she distinguishes art from actuality.

Her third pensée follows hard on, for she ends "Art & Thought" with the word "Next," leading to "Writing by living people," a meditation on the novel Clarence given her by its author, Maurice Baring. Admitting that she scarcely ever reads "[w]riting by living people," she admits:

I am surprised to find it as good as it is. But how good is it? Easy to say it is not a great book. But what qualities does it lack? That it adds nothing to one's vision of life, perhaps. Yet it is hard to find a serious flaw. . . . Never reading it, I get into the way of thinking it non-existent. So it is, speaking with the utmost strictness. That is, it will not exist in 2026; but it has some existence now; which puzzles me a little. Now Clarence bores me; yet I feel this is important. And why? (*D* 3: 102–3)

Here is another pensée composed of questions, and one that repeats her April recognition that worlds "exist" outside herself and her art.

Male writers—Hardy, Baring—appear to engage her at this moment. In fact, one wonders if the male voice casts a chill that stiffens her and keeps her from her novel. Between her London Strike Diary and her country probes appear portraits of three senior literary statesmen—H. G. Wells, Robert Bridges, and Thomas Hardy—and hardly anything else. Three of the six entries before Rodmell examine Wells, whose fiction Woolf rejected as "materialist" rather than interior in her 1923 fiction credo "Mr Bennett and Mrs Brown" and whose invitations since she has dodged. She takes time, nevertheless, to record Leonard's lunch on June 9 with Wells. Wells calls her "'too intelligent—a bad thing,'" she reports, and then she speaks of his renown: "Leonard asked for him at the Automobile Club; 'A very famous name' said the man. And the warmth & clamour of Wells' fame seems to reach me, this chilly rainy evening; & I see how, if I stayed there, as he asks us, he would overwhelm me" (*D* 3: 90).

A July 1 lunch with the Wells at the Keynes' provides a Bloomsbury buffer. The meeting humanizes Wells for Woolf. "These great men are so much like the rest of us," she writes of Wells and Bridges at the start of her entry (*D* 3: 91). Nevertheless, as she will do with her tea with Hardy, she brings Mrs. Wells forward and imagines her fate: "I could see from the plaintive watery look on Mrs Wells' face (she has widely spaced teeth & in repose looks very worried, at the same time vacant) that he is arrogant lustful & bullying in private life" (*D* 3: 92). Woolf primes Wells to talk of Hardy and Henry James when he and Desmond MacCarthy lunch at the Woolfs' home the next day, and although she notes that Wells insists women are "even more suggestible than men," she closes her portrait by marking his aplomb at age sixty: "In all this he showed himself . . . perfectly content to be himself, aware of his powers,—aware that he need not take any trouble, since his powers were big enough" (*D* 3: 95).

Her visits with Robert Bridges and Thomas Hardy bring similar recognition of their gifts—and, in their cases, praise unalloyed. She finds Bridges "a very lean tall old man . . . very active" when she visits him at his home near Oxford (*D* 3: 92). He shows her his garden, asks her to come again when he will read her his later poems, and she comes away "mainly pleased & gratified to find him so obliging & easy & interested" (*D* 3: 93). Hardy, too, appears completely content and at ease, "the whole aspect cheerful & vigorous," in her extended description of her visit that makes up her July 25 entry, the last entry before the country pensées: "He seemed perfectly aware of everything; in no doubt or hesitation; having made up his mind; & being delivered of all his work; so that he was in no doubt about that either" (*D* 3: 96, 98). She seeks his counsel on questions that nag her. "Did you write poems at the same time as your novels?" (*D* 3: 98); "Do you think one can't write poetry if one sees people?" (*D* 3: 99).

Do Wells's "big powers" and Bridges' and Hardy's ease shadow and stall Woolf as she faces the hard task of completing *To the Lighthouse*? We cannot know for sure. However, her "state of mind" probes become her tack toward the challenge. Her fourth pensée—following "Rodmell. 1926," "Art & Thought," and "Writing by living people"—turns further inward: the stunning "My own Brain." Just as her October 15, 1923, diary entry captured a single night of psychic anguish, she preserves in 1926 "a whole nervous breakdown in miniature" that touched her first Rodmell days. The entire entry merits quoting, for it illuminates what may have occurred across *months* the year before:

> We came on Tuesday. Sank into a chair, could scarcely rise; everything insipid; tasteless, colourless. Enormous desire for rest. Wednesday— only wish to be alone in the open air. Air delicious—avoided speech; could not read. Thought of my own power of writing with veneration, as of something incredible, belonging to someone else; never again to be enjoyed by me. Mind a blank. Slept in my chair. Thursday. No pleasure in life whatsoever; but felt perhaps more attuned to existence. Character & idiosyncracy as Virginia Woolf completely sunk out. Humble & modest. Difficulty in thinking what to say. Read automatically, like a cow chewing cud. Slept in chair. Friday. Sense of physical tiredness; but slight activity of the brain. Beginning to take notice. Making one or two plans. No power of phrase making. Difficulty in writing to Lady Colefax. Saturday (today) much clearer & lighter. Thought I could write, but resisted, or found it impossible. A desire to read poetry set in on Friday. This brings back a sense of my own individuality. Read some Dante & Bridges, without troubling to understand, but got pleasure from them. Now I begin to wish to write notes, but not yet novel. But today senses quickening. No "making up" power yet; no desire to cast scenes in my book. Curiosity about literature returning: want to read Dante, Havelock Ellis, & Berlioz

autobiography; also to make a looking glass with shell frame. These processes have sometimes been spread over several weeks. (*D* 3: 103)

Woolf's honesty and powers of self-observation impress. She acknowledges a near nervous breakdown but neither recoils from it nor veils it; rather, she seeks to record and understand the workings of "[Her] own Brain."

Her eighth pensée, titled "Returning Health," completes the breakdown saga. Her health's return "is shown by the power to make images: the suggestive power of every sight & word is enormously increased," she explains. "Shakespeare must have had this to an extent which makes my normal state the state of a person blind, deaf, dumb, stone-stockish & fish-blooded. And I have it compared with poor Mrs Bartholomew almost to the extent that Sh[akespea]re has it compared with me" (*D* 3: 104). The above lines offer insight into Woolf's particular creative process: the suggestive power of both sights and words.

Her seventh pensée, titled "Wandervögeln" ("Birds of Passage"), relates to the whole series' exploration of the "integrity of one's thoughts" and their transmutation. It links as well to her interest since April in worlds that "exist" beyond herself and her art. Woolf offers the metaphor of birds of passage "of the sparrow tribe" for two "resolute, sunburnt, dusty girls" seen "tramping along the road in the hot sunshine" on July 31. She recognizes that her thoughts of them become screens that intrude between her and their "reality." On sight of them:

> My instinct at once throws up a screen, which condemns them: I think them in every way angular, awkward & self assertive. But all this is a great mistake. These screens shut me out. Have no screens, for screens are made out of our own integument; & get at the thing itself, which has nothing whatever in common with a screen. The screen making habit, though, is so universal, that probably it preserves our sanity. If we had not this device for shutting people off from our sympathies, we might, perhaps, dissolve utterly. Separateness would be impossible. But the screens are in the excess; not the sympathy. (*D* 3: 104)

Across all eleven country probes we see Woolf's wish to press beyond structures that *transform* life (into thought, into art), yet also her sense that this screening or shaping process is essential to (sane) life.

These probes of art and thought occur as Woolf prepares to finish *To the Lighthouse*. One follows the novel's progress with ease across the 1926 diary. Woolf's second entry, February 23, reports her continued creative gush:

I think it is worth saying for my own interest that at last at last, after that battle Jacob's Room, that agony—all agony but the end, Mrs Dalloway, I am now writing as fast & freely as I have written in the whole of my life; more so—20 times more so—than any novel yet. I think this is the proof that I was on the right path; & that what fruit hangs in my soul is to be reached there.[2] Amusingly, I now invent theories that fertility & fluency are the things: I used to plead for a kind of close, terse, effort. (*D* 3: 59)

On March 27, she reports trying to finish "the rather long drawn out dinner scene" in Part 1 of *To the Lighthouse* (*D* 3: 72). On April 29 she completes Part 1 and starts on Part 2 the next day. Of this ten-section "Time Passes" tour de force, she declares: "I have to give an empty house, no people's characters, the passage of time . . . I rush at it, & at once scatter out two pages. . . . Why am I so flown with words, & apparently free to do exactly what I like?" (*D* 3: 76).

However, during the days the novel reaches its close Woolf's diary reveals a fierce struggle between despair and country contentment—despair again that centers on motherhood and "natural happiness." After boasting confidently that she will "solve . . . somehow" the close of *To the Lighthouse* and starting even to imagine her next work, Woolf declares September 5 (perhaps protesting a bit much): "I am frightfully contented these last few days, by the way. I dont quite understand it. Perhaps reason has something to do with it. Charleston & Tilton knocked me off my perch for a moment: Nessa & her children: Maynard & his carpets. My own gifts & shares seemed so moderate in comparison; my own fault too—a little more self control on my part, & we might have had a boy of 12, a girl of 10: This always rakes me wretched in the early hours" (*D* 3: 106, 107).

She uses her diary to talk herself through this grief as she has done so often before. She determines to "exploit" her own gifts and offers a hymn to the country. "Then, I am extremely happy walking on the downs," she reflects: "I like to have space to spread my mind out in. Whatever I think, I can rap out, suddenly to L. We are somehow very detached, free, harmonious. I don't in the least want to hurry up & finish the time here. I want to go to Seaford & walk back over the downs; . . . to breathe in more light & air; to see more grey hollows & gold cornfields & the first ploughed land shining white, with the gulls flickering. No: I dont want anyone to come here & interrupt" (*D* 3: 107).

Her next entry, September 13, talks again of the close of *To the Lighthouse* and again praises the country. "I'm astonishingly happy in the country—a state of mind which, if I did not dislike hyphens, I should hyphen, to show that it is a state by itself" (*D* 3: 110). In point of fact, her diary has claimed the country as a state of mind since 1903, when she declared her aim to "forget" London voices and the male literary tradition and commune with nature in the country (*PA* 178). Two days later, she continues the reflection. Her September 15 entry begins, "Sometimes I shall use the Note form: for instance this," and then comes the 1926 diary's last titled pensée, called revealingly "A State of Mind" (*D* 3: 110). This important entry links to her September 5 entry confessing envy of Vanessa's family life and her parallel April envy of the Leaf family's "natural happiness." Again we see her shorn of ego:

> Woke up perhaps at 3. Oh its beginning its coming—the horror—physically like a painful wave swelling about the heart—tossing me up. I'm unhappy unhappy! Down—God, I wish I were dead. Pause. But why am I feeling this? Let me watch the wave rise. I watch. Vanessa. Children. Failure. Yes; I detect that. Failure failure. (The wave rises). Oh they laughed at my taste in green paint! Wave crashes. I wish I were dead! I've only a few years to live I hope. I cant face this horror any more—(this is the wave spreading out over me). . . . At last I say, watching as dispassionately as I can, Now take a pull of yourself. No more of this. I reason. I take a census of happy people & unhappy. I brace myself to shove to throw to batter down. I begin to march blindly forward. I feel obstacles go down. I say it doesn't matter. Nothing matters. I become rigid & straight, & sleep again, & half wake & feel the wave beginning & watch the light whitening & wonder how, this time, breakfast & daylight will overcome it; & then hear L. in the passage & simulate, for myself as well as for him, great cheerfulness; & generally am cheerful, by the time breakfast is over. Does everyone go through this state? Why have I so little control? It is not creditable, nor lovable. It is the cause of much waste & pain in my life. (*D* 3: 110–11)

She records here another flood of psychic anguish. The crisis reprises her October 15, 1923, night terror when she bicycled to Lewes. Her body becomes rigid—as it did then. She begins to march blindly forward (now in her mind) and takes pleasure in "being matched with powerful things," as she wrote in 1923 (*D* 2: 270). In 1926, she "brace[s] [her]self to shove to throw to batter down" (*D* 3: 110). Both times she sees others as happy, herself as outcast, and she feigns cheerfulness to Leonard. Her first diary words of 1923, in fact, confessed her envy of Vanessa's children and resolution to "never pretend that the things you haven't got are not worth having. . . . Never pretend that children, for instance, can be replaced by other things" (*D* 2: 221). On January 2, 1923, she leaves this matter "unfinished, a note of interrogation—signifying some mood that recurs, but is not often expressed" (*D* 2: 222).

The mood recurs in 1926, perhaps not surprisingly, as she finishes *To the Lighthouse*, a work that brilliantly depicts children and maternal yearning in tension with Lily's art. *To the Lighthouse* represents a rich rendering of this conflict—and perhaps a resolution, a laying to rest of the theme. Woolf in 1926, at the age of forty-four, seems to accept her childless state, embraces her "glooms" (as she writes in her next entry, September 28), and begins to think, as she writes in her October 30 entry, "of a solitary woman musing [?] a book of ideas about life. . . . [I]t is a dramatisation of my mood at Rodmell. It is to be an endeavour at something mystic, spiritual; the thing that exists when we aren't there" (*D* 3: 112, 114).

Woolf's 1926 diary should be remembered as one of her most distinctive diaries, one like her 1923 diary with its six play scenes. A bit more than a fifth of the 1926 diary—eleven entries of fifty-one—is given over to a public Strike Diary, while another fifth turns inward to private flashes of thought (in fact, eleven titled states of mind). During the "[i]ntense depression," the "season of profound despondency" that shadows her triumphant close of *To the Lighthouse*, Woolf observes: "I saw myself, my brilliancy, genius, charm, beauty (&c. &c.—the attendants who float me through so many years) diminish & disappear. One is in truth rather an elderly dowdy fussy ugly incompetent woman vain, chattering & futile. I saw this vividly, impressively" (*D* 3: 111, 112). However, she then embraces even this figure as part of her emerging vision of the solitary woman musing. "[O]ne will be left alone with this queer being in old age," she notes. "I am glad to find it on the whole so interesting, though so acutely unpleasant" (*D* 3: 112).

Her interest persists as the months unfold. "Life is as I've said since I was 10, awfully interesting," she declares in her November 23 entry, "—if anything, quicker, keener at 44 than 24—more desperate I suppose, as the river shoots to Niagara—my new vision of death; active, positive, like all the rest, exciting; & of great importance—as an experience" (*D* 3: 117). Metaphors of rushing water, fluency, and fruition dominate the 1926 diary. The opening of her September 30 entry, which reflects on her nine-week country "plunge into deep waters," links her September 15 wave of despair to the start of a new book:

I wished to add some remarks to this, on the mystical side of this solitude; how it is not oneself but something in the universe that one's left with. It is this that is frightening & exciting in the midst of my profound gloom, depression, boredom, whatever it is: One sees a fin passing far out.... The interesting thing is that in all my feeling & thinking I have never come up against this before. .... All I mean to make is a note of a curious state of mind. I hazard the guess that it may be the impulse behind another book. (*D* 3: 112, 113)

That Woolf continues to reread her growing diary is seen in the asterisk and margin note she places beside this 1926 passage and dates October 1929. "Perhaps *The Waves* or moths" she suggests of this "impulse behind another book" (*D* 3: 113).

In 1926, Woolf shows herself totally at ease with her diary and ready to expand it and press it toward "serious literature." "Just back from Rodmell—to use again the stock opening," she begins her first entry, February 8, and then reaffirms the diary's mission for public prose: "But undoubtedly this diary is established, & I sometimes look at it & wonder what on earth will be the fate of it. It is to serve the purpose of my memoirs. At 60 I am to sit down & write my life. As rough material for that masterpiece—& knowing the caprice of my own brain as record reader for I never know what will take my fancy, I here record that I come in to find the following letters waiting me" (*D* 3: 58). She opens her March 20 entry with the same query, "But what is to become of all these diaries," and now sees "a little book in them" for the Hogarth Press (*D* 3: 67).

In September, as she finishes *To the Lighthouse*, already rising in her diary is her great novel-to-come, *The Waves* (1931); however, the 1926 diary ends with intimations of her more imminent novel-biography, *Orlando* (1928). The 1926 diary closes in mid-sentence, following Woolf's portrait of Vita Sackville-West at Knole:

[S]talking in her Turkish dress, attended by small boys, down the gallery, wafting them on like some tall sailing ship—a sort of covey of noble English life: dogs walloping, children crowding, all very free & stately: & [a] cart bringing wood in to be sawn by the great circular saw. How do you see that? I asked Vita. She said she saw it as something that had gone on for hundreds of years. They had brought wood in from the Park to replenish the great fires like this for centuries: & her ancestresses had walked so on the snow with their great dogs bounding by them. All the centuries seemed lit up, the past expressive, articulate. (*D* 3: 125)

Orlando, of course, becomes Ambassador to Turkey, wears Turkish dress, and, back home in England, sees "heavy carts coming along the roads, laden with tree trunks, which they were taking, she knew, to be sawn for firewood.... Now, calling her troop of dogs to her she passed down the gallery whose floor was laid with oak trees sawn across" (99, 208).

The 1926 diary expands in form and in psychological and philosophical reach. Woolf moves her diary toward literature—and beyond. The diary reaches outward to the General Strike and then inward to a *personal* strike: her own brief nervous breakdown. Woolf strives in this diary to catch thoughts "before they become 'works of art'" (*D* 3: 102). Such thoughts, rising "hot & sudden," are intimations of life beyond human structures. For Woolf, they would compose "the greatest book in the world."[3]

The Diaries of Beatrice Webb

"I am reading Mrs Sidney Webbs autobiography and find it enthralling," Virginia Woolf writes to Clive Bell on April 9, 1926 (*L* #1627, 3: 252). She refers to Beatrice Potter Webb's *My Apprenticeship*, the Fabian socialist's memoir of her early years, 1858 to 1892, built around diary extracts. Woolf, of course, had known of Beatrice and Sidney Webb from at least January 23, 1915, when she records in her diary becoming herself a Fabian at a Fabian meeting: "The interest was watching Mrs Webb, seated like an industrious spider at the table; spinning her webs (a pun!—) incessantly."[4] Across the next eleven years, labor politics meant countless Webb lunches and dinners. However, the Webbs were an older generation. Virginia may not have known until she read *My Apprenticeship* in 1926 the many parallels between this diarist's life and her own.

Beatrice Potter, like Woolf, sprang from a large Victorian family of diarists. Beatrice's father kept a diary and read to her from it. Her mother also kept a journal, and her older sister Kate not only shared her diary with Beatrice but left it to Beatrice at her death.[5] If Virginia was the second-to-last of eight children, Beatrice was the second-to-last of nine *daughters*; in fact, she complains in *My Apprenticeship* of her neglect within a large and mobile household. Her mother "disliked women," Beatrice writes, noting the irony (*MA* 13). "I spent my childhood in a quite special way among domestic servants, to whom as a class I have an undying gratitude," she writes. "I was neither ill-treated nor oppressed: I was merely ignored" (*MA* 58).

Like Woolf, Beatrice suffered chronic ill health and nervous exhaustion as a child. In the 1860s and 1870s, the Potter family doctor prescribed the same regimen Virginia would receive in the 1890s: "no lessons, more open-air exercise, if possible a complete change of scene" (*MA* 60). Norman and Jeanne Mac-

Kenzie, who edited in the 1980s a four-volume edition of Webb's vast diaries, report that Beatrice "was apparently so sickly that she was thought incapable of sustained intellectual effort, and she was left so much to her own devices that her only formal education was a few uncomfortable months at a small 'finishing' academy for girls in Bournemouth."[6]

Like Woolf, Beatrice responded to denial of formal education by devouring books and scribbling. She had the run of her father's library and writes in *My Apprenticeship* that when they complained to their father that a book they wanted to read was banned by the libraries: "'Buy it, my dear,' was his automatic answer" (56). In *My Apprenticeship*, Webb stresses that her diary became an essential tool for "self-culture—reading the books of my free choice, and in my private manuscript book extracting, abstracting and criticising what I had read" (60). She continues this diary practice across seventy years. In *My Apprenticeship* she reports devoting the best part of a year, during her late teens and early twenties, to translating Greek classics, a practice Woolf followed as well (95).

Beatrice's first extant diary, like Virginia's, covers her fifteenth year.[7] Like Woolf, she was a periodic diarist who wrote a mostly unrevised diary slapdash (with initials and ampersands) in a "scarcely legible" hand (MacKenzies 1: xx). Like Woolf, Webb exhorted herself in her diary with the fortifying word "courage,"[8] and both diarists used the diary form for early literary works: Virginia for the unpublished short story titled today "The Journal of Mistress Joan Martyn," and Beatrice for her most successful (and most literary) early published work, "Pages from a Work-Girl's Diary." Like Woolf, Webb wrote more in her diary as she aged, and since she lived to be eighty-five and kept her diary till eleven days before her death in 1943, fifty-seven exercise books contain her manuscript diaries, as opposed to Woolf's thirty-eight.

At age twenty-one, Woolf grappled with social pressures in such 1903 diary essay-entries as "A Dance In Queens Gate," "A Garden Dance," "An Artistic Party," "Thoughts Upon Social Success," and "The Serpentine." *My Apprenticeship* showed her that Beatrice Potter faced a similar ordeal. When Beatrice's mother dies unexpectedly in 1882, twenty-four-year-old Beatrice (like Woolf, a lifelong beauty) is pressed into her father's service, since all seven of her older sisters are married. "The following entries in my diary, during the first year of my newly found position of an independent hostess in London society, reveal the strain and stress of this internal struggle between the desire for self-development and self-expression and the more conventional calls of family duty, reinforced by the promptings of personal vanity and social ambition," Webb writes in *My Apprenticeship* (118):

March 1, 1883 diary: "Find it so difficult to be the universally pleasant. Can't think what to say.... How can intelligent women wish to marry into the set where this is the social regime?" (*MA* 120–21)

April 24, 1883: "But it is a curious experience, moving about among men and women, talking much, as you are obliged to do, and never mentioning those thoughts and problems which are your *real life*, and which absorb, in their pursuit and solution, all the earnestness of your nature. This doubleness of motive, still more this dissemblance towards the world you live in, extending even to your own family, must bring with it a feeling of unreality; worse, a loss of energy in the sudden transitions from the one life to the other. (*MA* 122)

Like diarist Fanny Burney before her, who deferred her writing until the afternoon when she had finished her family chores, Beatrice Potter began "the habit of getting through [her] intellectual work in [her] own room between five and eight in the morning, leaving the rest of the day for domestic cares and social duties."[9] However, four years later, her diary records her continued struggle. "I do not wish to forgo the society of my own class—and yet to enjoy means wasted energy," she tells her December 1887 diary when she is twenty-nine:

Late hours, excitement, stimulants and unwholesome food, all diminish my small stock of strength available for actual work. And society has another drawback; it attracts one's attention away from the facts one is studying, so that the impression is not so keen and deep. To take a clear impression, the intellect must be in a peculiar state—strong, and yet for the moment blank.... Gradually, if you give way, the ogre, society, sucks you in. (*MA* 318, 319)

Compare this with Woolf's 1903 diary essay-entry "A Dance In Queens Gate," in which the dance represents Society: "[The dance] sounds louder & louder—it swings faster & faster—no one can stop dancing now. They are sucked in by the music" (*PA* 166).

Beatrice's "doubleness" particularly hampers, for like Woolf, she wished to write. In *My Apprenticeship* Webb quotes her January 1874 diary entry at age sixteen: "Sometimes I feel as if I must write, as if I must pour my poor crooked thoughts into somebody's heart, even if it be into my own" (74). To this end, Beatrice enjoyed advantages neither Woolf nor Fanny Burney shared. Beatrice's father possessed greater wealth than either Leslie Stephen or Dr. Burney. A timber and railroad baron, he directed the Grand Trunk Railway of Canada for ten years. His frequent inspections of his railroads and other domains gave teenage Beatrice the chance for travel to the United States and Canada that Virginia Stephen never enjoyed. Beatrice began her diary at age fifteen during "this exciting episode" of travel (*MA* 64).

Her family also knew great men.[10] She writes in *My Apprenticeship* that her father "delighted in talks" with T. H. Huxley, John Tyndall, and James Martineau, as well as in walks with his friends James Anthony Froude and Thomas Carlyle (24). From this "unusually varied mental environment," Beatrice gained a mentor, a boon Woolf never secured (*MA* 61). He was the Potter family's "oldest and most intimate friend" Herbert Spencer, her mother's "intellectual associate" (*MA* 21, 23). "It was the philosopher on the hearth who, alone among my elders, was concerned about my chronic ill-health, and was constantly suggesting this or that remedy for my ailments," Beatrice writes in *My Apprenticeship*:

> who encouraged me in my lonely studies; who heard patiently and criticised kindly my untutored scribblings about Greek and German philosophers; who delighted and stimulated me with the remark that I was a "born metaphysician," and that I "reminded him of George Eliot"; who was always pressing me to become a scientific worker, and who eventually arranged with Knowles of the *Nineteenth Century* for the immediate publication of my first essay in social investigation. (29)

Webb reprints in *My Apprenticeship* her 1903 diary tribute at Spencer's death:

> [H]e was perhaps the only person who persistently cared for me—or rather who singled me out as one who was worthy of being trained and looked after. . . . He taught me to look on all social institutions exactly as if they were plants or animals—things that could be observed, classified and explained, and the action of which could to some extent be foretold if one knew enough about them . . . to listen for voices in the great Unknown, to open my consciousness to the non-material world. (38)

Beyond an eminent mentor and the vistas opened through early travel, Beatrice Potter enjoyed a crowning advantage: a legacy of £1,500 a year at her father's death in 1892.[11] It allowed her to pursue her social investigations throughout her life (employing full-time research helpers) and enabled Sidney Webb to quit the Civil Service in 1891 during their courtship and devote himself throughout his long life to unpaid public service. The Webbs did not need to rely on journalism for their daily bread as the Woolfs did for many years.

Virginia likely knew that by 1905 the Webbs were, as the MacKenzies assert, "the best-known couple in [English] public life" (3: xi). She likely saw her marital similarities: a late and childless marriage (Virginia married at thirty; Beatrice, thirty-four); a close intellectual and publishing partnership;[12] a shared interest in the co-operation, labor, and socialist movements. Could Woolf have escaped the notion that she and Leonard were the Webbs' successors as England's best-known public couple?

Woolf devotes unusual time in 1926 to *My Apprenticeship*, published on February 25. "Mrs Webb's book has made me think a little what I could say of my own life," Woolf tells her diary on February 27 (*D* 3: 62). She first notes the ardent curiosity she shares with this diary foremother. Webb defines herself as a "social investigator" in *My Apprenticeship*, and she structures her artful memoir upon two questions, which give birth to many more.[13] "[U]ntil I can take to enquiry as a life-work, and not only as a holiday task, I shall do very little good with it," Beatrice laments in her 1887 diary when she must nurse her ailing father (*MA* 296).

In her first diary mention of *My Apprenticeship*, Woolf senses that Webb's investigations are more focused, more disciplined, than her own. "But then there were causes in her life: prayer; principle. None in mine," Woolf notes and analyzes her own quest: "Great excitability & search after something. Great content—almost always enjoying what I'm at, but with constant change of mood. . . . Yet I have some restless searcher in me. Why is there not a discovery in life? Something one can lay hands on & say 'This is it?' My depression is a harassed feeling—I'm looking; but that's not it—thats not it. What is it? And shall I die before I find it?" (*D* 3: 62). The difference between "restless searcher" and "social investigator" neatly defines the difference between Virginia Woolf and Beatrice Webb.

Woolf continues to read and to reflect on Webb's memoir, for forty-three days later her April 11, 1926, diary entry opens: "Cannot read Mrs Webb because at any moment S[tephen]. Tomlin may ring the bell" (*D* 3: 74). And then, after a suggestive digression to the Leaf family and "natural happiness," she returns to the theme of her February 27 entry:

Mrs Webb's Life makes me compare it with mine. The difference is that she is trying to relate all her experiences to history. She is very rational & coherent. She has always thought about her life & the meaning of the world: indeed, she begins this at the age of 4. She has studied herself as a phenomenon. Thus her autobiography is part of the history of the 19th

Century. She is the product of science, & the lack of faith in God; she was secreted by the Time Spirit. Anyhow she believes this to be so; & makes herself fit in very persuasively & to my mind very interestingly. She taps a great stream of thought. (*D* 3: 74)

My Apprenticeship influences Woolf's thought and works for many years to come. Webb's clear-eyed view of her father and mother may have helped Woolf as she finishes *To the Lighthouse*. Webb acknowledges her father's charm and liberality with his daughters but also describes him as a "capitalist at large": "[H]e thought, felt and acted in terms of personal relationship and not in terms of general principles; he had no clear vision of the public good. . . . Hence he tended to prefer the welfare of his family and personal friends to the interests of the companies over which he presided, the profits of these companies to the prosperity of his country, the dominance of his own race to the peace of the world" (*MA* 3, 7). Despite his frequent absences, Richard Potter "was the central figure" in the family and "controlled the family destinies" (*MA* 10, 11). His gifted wife "lived where it suited him to live, and he came and went as he chose" (*MA* 11).

My Apprenticeship reveals a daughter's belated homage to a mother. "Throughout my childhood and youth [my mother] seemed to me a remote personage," Webb explains, " . . . poring over books in her boudoir; a source of arbitrary authority whose rare interventions in my life I silently resented. I regarded her as an obstacle to be turned, as a person from whom one withheld facts and whose temper one watched and humored so that she should not interfere with one's own little plans" (11–12). In fact, Laurencina Potter withdrew from "social intercourse" to write a novel, learn twelve languages, and devote herself to study.

In *My Apprenticeship* we hear a daughter's yearning and lament: "This absence of affection between us was all the more pitiful because, as we eventually discovered, we had the same tastes, we were puzzling over the same problems; and she had harboured, deep down in her heart, right up to middle life, the very ambition that I was secretly developing" (12). Laurencina Potter dies unexpectedly in 1882, but not before, Webb asserts, "a caressing glance and a sympathetic suggestion that I might succeed where she had failed, and become a writer of books" (*MA* 17). This leads Webb to declare that her mother "exercised a far greater influence over my life after her death than while she was living." She then quotes from her August 1882 diary:

I never knew how much she had done for me, how many of my best habits I had taken from her, how strong would be the influence of her personality when pressure had gone. . . . When I work with many odds against me, for a far distant and perhaps unattainable end, I think of her and her intellectual strivings which we were too ready to call useless, and which yet will be the originating impulse of all my ambition, urging me onward towards something better in action and thought. (*MA* 17)

Webb preserves a female legacy in her diary. Beyond the evocation (and interrogation) of Victorian parents parallel to Woolf's in *To the Lighthouse*, *My Apprenticeship* also set forth ideas Woolf will draw on in *A Room of One's Own* (1929). Webb does more in her memoir than just think back through her mother[14] and place her own story within history; she closes her book with a call for attention to economics and art. "How far, and by what means social organisation can promote and increase either inventive or artistic genius deserves further study," Webb suggests, and her volume's last words are these:

The inventor or the artist must have sufficient leisure of body and mind, and sufficient freedom from the incessant anxieties as to daily bread, to set his spirit free. Too severe and too prolonged a penury depresses genius, and finally kills off its possessors. . . . How much can be done for genius by universal education; by scholarships and fellowships (which might be instituted in connection with great industrial undertakings as well as universities); by lightly tasked professorships and even sinecure appointments with no other duties than observation and reflection; by "measurement and publicity," and even experimental execution at the public expense, must be left to other students to explore. (*MA* 452–53)

In *My Apprenticeship* Webb calls the exercise of power the prime—yet subconscious—force in British life. "The dominant impulse [of the governing class] was neither the greed of riches nor the enjoyment of luxurious living, though both these motives were present," she declares, "but the desire for power" (*MA* 54). Praising the "brilliant" memoir of another contemporary woman, Margot Asquith—a memoir, "owing to its frankness, of great value to the sociologist"—Webb probes the hidden motive behind the marriage game both she and Lady Asquith played:

There was of course a purpose in all this apparently futile activity, the business of getting married; a business carried on by parents and other promoters, sometimes with genteel surreptitiousness, sometimes with cynical effrontery. . . . But deep down in the unconscious herd instinct of the British governing class there *was* a test of fitness for membership of this most gigantic of all social clubs, but a test which was seldom recognised by those who applied it, still less by those to whom it was applied, *the possession of some form of power over other people.* (*MA* 48, 49, 50; italics Webb's)

In *My Apprenticeship*, Webb offers Woolf a living model for horrid Professor von X in *A Room of One's Own*, he of the monumental work *The Mental, Moral, and Physical Inferiority of the Female Sex* who must keep jabbing his pen in anger "as if he were killing some noxious insect" (31). In 1889, after she published her first work, Beatrice Potter met Professor Alfred Marshall, whom she describes in *My Apprenticeship* as "the greatest living economist" (*MA* 350). Proclaiming male preeminence all the while, Professor Marshall urges her to write next on "Woman's Work at the East End" rather than on "Co-operation." She quotes from her March 1889 diary:

> [H]e hold[s] that woman was a subordinate being, and that, if she ceased to be subordinate, there would be no object for a man to marry. That marriage was a sacrifice of masculine freedom, and would only be tolerated by male creatures so long as it meant the devotion, body and soul, of the female to the male. Hence the woman must not develop her faculties in a way unpleasant to the man: that strength, courage, independence were not attractive in women; that rivalry in men's pursuits was positively unpleasant. Hence masculine strength and masculine ability in women *must be firmly trampled on* and boycotted by men. . . . "If you compete with us we shan't marry you," he summed up with a laugh.[15]

Webb confesses she wrote on the history of Co-operation, rather than on "Woman's Work at the East End," partly to defy Professor Marshall.

Beyond offering topics and personages for the 1929 *A Room of One's Own*, Webb's *My Apprenticeship* sets forth the approach Woolf will follow in her famous 1931 address "Professions for Women." Webb offers her own *Apprenticeship* as a model for others to follow. *My Apprenticeship* leads to (and ends with) *Our Partnership*, Webb's next diary-memoir that takes up her life at her 1892 marriage to Sidney Webb. The book thus moves from the individual to the collective. Likewise she presents herself throughout her memoir as a "student," a "scientific worker," and a "social investigator" and includes material in *My Ap-*

prenticeship to assist those on the same path. Her volume's five appendices—"Personal Observation and Statistical Enquiry," "The Method of the Interview," "The Art of Note-taking," "On the Nature of Economic Science," and "Why the Self-governing Workshop has Failed"—give helpful tips to others. "[F]or the benefit of the reader who is also a student I give the gist of these unpublished essays in an appendix," Webb explains, "my excuse being that this intolerable toil of thought was an essential part of the apprenticeship I am trying to describe" (*MA* 292). In like manner Woolf describes her own early professional experiences as a writer in "Professions for Women."[16]

Webb's *My Apprenticeship* even serves as a bellwether for Woolf's 1931 novel *The Waves.* Beyond the nervousness and ill health young Beatrice and Virginia shared lay tendencies to melancholy and family histories of suicide. In *My Apprenticeship*, Webb reports her "vivid memory" of stealing and hiding a bottle of chloroform as a young girl "as a vaguely imagined alternative to the pains of life and the ennui of living" (59).

At age twenty-one, when Beatrice passes herself off as a farmer's daughter for her first social investigations, she learns that both a brother and a sister of her grandmother Heyworth committed suicide and that two or three other family members had been "threatened with suicidal mania" (*MA* 155). In 1905, Beatrice's sister Blanche committed suicide, and Blanche's daughter, Julia (also unhappily married), killed herself in 1921. Webb's 1889 diary entry during her father's illness prefigures Virginia's 1903 diary report of an unknown woman's suicide in "The Serpentine." Beatrice describes a woman *writer*'s death by her own hand. "The very demon of melancholy gripping me," Beatrice wrote, "my imagination fastening on Amy Levy's story, a brilliant young authoress of seven-and-twenty, in the hey-day of success, who has chosen to die rather than stand up longer to live" (*MA* 399). Beatrice then is thirty-one.

A dialectic of "unhappiness" and "happiness" undergirds *My Apprenticeship*. Webb includes an 1879 diary entry that asks: "Does my want of happiness come from my want of belief in the old faith which has helped so many thousands along this weary way?" (*MA* 98). I believe Woolf derives her 1926 concept of "natural happiness" from Webb's trenchant words on the subject.[17] "The sympathetic reader may have noted a black thread of personal unhappiness woven into the texture of my observations on East End life," Webb writes:

> From the entries in my diary I gather that I saw myself as one suffering from a divided personality; the normal woman seeking personal happiness in love given and taken within the framework of a successful mar-

riage; whilst the other self claimed, in season and out of season, the right to the free activity of "a clear and analytic mind." But did the extent of my brain power—I was always asking myself—warrant sacrificing happiness, and even risking a peaceful acceptance of life, through the insurgent spirit of a defiant intellect? For in those days of customary subordination of the woman to the man . . . it would not have been practicable to unite the life of love and the life of reason. (*MA* 279)

In another diary entry, Webb declares: "[I]f I had faith in my own power I could accept an existence of daily toil, devoid of excitement, or what most persons call pleasure, and wanting in the holier happiness of wife and mother" (*MA* 283). In this striking section of *My Apprenticeship*, which Webb titles "The Dead Point," she shares from her February 12, 1886, diary the low point of her life:

Life seems to my consciousness a horrible fact. Sometimes I wonder how long I shall support it. . . . I am not strong enough to live without happiness. . . . I struggle through each new day waking with suicidal thoughts early in the morning. . . . I look out to-night on that hateful grey sea, the breaking and the vanishing of the surf on the shore; the waves break and vanish like my spasms of feeling; but they return again and again, and behind them is the bottomless ocean of despair. Eight-and-twenty, and living without hope! . . . No future but a vain repetition of the breaking waves of feeling. (*MA* 282)

Woolf likely first read this passage in February, March, or April 1926. I believe that it haunts her and that she recasts it in her *own* September diary entries evoking the breaking waves of feeling and the fin: ("tossing me up. I'm unhappy unhappy! . . . Vanessa. Children. Failure. . . . (The wave rises). . . . I cant face this horror any more—(this is the wave spreading out over me). . . . The wave again!").[18] If Woolf was right in 1929, and these September 1926 diary entries offer the first glimpse of her novel *The Waves*, then that work, too, can be linked to Webb's diary, which likely spurred Woolf's pursuit of the mystical in 1926.

Yet there is more. Webb's *My Apprenticeship* makes us look again at Woolf's *Flush: A Biography*, published in 1933. Woolf's "Whitechapel" chapter can be seen as homage to Beatrice Potter's rent-collections in Whitechapel, the place where Beatrice, like that other privileged Victorian invalid Elizabeth Barrett in *Flush*, becomes aware (as Webb writes) "of the meaning of the poverty of the poor" (*MA* 93). Webb mentions Elizabeth Barrett Browning in *My Apprentice-*

ship. "To me," Webb writes, "'a million sick' have always seemed actually more worthy of self-sacrificing devotion than the 'child sick in a fever' preferred by Mrs. Browning's *Aurora Leigh*" (258).

Finally, a trace of *My Apprenticeship* can be found in Woolf's 1938 *Three Guineas*. Webb's memoir showed Woolf that letters and diaries can underwrite cultural criticism: that private prose can do public work. Furthermore, Webb includes in her memoir this charge from her 1887 diary: "Every woman has a mission to other women—more especially to the women of her own class and circumstances" (*MA* 319). Readers have long pondered Woolf's very precise projection of herself in *Three Guineas* as speaking as a "daughter of an educated man" for and to daughters of educated men (4, 9). Perhaps she drew this careful (ironic) language from Webb, who speaks in *My Apprenticeship* not only of "brainworkers" and "social investigators" but also of "the daughters of business and professional men" (45).

Woolf may have noticed in *My Apprenticeship* that she and Webb shared many of the same motives for diary-keeping. Webb confesses she uses her diary both to rid herself of painful emotions and "to enjoy the unwonted pleasure of self-expression" (*MA* 60). She includes an excerpt from her 1874 diary at age sixteen that declares her diary's great benefit as "a vent for one's feelings, for those feelings in particular that one cannot communicate to other people" (*MA* 76). For young Beatrice, perhaps even more than for young Virginia, a diary served as a confidante for a lonely child, someone with whom she can "chat" (*MA* 72). In fact, it serves as a "phantom" of herself, as she writes in her 1884 diary at age twenty-six:

> [T]here is a long lapse in my habit of writing down what I see, think and feel. And yet I am loath to say good-bye to an old friend, one who has been with me since I first had experiences, and wished to tell them to some one, tho' it were only to a phantom of myself. It would be curious to discover *who it is* to whom one writes in a diary? Possibly to some mysterious personification of one's own identity, to the Unknown, which lies below the constant change in matter and ideas, constituting the individual at any given moment. (*MA* 280; italics Webb's)

Webb also used her diary to clarify and to strengthen her thoughts (*MA* 280), to examine herself (*MA* 76), and to provide a record of her growth. Diary historian Harriet Blodgett calls Webb "an unusually frank and introspective woman" (*Centuries* 43). Once Beatrice starts her social investigations, she finds she must protect her diary from outside matter. "Otherwise," she writes in her 1887 diary:

the autobiography is eaten up by statistics of wages, hours of work, interviews with employers and workpeople—no space for the history of a woman's life. And without egotistical brooding, it is still necessary to keep a record of individual growth; not merely as a stepping-stone to higher life, but as a help in the future. How often have I found strength in turning over back pages, in watching the inevitable work its way in spite of my desperate clutches at happiness, which were seemingly fore-doomed to failure. (*MA* 280)

Early on Webb saw that her diary possessed historical and autobiographical value. "As it may be interesting in future years to know what my religious convictions were at nineteen," she declares in a diary passage included in *My Apprenticeship*, "I might as well state roughly what are my vague beliefs."[19] Five years later, Webb becomes a conscious diary portraitist: "[S]ince my life will be much spent in society, an attempt to describe the men and women I meet will add interest to it, and give me a more delicate appreciation of their characteristics" (*MA* 115). Later, she acknowledges her diary is, in fact, one of her "craftsman's tools" (*MA* 61).

Beatrice Webb and Virginia Woolf paid sympathetic, yet discriminating, attention to each other across the generational divide, and their writings stimulated each other. Not surprisingly, Webb appreciated Woolf's novels *Night and Day* and *The Years* more than her modernist experiments. In a letter to Leonard Woolf dated provisionally autumn 1920, Webb offered high praise of *Night and Day*:

I have just read your wife's book—will you tell her that she has won the admiration of an old woman. She has made the novel the form in which to present the most subtle criticism of character and the most poetic appreciation of nature—the whole harmonized by charming kindliness towards weary humanity. I wish I could see something of her; but I gather that she does not feel strong enough to come across new friends—do tell her that I shall now watch for her recovery with anxiety because I realise that she has an extraordinarily valuable instrument in her spiritual insight and literary gift—it would be a sin against humanity if it were lost to the world through continued ill health. *She must make herself well.* (*The Letters of Sidney and Beatrice Webb*, 3: 141; italics Webb's)

In February 1927, following the Woolfs' weekend stay at Passfield Corner, the Webbs' Surrey home, Webb's diary shows her still the good student trying to classify and summarize Woolf:

She is uninterested in politics—wholly literary—an accomplished critic of style and a clever artist in personal psychology, disliking the "environmental" novel of late Victorian times, especially its latest exponent, Arnold Bennett. Like other works of the new school of novelists, I do not find her work interesting outside its craftsmanship, which is excellent but *précieuse*. Her men and women do not interest me—they don't seem worth describing in such detail; the mental climate in which they live seems strangely lacking in light, heat, visibility and variety; it is a dank mist of insignificant and monotonous thoughts and feelings, no predominant aims, no powerful reactions from their mental environment, a curious impression of automatic existence when one state of mind follows another without any particular reason. To the aged Victorian this soullessness is depressing. Doubtless our insistence on a purpose, whether for the individual or the universe, appears to them a delusion and a pernicious delusion. (MacKenzies 4: 113)

Webb must have reason, purpose, and social improvement. However, fifteen months later, she turns to *To the Lighthouse* and asks her diary, "[C]ould I record my own consciousness?" (MacKenzies 4: 144). She returns to this question two months later as she seeks new directions. "What I should like doing would be to browse among books and write or not write as I felt inclined—perhaps try some new style of thought and expression," she tells her July 1928 diary. "To go back to Virginia Woolf's method of novel-writing; the description of the streams of consciousness of one or other of her characters. Can I describe my own?" (MacKenzies 4: 149).

In October 1939, after a lunch with Leonard and Virginia, eighty-one-year-old Beatrice admires *The Years* in her diary: "I asked her whether she was going to write a second volume of *Years*. I longed to hear how the family she described so vividly would respond to this new war. Would they be as unconcerned as they were during the great war of 1914–18?" (MacKenzies 4: 444). However, Webb still finds Woolf lacking a creed.

On the whole Woolf saw more. Both she and Webb suffered "nervous breakdowns" in 1915, and each used her diary to return to the world.[20] In her 1918 diary, Woolf captures the Webbs' first visit to Asheham House with first a comic entry and then a sober one. Many biographers speak of Beatrice Webb's impersonality; Woolf offers an explanation for this trait after first seizing on "the curious discomfort of soul which Mrs Webb produces" because "'I' was not exalted; 'I' was practically nonexistent" (*D* 1: 193): "On the way up the hill she stated her position that one should wish well to all the world, but discriminate no one. According to her the differences are not great; the defects invariable; one must cultivate impersonality above all things" (*D* 1: 196). In her next entry, Woolf seeks as usual to balance and deepen her portrait. Observing how easily a "half carping half humorously cynical view" steals into descriptions of the Webbs,[21] she declares her wish to make a "masterly summing up of the Webbs . . . to point out the good qualities which come from such well kept brisk intellectual habits; how open minded they showed themselves; how completely & consistently *sensible*. . . . How sensible it was not to fuss about goodbye, or a Collins; how sensibly they approach every question whether of servants or politics, putting their minds at your service without the least ostentation or flummery" (*D* 1: 196–97).

Beatrice Webb's "clear and analytic mind" and Woolf's acuity in capturing it is seen in the following 1918 Woolf diary passage preserving their "few private words": "She asked me about my novel [*Night and Day*], & I supplied her with a carefully arranged plot. I wished, so at least I said, to discover what aims drive people on, & whether these are illusory or not. She promptly shot forth: 'Two aims have governed my life; one is the passion for investigation by scientific means; the other the passion for producing a certain good state of society by those investigations'" (*D* 1: 196). In 1918, this is rather a full précis of the yet-to-be-written *My Apprenticeship*.

Woolf knew Webb kept a diary. Woolf's 1921 diary "disquisition on the return of peace" ends: "But I think you'll find all this written more accurately in other books, my dear Virginia: for instance in Mrs Gosse's diary & Mrs Webb's" (*D* 2: 92–93). I believe *My Apprenticeship* enhanced Woolf's respect for Beatrice Webb. Perhaps Webb knew of the Woolfs' admiration for her memoir, for in 1931 she sent them a draft of her sequel diary-memoir, *Our Partnership*, seeking their advice. Virginia's April 8, 1931, letter to Webb reveals her continued regard for Webb's diary:

> We are both agreed that it [*Our Partnership*] is extremely interesting, and that it would be a great pity to cut any of the diary. We feel that the reality that the diary gives is better than any more general account could be.[22] I was extremely interested and amused throughout, and this is a good test, as few people can know less about Trade Unions than I do. We only wish you could write it straight off, as your next book, so much do we want to see how your story with its most interesting commentary develops.[23]

Beatrice Webb's vast diary—like Virginia Woolf's—reached readers in tantalizing portions across the twentieth century.[24] Along the way, it has regularly been called one of the great English diaries.[25] In 1898, Charles Trevelyan traveled round the world with the Webbs and wrote home that "Mrs Webb . . . will be the Pepys of the nineteenth century" (MacKenzies 2: 142). *My Apprenticeship* received high praise from George Bernard Shaw in 1925 and from F. R. Leavis in 1949 and 1950.[26] By 1972, Samuel Hynes was declaring that the best writing in *My Apprenticeship* lies in the diary extracts (162). "A reading of the unpublished diaries at the London School of Economics confirms the sense that one gets from *My Apprenticeship*, that there is an even finer book to come," he declares, "and that when the full text [of Webb's diaries] is published Mrs Webb will take her place among the great diarists (her only modern rival will be Virginia Woolf)."[27]

I believe Woolf took much from Webb's diaries: thoughts for *To the Lighthouse, The Waves, Flush: A Biography, Three Guineas*—and especially for *A Room of One's Own* and "Professions for Women." Webb's diary extracts pressed Woolf beyond literature to the great Unknown. At the least, *My Apprenticeship* showed her that a woman at age sixty could craft a brilliant memoir from her diaries.

The *Journals* of Thomas Cobden-Sanderson

Thomas Cobden-Sanderson, the artist of *The Book Beautiful*, died in 1922. In the autumn of 1926 a beautiful two-volume edition of his *Journals* appeared, which offered Virginia Woolf a male complement to Beatrice Webb's suggestive diary extracts in *My Apprenticeship*. "I shall do Cobden Sanderson [*sic*] & Mrs Hemans & make something by them," Woolf boasts to her September 13, 1926, diary as she finishes *To the Lighthouse* (*D* 3: 109). Her review of the artist's *Journals* appeared in the October 9 *Nation and Athenaeum*.

Although a generation older than Beatrice Webb—he was born in 1840 and lived to be eighty-one—Cobden-Sanderson covers in his *Journals* much of the same terrain as Webb does in *My Apprenticeship*. Like Webb, he holds Herbert Spencer in high regard—so much so that he adds Spencer's portrait to the picture-gallery of great men that hangs over his bed (1: 43). Like Webb (and the Woolfs), Cobden-Sanderson favors trade unions, labor, and socialism. Also like Beatrice and Virginia, he forms a late but fruitful marriage partnership that leads to the production of books.[28] Following his marriage in 1882, he abandons law to begin an apprenticeship in bookbinding. He opens his own Doves Bindery in 1893, and in 1902 founds the Hammersmith Publishing Society as an arm of his 1900 Doves Press.[29] Like both Beatrice and Virginia, Cobden-Sanderson endures periods of depression throughout his life that lead to thoughts of suicide, and like them he seeks relief in his diary and through his own form of mystical belief.

While such parallels increase the *Journals'* interest, Cobden-Sanderson's diaries offered as well a very different male voice from those that sound in Beatrice Webb's diaries. Webb struggles across the 1880s with males who seek to narrow and trample her growth. Thomas Sanderson, in contrast, buys John Stuart Mill's *Subjection of Women* on October 31, 1881, and writes in his journal the next day (months before he meets his suffragist wife, Anne Cobden): "A whole social revolution yet to be made dawns before my eyes.... Shall I not recognize that there is a right yet to be won before the world is older, that women should be put upon an equality with men?... Let her win her laurels. Let her too have a life to lead, an independent life, a life that shall surpass this of man if it may" (1: 41, 42). At his marriage he joins his wife's name to his own, telling Professor John Tyndall: "[M]y wife was the daughter of Richard Cobden, and ... for her sake I had prefixed the name of Cobden to my own, that she might not altogether lose hers in it" (1: 121).

At home, he teaches his wife bookbinding, and he asks his own teacher in December 1883 "why women were not admitted to the higher branches of the work":

> He said that the men would not allow them, and if a woman were taken into a shop to learn, all the Trade Unionists would instantly object, and leave if she were not dismissed. He did not know if there was a trade rule to that effect, but certainly it is what would happen. He himself did not favour the admission of women into the business. It was no doubt a trade jealousy. But there were other professions open to women, and they were not wanted in the bookbinding trade, although no doubt many of the operations could as well be performed, or even better, by women than men. I said it was very disgraceful, and that all employment should be open equally to women as to men.
>
> Perhaps in time I may help to remedy this. (1: 169)

While in the 1880s, privileged Beatrice Potter disdains women's press for the vote, Anne Cobden-Sanderson is not only a labor leader but also a suffragist. In 1909, she is one of the eight suffragists arrested for trying to present a petition for the vote to Prime Minister Herbert Asquith. Her imprisonment and subsequent trial spur her sixty-nine-year-old husband to diary words that speak to Webb's condescending Professor Marshall:

The insurgent woman . . . is seeking not to separate herself from man, but, as a primitive force in co-operation with his own, to act directly on the world which hitherto she has entirely neglected, or acted on only indirectly through her action on man himself. It is indicative of and consequential upon the development itself of woman's will and intelligence. And it is opposed on the one hand by men who desire to have this larger world to themselves, and themselves to be the objects of women's devotion and flattery, and on the other hand by women of minor intelligence and instinctive outlook, who feel that the world of fiction and domestic office is sufficient, and the outer world an alien one, which they may comfortably leave to the coarse violence of the man nature to overcome and temper for their more delicate habitation.

In fact, the movement and problem involved are profound, and not on the surface, and involve a complete readjustment of the operative ideas and forces of mankind. (2: 156)

In short, much in Cobden-Sanderson's *Journals* might have interested Woolf in 1926. On the personal plain, he refers to her father, just as Webb had in *My Apprenticeship*; however, his references are more substantial. In the tenth entry of his published *Journals*, Sanderson writes in 1880: "I have just been looking into Leslie Stephen's review of Pollock's book on Spinoza. Leslie Stephen writes of Spinoza, 'He considered within himself that the common objects of human desire, wealth and power and pleasures, offered no certain or satisfactory reward. *The only security for happiness is to have a mind filled with a love of the infinite and eternal*'" (1: 9; italics Cobden-Sanderson's). Thirty-eight years later, when he puts his journals in order, the artist still finds Stephen's words resonant, for he repeats them in his March 1918 journal (2: 347). Cobden-Sanderson shares Leslie Stephen's alpine bent. "The air of the mountains is the air of my body, and of mind too," he tells his April 1882 journal during one of his regular trips to the Alps (1: 57). "To the mountains we should go for recovery from the overcharged life of the great cities," he declares at age seventy-one (2: 186).

Cobden-Sanderson's *Journals* resurrect Woolf's father, and they also appear to praise her sister. In November 1912, Cobden-Sanderson exhibits ten Doves Press books in the Arts and Crafts Exhibition at the New Grosvenor Gallery on Bond Street (2: 209). He may have known Vanessa through the arts and crafts movement—Roger Fry was preparing to launch the Omega Workshops at this time—for he speaks of "the Bells" approvingly in an August 12, 1912, journal entry. That month the Cobden-Sandersons rent Lollesley Farm in West Horsley for a six-week summer holiday, and on the twelfth enjoy a visit from the Bells, who "won all our hearts—so kind and unaffected, and so responsive to our simple means of pleasure" (2: 205).

The artist also engages his Press's first compositor on the recommendation of Mary Sheepshanks of Morley Hall and in December 1911 stays at Hilton Young's cottage called The Lacket, as a "quasi-gift" from Young (2: 4, 196). There the bookbinder entertains Augustine Birrell and his son, Tony, and even Birrell's "detective, an amiable and undetective looking man" (2: 232). At age eighty-one, in his next-to-last journal entry, Cobden-Sanderson reports giving Birrell copies of his beautifully bound *Shelley*, his *Keats*, and his own the *Cosmic Vision*, "the last my own copy, the only one I had" (2: 429).

Cobden-Sanderson's world thus touched on Woolf's own. It also offered her firsthand views of other artists. It shows Jane and William Morris, who invite Cobden-Sanderson into the world of art; Edward Burne-Jones, who assists and inspires him; and John Ruskin, who most fires his search for the cosmic ideal. "I think Ruskin the greatest and most worshipful man in all the British Isles," the bookbinder tells his journal. "I am going humbly to bind [his] *Unto this Last*, and to lay it humbly at his feet" (1: 234). In 1886, Cobden-Sanderson despairs to his journal: "To-day there is a notice in the *Daily News* that Ruskin is threatened with a return of insanity. I have not yet sent him my book. I must send it away to-day. I must be in conscious communication with him once before the end" (1: 248).

In April 1890, Cobden-Sanderson attends the opening of the Ruskin Museum and sees his book on the bookcase, and when Ruskin dies in 1900, the diarist declares: "I am glad that the poor, worn body may now be returned to the earth, and the spirit liberated. Ruskin's is now the voice of the universal world: disembodied, and re-embodied. It is the voice of nature's self. I begin the study of that voice to-day, and as I listen to it, river and lake and mountain and sky speak, too, and say, 'That voice is mine'" (2: 2). Cobden-Sanderson meets William James during his American lecture tour on the book beautiful and copies into his 1908 journal James's letter calling his *Credo*, "in addition to its physical beauty . . . a wonderfully fine expression of a naturalistic faith, a precious document on that account" (2: 115).

In 1915, the diarist joins his wife, Anne, on the platform at a meeting on behalf of peace. (Leonard Woolf attends this meeting.) Cobden-Sanderson gives to Jane Addams, the American social worker and peace advocate who is the evening's principal speaker, a copy of the Doves Press edition of Shelley "bound in blue morocco (Grolier pattern with wreath and trefoils), with this inscription:

'To Jane Addams, In affectionate memory of the Hague Congress and of her visit to England on behalf of the 'World's Great Age'—World Peace" (2: 264).

Sanderson enjoyed deep ties with Bertrand Russell's diary-keeping parents in his early years;[30] in fact, he is named one of Bertrand's guardians at his parents' early deaths. In 1912, Cobden-Sanderson offers his own home to the struggling Russell, and his 1916 journal entries include Anne's letters providing firsthand reports of Russell's trial as a conscientious objector to war (2: 292, 293). On February 9, 1918, Cobden-Sanderson himself, now seventy-seven, goes "to stand by Bertie Russell, on trial for some writing which I had not seen in some obscure pacifist journal. He was sentenced to six months' imprisonment. . . . He appealed, and Frank [Bertrand's brother] and I bailed him out, otherwise he would have gone straight to prison" (2: 345).

As should now be clear, Cobden-Sanderson shared many of Virginia Woolf's views and values. He recoils from the Boer War, recording, appalled, in his July 1901 journal: "'To the last cartridge, to the last man'—(Botha), and thus on England shall be fixed for ever the indelible disgrace of the deliberate murder of a few people" (2: 11). He reports writing to the *Westminster Gazette* in September 1902, "that it was a pity we could not be a great nation, that having been extravagantly unjust we could not be extravagantly generous, and subscribe twice over all that South Africa wanted to restore its ruined farms. But England will not" (2: 36).

He senses the coming Great War and its meaning, for he writes in his August 2, 1914, journal: "Europe, the world, on the eve of a convulsion of change, more widespread and destructive than any which it has ever endured since the world was a world—destruction of man, and man's world, by man" (2: 251). On January 1, 1915, the seventy-four-year-old writes: "From the war as a war I withdraw myself. I will pray for a change of spirit, both in ourselves and in the 'enemy'; a change of spirit, for how otherwise shall there be peace?"—words that may have stayed in Woolf's mind as she evolved *Three Guineas* (2: 259). He turns instead to constructive measures. As a sign of faith, he builds a new house for his beloved Anne and their Doves Press and—more daringly, in those intensely anti-German times—publishes Goethe in 1915 "in honour of Germany's better past, and in hope of Germany's still greater future, when she shall have sloughed off the hate which, to-day, bedarkens both her and our Welt-Ansicht and World-Vision" (2: 261).

As Woolf will do twenty-three years later with *Between the Acts*, Cobden-Sanderson offers art as an answer to war. In June 1914, at age seventy-three, he closed his Doves Press; however, he writes in his December 1, 1914, entry: "I may note here a passing—or enduring?—desire to prolong in these sad days the life of the Press . . . a desire born of the sadness of the time, and the longing to keep in touch with beauty and the tenderer mind of man when all the world seems sick with sorrow, filled with man's own created horror; to keep in touch with Beauty, and the life supreme of Order" (2: 258–59).

Cobden-Sanderson questions nationalism and empire across his journals. "Is then the Empire of England a great idea, an idea worthy of such an immense devotion?" he asks in his June 1902 journal (2: 29). Three months later he declares: "I am neither for nor against Empires, just as I am neither for nor against elephants. But I do not want to trample, and I object to be trampled upon" (2: 37). In his August 1908 journal, he suggests: "The motto of the Cobden Club should not be Peace, Goodwill among *Nations*, but Peace, Goodwill among *Trades*, Trades taking the place of Nations. What is the *raison d'être* of 'Nations' as a system or scheme of organization? Is there anything in the nature of things to make them essential to human well-being, and to prevent its dissolution? What, if any, is their essential and indispensable function?" (2: 113).

A month earlier, the diarist reimagines education—as Woolf will later do in *Three Guineas*. "A scheme of education should above all things aim at providing modes for the evocation and expression of energy," he tells his journal: "So there should be singing, dancing and gymnastics, and declamation; also all the crafts should be introduced for the cultivation of constructive thought and imagination—not for the sake of the objects produced, nor even for the sake of the crafts which are their methods of creation, but for the sake of the bodies and souls of the children, and of the body and soul of the community of which they are in their maturity to form a part, and collectively the whole" (2: 108).

To that collective end Cobden-Sanderson rejects honors and courts obscurity. "I cannot abide such personal distinction," he writes an old schoolfellow who presses him to accept the "Victorian Degree" (2: 12). His April 17, 1889, entry includes his letter to "a young lady" who wishes to write of him and his work: "Dear Madam, I am sorry I cannot have the pleasure of seeing you on Thursday as you propose. I am much engaged, and if I may say so without seeming to reflect on your work, would prefer to remain in the obscurity I at present enjoy" (1: 280).

Cobden-Sanderson's *Journals* share many traits with Woolf's diary (and with Beatrice Webb's as well). He writes a periodic journal of vast length that he rereads and thinks to draw on for his memoirs (2: 341, 88). His journal from the first serves as his confidant, his "old companion" and "friend" (1: 265; 2: 139).

"I have left my diary at the Cottage," he writes in August 1908, "and as I must talk to myself I begin another book; a new one which, fortunately, I find ready to hand" (2: 111). He uses his diary both to record his world and to measure his growth: "I will now begin to keep a diary of work, that I may . . . have . . . an accurate measure or record of things done" (1: 221).

His journals, like Woolf's and Webb's, also preserve his responses to books, and, like them too, he uses his diary at times to vent. In March 1887, when he cannot wield his tools as he wishes, he writes:

> I am in a rage to murder. My binding of *In Memoriam* is in my own opinion a beastly performance, and I had hoped something of it. . . . I could spit upon the book, throw it out of the window, into the fire, upon the ground and grind it with my heel. . . . I am in a perfect frenzy and ecstasy of rage. . . . Well, I write it that I may an hour hence marvel. And in the meantime I turn from the whole petty turmoil to spread my mind over a wider theme, and to expand my soul to larger hopes. (1: 255–56)

The latter is the more frequent office of his journal: to record his mystical experiences. "I have been all this morning alone on the shore in dejection," he confesses to his diary in April 1883. "But I take up my journal now and read its first pages, and lo! another world than the one round about, or a larger of which it is a mystic part, rises up, and in *it* plays the music of the waves of this" (1: 70).

Woolf titles her review of Cobden-Sanderson's *Journals* "The Cosmos," and she develops at some length his lifelong—ultimately failed—drive to explain his mystic *Credo*. Like Woolf, Cobden-Sanderson was a searcher, a questioner who wanted to know "what life is" (1: 32). His questing *Journals* likely encouraged her own search in September 1926 (and after) for "the mystical side of this solitude," she writes on September 30, "how it is not oneself but something in the universe that one's left with" (*D* 3: 113). He withdraws himself from war and reimagines education, steps Woolf will follow, too, in *Three Guineas*.

Thomas and Anne Cobden-Sanderson have the two children—a boy and a girl—Woolf yearns for in her September 5, 1926, diary entry, and he speaks regularly of "happiness," as did Beatrice Webb. The artist's *Journals* likely evoked Woolf's September diary pensée, titled "A State of Mind," for he confesses to his 1912 diary: "For some time past life seems to have vanished out of the Press. . . . This no doubt represents a 'state of mind,' and has its causes within. What are they? Why are they?" (2: 207). The "candour with which these private struggles are laid bare," Woolf writes in her review, "is no small part of the deep interest of these diaries" (*E* 4: 370).

Benjamin Robert Haydon's Journals

"What a picture of life are my journals," exclaimed the English historical painter Benjamin Robert Haydon in his 1826 diary (Taylor 1: 382). One hundred years later Virginia Woolf wholly concurs. In late September 1926, Woolf writes to her sister, Vanessa: "I should be much obliged if you or Duncan could tell me on a card where I could see some of the historical pictures of Benjamin Haydon? [I]n some restaurant, I think. I have to write about him" (*L* #1676, 3: 295). "Genius," her review of a new reprint of Haydon's memoir and journals, appears in the December 18 *Nation & Athenaeum*.

Haydon's self-absorbed yet fascinating journals first saw print in June 1853—seven years after his dramatic suicide. At his widow's request, English scholar Tom Taylor compiled and edited a *Life of Benjamin Robert Haydon, Historical Painter, from his Autobiography and Journals*. Within five months a second edition was required. Woolf read a reprint of this second, corrected and slightly expanded, version, which now also sported (she wrote) a "brilliant" introduction by Aldous Huxley.[31]

Like Beatrice Webb's *My Apprenticeship*, which Woolf pondered at length this year, this Haydon text showed that a compelling memoir could be made from diaries. It revealed that diaries could, also, etch a world on their own. Haydon began to write his autobiography six years before his death, artfully weaving in journal entries to show his early stepping stones—just as Webb would do. He had reached only to 1820 at his 1846 end, but editor Taylor found he could easily continue the painter's story with his diary entries—to the very day of his death. These diaries supplied matter for Woolf's *To the Lighthouse* (in progress), her 1929 *A Room of One's Own*—and more.

Haydon shared a birthday with Virginia Woolf. He was born January 25, 1786, to a prosperous Plymouth printer, stationer, and bookseller. Like young Virginia, he read avidly, with history his special love. Taylor reports that Haydon was "a copious" diary commentator on the books he read (Beatrice Webb's practice as well), "and these took in a range not often embraced by the [visual] artist" (1: 327). In his late teens, again like Woolf and Webb, he began to study Greek.

Beyond these biographical ties, Woolf also might have noted shared artistic traits. Haydon enjoyed spontaneous invention. In February 1828, he reports sitting in his son's sickroom "sobbing quietly, in bitter grief . . . when—will it be believed?—Punch, as the subject for a picture, darted into my thoughts, and I composed it, quite lost to everything else, till dear little Frank's feeble voice recalled me. This involuntary power it is which has always saved me" (2: 431).

In August 1836, he records: "Awoke at four with a terrific conception of Quintus Curtius" (2: 608).

Like Leo Tolstoy and fellow painter-diarist Eugène Delacroix (both of whose diaries Woolf will read in the 1930s), Haydon saw his spontaneous creations as "sparks" or "flashes" of insight. "Strange the action of the faculty called genius!" he exclaims to his 1844 diary: "I sketched Aristides, the populace hooting him. On Sunday I looked at it without thought or reflection. In flowed a brilliant flash of placing him in the middle. . . . [F]or five minutes I was lost to external objects; I saw the whole—never clearer—never stronger—never finer"(2: 778). In the famous passage in Woolf's *To the Lighthouse*, the first draft finished in late September 1926, the painter Lily Briscoe, at dinner, decides to move a tree to her painting's middle (86).

Along with the shared gift of spontaneous invention, Haydon reveled, as Woolf did, in street composition. "The moment my mind was relieved from these agonising pressures," he tells his 1827 diary, "it began conceiving subjects as I walked along the streets, with a sort of relishing delight" (1: 405). However, at times he also describes the creative shutdown Woolf has just limned in her autumn diary pensée "My own Brain." Haydon tells his 1841 diary: "Like [Dr.] Johnson in hypochondria, there I sit, sluggish, staring, idle, gaping, with not one idea. Several times do these Journals record this condition of brain" (2: 702).

Haydon prized the sketch throughout his days—as did Woolf. In his third year as a professional painter, he tells his 1808 diary: "Put in the head of my hero, not at all satisfied; not half so well as the sketch. There is always something in a sketch that you can never after get when your feelings are quiescent. I look forward to that time, the result of many years' incessant study, when I shall be able to paint a picture warm from my brain with fire, certainty and correctness" (1: 73). Seeking to instruct future historical painters through his autobiography, he writes in 1841:

> My object in thus detailing the secret history of my mind in the progress of the Dentatus [his second picture], is to be useful to students in every way, to show them that before they can obtain the power of sketching instantaneously, which people applaud in me now at fifty-five, and which all young men are so ambitious of gaining, they must again and again begin, obliterate and recommence; they must go to nature, and study the antique, making separate studies of each part; they must fail, not be discouraged, but at it again. (1: 78)

Like Woolf, Haydon found vacancy a spur to invention. Taylor explains that the idea for Haydon's Lazarus—which Sir Walter Scott and others called his most brilliant achievement in paint—"flashed upon him when, in looking over prints in the British Museum, he saw an unfinished proof of the subject, in which the oval of the face of Lazarus remained a white spot. This his imagination at once worked to fill up" (1: 317–18).

Woolf's review suggests she identified with this historical painter. She takes time to describe his first days in London as a version of her own Bloomsbury Group:

> He lived and painted in one room, and there, night after night, Wilkie, Du Fresne, Dr Millingen, McClaggan, Allan ("the celebrated painter"), and Callender all met and drank his good tea out of his large cups, and argued about art and politics and divinity and medicine and how Marie Antoinette's head was cut off . . . while Liz of Rathbone Place, who loved their talk, but was otherwise cold, sided with one, attacked another, and was found studying Reid on the Human Mind "with an expression of profound bewilderment." "Happy period!" Haydon burst out, "no servants—no responsibilities—reputation on the bud." (4: 406–7)

Woolf found many of her favorite diarists in Haydon's *Journals*—and also some old diary friends. Haydon reads Pepys's diary in 1826, the year after it first appears, and personalizes the failing eyesight that halts Pepys's pen: "Finished Pepys' *Memoirs*, a Dutch picture of the times, deeply interesting. O God, grant me no longer life but while I can read and paint" (1: 386). In 1845, he visits painter Joshua Reynolds' niece and records this tale of young Fanny Burney, Woolf's diary "mother": Reynolds' niece "said she and her sister plagued Miss B. in the garden at Streatham to know who was the author of *Evelina*, never suspecting *her*. As they rode home Sir Joshua said, 'Now you have dined with the author—guess which of the party.' They could not guess, when Sir Joshua said, 'Miss Burney'" (2: 795).

Haydon does better than the nieces in 1820 during a similar evening with Woolf's diary "father" Walter Scott. "One talk satisfied me who was the author of *Waverly*," Haydon begins his deft Scott portrait:

> His expression denoted a kind, keen, prudent, deep man. His conversation showed great relish of what is nature, and for no part of her works so much as where vice and humour are mingled.
>
> He told us a story of one Dick, a smuggler. . . . The detail of Dick's dress,

his large buttons, his dog, and other peculiarities of description, so convinced me who wrote the novels, that I could hardly help thinking that
Scott took a pleasure in exciting your suspicions that he was the author,
without confessing it, chuckling that good breeding prevented you from
opening your lips. . . . He paid me high compliments; said he was anxious to see a picture the world was talking of [Haydon's *Jerusalem*], and
the next morning, when Sammons came down to open the gallery, who
should be sitting on the stairs outside of the door, with simple patience,
but the mysterious author of *Waverley*! . . . This always appeared to me
a beautiful trait of the natural character of this great genius. (1: 285–86)

Mutual regard thus blooms. In December, Scott sends Haydon an outline of
a course in Scottish history and in January 1821 the story "The Laird's Jack" as
"a good subject for a sketch . . . though perhaps better adapted for sculpture"
(1: 299). In March 1821, Haydon describes a joyous morning visit from Scott,
Charles Lamb, and the painter David Wilkie. "Scott operated on us like cham-
pagne and whisky mixed," Haydon tells his diary and then offers an extended
contrast of Scott and William Wordsworth—to Scott's advantage—ending,
"Scott is the companion of Nature in all her feelings and freaks, while Wordsworth follows her like an apostle, sharing her solemn moods and impressions"
(1: 302, 303).

Did it gratify Woolf to find here such an admirable Walter Scott? When Haydon sinks into debt, Scott always sends cash. His encouraging 1823 letter to a
Haydon locked now in debtor's prison resonates richly, for it comes three years
before Scott's own financial woes and foreshadows Scott's response:

They have much to answer for, who proceed as your creditors have done,
not only in the depreciation of your property, and the interruption at
once of your domestic happiness and professional career, but in the deprivation of your personal liberty, by means of which you could in so
many ways have been of service to yourself, and even to them. There is
one advantage, however, in your situation which others cannot experience, and which ought to give you patience and comfort under your severe affliction. What real means of eminence and of future success you
possess lie far beyond the power of the sheriff's writ. . . . [N]o species of
legal distress can attack the internal resources of genius, though it may for
a time palsy its hand. . . . [T]he exertion of your own talents would soon
retrieve the comforts you have lost for the present. (1: 336–37)

It is of Walter Scott in 1826 that Haydon exclaims, "What a picture of life are my journals." He continues: "Two [journal] volumes ago, Scott sent me £10 for [William] Godwin, then £20 for myself, and now he writes me he has lost a large fortune, and is in distress" (1: 382). Does Haydon rush to Scott's rescue in return? His diary gives no sign, and it seems unlikely given the painter's chronic poverty. In fact, amid his own troubles, Scott sends funds in 1827 when Haydon lands in debtor's prison once more. The next year, Scott tries to help the painter by sitting for a sketch. "I hit his expression exactly," Haydon tells a May 1828 entry. "Sir Walter Scott has certainly the most penetrating look I ever saw, except in Shakespeare's portraits" (2: 441).

Haydon's final diary portrait of Scott in October 1831 offers a fair exhibit of his closely observed, animated, and penetrating diary portraits and illustrates Woolf's review assertion that Haydon's "painter's eye lights up his phrases":

> Called on dear Sir Walter yesterday, and was affected at the alteration in him. Though he was much heartier than I expected to find him, his mind seemed shaken. He said he feared he had occasionally done too much at a time, as we all do. . . . After a quarter of an hour I took my leave, and as I arose he got up, took his stick, with that sideling look of his, and then burst forth that beautiful smile of heart and feeling, geniality of soul, manly courage and tenderness of mien, which neither painter nor sculptor has ever touched. It was the smile of a superior creature who would have gathered humanity under the shelter of its wings, and while he was amused at its follies would have saved it from sorrow and sheltered it from pain. (*E* 4: 410; 2: 519–20)

Scott, in turn, in his own 1827 diary called Haydon "A man of rare genius" (Taylor 2: 838). Three months before his suicide, Haydon visits Abbotsford and is "much affected" by Dryburgh, Scott's burial site (2: 808), a trip Woolf will make herself in 1938. Haydon examines the manuscripts of Scott's novels and tells his diary that he is "astonished at the purity of the writing; like Shakespeare's, without blot" (2: 807).

Scott admired Haydon, but Aldous Huxley, in his 1926 introduction to the *Journals*, lends his weight to views launched as early as 1841: that Haydon mistook his genius, which lay in prose rather than paint. A *Morning Post* critic urged that year: "Let Mr Haydon rather write than paint. His pen is sometimes his friend; his brush is always his enemy" (Truss). Charles Dickens took up this theme at Haydon's death. "All his life he had utterly mistaken his vocation," the beloved writer declared, then sternly added: "No amount of sympathy with him and sorrow for him in his manly pursuit of a wrong idea for so many years—until, by dint of his perseverance and courage it almost began to seem a right one—ought to prevent one from saying that he most unquestionably was a very bad painter, and that his pictures could not be expected to sell or to succeed."[32]

Huxley makes these twin thoughts his introduction's core. Haydon was "a bad and deservedly unsuccessful painter," he declares; "he was . . . a born writer who wasted his life making absurd pictures when he might have been making excellent books" (1: xvi). Woolf agreed, but more gently, in her 1926 review: "[W]e catch ourselves thinking, as some felicity of phrase flashes out, or some pose or arrangement makes its effect, that his genius is a writer's. He should have held a pen. . . . It was some malicious accident that made him, when he had to choose a medium, pick up a brush when the pen lay handy" (*E* 4: 410).

The conflict of brush and pen unfurls in the journals. At age twelve, Haydon enters Sir Joshua Reynolds' own grammar school, Plympton St Mary. A passionate, dreamy boy, he spends his days peering at a Reynolds sketch in burnt cork on the classroom ceiling. However, Reynolds' *Discourses*—his *prose* not his *painting*—seal Haydon's fate. Reading the *Discourses*, Haydon writes in his memoir, "I felt my destiny fixed. The spark which had for years lain struggling to blaze, now burst out for ever" (1: 14). Yet at this crossroads, the young man misreads the blaze. His mother begs him to stay in Plymouth to take over the family book store, but he replies, "Do not, my dear mother, think me cruel; I can never forget your love and affection; but yet I cannot help it—I must be a painter" (1: 15). He is eighteen. "I thought only of LONDON—Sir Joshua—Drawing—Dissection—and High Art," he writes in his fervent uppercase way (1: 16). His parents at last relent. In 1804 they give him £20 and he boards the stage to London. The next year he enters the Royal Academy to study historical painting—and he is launched.

But he cannot give up his pen. In his memoir he explains that he "was animated by a desire to write in early life, because Reynolds, having deferred composition till late in life, was accused of not writing his own lectures" (1: 124). At only twenty-two, offended that the Academy hangs his second picture, *The Assassination of Dentatus*, in a small side room rather than in the main hall, Haydon's grandiose sense of himself and his art impels him to lash back in the press. This brash act offers an early instance of what editor Taylor calls "the gigantic proportions which trifles assumed in the strangely distorting mirror of his mind, the moment they related to himself" (2: 551). The attack places Haydon at odds forever with the English art hierarchy. That he often is right and ahead of his time only makes his war more poignant—overwrought though it be.

Soon after, Lord Elgin returns to England with the Greek marbles he hopes the English government will buy. Haydon, with his attractive youthful zeal, convinces the Lord to let him copy the Greek sculptures. As a result, Haydon becomes the most knowledgeable, as well as the most eloquent, defender of the marbles' worth when Payne Knight and other critics belittle the marbles as shoddy and inauthentic. Haydon writes in 1816: "I told Lord Elgin I would make Knight remember the Elgin Marbles as long as he lived; Lord Elgin smiled incredulously, but I knew my power, and retiring to my painting-room with my great picture of Jerusalem before me I dashed down on the paper thoughts and truths which neither nobility nor patrons ever forgave.... [the painter Thomas] Lawrence said, 'It has saved the Marbles, but it will ruin you.'"[33]

But ruin for art hardly daunts Haydon; rather, he seems to seek it. "While I live, or have an intellect to detect a difference or a hand to write," he vows, "never will I suffer a leading man in Art to put forth pernicious sophisms without doing my best to refute them.... I should consider myself a traitor to my art, and my country's taste, and the dignity of my pursuits if I suffered them to pass unnoticed; to these divine things I owe every principle of Art I may possess" (1: 237).

Haydon's more cautious friend Wilkie begs him to cool his pen, and an early patron, Sir George Beaumont—friend of Reynolds and David Garrick—urges him to *paint* them down" (1: 215). But Haydon finds the pen "irresistible"—a telling remark:

> It was a pity I allowed my mind to act again through the pen when the pencil was my real instrument, but the temptation was irresistible; and then I thought of doing good by implanting sound principles of patronage in a proper quarter. I might perhaps have done this without irritating and exasperating the Academicians. Yet, regarding them as a great body who influenced and prejudiced the aristocracy, it was impossible to touch on Art without finding the Academy at every point checking, misleading, and obstructing. Every weapon of attack was resorted to—ridicule, sarcasm, allegory and insinuation. (1: 249)

The Academy now his enemy, Haydon pens appeals to political leaders and to the press to win the reforms he seeks. He calls for art professorships at the universities and schools of design in the towns—and both appear within his lifetime. In 1818, he conceives of government support for the arts—in fact, foresees the now frequent policy of legislating a percentage of building funds for art. The early 1830s find him writing for the Reform Bill. "I have been again writing in newspapers, which is wrong," he confesses guiltily to his diary on April 28, 1832. "Yet I hardly see how I could avoid it; God knows what will become of me" (2: 530).

As Woolf notes in her review, Haydon not only finds the pen magnetic but he also cannot part from his books. She quotes his confession to his diary, "The truth is, I am fonder of books than of anything else on earth," and points out that he clings to his Shakespeare and Homer while he pawns his art (*E* 4: 410; 1: 387). "[H]is instinct to express himself in words was undeniable," she asserts. "Overworked as he was, he always found time to write a diary which is in no way perfunctory, but follows with ease and sinuosity the ins and outs of his life" (*E* 4: 410).

In truth, Haydon *needed* his diary just as Woolf needs hers, for it made possible his public work. He writes his diary and then his autobiography and public lectures from it. In 1842, he explains that he "acquired in early life a great love of the journals of others, and [Dr.] Johnson's recommendation to keep them honestly I always bore in mind. I have kept one now for thirty-four years. It is the history, in fact, of my mind, and in all my lectures I had only to refer to my journals for such and such opinions, to look when such and such thoughts had occurred, and I found them an absolute capital to draw upon."[34]

Twenty-six bulky ledger-like folio volumes, parchment-bound, preserve Haydon's impassioned days. He rereads his diaries more avidly than Woolf rereads hers and annotates them with side notes. In a revealing 1832 entry after a brief lapse, he suggests his mind would be "injured" if he did not keep a "regular account of how I have passed my time" (2: 512). Thus when his eyes go bad in 1814, he dictates his diary to friends "so that nothing was lost" (1: 165).

Haydon differs greatly from Woolf, however, in seeing his diary as a great moral lesson. He equates his own progress with that of English historical painting and, by extension, the fate of the English nation itself. His personal plight, in his own mind, assumes national import. He writes for history—his journals as well as his memoir. "I shall read this again with delight—and others will read it with wonder," he tells his 1822 diary (1: 317).

More than Woolf, however, he needs his diary to propel himself on (although Woolf uses her diary for this purpose as well). He starts each new diary book with one or two "mottoes" drawn from literature or the Bible. Their common thread: work hard and trust in God. He surveys his "state of mind" on each birthday and summarizes each year at its end (2: 622). In this way he (and we) can easily track his progress. "I always concluded the year with a review and a thanksgiving to God, and always opened it with a prayer for His blessing," he explains in his memoir. "I have no pleasure so great as the belief in the perpetual and secret intercourse with my Creator" (1: 257).

The journals harbor this "secret intercourse"; they supplicate the divine "whisper."[35] Haydon affirms repeatedly his trust in God to provide, and the journals record the trust fulfilled—though often after the harshest trials—until the very end. Can diaries be enablers? Indubitably. Haydon's journals foster a life of grandiose art eked from debasing poverty. The painter regularly records rising without a sovereign, or a crust in the house, or a way to pay his son's Oxford bill, and, after hours of frantic writing to friends or pleading with creditors, £20 will arrive from Walter Scott, or King George will buy his Hogarthian *Mock Election,* or he will sell yet another copy of his *Napoleon at St Helena Contemplating the Setting Sun.*

Haydon's diary hints that he welcomed this precipice life. In 1823, he observes to his diary that "[t]he faculties of some men only act in situations which appal [*sic*] and deaden others. Mine get clearer in proportion to the danger that stimulates them. I gather vigour from despair, clearness of conception from confusion, and elasticity of spirit from despotic usage. . . . [W]ant and necessity, which destroy others, have been perhaps the secret inspirers of my exertions" (1: 326).

Twenty-two years of harried struggle later he repeats: "An anxiety is a necessary sweater, or I should be too buoyant" (2: 797). He seems to sense here his manic bent. Thirty years before, he tells his 1815 diary: "Never have I had such irresistible and perpetual urgings of future greatness. I have been like a man with air-balloons under his armpits, and ether in his soul. While I was painting, walking, or thinking, beaming flashes of energy followed and impressed me. O God! grant they may not be presumptuous feelings" (1: 204).

Huxley called Haydon a "great personality" as well as a born writer (1: xvi). In 1962, scholar Norman Gash suggested that the painter's "literary self-portrait . . . compares with Pepys, Boswell and Kilvert as a revelation of human nature" (178).[36] The painter meant his work to be instructive, and in 1853 editor Taylor commends the memoir and journals to readers as a "curious piece of psychological revelation and a not uninteresting though mournful picture of artist life" (1: xxx).

The journals beg for psychological probe. Haydon's life seems shaped by a Messianic motive. Woolf calls it a persecution complex (*E* 4: 409). He must ever be in "secret intercourse" with his God, who will sustain him despite his trials. He paints *Christ's Entry into Jerusalem; Christ's Agony in the Garden; Christ*

Rejected; the *Crucifixion; The Raising of Lazarus; The Banishment of Aristides* ["The Just"]; *The Assassination of Dentatus;* and *Curtius Leaping into the Gulf.*[37] Haydon seems also an archetypal Chekhov character: blind to failure, deaf to appeal, repeating his refrains as the cherry orchard falls.

Where did his high hopes miscarry? Perhaps at the start when he chose the brush over the pen. He might, however, have avoided some of his financial stress and achieved more as an artist had he adopted Delacroix's path and put marriage aside. At age thirty, Haydon falls in love at first sight with Mary Hyman, captivated by her beauty and her devoted care for her dying husband. At age thirty-five, he marries the now penniless widow with two children, increasing three-fold his cares. At least eight more children of their own soon arrive, the painter a devoted father and husband. Mary brings him comfort and solace. Why should he be denied "natural happiness"—as Woolf calls family life across her 1926 diary (*D* 3: 73)?

In truth, Haydon's debts start even before he weds. However, support of twelve, or even five (when deaths shrink the family circle) tasks the soul and body more than support of one. Three years after his marriage, he confesses to his 1824 diary: "Alas! I have no object in life now but my wife and children, and almost wish I had not them, that I might sit still and meditate on human ambition and human grandeur till I died. I really am heartily weary of life" (1: 355).

Huxley describes, nevertheless, a "magic" in Haydon (1: xii). With his handsome head, exalted talk, and fervor for art, he charmed landlords into foregoing his rent and inns into gifting him meals—all for the sake of England's historical art.[38] The most esteemed men, as well as landlords, valued this man. John Keats wrote three sonnets to Haydon; Wordsworth did the same. Scott thought him "a man of rare genius" well worth support. Haydon's four stays in debtor's prison come after his marriage. To his credit—or perhaps his folly—he would educate his sons as gentlemen and educate his daughter too. The family compounds his happiness but also his bills.

Editor Taylor places the mortal blow in 1843 when Haydon's designs for the new houses of Parliament fail in the national competition. In 1812, when Haydon saw Lord Wellesley address the House of Lords surrounded by "miserable tapestry," he conceived "a grand series of designs to adorn the ample sides of the House": "I became gloriously abstracted, and settled that an illustration of the best government to regulate without cramping the energy of man would do: first to show the horrors of anarchy; then the injustice of democracy; then the cruelty of despotism; the infamies of revolution; then the beauty of justice [and trial by jury]; and to conclude with limited monarchy and its blessing" (1: 147).

The 1834 fire that destroys Parliament must have seemed to Haydon a divine act to further his plan. In 1835, he petitions the government to decorate the new Houses of Parliament with historical paintings. "I am most anxious about this matter," he tells his March 7 journal, "because it really is the climax of my efforts, to obtain which I have staid in England, neglected to go to Italy and devoted my whole life to the accomplishment of this great national object" (2: 586). Taylor believes Haydon died in 1846 "a victim to disappointment; that his exclusion from all share in the decoration of the New Houses of Parliament broke his heart; and that all his subsequent efforts to reassert his claims, through the Public, instead of the Fine Arts Commission, were void of true hope" (2: 824).

Perhaps. However, beyond the mania, the Messianic (or persecution) complex, a related "curious piece" of psychology may also shed light on his end. A man small in stature, Haydon fixates on the large. He writes his diaries in large folios, and he never feels so happy as in his studio with a canvas towering above him. Napoleon enthralls him: the small man become great. On many journal pages Haydon ponders the general's character and conduct. In fact, his most popular paintings depict Napoleon against a series of changing backgrounds: Saint Helena, Fontainebleu, even the Egyptian pyramids. In the 1820s, Haydon sees that the huge size of his canvases hinders his sales and attempts to reduce his scale. He tells his 1827 diary: "It is curious that I have at this moment a positive passion to try my hand at the cabinet size; to work it up like Rembrandt's small works—gemmy, rich and beautiful. . . . If I had begun in this size I should have made my fortune" (1: 409).

But small works do not create the anxiety he needs. In October 1831 he tells his diary: "Now Xenophon is done, I feel the want of a great work to keep my mind excited. A number of small things does not do so; it is not enough" (2: 519). Revealing, too, is the 1840 journal: "I feel with small pictures as if I had nothing on my shoulders, which I always like to have. I'll soon be at my large canvas" (2: 678). Just as *diary* pen strokes soothe Virginia Woolf, *brush* strokes salve Haydon's psychic stress. "If it was not for my divine art I should certainly go mad; but the moment I touch a brush all pain vanishes," he tells his 1822 diary (1: 322). Nineteen years later, he writes: "When a great canvas is up I feel sheltered, though I have not one farthing in my pocket" (2: 697). In eight months, he again exclaims: "There is nothing like a large canvas. Let me be penniless, helpless, hungry, thirsty, croaking or fierce, the blank, even space of a large canvas restores me to happiness, to anticipations of glory, difficulty, danger, ruin or victory. My heart expands, and I stride my room like a Hercules" (2: 718).

And he must be a Hercules—or a Napoleon. Four months before his death, Haydon confesses to his journal: "In the greatest anxiety about money matters. . . . I have lost three glorious days, painted hardly at all, and have not succeeded in getting £5, with £62 to pay. I must up with my new canvas, because without a new large picture to lean on I feel as if deserted by the world" (2: 804).

How could a mere writer's sheet of paper compete with the colossal canvas? The mortal blow to Haydon may, in fact, have come in April 1846—two months before his suicide. His Parliamentary paintings passed over in 1843 by a government panel headed by his own first pupil, Charles Eastlake, Haydon as usual turns to the public as the true jury. The people, he believed, always held him in their heart—as they did Shakespeare and Milton (he grandly adds) (2: 740). For his public vindication—and to earn money too—he hires a hall to exhibit his *Banishment of Aristides* ["the Just"] and the *Burning of Rome by Nero*.

However, a "malicious accident" once more occurs. The adjoining hall exhibits not huge historical paintings but tiny Tom Thumb. Is the final insult to be bested by this dwarf? Haydon's April 1846 journal entries disclose that his last resort, John Bull, now turns from him as well. "They rush by thousands to see Tom Thumb. They push, they fight, they scream, they faint, they cry help and murder! and oh! and ah!," he exclaims to his April 13 entry: "They see my bills, my boards, my caravans, and don't read them. . . . I would not have believed it of the English people" (2: 810). Eight days later, he records: "Tom Thumb had 12,000 people last week; B. R. Haydon, 133 1/2 (the 1/2 a little girl). Exquisite taste of the English people!" (2: 811–12).

One never can know the final motive for suicide. Was it his failure in the 1843 competition? Was it the public's preference for Tom Thumb? The lucid letter and scrupulous will Haydon leaves behind disclose that he owed at least £3,000 on the day of his death—not a sum readily managed with £20 gifts from friends or another sale of Napoleon contemplating the setting sun. Perhaps at age sixty he was simply tired. Or perhaps he reckoned Mary and the children would do better without him. Aldous Huxley marvels at Haydon and his death, calling him "one of these glorious lunatics," though possessing an "insanity . . . of good quality" (1: xix). "One can only feel astonished," Huxley writes, "that he did not kill himself before" (1: xii). In her review, Woolf treats the death with unflinching sympathy: "One morning after quoting Lear and writing out a list of his debts and his thoughts, he put a pistol to his forehead, gashed a razor across his throat, and spattered his unfinished picture of Alfred and the first British Jury with his blood. He was the faithful servant of his genius to the last."[39]

Time has turned a kinder eye on Benjamin Haydon's labors.[40] In 1934, scholar Clarke Olney published an article that hailed Haydon's crucial role in Keats's art. Noting that the two "were intimate friends during the greater part of Keats's active creative life," Olney reminds readers that it was Haydon who took Keats to see the Elgin Marbles (which led to the famous sonnet); Haydon who in 1817 gave Keats Goldsmith's *The History of Greece*; and Haydon who lent Keats his copy of Chapman's *Homer* (258). Olney calls Haydon's memoir and journal words on Keats "among the finest and most discriminating things ever said about the poet" and suggests that Haydon's "ideas and example may have encouraged Keats to attempt his more 'bold,' more 'grand,' and more 'powerful' *Endymion*" (273, 275). We know Haydon encouraged the poet throughout the poem's composition. Olney argues that "when Keats came more fully under Haydon's influence, his poetical calling took on new significance, new dignity, the grand calm beauty which Haydon had showed him in the Elgin marbles.... On the whole, then, Haydon's influence on Keats was wholesome; for by showing him the seriousness and dignity of the poet's calling, he helped make Keats dissatisfied with the trivialities of the Cockney school" (275).

Olney lamented in 1934 that Haydon's full journals were "not available" (262n18). In 1853 Taylor published, of course, only a portion of the painter's twenty-six bulky journal volumes. He also shied from hurting living persons, so he tantalizes us with initials and blanks for names.[41] Readers, however, clearly wanted more. In 1927, Alexander P. D. Penrose followed the two Huxley volumes with a one-volume *The Autobiography and Memoirs of Benjamin Robert Haydon, 1786–1846, compiled from his "Autobiography and Journals" and "Correspondence and Table-Talk."*[42] In 1950, Malcolm Elwin edited another one-volume version of the *Autobiography and Journals*, and finally, starting in 1960, Willard Bissell Pope brought forth the (almost) complete *Diary of Benjamin Robert Haydon*, in five volumes.[43] In 1990, for those thirsting for the journals distilled, John Jolliffe offered the short *Neglected Genius: The Diaries of Benjamin Robert Haydon, 1808–1846*.

Haydon's dramatic life has also cried out for the stage. In 1977, John Welles wrote *The Immortal Haydon*. In 2007, the Nunkie Theatre Company premiered *Blood, Bone and Genius*, another one-man play based on Haydon's life and diaries, written and performed by Robert Lloyd Parry. Ironically and in full circle, it was staged in the Royal Academy School's historic life-drawing classroom to tie in with an exhibition of Haydon's anatomic drawings at the Royal Academy of Art. Would Haydon have smiled at the exhibition title: "The Body Politic"? By design, the play premiered on June 22, 2007, the 161st anniversary of Haydon's suicide.[44] The next year, in Vancouver, Canada, Janet Munsil's play *Influ-*

ence premiered. The work dramatizes Keats first visit to the Elgin Marbles as Haydon's guest.

Thus Haydon's life and journals have now fully reached the public, as he wished. The diaries, however, stand forth today as his greatest work. In 1965, Frederick Cummings called Haydon's diary his "most important legacy" and "one of the most important literary, art historical, and social documents of the nineteenth century" (397). Marcia Allentuck declared that "[t]here are few such packed and many-levelled documents in western literature as this great diary" (77).

Haydon's diary figures fascinatingly in Woolf's own life and art. The brush and pen rivalry she describes in her review—with genius lodged in the pen—mirrors her own rivalry with Vanessa disclosed movingly in *her* diary this year, in fact, as recently as her September 15 "A State of Mind" diary pensée with its "painful wave swelling about the heart. . . . Vanessa. Children. Failure" (*D* 3: 110). In her review, Woolf writes of Haydon: "He had, above all, a mind which was for ever tossing and tumbling like a vigorous and active dolphin in the seas of thought" (*E* 4: 409). Since "dolphin" is her pet name for Vanessa, this line may offer a private bow to Vanessa as possessing a "vigorous and active" mind—or a subtle slap (since Haydon is shown a failed painter).

In respect to Woolf's own works to come, beyond the figure moved to the middle of the painting that she will borrow for *To the Lighthouse*, Woolf also meets in Haydon's *Journals* the generous Mary Russell Mitford. Kindly Mitford introduces Haydon to her friend, the invalid poet Elizabeth Barrett of Wimple Street. (In Woolf's 1933 *Flush: A Biography*, Mitford gives Flush, the spaniel, to Barrett.) One of Haydon's "truest and kindest friends," Miss Mitford pens a sonnet that opens: "Haydon! this dull age and this northern clime / Are all unripe for thee!" (1: 278, 341).

In October 1842, at Mary Mitford's request, Haydon sends his sketch of *Curtius Leaping into the Gulf* to Elizabeth Barrett, together with his portrait of *Wordsworth Musing on Helvellyn*, also painted that year. Has any painter inspired so many sonnets?[45] Elizabeth Barrett, from her couch, is so moved by the Wordsworth portrait that she seeks to capture it in a sonnet that ends:

No portrait this with academic air,
This is the poet and his poetry. (2: 741)

Before his death, Haydon sends his memoir and journals in a chest to "Miss Barrett, 50 Wimple Street" with the hope of publication. "I wish Longman to be consulted," he directs in his will. "My memoirs are to 1820; my journals will supply the rest" (2: 821). Thus Miss Mitford and Elizabeth Barrett cross Woolf's mind's eye in September 1926. Haydon's journals also offer a striking line on death and waves. Six months before his death, he exclaims to his diary: "This year is closing rapidly. I almost hear the rush and roar of the mighty wave from eternity that will overwhelm it for ever!" (2: 799).

However, beyond these sparks for Woolf works to come, Haydon's *Journals* offered her in 1926 a painfully detailed portrait of genius maimed by poverty. Haydon's stepson, named Orlando as it happened, attends Wadham College, Oxford. "There is some pleasure in suffering for a boy like this," Haydon tells his 1830 journal (2: 490). The next year, he records of Oxford: "I never saw a place that has so much the air of opulence and ease" (2: 511). In 1840, he is invited himself to Oxford to lecture and gives his six lectures for free. His diary records the privileged aura he senses there. "Oxford affects my imagination vastly," he notes; "such silence, and solitude, and poetry, such unquestionable antiquity, such learning, and means of acquiring it" (2: 671).

Haydon thinks he needs some "anxiety" as a sweater to cloak his mania. However his *Journals* also record the toll his perpetual poverty takes. In her 1929 *A Room of One's Own*, Woolf describes the "incandescent" mind needed for optimum creation: an "artist's" mind must be free of "impediments" such as "grudges" and "[a]ll desire to protest, to preach," which can warp the vision (56–57, 59). Haydon writes of this in his *Journals*. Six months before his suicide, he observes, "Out of what a mass of indigestion, fog, debt, discontent, opposition, vice, temptation and trial is every work of intellect accomplished" (2: 801). In 1834, he is more direct: "I am convinced long suffering from pecuniary necessity affects the imagination. It magnifies difficulties" (2: 573). Editor Taylor writes that by 1843 "[i]t was apparent to all, and to none more than to his warmest and truest friends, that years of harass, humiliation, distraction, and conflict had enfeebled his energies, and led him to seek in exaggeration (to which even in his best days he had been prone) the effect he could no longer attain by well-measured force" (2: 743). Haydon himself told his 1836 diary: "These Journals testify that whenever I have been free, I have flown to my canvas as a relief and a blessing. The Mock Election was the fruits of the peace I enjoyed in 1827. The Chairing the result of George IV.'s purchase. In fact, if I had £500 a year regularly, never would I cease painting, morning, noon, or night, and never have a debt" (2: 608). Here is the £500 for *A Room of One's Own*.

8

The Loose-Leaf Diary

"What Liberty / A loosened spirit brings," Emily Dickinson declared. In 1927, Virginia Woolf embarks on a two-and-a-half-year experiment with a loose-leaf diary. To be *loose* is "not to be fastened, restrained, or contained"; to be "unfettered; free from confinement or imprisonment." One "loose" is one "not taut, fixed, or rigid"—states anathema to Woolf. To be "loose," moreover, is to be "lacking conventional moral restraint in sexual behavior."

A loose-leaf diary allows its "leaves," its *traces*, to be easily shifted, replaced, or removed. Woolf's 1927 loose-leaf diary seems to plunge her into her creative unconscious. An offhand air emerges from this diary, which seems a holding pond spontaneously spouting scenes. These scenes most often are of death, yet Woolf answers each with renewed creation. The first traces of *Orlando* appear in this diary, along with the "play-poem" that becomes *The Waves*. The loose-leaf diary invites such unfettered fancy; however, it serves, too, as a site to *contain* Woolf's "gushing mind" as she savors the "ardour & lust of creation" (*D* 3: 129).

Touchingly, at this time when Woolf is awash in spontaneous invention, she reads in August 1927 the first published version of Katherine Mansfield's *Journal*. She could hardly fail to note there Mansfield's greater struggle and self-doubt. Although Mansfield promised to send Woolf her diary in 1920—and then failed to do so—Woolf exudes generosity in her review. She pays public tribute to this valued friend and fellow artist, perhaps not only because in late 1918 Mansfield meant for her a Hampstead "public of two" but also because her *Journal* offered nourishing matter for Woolf's own works to come (*D* 1: 222).

Virginia Woolf's 1927 Diary

> *"I amuse myself by watching my mind shape scenes."*
>
> (September 4, 1927; *D* 3: 154)

Nonchalance emanates from Woolf's 1927 diary. We meet an artist deeply submerged in creation yet also riding a wave of health and happy distractions. A mere thirty-three entries comprise the 1927 diary, so distracted is Woolf by European travel and by the wealth and new "motor car" *To the Lighthouse* brings, so buoyed, too, by Vita Sackville-West, who "refreshes" and "solaces" her soul (*D* 3: 149).

"[B]ut here's an innovation: this is not a book but a block—so lazy am I about making writing books nowadays," Woolf whispers in parentheses in her first entry, February 3, 1927, disclosing her casually inventive diary ways (*D* 3: 125). This diary's burnt-orange calfskin cover sports two punched holes, making it a loose-leaf notebook filled with white paper printed with a thin pink vertical line 1 ½ inches from the left-hand edge—the line Woolf used to rule herself.[1] This "block" diary fulfills Woolf's December 1918 diary vision: "Suppose I buy a block, with detachable leaves, I think I shall snare a greater number of loose thoughts. No doubt this is pure fancy, but then so much of one's mental affairs are controlled by fancy" (*D* 1: 228).

Many *scenes* are snared in this 1927 diary, and Woolf sees them as unbidden gifts. Does the loose-leaf diary invite them? "I can make up situations, but I cannot make up plots," Woolf admits in her October 5 entry. "That is: if I pass the lame girl, I can without knowing I do it, instantly make up a scene. . . . This is the germ of such fictitious gift as I have" (*D* 3: 160). Scenes flourish particularly in the country, which she describes, revealingly, in her June 6 entry as her "freedom from inspection" (*D* 3: 137).

"Some little scenes I meant to write down," she opens her August 21 entry and then preserves hymn singing on the flats on a blazing hot day (*D* 3: 153). "Many scenes have come & gone unwritten" begins her next entry, September 4; "I amuse myself by watching my mind shape scenes" (*D* 3: 153, 154). She then offers two scenes: one of the field at Michelham Priory that dissolves into a quarrel with Leonard; the other set apart as a "Note," like the eleven titled probes of her 1926 diary. Titled "A graveyard scene," this note actually offers two scenes of death. The first occurs close to home, and Woolf views it as an artist. She takes her eight-year-old niece, Angelica, to the churchyard next to Monks House and finds Avery digging a grave, "throwing up heavy showers of the yellow earth," and Mrs. Avery, "immensely fat & florid, . . . sprawling on the edge of the grave, with her small children playing about. They were having tea, & dressed in their reds & blue looked more like a picture, by Millais, or some other Victorian, of life & death, youth & the grave, than any real sight. It was quite unconscious; yet the most deliberate picture making; hence, unreal, sentimental, overdone" (*D* 3: 154).

She follows this rejected actual graveyard scene with a totally imagined watery death scene of her own creation. Her scene-making gift delivers to her whole the unknowable recent death of the German Princess Löwenstein-Wertheim in the Atlantic Ocean as she sought to make the first westbound transatlantic flight. Next day, Woolf opens her diary to confess that solidifying "the vision of the flying Princess into words . . . laid a phantom" to rest that had been "very prominent" before her eyes (*D* 3: 155).

She declares in her next entry, September 20, "One might write a book of short significant separate scenes," for she has just offered another titled scene of life and death (*D* 3: 157). Called "Laughton Place & Philip Ritchie's death," it preserves her response to Ritchie's shocking death at age twenty-eight. She joins house and death because "[t]hese as it happened, synchronised" (*D* 3: 156). She and Leonard arrange to see Laughton Place, the remains of a sixteenth-century moated mansion on the flats, with the thought it might replace Monks House:

> This arranged, & our hopes very high, I opened the Morning Post & read the death of Philip Ritchie. "He cant take houses, poor Philip" I thought. And then the usual procession of images went through my mind. Also, I think for the first time, I felt this death leaves me an elderly laggard; makes me feel I have no right to go on; as if my life were at the expense of his. . . . So the two feelings—about buying the house & his death—fought each other: & sometimes the house won & sometimes death won. (*D* 3: 156)

Woolf seems to hold up for study in this diary the opposing poles of death and life—here as the "shivering fragments" and "discords" she envisioned as her aesthetic in her 1908 diary (*PA* 393). A month later, she takes time to record Jane Wells's funeral: H. G. Wells in his blue overcoat sobbing, Lydia Lopokova weeping, and George Bernard Shaw declaring, "You mustnt cry. Jane is well— Jane is splendid" (*D* 3: 163–64). Earlier, in her much-admired June 30 diary reprise of the solar eclipse, Woolf pictures the whole Earth dead, extinct: "How can I express the darkness?" (*D* 3: 143, 144).

Alongside these many 1927 scenes of death—in answer to them perhaps— are multiple acts of spontaneous creation. Woolf opens her sixth entry, March 14, to record "the conception last night between 12 & one of a new book" (*D* 3: 131). It is *Orlando*, and again we find the blend of Vita, sexual desire, and prose: "For some weeks, since finishing The Lighthouse I have thought myself virgin, passive, blank of ideas. . . . Suddenly between twelve & one I conceived a whole fantasy to be called 'The Jessamy Brides'—why, I wonder?... Sapphism is to be suggested.... I want to embody all those innumerable little ideas & tiny stories which flash into mind at all seasons" (*D* 3: 131).

But she must see *To the Lighthouse* through the Press before she can "touch" *Orlando* (*D* 3: 131), so the Jessamy Brides remain virgin till fall. This diary reveals the porous nature of Woolf's semiprivate diary, memoir, and fictional prose. In her first 1927 entry, Woolf once more justifies her continued diary-writing with the promise: "[O]h yes, I shall write my memoirs out of [these diaries], one of these days" (*D* 3: 125). More than seven months later, diary-memoirs still engage her, for she declares in her September 20 entry: "One of these days, though, I shall sketch here, like a grand historical picture, the outlines of all my friends.... It might be a way of writing the memoirs of one's own times during peoples lifetimes" (*D* 3: 156–57). In the next sentence, however, diary-memoirs become *Orlando*. "It might be a most amusing book. The question is how to do it," she muses. "Vita should be Orlando, a young nobleman" (*D* 3: 157).

Beyond *Orlando*, another work bursts forth in this fecund 1927 diary. Woolf's third entry, February 21, opens, "Why not invent a new kind of play—as for instance

> Woman thinks:...
> He does.
> Organ Plays.
> She writes.
> They say:
> She sings:
> Night speaks:
> They/miss

The entry continues: "I think it must be something in this line—though I cant now see what. Away from facts: free; yet concentrated; prose yet poetry; a novel & a play" (*D* 3: 128).

In the country four months later, the vision emerges further. "[S]uddenly unfolding before me spontaneously," she tells her June 18 entry, "suddenly I rhapsodised (the night L. dined with the apostles) & told over the story of the Moths, which I think I will write very quickly.... Now the moths will I think fill out the skeleton which I dashed in here: the play-poem idea: the idea of some continuous stream, not solely of human thought, but of the ship, the night&c" (*D* 3: 138, 139).

On September 4, 1927, she recalls—or perhaps even rereads—her September 1926 diary, for she writes that she has never forgotten her "vision of a fin rising on a wide blank sea," her first intimation of *The Moths/Waves* (*D* 3: 153). Then she offers one of her profound insights on the writing of lives. "No biographer could possibly guess this important fact about my life in the late summer of 1926"—her vision of a fin on a wide blank sea—"yet biographers pretend they know people" (*D* 3: 153). In fact, her glimpses of works to come are all subterranean, private visions, the diary the sole interface.

But on the surface she must prepare *To the Lighthouse* for the Press. She reverts to her turn-and-turn-about tack to counter projected failure. "If they— the respectables, my friends, advise me against The Lighthouse, I shall write memoirs; have a plan already to get historical manuscripts & write Lives of the Obscure: but why do I pretend I should take advice?" she asks, revealing her self-possession. And she takes further heart from thoughts of travel refreshment: "After a holiday the old ideas will come to me as usual; seeming fresher, more important than ever; & I shall be off again, feeling that extraordinary exhilaration, that ardour & lust of creation."[2]

Like her 1925 diary, which tallies the sales of *Mrs. Dalloway* and *The Common Reader*, the 1927 diary records the mounting sales and triumph of *To the Lighthouse*. The work, in fact, begets a motorcar: a dark blue secondhand Singer. Woolf learns to drive in the country—although she swiftly cedes the wheel to Leonard—and country drives furnish fall diary scenes. A car is more to Woolf than a mere sign of financial ease. It offers *movement*, that vital Woolf need, and new vistas as well. On August 21, Woolf suggests that the car takes her beyond herself: "What I like, or one of the things I like, about motoring is the sense it gives one of lighting accidentally, like a voyager who touches another planet with the tip of his toe, upon scenes which would have gone on, have always gone on, will go on, unrecorded, save for this chance glimpse. Then it seems to me I am allowed to see the heart of the world uncovered for a moment" (*D* 3: 153). Her August 10 entry suggests that motoring creates the traits she likes in her diary: "We spin off . . . as light & easy as a hawk in the air" (*D* 3: 151).

Vita, too, remains a liberating diversion. "[W]ith so much Vita & Knole & staying away: we have launched ourselves a little more freely perhaps from work & the Press," Woolf acknowledges in her second entry, February 12 (*D* 3: 127). Her loose-leaf diary offers similar increased freedom to court separate traces and fancy. While the diary records first vestiges of *Orlando* and *The Waves*, Woolf simultaneously, offhandedly, fulfills her September 20 diary promise to "sketch here, like a grand historical picture, the outlines of all my friends" (D 3: 156–57). The 1927 diary offers a gallery of Bloomsbury portraits: Bloomsbury at midlife.

Vanessa appears in what now seems to be a recurring diary role. Woolf ends her 1927 diary in the manner of her 1921 and 1922 diaries. That is, she trumpets happiness in one entry and then tempers it in the next. "Yes, I repeat, a very happy, a singularly happy autumn," she crows near the end of her December 20 entry, only to add a more somber closing to her diary two days later: "I just open this for a moment . . . to enter a severe reprimand of myself to myself. . . . I am meretricious. mediocre; a humbug; am getting into the habit of flashy talk. . . . So easily might I become a hare brained egotistic woman, exacting compliments, arrogant, narrow, withered. Nessa's children (I always measure myself against her, & find her much the largest, most humane of the two of us[)]" (D 3: 168). Vanessa remains the measure—and the discipline.

On the one hand, *To the Lighthouse* appears to help Woolf accept her childless state. Thinking of Vanessa's children in her December 20 entry (as she did at the close of her 1922 diary), Woolf tells her diary: "And yet oddly enough I scarcely want children of my own now. This insatiable desire to write something before I die, this ravaging sense of the shortness & feverishness of life, make me cling, like a man on a rock, to my one anchor. I don't like the physicalness of having children of one's own. This occurred to me at Rodmell; but I never wrote it down" (D 3: 167).

The "insatiable desire to write" dominates the 1927 diary, a diary that should be seen as a reservoir, a nurturing holding tank for literary works that spurts forth scenes in profligate profusion, a holding pond teeming with life (and death) while she kicks up her heels abroad and at home. The loose-leaf diary becomes a tool both to admit and to avoid death: Woolf depicts death in scene after scene but also finesses a bound diary book's final page.

Across the year she again uses her diary for multiple aims. On June 6, emerging from a week in bed "with a sudden & very sharp headache," Woolf turns to her diary "to test [her] brain" (D 3: 136). She uses her diary again and again to envision her work, and in September she turns to it to calm her teeming mind: "[T]o soothe these whirlpools, I write here" (D 3: 155). At the end of the year, she takes up her diary not only to soothe but also to restrain her gushing mind. The unwilled, spontaneous rush of Woolf's creativity emerges again and again across the new loose-leaf 1927 diary as she amuses herself "watching [her] mind shape scenes" (D 3: 154). Metaphors of passion mix with the continued flood of water tropes[3] as she preserves the "ardour & lust of creation" (D 3: 129).

Katherine Mansfield's 1927 *Journal*

"I've been reading Katherine Mansfield with a mixture of sentiment and horror," Virginia Woolf ends a letter to Vita Sackville-West dated August 5, 1927. "What odd friends I've had—you and she—" (*L* #1796, 3: 408). She refers to the first version of Mansfield's *Journal*, just published by Mansfield's husband, John Middleton Murry. At last, Woolf might have thought, she now could read the "diary" Mansfield promised to send her in 1920, the diary she recalled instantly in 1923 in the shock of Mansfield's death. To hold the actual diary sent personally to her would have been more intimate. Now the 1927 published *Journal* must suffice.

Today we understand more fully why Mansfield never sent Woolf her "diary." Mansfield's illness offers one excuse; her general aloofness from humankind supplies another.[4] Mansfield was keeping a commercial engagement diary in 1920 that she might have sent to Woolf; however, it included only brief daily entries from December 29, 1919, through February 13, 1920 (a mere month and a half), five entries in April, and one in July. It was, in short, a dying diary.

Those who have studied the mass of manuscript material that came to the Alexander Turnbull Library in Wellington, New Zealand, following Murry's 1957 death, have penetrated the artful, scented mist Murry formed from Mansfield's papers. In point of fact, Mansfield kept exercise books: fifty-three surviving "notebooks" along with more than one hundred unbound pages of further "notes."[5] Among these notebooks are just four stationer's diaries, "pocket diaries" (as biographer Ian Gordon describes them) for the years 1914, 1915, 1920, and 1922 (*Katherine Mansfield* 30). Murry crafted his 1927 *Journal of Katherine Mansfield*, his 1939 *Scrapbook of Katherine Mansfield*, and his 1954 enlarged, so-called definitive, *Journal of Katherine Mansfield* from this mass of material left him at Mansfield's death.

For the first *Journal*, published in 1927, Murray combined many of the genuine diary entries with story fragments, poems, titled and untitled reflections, and unposted letters from the notebooks and unbound papers—most of these items undated. Although readers must be grateful for Murry's devotion and skill in transcribing Mansfield's almost illegible hand, the 1927 *Journal* is astonishingly unreliable and self-serving.[6] It also serves Mansfield in a misguided way, for it projects an image of a pure soul, a saintly suffering mystic, that in the full spread of her notebooks and papers proves simple, sentimental, and false. Margaret Scott rightly titled her transcription of the full material *The Katherine Mansfield Notebooks* when she published it in 1997.

Murry's 1927 *Journal of Katherine Mansfield* belongs then among the fictive diaries—belongs with Lady Charlotte Bury's *Diary of a Lady-in-Waiting*, which Woolf read in 1908, Barbellion's *Journal of a Disappointed Man*, which she read in 1920, and the diaries of Anaïs Nin—for as several critics have noted, Mansfield only intermittently kept a journal in the way Woolf did or in the manner of most diarists: that is, as a sequence of dated entries in one or more discrete books.[7] Discredited and supplanted today by the *Notebooks*, Murry's 1927 *Journal of Katherine Mansfield* stands as a curious yet brilliant monument to reputation-making, to a husband's mythologizing a dead wife.

But Woolf likely knew nothing of this in 1927. Like everyone else, she thought she was reading Mansfield's journal. In fact, the text she read foregrounded many of the experiences and passions the two writers shared and so may have renewed Woolf's "queer sense of being 'like'" the younger writer—as she wrote in her 1920 diary (*D* 2: 45).

The 1927 *Journal* highlights Mansfield's loss of a beloved brother, a blow Woolf knew too well. Leslie Beauchamp's death early in the Great War leads to a shift in Mansfield's diary audience and purpose that assists her public prose. This shift anticipates Woolf's 1919 shift as she enters her own mature, modernist phase. "Dear brother, as I jot these notes, I am speaking to you," Mansfield writes in a notebook entry dated February 14, 1916 (just as Woolf will project and talk to Elderly Virginia): "To whom did I always write when I kept those huge complaining diaries? Was it to myself? But now as I write these words and talk of getting down to the New Zealand atmosphere, I see you opposite to me, I see your thoughtful, seeing eyes. Yes, it is to you. . . . It is with you that I see, and that is why I see so clearly. . . . However often I write and rewrite I shall not really falter, dearest, and the book shall be written and ready."[8]

Beyond a lost brother, Mansfield's 1927 *Journal* also reveals her recoil from society, disgust Woolf sometimes shares. "I have nothing to say to 'charming' women," Mansfield writes in a March 1914 diary entry at age twenty-five. "I feel like a cat among tigers" (*Journal* 10). Five days later, when Murry speaks of parties with pleasure, Mansfield writes: "I nearly groaned. . . . I've done with [society], and can't combat it at all now. I had so much rather lean idly over the bridge and watch the boats and the free, unfamiliar people and feel the wind blow. No, I hate society" (*Journal* 12). More than a year after reading Mansfield's *Journal*, Woolf adopts (and transforms) Mansfield's bridge trope for her own October 27, 1928, diary entry: "A scandal, a scandal, to let so much time slip, & I leaning on the Bridge watching it go. Only leaning has not been my pose: running up & down, irritably, excitedly restlessly. And the stream viciously eddying. Why do I write these metaphors?" (*D* 3: 199). Because she soaks up others' diaries.[9]

Mansfield's 1927 *Journal* also offers acute thoughts on women. An undated, untitled notebook item Murry titles "Travelling Alone," and places in 1915, seeks to answer a question:

> Was it simply her own imagination, or could there be any truth in this feeling that waiters—waiters especially and hotel servants—adopted an impertinent, arrogant and slightly amused attitude towards a woman who traveled alone? Was it just her wretched female self-consciousness? No, she really did not think it was. For even when she was feeling at her happiest, at her freest, she would become aware, quite suddenly, of the "tone" of the waiter or the hotel servant. And it was extraordinary how it wrecked her sense of security, how it made her feel that something malicious was being plotted against her and that everybody and everything—yes, even to inanimate objects like chairs or tables—was secretly "in the know," waiting for that ominous infallible thing to happen to her, which always did happen, which was bound to happen, to every woman on earth who traveled alone![10]

In an undated and untitled fragment that Murry dates May 1919 and titles "The Angel of Mercy," Mansfield describes a housemaid who "had to leave because her husband 'didn't want her to work no more' and, to consolidate his authority, had punched her so hard in the neck that she had a great red swelling under ear."[11]

Woolf may have been most struck, however, by Mansfield's 1922 analysis of her doctor, Bernard Hudson: "Off his guard, speaking of Miss S_____ he declared, 'Well, the fact is she is not normal. And anyone who is not normal I call *mad*. She is unconventional, that is to say, and people who are that are no good to anyone except themselves.' When he said 'mad,' a look came into his eyes—a flash of power—and he swung the stethoscope, then picked up my fan and rattled it open."[12] Dr. Hudson supplies another real-life model (with Beatrice Webb's Professor Marshall) for Professor von X of *A Room of One's Own*. Dr. Hudson swings his stethoscope while Professor von X is "labouring under some emotion that made him jab his pen on the paper as if he were killing some noxious insect as he wrote" (31). Hudson "is a man to remember," Mansfield's January 18, 1922, entry stresses: "One must remember, too, his extraordinary insecurity. The world rocks under him, and it's only when he has that stethoscope that he can lay down the law. *Then* lay it down he does. . . . And you hear pride in his voice; you hear the unspoken" (*Journal* 221, 222). After introducing Professor von X with his jabbing pen, Woolf goes on to describe his insecurity, his inferiority complex, which motivates his anger at women.

Mansfield turns to nature, just as Woolf does, in her recoil from society and its disdain for women. "The lovely world (God, how lovely the external world is!) is there and I bathe in it and am refreshed" Mansfield exclaims in a May 1919 item.[13] The 1927 *Journal* shows Mansfield's love of birds and shifting light—so like Woolf's. "I am getting all *my* spring out of the sunsets," Mansfield ends a March 1914 diary entry (*Journal* 10). In an undated item in the unbound papers that Murry dates December 1915, she writes, "Every moment the light changes. Even as I write, it is no longer hard.... And now a purple colour, very menacing and awful, is pulling over the sky. The trees tumble about in the unsteady light," reminding us of Woolf's own aesthetic of changing light given in a passage on sunsets in her 1899 Warboys diary (*Journal* 40).[14] Mansfield's January 1, 1922, diary entry ends: "I want to remember how the light fades from a room—and one fades with it, is *expunged*...." (*Journal* 210).[15]

Woolf could not help reading Mansfield's *Journal* as many have read *her* diary: as a life unfolding in the shadow of death. Murry invites this reading, for he crafts the 1927 *Journal* as a diary of illness. Had he wished, he could have started the 1927 *Journal* with the first dated diary entry available to him in the notebooks: Mansfield at age fifteen. This charming robust entry, with its nature personification (like those in Woolf's 1899 Warboys diary at age seventeen) betrays no sign of ruptured health. Murry, in fact, passed over *all* the teenage diary entries available to him: eighteen dated entries from March 30, 1907, to December 21, 1908, that begin with observations on "poses" (*Notebooks* 1: 99); and twenty more entries in a separate travel diary Mansfield kept of her 1907 Urewera camping trip at age nineteen, to which she added seven more dated diary entries.

But Woolf saw none of Mansfield's teenage diary. Instead, like other readers, she read the 1910 Camille-like entry Murry chose to start the *Journal*:

> *June.* It is at last over, this wearisome day, and dusk is beginning to sift in among the branches of the drenched chestnut tree. I think I must have caught cold in my beautiful exultant walk yesterday, for today I am ill. I began to work but could not.[16]

The 1927 *Journal* closes twelve years later with Mansfield's acceptance of her pain and coming death with the final words "*All is well*" (255; emphasis Mansfield's). In reality, her final (1922) diary ends with her carefully kept financial records and the more sophisticated observation in German: "For everyone sees and presents things differently, in his own way" (*Notebooks* 2: 330–31; n301).

In between "today I am ill" and *"All is well,"* the *Journal* unfolds as a diary of creeping disease. In an undated item in the unbound papers (which Murry dates February 1918) Mansfield records the fatigue and "blankness" Woolf described as part of a miniature nervous breakdown in her 1926 diary "note" "My own Brain." "What happens is that I come in absolutely exhausted, lie down, sit up and sit in a daze of fatigue—a horrible state—until 7 o'clock," Mansfield writes. "I can barely walk—can't think. . . . I am simply a blank" (*Journal* 76). In 1920, Mansfield starts to hear voices. After working nearly fifteen hours to finish a story, she writes from Casetta in a January entry: "In the sea drowned souls sang all night. . . . These are the worst days of my whole life."[17] From a nursing home in Mentone, France, her February 1, 1920, entry ends: "At night *old Casetta* feelings, like madness."[18]

Thoughts of suicide and death pervade the 1927 *Journal* long before Mansfield's final illness. Her brother's death in 1915 effects a shift not only in her notebook audience and professional prose but also in her attitude toward death. "I welcome the idea of death," she writes in an item in her unbound papers dated October 29, 1915. "I believe in immortality because he is not here, and I long to join him. First, my darling, I've got things to do for both of us, and then I will come as quickly as I can."[19] She continues the thought in the undated next item headed "Brother":

> I think I have known for a long time that life was over for me. . . . Yes, though he is lying in the middle of a little wood in France and I am still walking upright and feeling the sun and the wind from the sea, I am just as much dead as he is. The present and the future mean nothing to me. I am no longer "curious" about people; I do not wish to go anywhere; and the only possible value that anything can have for me is that it should put me in mind of something that happened or was when he[20] was alive. . . . Then why don't I commit suicide? Because I feel I have a duty to perform to the lovely time when we were both alive. I want to write about it, and he wanted me to. (*Journal* 38)

Four years later, Mansfield continues to find motive for life in her work. "Life without *work*—I would commit suicide," she writes in an item Murry dates June 10, 1919—although it follows a November 10, 1919, item in the *Notebooks*.[21]

With items from late 1919 and 1920, Murry portrays Mansfield's drive to transform suffering and death. He invents the title "Death" for the opening item in Notebook 26 (although it bears the title "The Walking Stick").[22] In this item, Mansfield describes a dream of her "whole body *breaking up*": "It slowly dawned upon me—the conviction that in that dream I died. . . . The *spirit* that is the enemy of death and quakes so and is so tenacious was shaken out of me. I am (December 15, 1919) a dead woman, and *I don't care.* It might comfort others to know that one gives up caring; but they'd not believe any more than I did until it happened. And, oh, how strong was its hold upon me! How I *adored* life and *dreaded* death!"[23]

A year later, in an item in the unbound papers Mansfield titles "Suffering" and signs with her name and the date December 19, 1920, she declares:

> I should like this to be accepted as my confession.
> There is no limit to human suffering. When one thinks: "Now I have touched the bottom of the sea—now I can go no deeper," one goes deeper. And so it is for ever. . . . Suffering is boundless, it is eternity. . . .
> I do not want to die without leaving a record of my belief that suffering can be overcome. For I do believe it. What must one do? There is no question of what is called "passing beyond it." This is false.
> One must *submit.* Do not resist. Take it. Be overwhelmed. Accept it fully. Make it *part of life.*
> Everything in life that we really accept undergoes a change. So suffering must become Love. This is the mystery.[24]

Amid this painful struggle with illness and death, Woolf found confirmed her greatest affinity with Mansfield: their shared passion for their art.[25] The 1927 *Journal* is a writer's notebook, like Woolf's own diary-in-progress. In an item in the unbound papers dated May 19, 1919, Mansfield declares: "I really only ask for time to write it all—time to write my books. Then I don't mind dying. I live to write" (*Journal* 104). She again asks herself in an undated item headed "Work" that Murry dates May 31, 1919: "Shall I be able to express one day my love of work—my desire to be a better writer—my longing to take greater pains. And the passion I feel. It takes the place of religion—it *is* my religion—of people— I create my people: of 'life': it *is* Life" (*Journal* 112). Woolf perhaps would own *some* of these drives, although at this time she is carefully probing the *differences* between life and art.

In the last year of her life, Mansfield tells her January 1922 diary, "There is no feeling to be compared with the feeling of having written and finished a story," and she writes in the 1927 *Journal*'s last item: "Then I want to *work.* At what? I want so to live that I work with my hands and my feeling and my brain. I want a garden, a small house, grass, animals, books, pictures, music. And out of this, the expression of this, I want to be writing" (*Journal* 217, 254–55). Woolf quotes these words in her review (*E* 4: 448).

In a fascinating undated and untitled notebook item that Murry dates December 1919, Mansfield describes something like Woolf's "scene-making" gift, a faculty intensified by illness (in Mansfield's case, at least). "It often happens to me now that when I lie down to sleep at night, instead of getting drowsy, I feel more wakeful and, lying here in bed, I begin to *live* over either scenes from real life or imaginary scenes," Mansfield explains:

> It's not too much to say they are almost hallucinations: they are marvel-lously vivid. I lie on my right side and put my left hand up to my forehead as though I were praying. This seems to induce the state. . . . All these things are far realer, more in detail, *richer* than life. And I believe I could go on until . . . There's *no end* to it.
>
> I can do this about everything. . . . I could always do this to a certain extent; but it's only since I was really ill that this—shall we call it?— "consolation prize" has been given to me. My God! it's a marvellous thing.[26]

This passage may have prompted Woolf's own autumn diary scenes. How suggestible Woolf is!

Mansfield reread her notebooks—as did Woolf.[27] Her exercise books served many uses that Woolf's own diary serves. Mansfield used her notebooks for writing warm-up. The fifth item Murry offers in the *Journal* is a sentence Mansfield copied from another writer followed by her words, "That's the sort of strain—not for what it says and means, but for the 'lilt' of it—that sets me writing" (4). Notebook "talk" also helped her to ease into public prose. In an item likely written on July 14, 1921, Mansfield records a dialogue with herself:

> I don't want to write anything. It's grey; it's heavy and dull. And short stories seem unreal and not worth doing. I don't want to write; I want to *live*. What does she mean by that? It's not easy to say. But there you are!
>
> Queer, this habit of mine of being garrulous. And I don't mean that any eye but mine should read this. This is—*really private*. And I must say—nothing affords me the same relief. What happens as a rule is, if I go on long enough, I *break through*.[28]

Four months later, the sole item of Notebook 6, dated November 13, 1921, begins (like Beatrice Webb): "It is time I started a new journal. Come, my unseen, my unknown, let us talk together" (*Journal* 199). Woolf quotes these words in her review (*E* 4: 446).

Mansfield also used her notebooks, as Woolf does, to ask questions of her art. "What is it that stirs one so?" she asks herself in a May 1922 item from Paris. "What is this seeking—so joyful—ah, so gentle! And there seems to be a moment when all is to be discovered."[29] In an earlier notebook entry dated February 13, 1916, the questions are: "Why do I hesitate so long [to write]? Is it just idleness? Lack of will-power? Yes, I feel that's what it is, and that's why it's so immensely important that I should assert myself" (*Journal* 45). Two years later, in an untitled note Murry titles "The Eternal Question," Mansfield confesses: "I pose myself, yet once more, *my* Eternal Question. What is it that makes the moment of delivery so difficult for me? . . . And don't I want to write them? Lord! Lord! it's my only desire—my one *happy issue*" (*Journal* 94).

Like Woolf, Mansfield sees egotism as a barrier to her art. "I am a *sham*," she berates herself in a February 1922 diary entry, a sentiment Woolf repeats in her 1927 diary's final disciplining entry. "I am also an egoist of the deepest dye— such a one that it was very difficult to confess to it in case this book should be found," Mansfield continues. "Even my being well is a kind of occasion for *vanity*. There is nothing worse for the soul than egoism" (*Journal* 229). Mansfield also turns to her notebooks to record her work. "I must keep this book so that I have a record of what I do each week," she writes near the close of that sole notebook entry dated November 13, 1921—ironic words, for the empty pages that follow lay bare the truth that she often failed to fulfill her plans.[30] One of the last items in the 1922 diary is a list of three completed stories and fourteen unwritten ones. Of the latter, Murry reports, only one, "The Fly," was written.[31]

Like Woolf, Mansfield worked out problems in her professional prose in the pages of her notebooks. "To-day I began to write, seriously, *The Weak Heart*,—a story which fascinates me *deeply*," she writes November 21, 1921. "What I feel it needs so peculiarly is a very subtle variation of 'tense' from the present to the past and back again—and softness, lightness, and the feeling that all is in bud, with a play of humour over the character of Ronnie. And the feeling of the Thorndon Baths, the wet, moist, oozy . . . no, I know how it must be done" (*Journal* 200).

Mansfield used her notebooks more directly (and fully) than Woolf as a literal practice ground for her fiction. In an item Murry places in 1920, Mansfield writes: "Let me remember when I write about that fiddle how it runs up lightly and swings down sorrowful; how it *searches*—" (*Journal* 173). Woolf quotes this in her review (*E* 4: 447). Mansfield's January 22, 1922, diary entry repeats the pattern: "*Lumbago*. . . . I must remember it when I write about an old man. The start to get up—the pause—the look of fury—and how, lying at night, one seems to get *locked*. To move is an agony; till finally one discovers a movement which is possible. But that helpless feeling about with the legs first!" (*Journal* 224). Two weeks later she exclaims to her diary: "And my sciatica! Put it on record, in case it ever goes, what a pain it is. Remember to give it to someone in a story one day" (*Journal* 230). The *Notebooks* exude story fragments: life and art intermingle chaotically, for Mansfield (unlike Woolf) makes no effort to distinguish between the two.[32]

Woolf may have noted further differences between her own diary and Mansfield's *Journal*—as well as the many parallels. Mansfield was six years younger than Woolf and in the *Journal* she again and again yearns for children—sometimes for a boy, sometimes for a girl—deep desires Woolf now seeks to lay aside. An undated notebook item that Murry places in 1919 offers a scene between a woman (Mansfield?) and her doctor: "But what would he have said if I'd told him that until a few days ago I had had a little child, aged five and three-quarters, of indeterminate sex? Some days it was a boy. For two years now it had very often been a little girl" (*Journal* 136–37). This passage may have inspired *Orlando*'s gender switch, first articulated in Woolf's diary on October 5, 1927. While the two writers mutually revered Shakespeare, Mansfield's passion for Chekhov passed all bounds. "I want to adopt a Russian baby, call him Anton, and bring him up as mine, with K[oteliansky]. for a godfather and Mme. Tchehov for a godmother. Such is my dream," Mansfield writes in her January 12, 1922, diary, displaying her bald wish for literary lineage (*Journal* 218).

Her next words, "I don't feel so sinful this day as I did, because I have written something," reveal another difference in the two writers' notebooks: Mansfield's religious bent, likely one source of the "horror" with which Woolf read the *Journal* (218). In the next month, Mansfield again treats story failures as sins and bad faith: "To do anything, to be anything, one must gather oneself together and 'one's faith make stronger.' . . . But remember *The Daughters* [*of the Late Colonel*] was written at Mentone in November when I was not so bad as usual. I was trying with all my soul to be good. Here I try and fail, and the fact of consciousness makes each separate failure very important—each a *sin*" (*Journal* 229). After telling herself how to write "The Weak Heart" in November 1921, Mansfield exclaims, "Lord, make me crystal clear for thy light to shine through!"[33]

In August 1927, awash in spontaneous invention, Woolf could hardly fail to note Mansfield's greater creative pain. Despair at her failure to write is one of

Mansfield's habitual *Journal* themes. "I've decided to tear up everything that I've written and start again," she confesses in an April 1914 diary entry at age twenty-five. "If I could write with my old fluency for *one day*, the spell would be broken" (*Journal* 12). Two days later, she asserts: "Nothing that isn't satirical is really true for me to write just now. If I try to find things lovely, I turn pretty-pretty. And at the same time I am so frightened of writing mockery for satire that my pen hovers and won't settle" (*Journal* 13). Woolf reads this as she is about to launch the satiric *Orlando*.

In an undated notebook entry that Murry dates May 1914, Mansfield cries, "I long and long to write, and the words just won't come," and in November she records: "But the book to be written is still unwritten. I can't sit down and fire away like J [Murry]." (*Journal* 14, 16). And even with "Prelude" and a measure of fame behind her, she despairs in July 1921: "Look at the stories that wait and wait just at the threshold. Why don't I let them in? And their place would be taken by others who are lurking beyond just out there—waiting for the chance" (*Journal* 185). Woolf quotes some of this in her review.

Again four months later comes the biblical wail: "Why do ye tarry? Ah, why indeed? My deepest desire is to be a writer, to have 'a body of work' done. And there the work is, there the stories wait for me, *grow tired*, wilt, fade, because I will not come. And I hear and I *acknowledge* them, and still I go on sitting at the window, playing with the ball of wool."[34] Mansfield's perfectionism caused her to castigate herself even in these years of impressive output: 1920 and 1921. Woolf sees this and may have marked gratefully her own greater creative flow.

And was Woolf hurt that her name appears nowhere in the published 1927 *Journal*? Was she especially pained at her omission from Mansfield's January 20, 1922, diary sentence: "I suppose it is the effect of isolation that I can truly say I think of [Walter] de la Mare, Tchehov, Koteliansky, [H. M.] Tomlinson, Lawrence, [A. R.] Orage, every day. They are part of my life" (*Journal* 223)? These words bolster Woolf's sense of Mansfield's cooler regard. She would have been further struck to learn that, for reasons of his own, Murry added D. H. Lawrence's name to Mansfield's list (*Notebooks* 2: 318).

Whatever her deepest response to the 1927 *Journal*—perhaps "sentiment and horror," as she writes to Vita—Woolf displays generosity in her September 10, 1927, *Nation & Athenaeum* review. In her opening, she merely lifts an elegant eyebrow as she passes swiftly over Murry's snub of her in the *Journal's* introduction and his oddly nebulous claim that as an artist Mansfield was *hors concours* (beyond competition). Declaring that *The Garden Party* established

Mansfield "as the most remarkable short-story writer of her generation in England," Murry continued:

> It is noticeable, however, that the most whole-hearted admiration her work has received comes preeminently from the most distinguished short-story writers we have in England—H. G. Wells, John Galsworthy, Walter de la Mare, H. M. Tomlinson, Stacy Aumonier, Barry Pain, Ethel Colburn Mayne. These practitioners of the art, with one voice, salute her as *hors concours*, though they find it as difficult as any critic to say wherein her superiority consists. (*Journal* xiii, xiv–v)

Woolf implies a different view in her review's opening by simply quoting Murry's words back at him: "The most distinguished writers of short stories in England are agreed, says Mr Murry, that as a writer of short stories Katherine Mansfield was *hors concours*. No one has succeeded her, and no critic has been able to define her quality. But the reader of her journal is well content to let such questions be" (*E* 4: 446).

Instead, in this review titled "A Terribly Sensitive Mind," Woolf offers her own estimate of Mansfield's gifts. "It is not the quality of her writing or the degree of her fame that interest us in her diary," she continues, carefully distinguishing her focus, "but the spectacle of a mind—a terribly sensitive mind—receiving one after another the haphazard impressions of . . . life" (*E* 4: 446). Woolf takes her review's title and theme from Mansfield's own 1922 diary words: "I have a terribly sensitive mind which receives every impression, and that is the reason why I am so carried away *and* borne under."[35] Woolf, of course, harbored keen senses herself and had noted Mansfield's radar long before she read this *Journal* confirmation. "Her senses are amazingly acute," Woolf had observed in her own 1920 diary in the entry that reported that Mansfield "will send me her diary. . . . Will she? If I were left to myself I should; being the simpler, the more direct of the two" (*D* 2: 62).[36]

Mansfield's "diary was a mystical companion," an outlet for talk, Woolf goes on to declare in her review (*E* 4: 446–47). Then, drawing on the phrase she had used to sum up John Evelyn's diary in 1920, she again bows to diaries' accretive force: "But then as the scraps accumulate," Woolf writes, "we find ourselves giving them, or more probably receiving from Katherine Mansfield herself, a direction" (*E* 4: 447). The direction is rather an impression: the impression that Mansfield is "a born writer" (*E* 4: 447).

This is high praise, and Woolf adds to it the suggestion that Mansfield's passion for their "precious art" even surpassed her own. "No one felt more seriously the importance of writing than she did," Woolf declares. "In all the pages of her journal, instinctive, rapid as they are, her attitude to her work is admirable; sane, caustic and austere" (*E* 4: 448). Woolf praises Mansfield's *Journal* for traits her own diary lacks. "There is no literary gossip; no vanity; no jealousy," she continues. "Although during her last years she must have been aware of her success she makes no allusion to it" (*E* 4: 448).

Woolf repeatedly notes the fragmentary nature of the 1927 *Journal*, fragments, however, in Woolf's view, nearly coalescing into art: "Everything she feels and hears and sees is not fragmentary and separate; it belongs together as writing. . . . In all this we seem to be in the midst of unfinished stories; here is a beginning; here an end. They only need a loop of words thrown round them to be complete."[37] Woolf closes her review with a final raised eyebrow regarding the end Murry gives to the 1927 *Journal*; however, again she replaces her doubts with more generous hopes. "The diary ends with the words 'All is well,'" she writes. "And since she died three months later it is tempting to think that the words stood for some conclusion which illness and the intensity of her own nature drove her to find at an age when most of us are loitering easily among those appearances and impressions, those amusements and sensations, which none had loved better than she" (*E* 4: 448).

Perhaps Woolf saw her review as a chance to pay public tribute to this valued friend and fellow artist. "I have the feeling that I shall think of her at intervals all through life," she told her diary on January 16, 1923, when she first recorded Mansfield's death (*D* 2: 227). Perhaps Woolf also pays tribute because this *Journal* offered useful matter for her own work. In the third item in the 1927 *Journal*, Mansfield quotes from and then comments caustically on Dorothy Wordsworth's *Journal*, a diary Woolf will take up herself (and defend) in 1929.[38]

And as Woolf mulls her own next work, *Orlando*, in August 1927, she reads these words from an untitled, undated notebook item Murry titles "Love" and dates August 1921: "We are neither male nor female. We are a compound of both. I choose the male who will develop and expand the male in me; he chooses me to expand the female in him. Being made 'whole'" (*Journal* 191). Thus, beyond its report of an imaginary child who changes gender, Mansfield's 1927 *Journal* offers this endorsement of androgyny as well.

Passages in the *Journal* also resonate uncannily with Woolf's own growing ideas for *The Waves*.[39] In a kind of manifesto signed "K. M." and dated January 22, 1916, Mansfield anticipates Woolf's 1927 desire for a new kind of prose poem: "I feel always trembling on the brink of poetry. . . . But especially I want to write a kind of long elegy to you [her dead brother] . . . perhaps not in poetry. Nor perhaps in prose. Almost certainly in a kind of *special prose*."[40] In an untitled, undated item Murry titles "The Glimpse" and places in February 1920, Mansfield writes in a notebook separate from her 1920 diary:

> And yet one has these "glimpses," before which all that one ever has written...—all (yes, all) that one ever has read, pales.... The waves, as I drove home this afternoon, and the high foam, how it was suspended in the air before it fell.... What is it that happens in that moment of suspension? It is timeless. In that moment (what *do* I mean?) the whole life of the soul is contained. One is flung up—out of life—one is "held," and then,—down, bright, broken, glittering on to the rocks, tossed back, part of the ebb and flow. (*Journal* 150)

Here is a "glimpse" not of a fin but of the waves.

Mansfield's *Journal* reinforced Woolf's own sense of time's evanescence. "I am pursued by time myself," Mansfield declares in a January 1922 diary entry, words Woolf herself will repeat in 1928 (*Journal* 221). Mansfield writes in a 1914 notebook: "It is as though God opened his hand and let you dance on it a little, and then shut it up tight—so tight that you could not even cry" (*Journal* 6).

The 1927 *Journal* even offers a word (and idea) Woolf will take forward for *Three Guineas*. In an undated notebook item Murry dates October 1922, Mansfield writes: "It is of immense importance to learn to *laugh at ourselves*. What Shestov calls 'a touch of easy familiarity and derision' has its value" (*Journal* 248). In her 1938 *Three Guineas*, Woolf makes "derision" one of the "teachers" one should never desert (78). In so doing, she bows to Mansfield and her *Journal*. And perhaps as suggestive as Mansfield's visions of androgyny and her glimpses of the waves and of a "special prose" were her *Journal* words and the very picture the *Journal* paints of a "born writer" wandering, nomadic with neither money nor a room of her own. In an item Murry dates October 1921, Mansfield once more berates herself for pride. "This interferes very much with work," she declares. "And anything that I write in this mood will be no good; it will be full of *sediment*" (*Journal* 198). Here Mansfield describes impediments to what Woolf in her review calls "the crystal clearness which is needed if one is to write truthfully"—the sediment-free, impediment-free "incandescent mind" Woolf will extol in *A Room of One's Own* (*E* 4: 448; 59).

Yet, like Judith Shakespeare, how far Mansfield stood from achieving this state! Mansfield declares in her first diary entry of 1915: "For this year I have two wishes: to write, to make money. Consider. With money we could go away as we liked, have a room in London, be as free as we liked, and be independent and proud with nobodies. It is only poverty that holds us so tightly" (*Journal* 18). Part of the "Eternal Question" of her failure to write in 1918 is the complaint "I haven't a place to write in or on," and a 1921 item reprises: "But I bitterly long for a little private room where I can work undisturbed."[41] *A Room of One's Own* may be Woolf's private gift to Katherine Mansfield.

9

Artist at a Crossroads

Virginia Woolf's second diary stage opens to answer a crisis. It closes at a crossroads, another "crucial point." Her 1928 diary book reveals an artist at a juncture: "some uneasy sense, of change," Woolf writes in her first entry (*D* 3: 174). *Orlando*'s completion and surprise success dominates the 1928 diary. However, the problem, as she writes in November, is what to write next. The artistic crossroads she faces involves nonfiction versus fiction, the external and the internal, a possible new combination, and the will to explore.

Her loose-leaf diary experiment ends with the first 1929 diary, the final diary in Woolf's second, lean modernist stage. If *Orlando* unfurled across the 1928 diary, then the first 1929 diary resounds with *A Room of One's Own*. However, Woolf readies herself at the same time for her coming attack on *The Waves*. She will need all her courage as she lets herself down into her mind, begins "a time of adventure & attack, rather lonely & painful" (*D* 3: 219). But her diary continues to help her; in fact, she moves at the end to give it even firmer life in a bound diary book.

Virginia Woolf's 1928 Diary

> *"And what remains of Eddy is now in some ways more vivid, though more transparent, all of him composing itself in my mind, all I could get of him, & making itself a landscape appropriate to it; making a work of art for itself."*
>
> (August 8, 1928; *D* 3: 189)

The reflective year of an artist at a crossroads emerges from the 1928 diary. Gone today is the cover of this large diary book, ripped away, perhaps, in 1940 when the bombs dropped on Woolf's London home. Woolf continues the loose-leaf format of the 1927 diary, down to its white pages with their printed pink margin line.[1] Thirty entries preserve the 336 days from January 17 to December 18, 1928, the leanest diary in entry number of the 1920s.

This diary opens on a note of dispersal, death, and despair. Woolf turns to her diary for comfort—for Bloomsbury scatters this day. Vanessa and Duncan are off to France; Clive and Quentin to Germany, with Vita soon to follow. Woolf records their exits and then recalls Thomas Hardy's recent funeral, her words famously reprised in composer Dominick Argento's 1975 Pulitzer Prize–winning song cycle *From the Diary of Virginia Woolf*. "Over all this broods for me, some uneasy sense, of change," she closes this first entry, "& mortality, & how partings are deaths; & then a sense of my own fame—why should this come over me?—& then of its remoteness . . . & a sense of the futility of it all" (*D* 3: 174).

Twenty-four days pass before her next entry, February 11, which picks up the thread of despair. "The futility of it all—so I broke off," she writes, "& have indeed been feeling that rather persistently, or perhaps I should have written here. Hardy & Meredith together sent me torpid to bed with headache. I know the feeling now, when I can't spin a sentence, & sit mumbling & turning; & nothing flits by my brain which is as a blank window" (*D* 3: 174). The male voice has chilled her once more. Lord Sackville also has died on January 28, leaving Vita bereft, not just of a father but also of Knole.

Once more Woolf turns to work, to art, to answer death. She must finish *Orlando*, who never dies, who never loses her estate. In this second entry, Woolf admits to "hacking rather listlessly" at the book's last chapter (*D* 3: 175). She hopes for a "fresh wind" and misses "the fun, which was so tremendously lively all October, November & December" (*D* 3: 175). She opens her diary on March 18 to announce the book's finish the day before and confesses, "Since February I have been a little clouded with headache, had a touch of influenza; & so . . . all energy turned to forcing my book along, have not written here" (*D* 3: 177).

She has rushed to finish *Orlando* before her March 26 departure with Leonard for three weeks motoring in France. "Anyhow the canvas is covered," she sighs in this fourth diary entry. "There will be three months of close work needed, imperatively, before it can be printed; for I have scrambled & splashed, & the canvas shows through in a thousand places. . . . I have written this book quicker than any. . . . I feel more & more sure that I will never write a novel again" (*D* 3: 176, 177).

She returns from France to find *Orlando* "to tell the truth, damned rough" (*D* 3: 180). Her important April 21 entry reveals a surprise change in her artistic standards, which she seems to relax for this work. "I vow I wont spend longer at Orlando, which is a freak," she declares, suggesting she sees the work as separate from her regular art. "[I]t shall come out in September, though the perfect artist would revoke & rewrite & polish—infinitely" (D 3: 180–81). However, she labors hard during the now not even month-and-a-half she gives herself for revision: ten pages a day till June 1.

She opens her diary May 31 to report that "Leonard is reading Orlando, which goes to the printer tomorrow" (D 3: 183). She takes her own measure of the book before hearing Leonard's and again finds it less than her best: "I think it lacks the sort of hammering I should have given it if I had taken longer: is too freakish & unequal. Very brilliant now & then. As for the effect of the whole, that I cant judge. Not, I think 'important' among my works. L. says a satire" (D 3: 184). Leonard causes her, however, to revalue the work. "L. takes Orlando more seriously than I had expected," she records. "Thinks it in some ways better than The Lighthouse; about more interesting things, & with more attachment to life, & larger" (D 3: 185).

In what has become a habitual diary gesture, Woolf again projects failure before the book appears.[2] When one expects darkness, the slightest light warms. Orlando is published on October 11, and Woolf is able to report dryly in her next entry, October 27: "The reception, as they say, surpassed expectations. Sales beyond our record for the first week" (D 3: 200). But the problem, as she writes on November 7, is what to write next. "The Moths," she notes in August, "hovers some where at the back of my brain" (D 3: 190). In one of the most important of all Woolf's diary entries, before Orlando's triumph unfolds, she confesses on September 10:

> Often down here [in the country] I have entered into a sanctuary; a nunnery;[3] had a religious retreat; of great agony once; & always some terror: so afraid one is of loneliness: of seeing to the bottom of the vessel. That is one of the experiences I have had here in some Augusts; & got then to a consciousness of what I call "reality": a thing I see before me; something abstract; but residing in the downs or sky; beside which nothing matters; in which I shall rest & continue to exist. Reality I call it. And I fancy sometimes this is the most necessary thing to me: that which I seek. But who knows—once one takes a pen & writes? How difficult not to go making "reality" this & that, whereas it is one thing. Now perhaps this is my gift; this perhaps is what distinguishes me from other people; I think it may be rare to have so acute a sense of something like that—but again, who knows? I would like to express it too. (D 3: 196)

What is this necessary "reality" she seeks, where she "shall rest & continue to exist"? This entry links to—and elaborates—her September 28 and 30, 1926, diary entries, where she first glimpsed "an edge . . . of great importance," "the mystical side of this solitude; how it is not oneself but something in the universe that one's left with. . . . One sees a fin passing far out" (*D* 3: 112, 113).

Also hovering in her mind, however, are her talks on women and fiction that will become *A Room of One's Own* (1929). This groundbreaking work figures in the 1928 diary from start to end. In January, Woolf agrees to speak to the Arts Society of Newnham College, Cambridge. When she asks herself in her first entry what she thought about at Hardy's funeral, she confesses to thinking of Max Beerbohm's letter, which praised her nonfiction over her fiction, and of "a lecture to the Newnhamites about women's writing."[4] In her third entry, February 18, she opens her diary when she "should be revising Lord Chesterfield," because her mind instead "is woolgathering away about Women & Fiction. . . . The mind is the most capricious of insects—flitting fluttering. . . . I've been racing up & down the whole field of my lecture" (*D* 3: 175).

While Leonard reads *Orlando* on May 31, Woolf tells her diary: "Now I want to write some very closely reasoned criticism; . . . an essay of some sort. . . . Dr Burney's evening party I think for Desmond" (*D* 3: 185). Her mind turns to Fanny Burney, the "mother" of English fiction—and to Burney's diaries where Dr. Burney's evening parties appear.[5] Tellingly, she returns to Burney's diaries *after* her Cambridge lectures in late October. "My ambition is from this very moment . . . to attain complete concentration again," she writes on October 27. "When I have written here [in her diary], I am going to open Fanny Burney's diaries, & work solidly at that article" (*D* 3: 199–200). Woolf's diary mother and her diaries thus cradle *A Room of One's Own*.

Woolf begins to amass in the second half of 1928 a string of diary reflections on gender and art. On September 3, in a lively portrait of Leonard's mother, Woolf probes the link between care and art: "But to be attached to her as daughter would be so cruel a fate that I can think of nothing worse; & thousands of women might be dying of it in England today: this tyranny of mother over daughter, or father; their right to the due being as powerful as anything in the world. And then, they ask, why women dont write poetry. Short of killing Mrs W. nothing could be done. . . . Nothing has ever been said of this" (*D* 3: 195). But soon something will.[6]

In her next entry, September 10, she reports Desmond MacCarthy's continued belittling of women. In the August issue of his new magazine, MacCarthy had written: "If, like the reporter, you believe that female novelists should only aspire to excellence by courageously acknowledging the limitations of their sex (Jane Austen and, in our own time, Mrs Virginia Woolf, have demonstrated how gracefully this gesture can be accomplished), Miss du Coudray's first novel may at the outset prove a little disappointing, since here is a writer definitely bent upon the attainment of masculine standards" (D 3: 196n5).

In November, MacCarthy continues to annoy. "And the egotism of men surprises & shocks me even now," Woolf writes:

> Is there a woman of my acquaintance who could sit in my arm chair from 3 to 6.30 without the semblance of a suspicion that I may be busy, or tired, or bored; & so sitting could talk, grumbling & grudging, of her difficulties, worries; then eat chocolates, then read a book, & go at last, apparently self-complacent & wrapped in a kind of blubber of misty self satisfaction? Not the girls at Newnham or Girton. They are far too spry; far too disciplined. None of that self-confidence is their lot. (D 3: 204)

A month later she marks and probes Christabel MacClaren's attitude to men, "the adoring, flattering woman's attitude, which I so seldom see so purely":

> Like a flame leaping up. Clive "the most honourable of men"—yes but said with a devoutness, a radiancy, that made me laugh. Is this the "natural" attitude between the sexes? . . . So cordial, so appreciative; I could hear it kindling her voice. . . . And I can see man after man, Desmond, Clive &c, Wells, Shaw, warming his hands at this natural warmth, & expanding. It amused me. (D 3: 210)

Enough for *A Room of One's Own*? "A woman is in some ways so much better than a man," she has told her diary on September 22, "more natural, juicy, unfettered" (D 3: 199). Compare this with "The truth is, I often like women. I like their unconventionality. I like their subtlety. I like their anonymity" in *A Room of One's Own* soon to come (111).

And when she returns from her Cambridge lectures, her impression is of "[s]tarved but valiant" young college women, "[i]ntelligent eager, poor; & destined to become schoolmistresses in shoals," she writes in her October 27 entry. "I blandly told them to drink wine & have a room of their own. Why should all the splendour, all the luxury of life be lavished" on the men and not the women, she asks (D 3: 200). In her final entry she links economic ease and art. *Orlando*, now in its third printing, puts coins in her pocket beyond her "weekly 13/—which was always running out, or being encroached upon" (D 3: 212). "I think one's soul is the better for this lubrication," she writes on December 18; "& I am going to spend freely, & then write, & so keep my brain on the boil" (D 3: 212).

However, the November crisis persists: what to write next? Woolf faces an artistic crossroads at this moment involving nonfiction and fiction, the outer and the inner. On the one hand, she feels a tug to continue her (clearly successful) Orlando-style "memoirs," these "[b]iographies of living people," as she calls them in her May 31 entry (*D* 3: 185). On the other hand flutters The Moths. Woolf both probes and resolves the tension in conversation with herself in her November 7 and 28 diary entries. "I mean the situation is, this Orlando is of course a very quick brilliant book," she begins probing November 7. "Yes, but I did not try to explore. And must I always explore? Yes I think so still. Because my reaction is not the usual" (*D* 3: 202–3).

Orlando taught her to write "a direct sentence," taught her continuity and narrative (*D* 3: 203). But she "purposely avoided of course any other difficulty"; she never got down to her depths and "made shapes square up" as she did in *The Lighthouse*, she confesses (*D* 3: 203). Once more she intimates to her diary that she did not bring the same time and intensity to *Orlando* that she has to her previous books, and we wonder what that novel-biography would have looked like if she had.

And then she owns the force of the dilemma: "Well but Orlando was the outcome of a perfectly definite, indeed overmastering impulse. I want fun. I want fantasy. I want (& this was serious) to give things their caricature value. And still this mood hangs about me. I want to write a history, say of Newnham or the womans movement, in the same vein. The vein is deep in me—at least sparkling, urgent" (*D* 3: 203). These last words recall those of another crossroads: the 1923 crisis that saw the move from Richmond to London, when Woolf told her diary, "This social side is very genuine in me. Nor do I think it reprehensible. It is a piece of jewellery I inherit from my mother" (*D* 2: 250).

She resolves the matter by refining her turn-and-turn-about tack: "My notion is that there are offices to be discharged by talent for the relief of genius: meaning that one has the play side; the gift when it is mere gift, unapplied gift; & the gift when it is serious, going to business. And one relieves the other":

Yes, but The Moths? That was to be an abstract mystical eyeless book: a playpoem. And there may be affectation in being too mystical, too abstract; saying Nessa & Roger & Duncan & Ethel Sands admire that: it is the uncompromising side of me; therefore I had better win their approval—

Again, one reviewer [says] that I have come to a crisis in the matter of style: it is now so fluent & fluid that it runs through the mind like water....

I rather think the upshot will be books that relieve other books: a variety of styles & subjects: for after all, that is my temperament, I think: to be very little persuaded of the truth of anything . . . always to follow, blindly instinctively with a sense of leaping over a precipice—the call of—the call of—now, if I write The Moths I must come to terms with these mystical feelings. (*D* 3: 203)

She will now leap the tragic precipice first mentioned in her 1920 diary. As with the country and/in London, the turn-and-turn-about approach will both relieve her and cast each terrain in higher relief. Three weeks later, the two paths—heightened nonfiction or "playpoem"—still draw her; however, she reaches toward a deeper mix. "As for my next book," she resumes the query on her father's birthday, November 28, treating her books as offspring:

Orlando has done very well. Now I could go on writing like that—the tug & suck are at me to do it. People say this was so spontaneous, so natural. And I would like to keep those qualities if I could without losing the others. But those qualities were largely the result of ignoring the others. They came of writing exteriorly; & if I dig, must I not lose them? And what is my own position towards the inner & the outer? I think a kind of ease & dash are good;—yes: I think even externality is good; some combination of them ought to be possible. The idea has come to me that what I want now to do is to saturate every atom. I mean to eliminate all waste, deadness, superfluity: to give the moment whole; whatever it includes. . . . Why admit any thing to literature that is not poetry—by which I mean saturated? Is that not my grudge against novel[ist]s—that they select nothing? The poets succeeding by simplifying: practically everything is left out. I want to put practically everything in; yet to saturate. That is what I want to do in The Moths. It must include nonsense, fact, sordidity: but made transparent. (*D* 3: 209–10)

In her 1919 diary credo, Woolf declared her wish to create a diary "so elastic that it [would] embrace any thing," a work "transparent enough to reflect the light of our life" (*D* 1: 266). In 1928, saturation again leads to transparency.

In the country more than two months before, Woolf had first posed the outer and the inner and recognized the seeming paradox that *saturation*, the flooding of facts, thoughts, and sensations—in a diary or other form—creates the ideal state for the *distillation* of art. On August 8, in her first entry in the diary section she heads "Rodmell," Woolf explores, yet again, the tension that rises when the outer world intrudes on her country retreat. This August, the male voice belongs to fellow diarist Eddy Sackville-West, and Woolf captures her divided state. "Yet his presence somehow checked the flow of sub-cutaneous life. I was always having to think what comes next? How am I to break into this other life [Eddie's] which is 6 inches off mine in the deck chair in the orchard? So that my own thoughts could not flow deep or rapid, as they are doing now that Eddy is on his way to Tunbridge Wells," she explains, seeming to resent the need to halt the deep flow (*D* 3: 188–89).

And then she sees the distillation of her art: "And what remains of Eddy is now in some ways more vivid, though more transparent, all of him composing itself in my mind, all I could get of him, & making itself a landscape appropriate to it; making a work of art for itself" (*D* 3: 189). Here art again appears to be unwilled: acting *for itself* on "all [she] could get of him." She continues in this entry to value the collection, the surfeit, of material in her diary for the purpose of art. "Yet no doubt I shall be more interested, come 10 years, in facts; & shall want, as I do when I read, to be told details, details," she writes, "so that I may look up from the page & arrange them too, into one of those makings up which seem so much truer done thus, from heaps of nonassorted facts, than now I can make them, when it is almost immediately being done <by me> under my eyes" (*D* 3: 189; cross-outs in <> here and below). Here she hints at slightly more command of the process over time ("*I may* . . . arrange them")—although she elides "by me" at the end.

The 1928 diary exudes writerly thoughts like these as Woolf senses change and works toward further forms of her art. In the country on August 12, she admits that, beyond words, the "look of things has a great power over me" (*D* 3: 191). We then see her compose: catch another glimpse of life turning into art. "Even now," she continues, "I have to watch the rooks beating up against the wind, which is high. & still I say to myself instinctively 'Whats the phrase for that?' & try to make more & more vivid the roughness of the air current & the tremor of the rooks wing <deep breasting it> slicing—as if the air were full of ridges & ripples & roughnesses; they rise & sink, up & down, as if the exercise <pleased them> rubbed & braced them like swimmers in rough water" (*D* 3: 191).

Nineteen days later, the country offers a glimpse (yet again) of her aesthetic of changing light: "Each day is . . . full of wandering clouds; & that fading & rising of the light which so enraptures me in the downs . . ."[7] She admits on August 14 to feeling now (like Katherine Mansfield) "a pressing sense of the flight of time"; in fact, she feels "on the verge of the world, about to take flight" herself (*D* 3: 191). She reads Proust and *Moby-Dick* across the year and affirms twice her continued need to experiment and explore. On April 21 she tells her diary: "At 46 I am not callous; suffer considerably; make good resolutions—still feel as experimental & on the verge of getting at the truth as ever" (*D* 3: 180).

The year that begins with death, loss, and "a sense of the futility of it all," ends with *Orlando* ascendant and a continued drive to explore. If 1928 began with the death of old men—Thomas Hardy and Lord Sackville—the diary closes in December with old age triumphant. In February, Woolf visits the dying scholar Jane Harrison and finds her "with her old white head lifted up, on pillows, very aged & rather exalted" (*D* 3: 176). In April, when she hears of Harrison's death, she recalls that encouraging sight: Harrison "raised on her pillows, like a very old person, whom life has tossed up, & left; exalted, satisfied, exhausted" (*D* 3: 180).

When she and Leonard dine with Maynard and Lydia Keynes, Woolf records "two couples, elderly, childless distinguished" (*D* 3: 181), and as she feels the press of time and moves toward her mystical vision, thoughts of children continue to recede. "I dont want them any more, since my ideas so possess me," she declares in the country in August, "& I detest more & more interruption; & the slow heaviness of physical life, & almost dislike peoples bodies, I think, as I grow older; & want always to cut that short, & get my utmost fill of the marrow, of the essence" (*D* 3: 189).

The 1928 diary closes with portraits of two writers who exude vigor in old age. Woolf finally meets Max Beerbohm in December, and this allows her to bring the 1928 diary to an artful full-circle close. She describes him as "a thick set old man" and seems pleased that he treats her as "one of his colleagues & fellows in the art of writing; but not I hoped quite so old."[8] She offers a metaphor for his work that reveals why she so admires him. She likens his prose to a jewel "which is hard & flawless, yet always changing" (*D* 3: 213).

She follows Beerbohm's portrait—and closes her 1928 diary—with another admiring portrait of an older writer, George Moore, who is like "an old silver coin" (*D* 3: 214). Moore always says "the thing that comes into his head; fresh, juvenile almost for that reason; & very shrewd" (*D* 3: 214). She admires in him the traits she now seeks herself. "[T]he great are very simple; quick to come to terms with; reserved; & dont pay any attention to other peoples books . . . & live in an atmosphere very serene, bright, & fenced off: for all that they are more to the point than ordinary people; go to the heart of things directly" (*D* 3: 214).

The 1928 diary arrests us with its thoughts on writing as Woolf senses change and ponders her next leap. With *Orlando* she opens a new vein—her vein of fantasy and satire—yet she struggles to mediate speed versus polish, the external versus the internal, and finds some answer in her turn-and-turn-about tack, in "books that relieve other books," yet also in some finer blend: the saturation of each atom (*D* 3: 203, 209).

Her diary once more aids her. Her now exquisite diary command appears in her first "Rodmell" entry in the country, where she writes that she no longer wants children and then starts a new paragraph: "I write thus partly in order to slip the burden of writing narrative, as for instance; we came here a fortnight ago. And we lunched at Charleston & Vita came & we were offered the field . . ." (D 3: 189). We see her here skirt one of the readiest diary traps: rote recital of events. Her next entry, August 12, opens, "Shall I now continue this soliloquy, or shall I imagine an audience, which will make me describe?" (D 3: 190). In December, she takes up her diary as warm-up: "to get the taste of a sentence into my mouth again" (D 3: 211). A month earlier, she declares journalism and letter writing "unworthy the sacred morning hours. Phrase tossing can only be done then; so I toss them privately here . . ."—a sign of the continued "sacred" space she gives her diary prose (D 3: 206).

However, most haunting is her September 10 country vision of something before her: "something abstract; but residing in the downs or sky; beside which nothing matters; in which I shall rest & continue to exist" (D 3: 196). She calls this "reality" and "the most necessary thing to me: that which I seek" (D 3: 196). Does she find it in The Moths/The Waves? Does she find it ever—or at her death? In 1928, this "reality" remains in the downs or sky. Meanwhile, Orlando has sold six thousand copies (as she writes in her final diary entry), and her "room is secure" (D 3: 212).

Virginia Woolf's First 1929 Diary

> "[I]slands of light—islands in the stream that
> I am trying to convey: life itself going on"
>
> (D 3: 229)

The loose-leaf diary meets its end with the first 1929 diary. After only ten entries across the 163 days from January 4 to June 15, 1929, Woolf abandons her two-and-a-half-year loose-leaf diary experiment in despair and starts again in a new, bound diary book. She does so to preserve life: her diary's life. "I can't write any longer in books whose leaves perish. I don't know how to keep them," she confesses of the loose-page format meant to capture more stray thoughts. "[I]n a bound volume, the year has a chance of life. It can be stood on a shelf" (D 3: 233). The front cover of this diary has, in fact, perished (like the front and back covers of the 1928 loose-leaf diary). Only a brown back cover bearing two punched holes remains to support the diary's white pages, the whole held together with two gold-colored rings. Despite such tenuous bindings, this diary shows a writer on the brink of attack.

While the 1928 diary began in a somber mood of dispersal, death, and "the futility of it all," the first 1929 diary sounds an opening note of triumph that rarely abates (D 3: 174). "How odd to think that I have given the world something that the world enjoys," Woolf muses to start this diary. "I refer to the Manchester Guardian—Orlando is recognised for the masterpiece that it is" (D 3: 217). While *Orlando* unfolded across the 1928 diary, the first 1929 diary reverberates with *A Room of One's Own*. A long—eighty-two-day—gap yawns between Woolf's first 1929 entry and her second, March 28, a gap caused by travel, then illness capped by another rush of art. Woolf's diary ease reveals itself, for she simply restarts her book. "It is a disgrace indeed; no diary has been left so late in the year," she begins. "The truth was that we went to Berlin on the 16th of January, & then I was in bed for three weeks afterwards, & then could not write; perhaps for another three, & have spent my energy since in one of my excited outbursts of composition—writing what I made up in bed, a final version of Women & Fiction [*A Room of One's Own*]" (D 3: 218–19). She closes this entry: "At anyrate [*sic*], without any trouble to write well, as there should have been, I have once more launched this diary" (D 3: 220). This sentence has the rhythm of Woolf's even more assured 1939 "A Sketch of the Past" words: "So without stopping to choose my way, in the sure and certain knowledge that it will find itself—or if not it will not matter—I begin . . ." (*MOB* 64).

With *Orlando* the Hogarth Press flourishes, and this surely adds to Woolf's verve, for she writes in her next entry, April 13: "And 7 people now depend on us; & I think with pride that 7 people depend, largely, upon my hand writing on a sheet of paper. That is of course a great solace & pride to me. Its not scribbling; its keeping 7 people fed & housed: a great big man like Percy; a carrot faced woman like Cartwright; they live on my words. They will be feeding off Women & Fiction next year for which I predict some sale" (D 3: 221). She then praises this artful work's "considerable conviction":

I think that the form, half talk half soliloquy allows me to get more onto the page than any how else. It made itself up & forced itself upon me (in this form—the thinking had been done & the writing stiffly & unsatisfactorily 4 times before) as I lay in bed after Berlin. I used to make it up at such a rate that when I got pen & paper I was like a water bottle turned upside down. The writing was as quick as my hand could write; too quick, for I am now toiling to revise; but this way gives one freedom & lets one leap from back to back of one's thoughts. (*D* 3: 221–22)

Her fluidity thus continues, and by her next entry, April 29, she can report achieving her own "room." They order two new rooms for Monk's House: a bedroom for Virginia leading to the garden and a writing room above.

A Room of One's Own comes literally to life across Woolf's first 1929 diary. At the same time she prepares herself for her coming attack on *The Waves*. In her March 28 entry, and in other entries in this diary, we catch a further glimpse of how semiprivate diary prose drifts toward public fiction. Woolf worries about *diary* repetition in this entry, and this leads her to consider invention in public prose as well. "Perhaps I ought not to go on repeating what I have always said about the spring," she writes:

> One ought perhaps to be forever finding new things to say, since life draws on. One ought to invent a fine narrative style. Certainly there are many new ideas always forming in my head. For one, that I am going to enter a nunnery these next months; & let myself down into my mind; Bloomsbury being done with. I am going to face certain things. It is going to be a time of adventure & attack, rather lonely & painful I think. But solitude will be good for a new book. Of course, I shall make friends. I shall be external outwardly. I shall buy some good clothes & go out into new houses. All the time I shall attack this angular shape in my mind. I think the Moths (if that is what I shall call it) will be very sharply cornered. . . .
>
> I feel on the verge of some strenuous adventure: yes; as if this spring day were the hatching; the portal; the opening through which I shall go upon this experience. So when I wake early, I brace myself out of my terrors by saying that I shall need great courage. (*D* 3: 219)

Similarly, a month and a half later, an entry that appears to exist to "try a new pen" leads to poetry and (now) waves. Woolf muses in her May 15 entry that "every gold pen has some fatal drawback. . . . And then one cant be sure till one's written a long screed [whether the pen suffices]. And then one's ashamed to go back—& then one does—& then it all begins again, like Mathew [*sic*] Arnold's river, or sea (brings in again &c &c)" (*D* 3: 226). Diary editor Olivier Bell pinpoints helpfully the precise "Dover Beach" lines Woolf is recalling here, which also mirror Katherine Mansfield's *Journal* words read almost two years before:

> Listen! you hear the grating roar
> Of pebbles which the waves suck back, and fling,

At their return, up the high strand,
Begin, and cease, and then again begin,
With tremulous cadence slow, and bring
The eternal note of sadness in.

Here is a *diary*'s rhythm as well ("Begin, and cease, and then again begin")—
its discontinuity yet renewal. Sixteen days later, Woolf once more evokes the
waves in her diary's next-to-last entry. The context: her visit to Leonard's
mother and thoughts of suicide. "One may get it too, when one is 76," Woolf
imagines:

> One may lie sobbing, & yet cry does doctor think I shall recover? One
> will not perhaps go to the writing table & write that simple & profound
> paper upon suicide which I see myself leaving for my friends. What a day
> it was—the sea flowing in & out of the bays, all the way, like the Adriatic,
> or Pacific; & the sand yellow; & the boats streaming along; & behind[,]
> the downs like long waves, gently extending themselves, to break very
> quickly; smooth & sloping like the waves. (*D* 3: 231)

Woolf's mind has been pressing toward the waves. Her fourth diary entry,
April 29, reports pragmatically: "This morning I began to revise Phases of Fiction, & with that done, I can see my way clear to a complete imaginative book"
(*D* 3: 223). On May 28, *Phases of Fiction* done and *A Room of One's Own* finished,
she starts anew: "Now about this book, The Moths. How am I to begin it? And
what is it to be? I feel . . . only a great pressure of difficulty" (*D* 3: 229). She
then moves closer with one of her useful diary feints: "I am not saying, I might
say, that these sketches have any relevance. I am not trying to tell a story. Yet
perhaps it might be done in that way. A mind thinking. They might be islands
of light—islands in the stream that I am trying to convey: life itself going on"
(*D* 3: 229).

Her diary reflects ideal conditions for her attack. She turns (once more)
from London and from chatter to country silence and her art. In her fourth
entry, April 29, she exclaims of Rodmell: "It was cold; but how silent, how safe
from voices & talk! How I resented our coming back; & quickly changed into
the social sphere of my soul; & went to lunch with Sibyl; & there had, for my
pains, precisely six minutes of tolerable talk with Max Beerbohm. But dear me,
how little talk with great men now disturbs me" (*D* 3: 222). Sixteen days later,
she still yearns to silence talk. "And then Roger wants to come to Rodmell, &
I don't like after my protests, to say no; & yet to have to talk & talk . . ." (*D* 3:

227–28). In this diary's final entry, Woolf imagines "silence, complete aloofness from London."[9]

She not only moves toward country silence—that is, to nature and her unconscious—but also fortifies herself with praise. Her first entry can report *Orlando* hailed as "the masterpiece that it is," and her second that she has now "many admiring letters to answer."[10] With her third entry she can record the Press for the first time earning more than £400 profit and the "great solace & pride" she feels to support seven people with her pen (*D* 3: 221). George Duckworth asks her to lunch to meet a French couple who admire her. All is flourishing and promising, in short. In April, Leonard hands out employee bonuses, sharing *Orlando*'s largesse. In May, the Hogarth Press begins work on the *Uniform Edition of the Works of Virginia Woolf*.

So flush is Woolf at this moment that she waves off all thoughts of old age. When her oculist tells her "Perhaps you're not as young as you were," she first records it and then rejects it. "This is the first time that has been said to me; & it seemed to me an astonishing statement," she reports. "It means that one now seems to a stranger not a woman, but an elderly woman. Yet even so, though I felt wrinkled & aged for an hour, & put on a manner of great wisdom & toleration, . . . even so, I forget it soon; & am 'a woman' again" (*D* 3: 230). She gives a full-circle close to this next-to-last entry by reasserting her essence and her diary's value: "I was in a queer mood, thinking myself very old: but now I am a woman again—as I always am when I write" (*D* 3: 231).

In fact, in her second entry, March 28, she has already dismissed old age. "Old age is withering us; Clive, Sibyl, Francis [Birrell]—all wrinkled & dusty; going over the hoops, along the track," she admits. "Only in myself, I say, forever bubbles this impetuous torrent. So that even if I see ugliness in the glass, I think, very well, inwardly I am more full of shape & colour than ever. I think I am bolder as a writer."[11]

She will need this courage as she lets herself down into her mind and begins "a time of adventure & attack, rather lonely & painful" (*D* 3: 219). But her diary continues its support; in fact, she moves at the end to give it even firmer life in a bound diary book. Like her 1928 diary that starts and ends with Max Beerbohm, her first 1929 diary also reflects full-circle art, for it opens and closes with Vanessa as the measure (as have several earlier diaries). If the first sentence of the 1929 diary basks in *Orlando*'s recognition for "the masterpiece that it is," the second looks to Vanessa: "The Times does not mention Nessa's pictures. Yet, she said last night, I have spent a long time over one of them. Then I think to myself, So I have something, instead of children, & fall comparing our lives. I note my own withdrawal from those desires; my absorption in what I call, inaccurately, ideas: this vision" (*D* 3: 217).

In spite of this, she closes her diary on June 15 with the rivalry still alive. The Woolfs have just returned from days with Vanessa and Duncan in France, and now, with the success of *Orlando*, Woolf can buy a home there. Amid this prospect's many pleasures, she pictures, too, "talk with people who have never heard of me & think me older, uglier than Nessa, & in every way inferior to her" (*D* 3: 232). To this she once more poses her writing triumph. She confesses:

> L. & I were very extravagant, for the first times in our lives, buying desks, tables, sideboards, crockery for Rodmell. This gave me pleasure; & set my dander up against Nessa's almost overpowering supremacy. My elder son is coming tomorrow; yes, & he is the most promising young man in King's; & has been speaking at the Apostles dinner. All I can oppose that with is, And I made £2,000 out of Orlando & can bring Leonard here & buy a house if I want. To which she replies (in the same inaudible way) I am a failure as a painter compared with you, & cant do more than pay for my models. And so we go on; over the depths of our childhood. (*D* 3: 232–33)

Yet even so, Woolf still rides the creative flood in 1929. Each of this diary's ten entries harbors water tropes. On May 28, Woolf pictures the "mind thinking" in The Moths as "islands of light—islands in the stream that I am trying to convey: life itself going on" (*D* 3: 229). "Islands in the stream . . . life itself going on" is also an apt picture of a diary.

Epilogue

An unplanned crisis in the fall of 1918 propels Virginia Woolf into her second diary stage: the era of her thirteen mature, spare, modernist diaries, written between 1918 and 1929. These semiprivate diaries allow us to follow, as the 1920s unfurl, her steady stretch as a diarist, as well as her growth into her distinctive modernist style. Woolf reaches toward new realms with her 1920 diary; she turns inward toward the soul and also outward toward literature, toward that "shadow of some kind of form which a diary might attain to," as she envisioned in her 1919 diary credo (*D* 1: 266).

She moves closer to her distinctive voice and activates her vital, rhythmic "turn-and-turn-about" movement in her 1922 and 1923 diaries. We see her pare her diary entries and then begin to flower into poetry in 1924. As Elizabeth Podnieks explains, Woolf's diary is itself a "valid and valuable modernist achievement" (12).

Most notably, Woolf never stops her intellectual and artistic stretch. In February 1926, she begins "a new convention" for her diary: she will start each entry on a new page, her "habit in writing serious literature" (*D* 3: 62). Later that year, she begins to probe that which exists now *beyond* literature. Her two-and-a-half-year experiment with a loose-leaf diary, begun in 1927, may be an effort to snare that stray, loose "beyond." Across Woolf's second diary stage, her movement is always toward greater and greater freedom.

Diary-keeping has become now a way of life for Virginia Woolf. In this second diary stage, her diary books become annual and more standardized in size: an annual "life insurance" that pays high returns. As the interface between her unconscious and her public prose, they also reveal the dangers always awaiting her hard work and intensive stretch.

Others' diaries, however, refresh and fortify her across the 1920s—and supply rich matter for modernist use. We see that several of Woolf's most memorable modernist images, phrases, and moments are offered to her in multiple diaries across her days: the lighthouse, "a room of one's own," Professor von X, and Judith Shakespeare. Other items she borrows from just one diary: *Monday or Tuesday* from Chekhov's notebooks; Mrs. Ramsay and summer holidays at the Scottish seaside with "a large and clever family" from Anne Chalmers' teenage journals, reviewed in early 1924; the figure moved to the middle of a painting and £500 from painter Benjamin Robert Haydon's *Journals*, reviewed in September 1926; and "derision," prized in Katherine Mansfield's *Journal*, published in 1927.

The lighthouse, an image today associated almost exclusively with Woolf, offers a rich illustration of the potent influence of Woolf's reading—and especially her diary reading—on her public prose. In the fall of 1917, Woolf reviewed (and praised) *The Life and Letters of Stopford Brooke*, a biography sprinkled throughout with extracts from the diaries Brooke kept across seventy years. Probably bipolar like Woolf (and extraordinarily gifted), Brooke was predominantly a writer, but he was also a painter. In 1865, he penned a description of Turner's etching "Lost Sailor" that was included in the biography Woolf reviewed. Right over the lost sailor, Brooke writes:

> [I]n the distance—on the cliff—seen through a wild light of foam there stands the lighthouse—its saving gleam has shone in vain for the victim of the waters. It is the one touch of fine imagination which adds to the picture an infinity of human thoughts, pity, despair—all the past story of the ship which had struggled all the night against its destiny. . . . And there he lies now—drowned in sight of shore. Everything else, in the room, of Turner's sinks into insignificance before this one print. (1: 186–87)

Brooke also called this work "almost the most wonderful piece of pure imagination in any branch of Art" (1: 186). Woolf may have filed this notion away, as well as the view that a lighthouse invites "an infinity of human thoughts." Then in March 1920, she reads in Barbellion's *Journal of a Disappointed Man* depictions of *two* journeys "to the lighthouse": the first thwarted by death and the second, one of extraordinary collector's luck.

Similarly, Woolf meets men like the unforgettable Professor von X of *A Room of One's Own* across thirty-three years of diary-reading, starting with Fanny Burney's diaries read when she was only fourteen and ending with Beatrice Webb's Professor Marshall (encountered in 1926) and Katherine Mansfield's stethoscope-waving Dr. Bernard Hudson (met in 1927). A cornerstone of Woolf's genius was her sense of the great treasure residing in diaries and her ability to absorb that bounty into her mind and transmute it into art. Anne E. Fernald has pointed out that Woolf's intertextuality "contrasts with [T. S.] Eliot's ambition to demonstrate mastery of a tradition that he at once continues and preserves[,] as well as with [James] Joyce's pranksterish interventions in a tradition that he knows well enough to mock from the outside" (55). Woolf's more subtle transformation of sources attests instead, as Fernald notes, to "both her feminism and her abiding pleasure in reading"—and also, I would add, to her sense of the continuity of the common mind.

<hr />

As her second, spare modernist diary stage comes to a close, Woolf is readying herself to "attack" her most difficult book: *The Waves*. She prepares to let herself down into her mind, to begin a time of loneliness and pain. She will enter now the final flowering of her diary life. From July 1929 to her death, in late March 1941, she will pen *many* more diary entries per year than in her spare second diary stage. She will write her diary more often in the morning than before, and she will turn more and more to others' diaries. As she confronts wars without and wars within as the 1930s unfold, she will reach out more and more to diaries for support—to those of others and to her own.

Notes

Introduction

1. See my *Becoming Virginia Woolf: Her Early Diaries and the Diaries She Read* (Gainesville: University Press of Florida, 2014).

2. Ricardo J. Quinones notes that "paradoxes seem to abound in Modernism" (105). Additionally, as Rachael Langford and Russell West observe, the diary's conventions are "uneasily balanced" between the private and the public, between the self and events, between "the spontaneity of reportage and the reflectiveness of the crafted text," in short, between historical and literary writing (8). This made the diary a challenging and attractive form for Woolf.

Chapter 1. Crisis Calls for a New Diary Audience and Purpose

1. I treat Woolf's Asheham Diary at length in *Becoming Virginia Woolf*.

2. Writing at breakneck speed, like Byron, Woolf often left out apostrophes. All quotations from her diaries and letters will reproduce her text.

3. In *Self-Harvest: A Study of Diaries and the Diarist*, P. A. Spalding wrote in 1949 that "there is no 'purer' diary" than Sir Walter Scott's (80n10). Woolf herself wrote in 1924 that "no woman can read the life of this man and his diary and his novels without being head over ears in love with Walter Scott" (*E* 3: 464).

4. Woolf continues to recoil from didactic writing in this second 1918 Hogarth diary—just as she did in the first. Part of her depression when she visits Janet Case on November 3 comes from her sense that she is "talking to some one who seems to want all literature to go into the pulpit; who makes it all infinitely worthy & safe & respectable" (*D* 1: 213).

5. Biographer Hermione Lee calls these Webb entries "one of the diary's most brilliant bursts of caricature" (343).

6. *D* 1: 214. She executes the same salvaging maneuver in the entry before, which first discloses Case's "chill": "I was also depressed at the implied criticism of The Voyage Out, & at the hint that I had better turn to something other than fiction. . . . Its the curse of a writers life to want praise so much, & be so cast down by blame, or indifference. The only sensible course is to remember that writing is after all what one does

best; that any other work would seem to me a waste of life; that on the whole I get infinite pleasure from it; that I make one hundred pounds a year; & that some people like what I write" (*D* 1: 214).

7. The new diary is exactly the size of her first 1918 Hogarth diary (7 inches wide and 8 ¾ inches long), boasts the same dark red binding that extends one inch onto the front and back covers, and differs from the first 1918 Hogarth diary only in the color of the membranes on the blue-gray marbled cover: those on the first 1918 Hogarth Diary are orange-red, on the third, orange-red and white.

8. *D* 1: 223. Carlyle was born on December 4, 1795.

9. As early as November 26, 1918, Virginia writes to pregnant Vanessa, "[I]ts the possibilities of womanhood derived from you that I dream of" (*L* #990, 2: 299).

10. Woolf may be recalling Fanny Burney's published memoirs and revised diaries here or the *Diary, Reminiscences, and Correspondence of Henry Crabb Robinson, Barrister-at-Law*, which she recently has read. Judy Simons reminds us that Burney's later diaries show her "literary powers at their height" (20). Michael Schmidt calls Burney's diaries "more valuable than her later fiction" and all of her plays (202).

11. *D* 1: 235; revisions in italics. Woolf also elaborates the sentence "As these words have occurred almost automatically, I daresay there is some truth in them" to the less qualified and more revealing "As these words have occurred automatically [not "almost automatically"], *& will tease me till written down*, I daresay there is some truth in them" (*D* 1: 327, 235; changes in italics.)

12. In her November 21, 1918, entry, Woolf preserves Stephen "who sat like a frog with his legs akimbo, opening & shutting his large knife, & asserting with an egoism proper to all Stephens, that he knew how to behave himself, & how other people ought to behave . . . at Calcutta" (*D* 1: 221). As she pours tea at the 1917 Club for Leonard's assistant, Miss Matthaei, December 7, Woolf wonders, "Why should a woman of her sense apologise all her life long because she is an unattractive woman? She looks up sidelong, like a child who has done wrong. And yet she has more in her head than all the cropheads put together" (*D* 1: 225).

13. With her March 19 entry the red line changes to blue and the left margin increases slightly, suggesting she prepares a new set of pages in advance. She stops ruling her pages altogether after her November 6 entry, although she maintains the same margin. Black ink predominates, although her March 7 entry is in purple ink and her final entry in blue.

14. *D* 1: 261. His decision to publish is confirmed in a letter described in Woolf's May 7 diary entry: "I suppose, as I go to the trouble of copying his words verbatim, that I was a good deal pleased by them" (*D* 1: 269).

15. "Eliot is to be there [at Garsington]," Woolf writes to Vanessa on June 18, 1919. "He and Murry were much abused in the Times for their works, and Murry a good deal depressed" (*L* #1061, 2: 370). Nevertheless, biographer Hermione Lee reports that the edition of Eliot's *Poems*, of about two hundred copies, "sold well" (818n36).

16. *D* 1: 315. In her September 12 diary entry reporting prepublication angst—depression described by Leonard as "deep," yet more sanguinely by Virginia as "of the consistency of September mist"—she intimates the stakes riding on *Night and Day*'s reception: "If that is pronounced a failure, I dont see why I should continue writing novels" (*D* 1: 297).

17. *D* 1: 312–13. Woolf's 1919 letters to Janet Case and Margaret Llewelyn Davies reveal her efforts to improve her Hampstead rapport. "I meant to enclose some words of friendship with the notice [for 'Kew Gardens']," Woolf writes to Case on May 4 (*L* #1043, 2: 353). On July 23 she writes to Case: "I was dreaming about you so vividly last night, that I must write and find out whether this means that you were thinking with kindness of me. I'm afraid not. In my dream you were entertaining a Princess, and you wouldn't look at me—whereupon I flew into a rage, and turned to Emphie [Janet's sister] for comfort, and she was immensely grand, and made me feel myself so much in the way that I marched down the garden and out into the road, and left you bowing over the hand of your Princess. What can it all mean?" (*L* #1069, 2: 378). Woolf is more direct in a November 16 letter to Davies: "We are imperfect human beings, but that's no obstacle to friendship, (on my side) in fact rather an incentive. You'll never like my books, but then shall I ever understand your Guild? Probably not. As to Night and Day, and our argument, I was pleased to find on the hall table this testimony to my sympathy" (*L* #1094, 2: 399). She quotes it and other responses to the novel and ends: "You see, its a question of the human heart, and cutting out the rotten parts according to ones convictions. Thats what I want to do, and thats where we differ, and thats why you'll dislike N. and D.; and I shan't mind much if you do; but I should mind quite enormously if you didn't like me" (*L* #1094, 2: 400).

18. *D* 1: 296. She starts this second, and slightly smaller, diary book (with a soft cover) as her Monk's House diary; however, its nine entries continue the style of the Hogarth diary, and she ends it with her October return to Richmond.

19. *D* 1: 255. This last sentence, and an April reference to the destructive Coles, seems warm-up for Dr. Bradshaw in *Mrs. Dalloway*.

20. Of the many questions in Woolf's final novel, *Between the Acts*, Melba Cuddy-Keane suggests that "it is precisely in such open questioning that the hope of community lies" (284n10).

21. I treat the journals of Mary (Seton) Berry, the Goncourt Brothers, and Stopford Brooke in *Becoming Virginia Woolf*.

22. He resigned, however, in 1893 when he felt the Society's strategy of little use to native peoples.

23. 2: 402. He also owned a house in Damascus.

24. They have not been published. The Blunt Papers reside in the Fitzwilliam Museum in Cambridge, England. They were sealed until 1972.

25. *My Diaries* is listed among the books in the Woolfs' library with notes in Leon-

ard's hand (Holleyman, Section VI: 1). The Woolfs also owned an 1898 copy of *The Poetry of Wilfrid Blunt* owned by "George H. Duckworth" (Section I: 40).

26. Woolf did not know that Blunt actually censored *My Diaries*. Elizabeth Longford, in her 1980 biography, *A Pilgrimage of Passion: The Life of Wilfrid Scawen Blunt*, reveals that Blunt omitted or softened some of his diary words when he came to publish them in *My Diaries*. Of an 1898 speech by the Queen, for instance, he wrote in his diary: "There were the usual lies." He was persuaded to change "lies" to "insincerities" (Longford 333). At Victoria's death, his entry in the published *My Diaries* reads: "As to Her Majesty personally, one does not like to say all one thinks even in one's journal. By all I have heard of her she was in her old age a dignified but rather commonplace good soul, like how many of our dowagers" (2: 1–2). In the original diary no "rather" can be found; "good soul" was "old soul"; and the words "and bourgeois" preceded "like how many of our dowagers" (Longford 344). In short, he actually wrote: "By all I have ever heard of her she was in her old age a dignified but commonplace old soul, and bourgeois like many of our dowagers.... Privately all lovers of liberty will rejoice at the end of a bloody and abominable reign" (Longford 344). He discreetly omitted the last sentence.

27. Woolf rejected Wilton and the Pembrokes in her pivotal 1903 diary.

Chapter 2. New Diary Realms: Talk, the Soul, and Literature

1. The diary is almost the same size as Woolf's previous (1919) diary: 10 ⅝ inches long and 8 ½ inches wide.

2. *D* 2: 29, 30. Woolf acknowledges that she, in turn, can check Leonard: "I can inhibit poor L. as I myself am inhibited. Your trick is repetition, I say: whereupon his pen sticks like a broken machine" (*D* 2: 31). Five months later, Eliot's shadow cools her amid the party scene in *Jacob* she was earlier writing with great pleasure. "Eliot ... cast shade upon me," she writes on September 26, "& the mind when engaged upon fiction wants all its boldness & self-confidence.... An odd thing the human mind! so capricious, faithless, infinitely shying at shadows" (*D* 2: 68–69).

3. *D* 2: 50. Woolf's 1920 letters, however, again show her wish for Hampstead affirmation. "Will there be a little preserve of praise for me in Hampstead," she asks Janet Case in a letter written on January 5, 1920, "—something moderately encouraging of poor denuded Mrs Woolf ... ?" (*L* #1112, 2: 416). On February 1, she whispers to Case in parentheses: "(did I make it plain to you and Margaret who say I'm no novelist, and only write for the parish of Bloomsbury that such is the demand among the lower middle classes for my work that new editions of the V.O. and N. and D. have to be prepared at once?)" (*L* #1118, 2: 420–21).

4. *D* 2: 71. Woolf's letters reprise these views. "But we have to be back on Thursday though its nicer than all London rolled in one here," she writes to Violet Dickinson from Monk's House on January 4, 1920 (*L* #1110, 2: 413). The next day she writes to

Janet Case: "It seems to me that all the virtues and all the humanities can only flourish in a country village. Don't you think human beings improve very much spaced out with fields between them? And then nature—no, I shall never say how much I adore and respect nature" (L #1112, 2: 415).

5. D 2: 82. Woolf's first letter of 1920 (January 1) foreshadows the year's ambivalence. Here Woolf associates London with whirlpool drowning just as she had in her 1903 diary at the age of twenty-one. "I highly commend you for living in the country," she writes Katherine Arnold-Forster. "Everything seems a hundred times nicer there. The whole of London is now concentrated into Gordon Square. . . . This being so, we've gone and bought Hogarth and the house next door [Suffield]. I saw myself being swept into the vortex, and there whirled like a drowning leaf, till I was stuck in the mud and decayed" (L #1107, 2: 411).

6. JDM 282; D 2: 34, 72. Intriguingly, Virginia used the "strip of pavement" figure in a December 29, 1910, letter to Clive Bell, linking the country/subconscious with life beyond the London pavement: "[A]nother side of life reveals itself in the country, which I cant help thinking of amazing interest. It is precisely as though one clapped on a solid half-globe to one's London life, and had hitherto always walked upon a strip of pavement" (L #548, 1: 446).

7. JDM 223. "This War is so great and terrible that hyperbole is impossible," Cummings writes in his July 31, 1916, entry. "And yet my gorge rises at those fatuous journalists continually prating about this 'Greatest War of all time,' this 'Great Drama,' this 'world catastrophe unparalleled in human history,' because it is easy to see that they are really more thrilled than shocked by the immensity of the War" (JDM 242).

8. In an essay titled "On Journal Writers" included in the 1919 volume Enjoying Life and Other Literary Remains rushed into print at the success of The Journal of a Disappointed Man, Cummings declares, "In all their infinite variety, real journals possess this much in common: they are one and all an irresistible overflow of the writer's life, whether it be a life of adventure, or a life of thought, or a life of the soul" (75–76).

9. 333, 344. He writes in his May 8, 1917, entry: "This and another volume of my Journal are temporarily lodged in a drawer in my bedroom. It appears to me that as I become more static and moribund, they become more active and aggressive. All day they make a perfect uproar in their solitary confinement—although no one hears it. And at night they become phosphorescent, though nobody sees it. One of these days, with continued neglect they will blow up from spontaneous combustion like diseased gunpowder, the dismembered diarist being thus hoist upon his own petard" (JDM 291).

10. Woolf's father also kept a diary.

11. Evelyn's father maintained 116 servants liveried in green satin doublets with white feathers in their hats (Bray 1: 6; Smith 49).

12. Although Woolf does not use the word "curiosity," Evelyn possessed in large measure this trait that marks many of the great diarists.

13. *E* 3: 264. When Woolf revises this sentence for her "Rambling Round Evelyn" essay for her 1925 first *Common Reader*, she elaborates her meaning and makes it more emphatic: "He was not an artist; *no phrases linger in the mind; no paragraphs build themselves up in memory*; but as an artistic method this of going on with the day's story circumstantially" (*CR* 1: 85; additions italicized).

Chapter 3. Jealousy, Illness, and Diary Rescue

1. Of Clive Bell's other mistress, Mary Hutchinson, Woolf harbors a similar inclination on September 14: "Now there's a chapter in a novel!" (*D* 2: 137).

2. *D* 2: 115. Woolf's 1921 letters underscore her sensitivity to writing styles at this time. Twelve days before their tearoom talk, she writes to Lytton: "Well, I feel I must write to you either in your own style or in Victoria's. There's no escaping you after reading the book [*Queen Victoria*]" (*L* #1174, 2: 465). She writes to him again on August 29, 1921: "But even [in the country] Lytton Strachey predominates. I want to turn an honest penny; and behold, when I come to write about old Mrs Gilbert, it runs of its own accord into two semicolons, dash, note of exclamation, full stop. Do you recognise your style?" (*L* #1187, 2: 479).

3. This large diary matches the size of the 1920 diary: 8 ½ inches wide and 10 ⅝ inches long. However, in place of tiny pagodas, bridges, and trees in aquamarine imagine larger black and brown oriental dragons alternating with rows of tiny flowers (red, green, and blue) and rows of small black birds within circles of beige on beige leaves. This cover unites nature and the imagination in a colorful yet orderly design. Once again Woolf draws a single line on her book's blank white pages. She rules in blue ink a vertical left-hand margin for herself 1½ inches from the left edge. Again she uses the margin to the left for entry dates placed within a >-shaped wedge.

4. *Monday or Tuesday* featured a Vanessa Bell cover and four of Vanessa's woodcuts; in October, Virginia offers to publish a separate volume of Vanessa's art (*L* #1195, 2: 483–84).

5. She repeats here the rhythm of her October 25, 1920, strip of pavement over an abyss litany: "Its having no children, living away from friends, failing to write well, spending too much on food, growing old" (*D* 2: 72).

6. Biographer Hermione Lee notes that Woolf's father, Leslie Stephen, exhibited "passionate reactions to criticism" (69). Woolf's diary "mother," Fanny Burney, whose diaries Woolf read before starting her own first extant diary at age fourteen, also was painfully sensitive to criticism throughout her life. See *Becoming Virginia Woolf*, 19–31. Alexandra Harris points out that Woolf "could never bank on her own success because she never did the same thing twice" (7).

7. *D* 2: 121. In her 1923 diary she speaks of accepting £13 and hoping for £15 (*D* 2: 239).

8. In the series of spring entries "medicining" her "disease," Woolf writes on April 13: "Now I note the latest symptom—complete absence of jealousy. What I mean is

that I shall feel instantly warm & pleased (not only after an hour & a sharp pang) if there's a long & sound & appreciative review of L. in the Lit Sup tomorrow. I think this is perfectly true. Most people, though, would not have to write this down" (*D* 2: 109–10).

9. Woolf anticipates this direction in an emblematic tableau in her September 15 entry in which she again links herself with Roger Fry. "There is one woman of genius among the cows," she writes as she gazes out her Rodmell window. "She has decided to leave the herd & eat the branches on the fallen tree. She has now one disciple. The rest utterly condemn. She is a Roger Fry. I heard from Roger the other day, all in a hubblebubble about Murry's sneering pinpricking article. . . . (the cow has 2 disciples). We must go on doing what we like in the desert Roger says" (*D* 2: 139).

10. Woolf writes in her November 13, 1920, diary entry, "L. now translating Tchekov, & I must set to on my share, I suppose" (*D* 2: 75); however, her translating may have been postponed, for her Russian lessons do not appear to start until February 5, 1921 (*D* 2: 89). Koteliansky and Leonard are listed as the sole translators of the *Note-book of Anton Chekhov*.

11. 16. Leonard calls the characters in *Jacob's Room* "ghosts" when he first reads the novel in July 1922 (*D* 2: 186).

12. In "Tchekhov on Pope," an unpublished 1925 holograph, Woolf wrote: "Our ligatures are loosened, our prejudices relaxed; we feel ourselves expanding. . . . [S]o the heart expands under the Russian influence, the features spread, the boundaries disappear" (Rubenstein 86).

13. Scholars have long noted that Woolf pays direct homage to Chekhov in her short stories "Uncle Vanya," "The Shooting Party," and "Happiness." Neglect of diaries, however, has caused readers to miss the even larger homage Woolf offers in giving the title *Monday or Tuesday* to her entire story collection.

Chapter 4. Voice and Motion

1. *D* 2: 176. She notes similar post-Rodmell depression in previous diaries, and her 1922 letters repeat the country's nurturing role. "The downs will cure me," she writes to Violet Dickinson on March 30, 1922, regarding her illness (*L* #1231, 2: 516).

2. *D* 2: 192. Interestingly, Katherine Mansfield also uses the word "enemy" for Sydney Waterlow. Woolf copies Waterlow's Collins letter into her diary the next day. "A headache: no writing; so I will copy," she writes (*D* 2: 193). His letter not only confirms amusingly Woolf's portrait of him as a "dull donkey"—he calls himself "a perfect ass"—but also contains Mansfield's question to him on her return to London: "Sydney, are you my enemy?" (*D* 2: 194).

3. *D* 2: 177. Woolf's November 27 entry opens, for instance, with her lament that she cannot retail a comic moment due to the press of "historic" Press news: "I need not say that my wild duck stank like old sea weed & had to be buried. But I cannot

dally over this incident, which in tamer days might have provided some fun, because I have such a congeries of affairs to relate" (*D* 2: 213).

4. *D* 2: 186. In her July 22, 1922, diary entry, Woolf writes, "[E]ven the servants notice his surliness" (*D* 2: 185).

5. In *Modernist Writers and the Marketplace*, Ian Willison, Warwick Gould, and Warren Chernaik suggest that the Hogarth Press facilitated modernism's entry into the more general literary arena (xv).

6. *D* 2: 217. In her fourth diary entry, February 6, Woolf describes Partridge as "hard & angular as a block of wood" (*D* 2: 160).

7. *D* 2: 161–62. Woolf retains these views beyond this day's record, for she writes Vanessa on February 20 that Elena Richmond "is quite the nicest human being I have ever met . . . so maternal to me that I fell in love with her at once—Perhaps I always have been in love with her. . . . [A]nd I told her the story of George [Duckworth's violation]" (*L* #1218, 2: 505).

8. The book's cover offers a small burgundy print on cream background: tiny burgundy flowers or stalks of grain alternating with minute burgundy birds in flight. In her second entry, Woolf halts her portrait of Lytton Strachey "in order to rule some blue lines" (*D* 2: 157).

9. In an October 29, 1922, letter to Katherine Arnold-Forster, Woolf writes: "It was a great pleasure to get your letter, for I wasn't at all sure that you would find anything good to say of my offspring [*Jacob's Room*]" (*L* #1307, 2: 576).

10. In April, Woolf lies to evade H. G. Wells. She writes to Vanessa on April 16, 1922: "At moments it is divinely lovely here [at Rodmell]. . . . Thank God we're not in Essex with the Wells,' as we should be had I not told a lie" (*L* #1240, 2: 523).

11. Badenhorst writes: "[T]here in the food-stores stood cases full of butter and jam piled up; but no, the women might have none of it" (261).

12. In June and July, Woolf inserts brief play scenes into letters to Katherine Arnold-Forster and Jacques Raverat (*L* #1404, #1414, 3: 49, 59).

13. This diary is the same large size as Woolf's 1919–1922 diaries: 8 ¼ inches wide and 10 ⅝ inches long. Its black paper cover is woven with faint horizontal and vertical beige threads. Woolf again rules a vertical left-hand margin for herself in blue ink 1 ½ inches from the left edge.

14. Diary historian Harriet Blodgett asserts that "plentiful soul does enter Woolf's diary. . . . Her soul, in fact, binds her diary into a unity" ("A Woman Writer's Diary" 59). In "The Russian Soul Englished," Catherine Brown describes the soul's special meaning for Woolf as the common "core": "The Russian Revolution did something to dampen English fervor for the Russian soul, and demanded some modification of its conception—but less so than would have been the case were that soul not already understood as on the one hand intrinsically contradictory, and on the other as having elements that were eternal" (139.)

15. *D* 2: 243, 244. In a letter to Gerald Brenan three weeks before, Woolf wonders

how to capture her reader's soul in her *fiction*. "But how does one make people talk about everything in the whole of life, so that one's hair stands on end, in a drawing room? How can one weight and sharpen dialogue till each sentence tears its way like a harpoon and grapples with the shingles at the bottom of the reader's soul? Did we discuss dialogue at Yegen?" (*L* #1388, 3: 36).

16. Woolf records a similar incident in her 1926 diary (*D* 3: 110–11).

17. In fact, Woolf uses her own past diaries to shore her memory of Mansfield. She writes to Mansfield's friend, Dorothy Brett, March 2, 1923, "I've been looking in my diary and see that I must have written to her sometime in March 1921. From what you say, perhaps she never did get my letter. It makes me sorrier than ever that I did not simply persist" (*L* #1365, 3: 17).

18. See also Beth Rigel Daugherty, "Taking Her Fences: The Equestrian Virginia Woolf," *Virginia Woolf and the Natural World: Selected Papers from the Twentieth Annual International Conference on Virginia Woolf*, ed. Kristin Czarnecki and Carrie Rohman. Clemson, S.C.: Clemson University Press, 2011: 61–70.

19. vii. In 1922 Woolf read the biography *Young Boswell*, and this might have piqued her interest in Boswell's early Corsican *Journal*.

20. 32. Boswell's thoroughness can be gauged from this *Journal* passage: "[Signor Gian Quilico Casa Bianca] instructed me fully with regard to the Corsican government. He had even the patience to sit by me while I wrote down an account of it, which from conversations with Paoli, I afterwards enlarged and improved" (50).

21. 40. Seneca and Lucan were both implicated in the plot to overthrow the tyrant, Nero, and were forced to commit suicide.

22. 64–65. Themistocles was often called the savior of Greece; furthermore, Britons would warm to Themistocles' advocacy of ships.

23. 61. In a later passage describing Paoli's ability to dream what will come to pass, Boswell explains: "He went into a most curious and pleasing disquisition, on a subject, which the late ingenious Mr. Baxter has treated in a very philosophical manner, in his Inquiry into the Nature of the Human Soul; a book which may be read with as much delight, and surely with more advantage than the works of those who endeavour to destroy our belief" (73). Earlier Boswell criticizes his age "when mankind are so fond of incredulity, that they seem to pique themselves in contracting their circle of belief as much as possible" (71).

24. In his preface to the *Journal*, Boswell wrote: "For my part, I should be proud to be known as an author. . . . [O]f all possessions I should imagine literary fame to be the most valuable" (xiv).

Chapter 5. Spare, Modernist Perfection

1. Her third diary entry, January 12, begins: "I have just introduced a great improvement in the cover of this book—a calendar" (*D* 2: 284).

2. *D* 2: 281. Her diary's cover is also vibrant and impressionistic: a marbled blend of purples, lavenders, teals, and pinks. Entries are written in matching purple ink, and Woolf rules her usual vertical margin in blue ink, now a two full inches from the left edge. This diary is the same large size as the 1919 through 1923 diaries: 8 ½ inches wide and 10 ¾ inches long.

3. Later in this entry, she declares she likes London for writing *Mrs. Dalloway* because she "can dart in & out & refresh [her] stagnancy" (*D* 2: 302).

4. In her November 29, 1924, letter to painter Jacques Raverat, Woolf writes: "Once [*sic*] reflection occurred to me, dealing with our Mrs Joad, the other basement dweller—how much nicer young women are than young men. I hope to get a rise out of you. Nicer, I say, humaner, less conceited, more sensitive,—not cleverer. But a man has to be very clever to balance what my dear Jacques I can only call his damned offensive good opinion of himself—of his sex" (*L* #1515, 3: 145).

5. In this same month, she attempts to describe Lytton Strachey's feelings as well as her own: "Oh I was right to be in love with him 12 or 15 years ago. It is an exquisite symphony his nature when all the violins get playing as they did the other night; so deep, so fantastic. We rambled easily. He is in love again with Philip Ritchie. And hurt, a little; still capable of pain; but knows it now ridiculous, which hurts him too. & he feels it. For when I asked if we could help he was touched" (*D* 2: 317).

6. Woolf acknowledges this in her October 17 entry heralding the completion of *Mrs. Dalloway*: "But in some ways this book is a feat; finished without break from illness, wh. is an exception; & written really, in one year; & finally, written from the end of March to the 8th of October without more than a few days break for writing journalism. So it may differ from the others" (*D* 2: 316–17).

7. This 1923 volume, in fact, is titled *Letters & Journals of Anne Chalmers Edited by Her Daughter*.

8. Anne Chalmers' journal at age seventeen resembles Virginia's at the same age in its self-consciousness regarding audience. "At this period I left the meeting, and shall presently take leave of the subject, begging my reader's pardon (that is, if I am so fortunate as to have one at this period of my history)," Chalmers explains in her May 15, 1830, entry (104). And just as seventeen-year-old Virginia eyed clergymen in life as well as in art, Chalmers writes on May 20, 1830: "I begin to like bishops very much. I regard them with the eye of a naturalist as a new species before unknown to me" (110).

9. *L* #378, 1: 304. She read the novel again during her 1912 honeymoon (*L* #646, 2: 8). In her October 1934 diary, Woolf reports meeting William Butler Yeats, who tells her that her novel *The Waves* "comes after Stendhal" (*D* 4: 255).

10. Woolf read Beyle's early journals in the 1923 French edition, edited by Henry Debraye and Louis Royer.

11. The manuscript was at Knole House until 1950, when it was given to the Centre for Kentish Studies in Maidstone as part of the Sackville/Knole papers (Acheson 17).

12. A copy is in the Woolfs' library (Holleyman, Section VI: 8). Woolf knew of Lady Clifford's diary from at least early 1923, for Vita sent her, at her request, her 1922 volume *Knole and the Sackvilles* soon after they met in December 1922 (*L* #1341, 3: 1). In *Knole and the Sackvilles*, Vita describes Lady Clifford's diary at length.

13. In *Knole and the Sackvilles*, Vita writes that Richard Sackville "is utterly eclipsed—weak, vain, and prodigal—by the interest of that woman of character, his wife . . . and by the faithful picture that is her Diary" (59).

14. In 1995, Katherine O. Acheson published *The Diary of the Lady Anne Clifford, 1616–1619: A Critical Edition*, drawing on a newly found manuscript in the Portland Papers in the collection of the Marquess of Bath. Acheson argues persuasively that Vita's Knole manuscript was likely copied from the slightly more extensive Portland manuscript.

15. Karen Z. Sproles calls the realization that her gender prevented her from inheriting Knole "the founding trauma of Sackville-West's life" (43).

16. In her introductory note, Vita reports that to support his intemperate ways, "He sold his lands, he sold his London estates, he almost sold Knole itself" (xxxvi).

17. On February 16, 1616, Lady Clifford writes: "My Coz. Russell came to me the same day and chid me and told me of all my faults and errors in this business; he made me weep bitterly" (18–19).

18. In January 1619, she tells her diary: "The 22nd here supped with me my Sisters *Sackville* and *Beauchamp, Bess Neville, Tom Glenham,* and my Brother *Compton* and his wife. I brought them to sup here on purpose hoping to make them friends" (85). Lady Clifford "was related to half the fashion and influence about the Court," Vita explains in her introduction (xxxi).

19. In *Vita and Virginia: The Work and Friendship of V. Sackville-West and Virginia Woolf,* Suzanne Raitt suggests that the attraction between the two writers grew from "[t]he nostalgia, even the mourning, which [the two] shared for a maternal femininity which was apparently lost" (16).

20. Although no one as yet has suggested it, it is possible—even likely—that Vita shared her 1920 journal with Woolf, the diary in which she sought to understand her identity and her attraction to Violet Trefusis. If Woolf read it, it offered her direct matter for *Orlando*, for Vita writes: "I advance . . . the perfectly accepted theory that cases of dual personality do exist, in which the feminine and the masculine elements alternately preponderate" (Nicolson 115).

Chapter 6. Rush, Urgency, Wound, and Rescue

1. The diary is the same large size as the 1919–1924 diaries—8 ½ inches wide × 10 ½ inches long—and written mostly in purple ink.

2. *D* 3: 6. Her 1903 diary closes with a woman's suicide in the Serpentine.

3. Intriguingly, she also allows little space *between* entries in her 1925 diary, marking

new entries only with dates within her wedge-shape ">" to the left of her blue ruled line. This gives the impression of a continuous text.

4. *D* 3: 5. Woolf ruled all the pages in this 1925 diary to give herself a vertical margin 1½ inches from the left-hand edge—a sign she planned to fill all the book's pages.

5. *D* 3: 34. While "making up" *To the Lighthouse* as she writes this diary entry, she records Hills's portrait of *his* mother as "a very selfish woman" (*D* 3: 34).

6. Susan M. Kenney and Edwin J. Kenny Jr. assert that Leonard concluded that heat stroke caused Woolf to faint (165n12).

7. *D* 3: 38. Vanessa offers a similar analysis in her September 11, 1925, letter to Roger Fry: "Virginia has been rather ill with headaches, etc., I suspect the result of her London season, but she's better now, although she will have people like the Bruce Richmonds to stay with her, enough to drive anyone silly" (*Selected Letters of Vanessa Bell* 286).

8. *D* 3: 46. Woolf wrote to Vita Sackville-West on September 7, 1925: "But I cant talk yet without getting these infernal pains in my head, or astonishingly incongruous dreams. Two dull people come to tea, and I dream of precipices and horrors at night, as if—can they keep horrors and precipices concealed in them, I wonder?" (*L* #1578, 3: 205).

9. The 1925 diary refers twice to an implied "you" that might be Old Virginia or some other future reader. Woolf's May 15 entry quotes words of praise from a young man in Earls Court but then says: "Please forgive this outburst, but further quotation is unnecessary" (*D* 3: 21). On June 8, she writes: "This is the hottest June on record. Do not take this seriously—only it is very hot" (*D* 3: 28).

10. *D* 3: 26. In her 1921 diary, she declared twice of *Jacob's Room* before her summer collapse: "I must pull myself together to bring it off," "But I must pull together & finish it off" (*D* 2: 86, 116).

11. Woolf begins a letter to Sackville-West on September 23, 1925, "Do keep it up—your belief that I achieve things. I assure you, I have need of all your illusions after 6 weeks of lying in bed, drinking milk, now and then turning over and answering a letter.... You will emerge like a lighthouse, fitful, sudden, remote (Now that is rather like you)" (*L* #1588, 3: 214, 215).

12. Woolf writes to Vita Sackville-West on May 27, 1925: "I cant stop writing. I'm ashamed to think how many stories I've written this month, and can hardly bear to keep my fingers off a new novel, but swear I won't start till August" (*L* #1556, 3: 185). On May 31, Woolf writes to Ethel Sands: "I have seen too many people lately, and cant stop writing stories all the time" (*L* #1558, 3: 187).

13. After declaring July 19 that she means to regulate her social life better, she dismisses the vow: "But I dont think of the future, or the past, I feast on the moment" (*D* 3: 36).

14. *D* 3: 39. Note the renewed self-doubt here compared with the confidence of her 1922 declaration that she is "beginning to learn the mechanism of [her] own brain—how to get the greatest amount of pleasure & work out of it" (*D* 2: 206).

15. Vita's "fluency was remarkable," Nigel Nicolson, her son, writes in *Portrait of A Marriage* (67).

16. Woolf likely read Wilmot's travel diary in August 1920. See *D* 2: 57.

17. 2: 333. Sir Walter Scott, whose edition of the *Journal to Stella* Woolf likely read, used Deane Swift's "Presto" in place of Swift's "Pdfr." I have substituted "Pdfr" as more accurate and moving. Deane Swift acknowledged that his "Presto" was a euphonic substitute for "Pdfr." The Woolfs owned Scott's nineteen-volume 1814 *The Works of Jonathan Swift*, which had copious notes in Leslie Stephen's hand. The *Journal to Stella*, volumes 2 and 3, will be used here.

18. 2: 117. Frederick Ryland reports that Swift refers to writing the *Examiner* here (2: 81n2).

19. I quote from the slightly elaborated version of the 1925 essay that Woolf published in the 1932 *Second Common Reader* (58).

20. Swift's widely known compulsion for order is captured in other moments in the *Journal*. On January 5, 1711, for instance, he writes, "Mr Secretary [of State] St John sent for me this morning so early, that I was forced to go without shaving, which put me quite out of method: I called at Mr Ford's, and desired him to lend me a shaving, and so made a shift to get into order again" (2: 137).

21. "I endeavour to act in the most exact points of honour and conscience, and my nearest friends will not understand it so," Swift writes October 22, 1710, of his efforts, misprized by Addison, to help Richard Steele retain his office (2: 55–56).

22. *CR* 2: 59. Her father alluded to this label in his *Swift* (56).

23. Scott, for instance, calls Swift's *Journal* "intimate and familiar, nearly as much so, indeed, as thought itself" (2: 3). Woolf writes: "They knew each other in and out . . . so that without effort or concealment he could use those precious moments late at night or the first thing on waking to pour out upon her the whole story of his day . . . as though he were thinking aloud" (*CR* 2: 60).

Chapter 7. Renewed Diary Experiment: The Reach for Literature and Beyond

1. Following the pattern of her 1919 to 1925 diaries, the 1926 diary is 8 ⅜ inches wide and 10 ¾ inches long, written mostly in purple ink, and ruled with a vertical line 1 ½ inches from the left-hand edge. The book's brown paper cover is water stained today.

2. Olivier Bell helpfully notes that Woolf's vision of her soul alludes to Shakespeare's *Cymbeline*: "Hang there like fruit, my soul, / Till the tree die!" (Act V, line 262; *D* 3: 59n5).

3. *D* 3: 102. Toward the close of this diary's time frame, Woolf tries to explain this notion in a letter to Vita Sackville-West: "My parting lecture was not very coherent. I was trying to get at something about the thing itself before its made into anything: the emotion, the idea" (*L* #1711, 3: 321).

4. *D* 1: 26. Biographer Hermione Lee writes that Leonard and Virginia went to their first Fabian Conference in the summer of 1913 (323).

5. Beatrice gives this description of Kate's diary in her own diary on August 12, 1923: "Just had a long morning's walk and talk with dear old Kate about her diary, which is full of interesting matter and which she is leaving to me. . . . She gave me some volumes of her diary to read afterwards—mostly reporting the facts of her life and Leonard's career, speeches, sayings, etc.—essentially the diary of a devoted wife of a 'great man' and the friend of distinguished people whose conversation is carefully noted—all useful matter for future historians, giving the impressions of an excellent and charming married woman with great intelligence but no intellect" (MacKenzies 3: 424).

6. 1: 6. At forty-two, Webb wrote in a "New Year's Day 1901" diary reflection: "Chronic bad health and constant physical pain made me, as a child and a girl, detestably aware of my body" (2: 189).

7. Webb, however, includes in *My Apprenticeship* this "jotting"—actually, a complaint—at about age ten that suggests her precocity: "I am quite confident that the education of girls is very much neglected in the way of their private reading. Take, for instance, a girl of nine or ten years old, she is either forbidden to read any but child's books, or she is let loose on a good library; Sir Walter Scott's novels recommended to her as charming and interesting stories, 'books that cannot do any possible harm,' her adviser declares. But the object in reading is to gain knowledge" (62).

8. At age twenty-one, missing her absent sister Maggie, Webb tells her diary: "I must go plodding on—towards some goal that may never be reached. Ah me! Courage, *mon amie*, courage," and seven years later she ends another entry: "Courage, my friend, courage" (*MA* 82, 295). Both entries appear in *My Apprenticeship*. Not included is Webb's exhortation of "Courage" in her May 1888 diary entry as she thinks back on her break with Joseph Chamberlain, or her 1889 diary entry: "The Booths think my paper on the Jewish community the best thing I have yet accomplished. Courage!" (MacKenzies 1: 252, 278–79).

9. *MA* 117. Also like Burney, Webb served as private secretary for her father, a duty that kept her from her own prose (*MA* 113).

10. In a footnote in *My Apprenticeship*, Webb mentions Leslie Stephen and Mrs. Richard Strachey as members of the "radical and free-thinking set" (*MA* 322n2).

11. MacKenzies 1: 369. Margaret Cole describes the income as only £1000 a year in the introduction to *Beatrice Webb's Diaries, 1924–1932* (xviii).

12. The Webbs always made their own printing and publishing arrangements for their books. Although they distributed their books through Longman's, they usually prepared cheap editions for Fabians, trade union members, and similar groups.

13. The "continuous debate between an Ego that affirms and an Ego that denies, resolves itself, in my case, into two questions intimately connected with each other, the answers to which yield to me a scheme of personal and public conduct," Webb

writes in her introduction. "Can there be a science of social organisation in the sense in which we have a science of mechanics or a science of chemistry, enabling us to forecast what will happen, and perhaps to alter the event by taking appropriate action or persuading others to take it? And secondly, assuming that there be, or will be, such a science of society, is man's capacity for scientific discovery the only faculty required for the reorganisation of society according to an ideal?" (*MA* xiv).

14. Webb writes: "I find the following entry in my diary, showing how closely my intellectual effort had become associated with the memory of my mother." She then quotes from her 1888 diary, when she is thirty and her mother six years dead: "These latter days [I] constantly think of mother: sometimes the feeling of her presence is so strong that I am tempted into a kind of communion with her" (*MA* 17).

15. *MA* 350–51; italics mine. Webb also includes in *My Apprenticeship* her January 1884 diary description of political powerhouse Joseph Chamberlain (without revealing he was her first love): "By temperament he is an enthusiast and a despot. A deep sympathy with the misery and incompleteness of most men's lives, and an earnest desire to right this, transforms political action into a religious crusade; but running alongside this genuine enthusiasm is *a passionate desire to crush opposition to his will, a longing to feel his foot on the necks of others*, though he would persuade himself that he represents the right and his adversaries the wrong" (*MA* 125; italics mine).

16. In *My Apprenticeship*, Webb includes a letter she wrote to her father in 1885 defending the unmarried woman: "I think these strong women have a great future before them in the solution of social questions. . . . I only hope that, instead of trying to ape men and take up men's pursuits, they will carve out their own careers, and not be satisfied until they have found the careers in which their particular form of power will achieve most" (276).

17. Woolf first uses the phrase "natural happiness" in her April 11, 1926, diary entry between references to *My Apprenticeship* (*D* 3: 74).

18. *D* 3: 110, 113. Woolf's September 2, 1926, letter to Margaret Llewelyn Davies reveals that *My Apprenticeship* is still on her mind: "The Keynes,' Lydia and Maynard, are both completely under the sway of the Webbs. . . . Maynard is deeply impressed by her book [*My Apprenticeship*]. . . . Anyhow, the great Keynes—and he gets greater and greater, and buys more and more pictures and builds more and more libraries and bathrooms—is at her feet" (*L* #1667, 3: 289).

19. *MA* 97. Margaret Cole noted in 1956 that the passing of the members of the first Labour Cabinet "without leaving intimate records behind" leaves Webb's *Diaries* "(apart from the highly individual account of Viscount Snowden in his own *Autobiography*) the most considerable first-hand source for the inner history of the experiment" (2: vii). *My Apprenticeship* may, in fact, have prompted Woolf's May 1926 Diary of the General Strike.

20. Woolf began her laconic Asheham House natural history diary while Webb bought a typewriter and began to retype her diary for use in *My Apprenticeship*. Webb

used the term "nervous breakdown" in her September 13, 1916, diary entry (MacKenzies 3: 265).

21. Leonard Woolf's first contribution to the 1917 "collaborative diary" had been just such a carping, humorous view of Beatrice tolling her committees at a Webb lunch (*D* 1: 74). In a March 2, 1915, letter to Margaret Llewelyn Davies during her illness (and therefore written in Leonard's hand), Virginia asked: "Did I tell you that I have decided to write all the novels of Mrs Humphry Ward and all the diaries of Mrs Sidney Webb? It will be my life work. (Leonard has not yet laughed at any of these jokes though I think them rather good)" (*L* #725, 2: 62).

22. Sidney Webb did not value his wife's diary. Beatrice writes in a 1904 diary entry: "When Sidney is with me I cannot talk to the 'Other Self' with whom I commune when I am alone—'it' ceases to be present and only reappears when he is absent" (MacKenzies 2: xi). In a March 19, 1925, diary entry, she writes of Sidney's response to *My Apprenticeship*: "I don't think Sidney quite likes it: he does his best to approve, still more to help me, but there is something about it that he—not exactly resents—but which is unsympathetic. In his heart he fears I am overvaluing it, especially the extracts from the diaries; the whole thing is far too subjective" (MacKenzies 4: 48–49).

23. *L* #2344, 4: 305. Woolf's letter continues: "I wanted to tell you, but was too shy, how much I was pleased by your views upon the possible justification of suicide. Having made the attempt myself, from the best of motives as I thought—not to be a burden on my husband—the conventional accusation of cowardice and sin has always rather rankled. So I was glad of what you said."

24. Webb's diary runs close to three million words; Woolf's, a spare 770,000 (MacKenzies 1: xvii). Following the 1926 *My Apprenticeship*, with its many diary extracts, the posthumous *Our Partnership* appeared in 1948, edited by Barbara Drake and Margaret I. Cole. Cole then edited a two-volume edition of Webb's diaries: *Beatrice Webb's Diaries, 1912–1924* (1952) and *Beatrice Webb's Diaries, 1924–1932* (1956). In their wake came editions of Webb's travel diaries: *Visit to New Zealand: Beatrice Webb's Diary with entries by Sidney Webb* (1959), *Beatrice Webb's American Diary* (1963), and *The Webbs' Australian Diary* (1965). Norman and Jeanne MacKenzie's four-volume *The Diary of Beatrice Webb* (published between 1982 and 1985) presents Webb's diaries from the beginning to the end of her life. Fifty-seven original manuscript diary books, along with Beatrice's (and others') typescripts of them, reside in the British Library of Political and Economic Science.

25. Barbara Caine uses these very words to launch her 1983 review of the first of the four-volume *Diary of Beatrice Webb*, and she describes "the enthusiasm already evident in regard to the *Diary*" as even greater than that for *My Apprenticeship* (81, 82–83).

26. After reading a draft of *My Apprenticeship*, Shaw, the Webbs' lifelong friend, suggested that "it may turn out to be one of the great books of the world" (Caine 82). In 1949, F. R. Leavis called for the volume's reprinting, calling *My Apprenticeship* "an

English classic that has a special value for the reader whose interests are in the first place 'literary'" (*Scrutiny* 173; *Mill on Bentham and Coleridge* 18).

27. 162. In this essay, titled "The Art of Beatrice Webb," Hynes stresses Webb's literary gifts, including her potential as a novelist, and ends: "I am persuaded that if she had made the other choice, and had committed herself to art, she might have been a considerable novelist, a sort of latter-day George Eliot. But I see no reason to regret that she did not. It is surely only literary sentimentality to think that it is more worthy to be a novelist than to be a diarist, or a social researcher, and I am content that we have what we have, one George Eliot and one Beatrice Webb" (171).

28. Cobden-Sanderson marries at age forty-one, even later than either Webb (thirty-four) or Woolf (thirty). He knows, in fact, the Meinertzhagens, Webb's older sister, Georgina, and her husband (2: 54–55).

29. Like the Hogarth Press's 1926 series of short essays, the Hammersmith Publishing Society arose to publish 1-pence tracts such as the lecture on "Socialism and Politics," which inspired it, and Cobden-Sanderson's lecture "Craft-guilds, old and new" (2: 19).

30. The Woolfs will publish these diaries as *The Amberley Papers* in 1937.

31. *E* 4: 406. This 1926 edition bore the more misleading title *The Autobiography and Memoirs of Benjamin Robert Haydon (1786–1846)*. Edited from his *Journals* by Tom Taylor.

32. "Benjamin Haydon," *Wikipedia*.

33. 1: 232. The Italian sculptor Antonio Canova, beloved by writer Mary (Seton) Berry, whose diary Woolf earlier read, comes to England in 1815, visits the marbles as Haydon's guest, and takes back to Italy a cast of one of Haydon's moulds. Haydon tells his February 7, 1816, entry that "Canova's decided opinion" on the marbles "and his letter to Lord Elgin, were [a] direct . . . blow at the opinion of Payne Knight" (1: 230).

34. 1: 77. Norman Gash, reviewing in 1962 the first two of what would be five volumes of Haydon's *Diary*, observes that in writing his memoir, "Haydon used his journals much as he would have used his sketch-books when composing a canvas. The basic words and situations are taken from the journals but the version that appears in the autobiography is often rearranged, touched-up and made artistically more striking" (178–79).

35. Of the year 1820 Haydon writes: "'Go on,' said the inward voice I had heard from my youth; 'work and trust'; and trust and work I did" (1: 293).

36. Woolf will read Francis Kilvert's diaries in 1938 and 1939. She had read Pepys's diary at age fifteen and Boswell's *Journal of a Tour of the Hebrides with Samuel Johnson* at age twenty-one. See my *Becoming Virginia Woolf*.

37. He titled his first painting *Joseph and Mary resting with our Savior after a day's Journey on the Road to Egypt*. His full title for the *Dentatus* further hints at the subject's appeal: *The Celebrated Old Roman Tribune, Dentatus, making his last desperate*

effort against his old soldiers who attacked and murdered him in a narrow pass. George Hamilton's 1832 description of the painting suggests even more: "This old soldier, whose courage had procured him the name of the Roman Achilles, had fought his country's battles for more than forty years, and had been present in one hundred and twenty engagements, had received forty-five wounds . . . [yet] was suffered to exist in poverty and want while others were enriched by the spoils of his valour. A case of such extreme hardship at length aroused the public indignation, & the Decemvirs . . . contrived that he should be assailed in a hollow of a mountain by a band of assassins. In this emergency he placed his back against a rock and withstood all their assaults for a long time, killing fifteen and wounding thirty" (3: 197). In the volumes Woolf read, no less a painter than G. F. Watts declared that Haydon's "pictures are themselves autobiographical notes of the most interesting kind" (2: 828).

38. His good friend William Hazlitt said that Haydon talked better than any painter he ever met (Olney 261). Haydon marvels himself to his 1842 diary: "Think of my influence with my species to induce them to trust me for papers, canvas, chalk, labour, rent, models, to get collectors to pay my taxes, and landlords to abstain from rent; but I always show them my work, and they acquiesce" (2: 739).

39. *E* 4: 410. Haydon's diary ends with this quotation from *King Lear*: "Stretch me no longer on this rough world."

40. In 1960, *The Judgement of Solomon*, one of Haydon's favorite works and his greatest painting according to G. F. Watts and Taylor, appeared at a London auction room rolled up in a dirty table-cloth, faded, cracked, and mislabeled "Italian school, circa 1730." Fortunately, a collector recognized its true provenance, and the painting has now been restored.

41. 2: 552. In his preface to the 1853 second edition, Taylor refuses to discuss questions raised by "omissions and retentions, . . . satisfied that the discussion would be useless" (1: xxxi). We now know he actually bowdlerized diary passages.

42. Haydon's son, Frederic Wordsworth Haydon, published his *Correspondence and Table-Talk* in 1876.

43. Haydon included in his diaries newspaper clippings, Italian exercises, and excerpts from the books he was reading. Pope excluded these from the five volumes.

44. The play's title comes from Haydon's *Diary*, although Parry omitted a telling word. At the end of a long tally of his parts, Haydon marvels: "such are the elements of the mysterious, incomprehensible, singular bit of blood, bottom, bone & genius, B. R. Haydon!" (Pope 2: 273).

45. Hazlitt and Leigh Hunt also wrote sonnets to Haydon.

Chapter 8. The Loose-Leaf Diary

1. Like her 1919–1926 diaries, Woolf's 1927 diary is large: 8 ⅝ inches wide and 11 inches long. Most of its entries are written in her favorite purple ink.

2. *D* 3: 129. In this year drenched in the lust of creation, Woolf's February 28 entry offers another of her diary's rare intimations of sex—or at least lovemaking: "Last night I crept into L's bed to make up a sham quarrel" (*D* 3: 130).

3. "My [diary] notes have been few," Woolf observes in her November 20 entry, "life a cascade, a glissade, a torrent: all together" (*D* 3: 164).

4. Woolf wrote in her May 31, 1920, diary: "It struck me that she is of the cat kind: alien, composed, always solitary & observant" (*D* 2: 44).

5. Forty-six notebooks and many unbound pages reside in the Turnbull Library; seven brief notebooks and further unbound sheets are housed in the Newberry Library in Chicago.

6. The *Journal* entries from January through April 1915 are particularly misleading, for Murry excised the entire context from which they sprang: Mansfield's passionate love affair with French writer Francis Carco that unfolded at this time. One senses, in fact, that the affair and its difficulties motivated the diary-keeping. See Ian A. Gordon's valuable 1959 article "The Editing of Katherine Mansfield's Journal and Scrapbook," which first called attention to Murry's maneuvers, as well as the postscript to his 1963 *Katherine Mansfield*.

7. See Anna Jackson's article "The *Notebooks, Journal,* and Papers of Katherine Mansfield: Is Any of This Her Diary?"

8. *Journal* 47, 48–49. I quote here and hereafter from the 1927 *Journal* because that is what Woolf read; however, throughout I will indicate in footnotes differences between Murry's transcriptions and the actual *Notebooks*.

9. Woolf's own answer to the question is "Because I have written nothing for an age" (*D* 3: 199).

10. *Journal* 33. Scott suggests a closer date might be 1917 and that this passage relates to fragments of a story on this topic written on unbound paper (*Notebooks* 2: 110n66).

11. *Journal* 112. Along with the title, Murry added the quotation marks around "didn't want her to work no more" and other punctuation: c.f. *Notebooks* 2: 169.

12. *Journal* 216. Mansfield underlined "power" and wrote "Off his guard" as a separate sentence (*Notebooks* 2: 315).

13. *Journal* 104. Scott transcribes this passage with two punctuation changes that create a slight shift in sense: "I live to write: the lovely world (God how lovely the external world is!)" (*Notebooks* 2: 154). Here the colon suggests more strongly than Murry's period that Mansfield lives to write "the lovely world"; furthermore, she is not exclaiming *to* God, as Murry's inserted comma suggests, but rather employing "God" for emphasis.

14. "One lives by the sky again—by the changes of cloud & light," Mansfield wrote to Woolf on December 27, 1920, from the nursing home in Mentone (*Letters* 4: 154). Three years earlier, Mansfield wrote to Woolf of her short story "Kew Gardens": "Theres a still, quivering, changing light over it all and a sense of those couples dissolving in the bright air which fascinates me" (Mansfield *Letters* 1: 327).

15. Scott transcribes Mansfield's signature three ellipsis dots—not Murry's period and ellipsis (*Notebooks* 2: 312).

16. *Journal* 1. Murry's disingenuousness appears from his first editor's note to the 1927 *Journal*, which begins, "K.M. ruthlessly destroyed all record of the time between her return from New Zealand to England in 1909, and 1914" (*Journal* 1). In reality, he possessed four notebooks and many unbound papers from this time frame (See *Notebooks* 1).

17. *Journal* 141. Murry's ellipsis in this passage obscures a more immediate cause of Mansfield's despair. The omitted words: "[I]t all came back so vividly—all is connected with this feeling that J. [Murry] and I are no longer as we were. I love him but he rejects my *living* love. This is anguish. These are the worst days of my whole life" (*Notebooks* 2: 188).

18. *Journal* 146. Scott transcribes "like madness" as a separate sentence (*Notebooks* 2: 191).

19. *Journal* 37. Murry omitted the words "to you" at the end of the final sentence: "[T]hen I will come as quickly as I can to you." He also left out his own loss of status in the remainder of the entry: "You know I can never be Jack's [Murry's] lover again. You have me, you're in my flesh as well as in my soul. I give Jack my 'surplus' love but to you I hold and to you I give my deepest love. Jack is no more than—-—anybody might be" (*Notebooks* 2: 15–16).

20. Sadly, Murry's transcription of this and the next word shifts Mansfield's continued projection of herself as dead. Scott transcribes the sentence: "[P]ut me in mind of something that happened or was when we were alive" (*Notebooks* 2: 16).

21. *Journal* 119. Once again Murry omits the full context, that these thoughts relate to Mansfield's unhappiness with him: "[H]ow little Jack shares with me. . . . He ought not to have married. There never was a creature less fitted by nature for life with *a woman*. And the strange truth is I don't WANT him to change. I want to see him and then adjust my ways & go on alone & WORK. Life without *work*—I would commit suicide" (*Notebooks* 2: 171, 172).

22. Scott reports that Murry's note beside the title is "Title of a story—quite irrelevant" (*Notebooks* 2: 179n127).

23. *Journal* 134. This dream revelation follows a lengthy analysis of the failures of her relationship with Murry—again omitted. Mansfield also capitalized "Life" and "Death" in the last sentence and connected the last two sentences (*Notebooks* 2: 180).

24. *Journal* 166–68. Once more Murry prevents us from seeing that this "confession" is embedded in Mansfield's disappointment with him. She actually wrote, "There is no question of what Jack calls passing beyond it: this is false," and she writes here of her knowledge "that Jack wishes me dead—and of his killing me" (*Notebooks* 2: 201, 202).

25. On June 10, 1918, Woolf wrote to Violet Dickinson to thank her for buying two copies of Mansfield's *Prelude* from the Hogarth Press: "She is a woman from New

Zealand, with a passion for writing" (*L* #941, 2: 248). Fourteen months later, Woolf defended Mansfield in a letter to Katherine Arnold-Forster: "You thought her too painted and posed for your more spartan taste I think. But she is all kinds of interesting things underneath, and has a passion for writing, so that we hold religious meetings together praising Shakespeare" (*L* #1073, 2: 383). In fact, Mansfield appears to have taken the lead in asserting their accord. In a letter to Woolf dated provisionally June 24, 1917, she writes, "But pray consider how rare is it to find some one with the same passion for writing that you have, who desires to be scrupulously truthful with you" (*Letters* 1: 313).

26. *Journal* 135–36. Murry omits matters of emphasis in this passage. In the *Notebooks*, Scott transcribes Mansfield as underlining "induce," capitalizing "Life," and adding an exclamation mark after "marvellous thing." In fact, she transcribes it: "My God, its [*sic*] a marvellous thing!" (2: 181). Additionally, in the first sentence Mansfield wrote "I feel wakeful"—not "I feel more wakeful" as Murry has it—and his penchant to add commas obscures the fact that Mansfield wrote the opening line as one long uninterrupted thought. Other small transcription errors also appear.

27. Woolf read this August 30, 1914, diary entry early in the *Journal*: "We go to Cornwall to-morrow, I suppose. I've re-read my diary. Tell me, Is there a God? I'm old to-night. Ah, I wish I had someone to love me, comfort me and stop me thinking" (15). The differences between this Murry transcription and Scott's in the *Notebooks* illustrate in miniature the maddening misprision of the entire 1927 *Journal*. Scott transcribes this entry: "Ive reread my diary. Tell me, is there a God! I do not trust Jack [Murry]. Im old tonight. Ah, I wish I had a lover to nurse me—love me—hold me—comfort me—to stop me thinking" (*Notebooks* 1: 284).

28. *Journal* 185. Scott transcribes Mansfield as capitalizing "Live," and writing the more logical "What does one mean by that?" rather than "What does she mean by that?" (*Notebooks* 2: 280).

29. *Journal* 237. Scott transcribes no exclamation mark after "gentle" (*Notebooks* 2: 293).

30. *Journal* 200. Anna Jackson, who has studied the actual notebooks and unbound papers at the Turnbull Library, writes vividly on this point: "The collection of her manuscripts at the Turnbull library is a huge archive of exercise books, engagement diaries and notebooks from the 1910s and 1920s, most of them barely written in. Of a 'Monster Exercise Book' of eighty pages, she used six. The disproportionate number of brief entries dated January in the *Journal* comes from her habit of filling the first few pages of her engagement diaries each year before abandoning the task. She is as quick to abandon projects she sets for herself. . . . Her practise of numbering the pages of an exercise book in advance of her filling it in gives a particularly clear picture of how far her resolve outdoes her industry" ("The *Notebooks*" 84).

31. *Journal* 236. Murry unaccountably dates this item "February" 1922 in the 1927 *Journal*, despite the fact that the list follows an item dated October 18 in the 1922 diary

and comes just before the next-to-last diary item, Mansfield's meticulous record of monthly expenditures for the year (*Notebooks* 2: 329–30).

32. Again, Anna Jackson explains this vividly: "Each notebook is in itself a collection of beginnings of various writing projects. Exercise books that begin being kept as a diary turn into recipe books or notebooks for first drafts of stories or are turned to some other use, while collections of poems, notes on Shakespeare, and other projects, are turned into diaries, or have diary entries randomly placed within them. Apart from the sporadic attempts to keep a diary, usually at the beginning of the year, most of the entries that Murry first put together to make up the *Journal* seem to have been written anywhere at all, in whatever piece of paper was handy at the time . . . and are different lengths depending in part on where they were written and how much space was allotted them" (85). Joanne Campbell Tidwell suggests Mansfield's notebooks may be more meaningful as a postmodern text of chaotic existence than as a diary (68).

33. *Journal* 201. Mansfield capitalized "Thy" (*Notebooks* 2: 290).

34. *Journal* 199. Murry unaccountably omitted this sentence following "because I will not come," which further attests to Mansfield's personification of her stories: "When first they knock how fresh and eager they are" (*Notebooks* 2: 277). Mansfield also used an exclamation point after "Why do ye tarry"—not a question mark as Murry has it.

35. *Journal* 226. Scott transcribes Mansfield as underscoring "borne" rather than "and," as Murry has it, which creates a slightly different sense (*Notebooks* 2: 320).

36. Several 1927 *Journal* passages disclose the burden of Mansfield's keen senses. In January 1920, for instance, she tells her diary: "In the afternoon Foster came and agreed I must leave here. . . . I couldn't rest or sleep. The roaring of the sea was insufferable" (*Journal* 141). An October 1921 notebook item complains: "But I could not get away from the sound of the sea, and Beryl fanning her hair at the window. These things would not *die down*" (*Journal* 196). In a July 30, 1923, letter to French painter Jacques Raverat after Mansfield's January death, Woolf urged: "Please read Katherine's works, and tell me your opinion. My theory is that while she possessed the most amazing *senses* of her generation so that she could actually reproduce this room for instance, with its fly, clock, dog, tortoise if need be, to the life, she was as weak as water, as insipid, and a great deal more commonplace, when she had to use her mind" (*L* #1414, 3: 59).

37. *E* 4: 447. In contrast, Anna Jackson stresses that, as opposed to either the 1927 *Journal* or the 1997 *Notebooks*, the manuscripts themselves "give a very clear sense of how unrelated all these fragments of writing are to each other" (94). Nevertheless, like Woolf, she acknowledges the shaping power of the diary form: "What is remarkable is how the diary form works to give significance to the kinds of juxtapositions that arise, how the diary form knits up fragments of writing into a complete text with its own surface, a surface it is tempting to read as a kind of mirror for the writer's self" (97).

38. Thomas Cobden-Sanderson also spoke of Dorothy Wordsworth's journal in *his* journals, which Woolf read in September 1926.

39. In her Collins letter after her Asheham visit in August 1917, Mansfield wrote to Woolf: "We have got the same job, Virginia & it is really very curious & thrilling that we should both, quite apart from each other, be after so very nearly the same thing. We are you know; there's no denying it" (Mansfield *Letters* 1: 327).

40. *Journal* 43–44. An important difference appears in Scott's transcription. While Woolf read Murry's "Nor perhaps in prose," Scott shows Mansfield writing: "No, perhaps in Prose—almost certainly in a kind of special prose" (*Notebooks* 2: 33).

41. *Journal* 94, 189. Mansfield wrote to Murry in November 1919 from Casetta: "How I envy Virginia; no wonder she can write. There is always in her writing a calm freedom of expression as though she were at peace—her roof over her—her own possessions round her—and her man somewhere within call. Boge what have I done that I should have *all* the handicaps—plus a disease and an enemy" (*Mansfield Letters* 3: 127–28).

Chapter 9. Artist at a Crossroads

1. This diary book is 8 ¼ inches wide and 10 inches long.

2. *D* 3: 198. Woolf writes to Leonard from France: "I think we shall have a very happy and exciting autumn, in spite of the complete failure of Orlando" (*L* #1932, 3: 539).

3. In a letter to Vanessa on December 27, 1928, Woolf continues to associate the country with female spiritual retreat: "We came here [Rodmell] this evening and I am at present in the exalted state of the newly veiled nun" (*L* #1973, 3: 566).

4. *D* 3: 173. According to Olivier Bell, Beerbohm wrote December 30, 1927 that "he rated *The Common Reader* 'above any modern book of criticism,' but that in her novels VW was 'so hard on us common readers'" (*D* 3: 173n2).

5. On August 12, 1928, Woolf writes to Saxon Sydney-Turner of her plan to do London Library research on Fulke Greville, who will appear in "Dr. Burney's Evening Party" (*L* #1913, 3: 516).

6. On her father's birthday, November 28, Woolf tells her diary: "He would have been 96, yes, today; & could have been 96, like other people one has known; but mercifully was not. His life would have entirely ended mine. What would have happened? No writing, no books" (*D* 3: 208).

7. *D* 3: 192. In her May 2, 1928, letter to Julian Bell, critiquing his poems, she gives him this advice, which reflects her diary's role in her own literary growth—and particularly her 1899 diary at age seventeen: "I think you want to write a great deal still so as to get things to run quickly in words. But I quite agree that one must begin by being a pettifogging character, with a note book, trying to get the colour of the sunset right, at the beginning" (*L* #1888, 3: 491). Recall her 1899 diary's "A Chapter on Sunsets" (*PA* 155–56).

8. *D* 3: 212, 213. Sarah Davison points out that Woolf may have drawn her famous "Mrs. Brown" from a little-known 1909 Beerbohm article titled "Middle-Class Life from Without," in which Beerbohm writes: "I have often urged our dramatists to give the aristocracy a rest, and write plays about the class to which they themselves belong. An intimate and complete study of Mrs. Brown is of more account than the present-ment of the Duchess of Hampshire as she is vaguely and respectfully supposed to be" (352).

9. *D* 3: 232. Woolf's letters across these six months reiterate this theme. "I want to write a serious book," she writes to Quentin Bell on March 20, 1929. "Now if one writes imaginative works one has to stop talking" (*L* #2012, 4: 34).

10. *D* 3: 217, 220. Woolf writes to Vita Sackville-West on February 4, 1929, "A woman writes that she has to stop and kiss the page when she reads O[rlando]" (*L* #1993, 4: 14).

11. *D* 3: 219. Woolf writes to Vanessa on May 18, 1929: "As for Molly [MacCarthy]— do we all look like old women now, sitting by the open window, sadly reminiscing and sighing and getting up with difficulty? I was taken aback, to think she is 6 months younger than I am; and I feel as young as a flea" (*L* #2031, 4: 59).

Works Consulted

Primary Sources

The Autobiography and Memoirs of Benjamin Robert Haydon (1786–1846). Edited from his *Journals* by Tom Taylor. Intro. Aldous Huxley. 2 vols. London: Peter Davies, 1926. Print.

Barbellion, W.N.P. *The Journal of a Disappointed Man and A Last Diary*. Intro. H. G. Wells. London: Chatto and Windus, 1919. Print.

Beatrice Webb's Diaries, 1912–1924. Ed. Margaret I. Cole. Intro. Rt. Hon. Lord Beveridge. London: Longmans, Green and Co., 1952. Print.

Beatrice Webb's Diaries, 1924–1932. Ed. Margaret Cole. London: Longmans, Green and Co., 1956. Print.

Blunt, Wilfrid Scawen. *My Diaries: Being a Personal Narrative of Events, 1888 to 1914*. Foreword Lady Gregory. 2 vols. New York: Knopf, 1921. Print.

Boswell, James. *The Journal of a Tour to Corsica; and Memoirs of Pascal Paoli*. Ed. and Intro. S. C. Roberts. Cambridge: Cambridge University Press, 1923. Print.

———. *The Journal of a Tour to the Hebrides with Samuel Johnson, LL.D.* Ed. Robert Carruthers. London: Office of the National Illustrated Library, 1852. Print.

Boswell's Journal of A Tour to the Hebrides with Samuel Johnson, LL.D. Pub. from the original ms. Ed. Frederick A. Pottle and Charles H. Bennett. New York: Viking Press, 1936. Print.

Cather, Willa. *The Song of the Lark*. Boston: Houghton Mifflin, 1937. Print.

The Collected Letters of Katherine Mansfield. Ed. Vincent O'Sullivan and Margaret Scott. 4 vols. Oxford: Clarendon Press, 1984, 1987, 1993, 1996. Print.

The Diary and Letters of Madame D'Arblay (Frances Burney). With notes by W. C. Ward and essay by Lord Macaulay. 3 vols. London: Frederick Warne, 1892. Print.

The Diary of a Country Parson: The Reverend James Woodforde. Ed. John Beresford. 5 vols. London: Oxford University Press, 1924–1931. Print.

The Diary of a Lady-in-Waiting: Being the Diary Illustrative of the Times of George the Fourth Interspersed with Original Letters from the Late Queen Caroline and from other Distinguished Persons. Ed. A. Francis Steuart. 2 vols. London: John Lane, 1908. Print.

The Diary of Beatrice Webb. Ed. Norman MacKenzie and Jeanne MacKenzie. 4 vols. Cambridge, Mass.: Belknap Press of Harvard University Press, 1982–85. Print.

The Diary of Benjamin Robert Haydon. Ed. Willard Bissell Pope. 5 vols. Cambridge, Mass.: Harvard University Press, 1960, 1963. Print.

The Diary of John Evelyn. Ed. William Bray. Intro. Richard Garnett. 2 vols. London: M. Walter Dunne, 1901. Print.

The Diary of Samuel Pepys. Ed. Robert Latham and William Matthews. 11 vols. Berkeley: University of California Press, 1970. Print.

The Diary of Samuel Pepys. Ed. Henry B. Wheatley. 8 vols. London: G. Bell, 1962. First published in 10 vols., 1893–1899. Print.

The Diary of the Lady Anne Clifford. Intro. V. Sackville-West. New York: George H. Doran, 1923. Print.

The Diary of the Lady Anne Clifford, 1616 to 1619: A Critical Edition. Ed. Katherine O. Acheson. New York: Garland, 1995. Print.

Diary, Reminiscences, and Correspondence of Henry Crabb Robinson, Barrister-at-Law, F.S.A. Ed. Thomas Sadler. 2 vols. Boston: Houghton, Mifflin, 1898. Print.

The Early Diary of Frances Burney, 1768–1778. Ed. Annie Raine Ellis. 2 vols. London: G. Bell and Sons, 1913. Print.

Enjoying Life And Other Literary Remains of W.N.P. Barbellion. London: Chatto and Windus, 1919. Print.

Extracts of the Journals and Correspondence of Miss Berry from the Year 1783 to 1852. Ed. Lady Theresa Lewis. 3 vols. London: Longmans, Green, 1865. Print.

The Famous Miss Burney: The Diaries and Letters of Fanny Burney. Ed. Barbara G. Schrank and David J. Supino. New York: John Day, 1976. Print.

The Goncourt Journals, 1851–1870. Ed. and trans. Lewis Galantière. Garden City, N.Y.: Doubleday, Doran, 1937. Print.

An Irish Peer on the Continent (1801–1803), Being a Narrative of the Tour of Stephen, 2nd Earl Mount Cashell, Through France, Italy, Etc., as Related by Catherine Wilmot. Ed. Thomas U. Sadleir, M.A., Barrister-at-Law. London: Williams and Norgate, 1920. Print.

Jacks, Lawrence Pearsall. *Life and Letters of Stopford Brooke.* 2 vols. New York: Charles Scribner's, 1917. Print.

The Journal of Elizabeth Lady Holland, 1791–1811. Ed. Earl of Ilchester. 2 vols. London: Longmans, Green, 1908. Print.

Journal of Katherine Mansfield. Ed. J. Middleton Murry. New York: Knopf, 1927. Print.

The Journal of Sir Walter Scott. Ed. W.E.K. Anderson. Oxford: Clarendon Press, 1972. Print.

The Journal of Sir Walter Scott, 1825–32. Ed. David Douglas. Edinburgh: Douglas and Foulis, printed from the stereotype plates made for the edition of 1891, with a few inaccuracies corrected. Print.

The Journals and Letters of Fanny Burney (Madame D'Arblay). Ed. Joyce Hemlow with Curtis D. Cecil and Althea Douglas. 12 vols. Oxford: Clarendon Press, 1972. Print.

The Journals of Thomas James Cobden-Sanderson, 1879–1922. 2 vols. London: Richard Cobden-Sanderson, 1926. Print.

The Katherine Mansfield Notebooks. Ed. Margaret Scott. 2 vols. Minneapolis: University of Minnesota Press, 1997. Print.

Kilvert's Diary: Selections from the Diary of the Rev. Francis Kilvert. Ed. William Plomer. 3 vols. London: Cape, 1938–1940. Print.

Letters and Journals of Anne Chalmers; Edited by Her Daughter. London: Chelsea Publishing, 1923. Print.

Letters of Leonard Woolf. Ed. Frederic Spotts. London: Bloomsbury, 1992. Print.

Lockhart, John G. *Memoirs of the Life of Sir Walter Scott*. 10 vols. Edinburgh: Robert Cadell, 1839. Print.

MacKenzie, Norman, ed. *The Letters of Sidney and Beatrice Webb*. Vol. 3, *Pilgrimage, 1912–1947*. Cambridge: Cambridge University Press, 1978. Print.

Meryon, Charles. *Memoirs of the Lady Hester Stanhope, as Related by Herself in Conversations with Her Physician*. 3 vols. London: Henry Colburn, 1845. Print.

———. *Travels of Lady Hester Stanhope: Forming the Completion of Her Memoirs Narrated by Her Physician*. 3 vols. London: Henry Colburn, 1846. Print.

Moore, Thomas. *The Life, Letters and Journals of Lord Byron*. London: John Murray, 1866. Print.

Note-Book of Anton Chekhov. Trans. S. S. Koteliansky and Leonard Woolf. New York: B. W. Huebsch, 1921. Print.

The Private Diaries of Stendhal (Marie-Henri Beyle). Ed. and Trans. Robert Sage. New York: Doubleday, 1954. Print.

Russell, Bertrand, and Patricia Russell. *The Amberley Papers: The Letters and Diaries of Bertrand Russell's Parents*. 2 vols. New York: Norton, 1937. Print.

Ryland, Frederick, George Ravenscroft Dennis, Sir Frederick Richard Falkiner, W. Spencer Jackson, Constance Jacob, and John Henry Bernard, eds. *The Prose Works of Jonathan Swift*. 12 vols. London: George Bell and Sons, 1900–1914. Print.

The Scrapbook of Katherine Mansfield. Ed. J. Middleton Murry. New York: Knopf, 1940. Print.

Selected Letters of Vanessa Bell. Ed. Regina Marler. New York: Pantheon, 1993. Print.

Silver, Brenda R. *Virginia Woolf's Reading Notebooks*. Princeton: Princeton University Press, 1983. Print.

Stead, C. K. *The Letters and Journals of Katherine Mansfield: A Selection*. London: Allen Lane, 1977. Print.

Stendhal: Journal. Texte établi et annoté par Henry Debraye et Louis Royer. Tome Premier, 1801–1805. Paris: Librairie Ancienne Honoré Champion, 1923. Print.

Sutton, Denys, ed. and intro. *Letters of Roger Fry*. 2 vols. New York: Random House, 1972. Print.

Swift, Jonathan. *The Journal to Stella*. Vol. 2 of *The Prose Works of Jonathan Swift, D.D.* Ed. Frederick Ryland et al. London: George Bell and Sons, 1900. Print.

——. *The Journal to Stella*. Vols. 2 and 3 of *The Works of Jonathan Swift*. Ed. Sir Walter Scott. Edinburgh: Constable, 1814. Print.

——. *Journal to Stella*. Ed. Harold Williams. 2 vols. Oxford: Clarendon Press, 1948. Print.

Tant' Alie of Transvaal: Her Diary, 1880–1902. Trans. from the Taal by Emily Hobhouse. London: George Allen and Unwin, 1923.

Webb, Beatrice. *My Apprenticeship*. London: Longmans, Green and Co., 1926. Print.

William Allingham: A Diary. Ed. H. Allingham and D. Radford. London: Macmillan, 1907. Print.

Woolf, Virginia. *The Common Reader*. Ed. and Intro. Andrew McNeillie. New York: Harcourt Brace Jovanovich, 1925. Print.

——. *The Complete Shorter Fiction of Virginia Woolf*. Ed. Susan Dick. New York: Harcourt Brace Jovanovich, 1985.Print.

——. *The Diary of Virginia Woolf*. Ed. Anne Olivier Bell. 5 vols. New York: Harcourt Brace Jovanovich, 1977–84. Print.

——. *The Essays of Virginia Woolf*. Ed. Andrew McNeillie and Stuart N. Clarke. 6 vols. New York: Harcourt Brace Jovanovich, 1986–2011. Print.

——. *The Letters of Virginia Woolf*. Ed. Nigel Nicolson and Joanne Trautmann. 6 vols. New York: Harcourt Brace Jovanovich, 1975–80. Print.

——. *A Moment's Liberty: The Shorter Diary*. Abridged and ed. Anne Olivier Bell. Intro. Quentin Bell. New York: Harcourt Brace Jovanovich, 1990. Print.

——. *Moments of Being*. Ed. and Intro. Jeanne Schulkind. 2nd. ed. New York: Harcourt Brace Jovanovich, 1985. Print.

——. *A Passionate Apprentice: The Early Journals, 1897–1909*. Ed. and intro. Mitchell A. Leaska. New York: Harcourt Brace Jovanovich, 1990. Print.

——. *A Room of One's Own*. New York: Harcourt Brace Jovanovich, 1929. Print.

——. *The Second Common Reader*. New York: Harcourt Brace Jovanovich, 1932. Print.

——. *Three Guineas*. New York: Harcourt Brace Jovanovich, 1938. Print.

——. *A Writer's Diary: Being Extracts from the Diary of Virginia Woolf*. Ed. Leonard Woolf. Afterword Louise Bogan and Josephine Schaefer. New York: New American Library, 1968. Print.

Secondary Sources

Allentuck, Marcia. Rev. of *The Diary of Benjamin Robert Haydon*, vols. 1 and 2. *Art Bulletin* 45.1 (Mar. 1963): 74–77. Print.

Argento, Dominick. "From the Diary of Virginia Woolf." Nashville: Gasparo, 1989. Print.

Balzac, Honoré de. "Preface." *The Charterhouse of Parma*. Trans. Lady Mary Loyd, rev. Robert Cantwell. New York: Heritage Press, 1955. Print.

Bell, Anne Olivier. *Editing Virginia Woolf's Diary*. London: Bloomsbury Workshop, 1990. Print.

Bell, Quentin. *Virginia Woolf: A Biography*. 2 vols. New York: Harcourt Brace Jovanovich, 1972. Print.

"Benjamin Haydon." Wikipedia. Online source.

Bishop, Edward L. "Metaphor and the Subversive Process of Virginia Woolf's Essays." *Style* 21.4 (Winter 1987): 573–88. Print.

Blodgett, Harriet, ed. *"Capacious Hold-All": An Anthology of Englishwomen's Diary Writings*. Charlottesville: University Press of Virginia, 1991. Print.

———. *Centuries of Female Days: English Women's Private Diaries*. New Brunswick, N.J.: Rutgers University Press: 1988. Print.

———. "A Woman Writer's Diary: Virginia Woolf Revisited." *Prose Studies: History, Theory, Criticism* 12.1 (May 1989): 57–71. Print.

Brown, Catherine. "The Russian Soul Englished." *Journal of Modern Literature* 36.1 (2012): 132–49. Print.

Bunkers, Suzanne L., and Cynthia A. Huff, eds. *Inscribing the Daily: Critical Essays on Women's Diaries*. Amherst: University of Massachusetts Press, 1996. Print.

Caine, Barbara. "Beatrice Webb and her Diary." *Victorian Studies* 27.1 (Autumn 1983): 81–89. Print.

Clark, Lorna. "The Diarist as Novelist: Narrative Strategies in the Journals and Letters of Frances Burney." *English Studies in Canada* 27 (2001): 283–302. Print.

Cottam, Rachel. "Secret Scratching: The Diary and Its Writing." Diss. University of Sussex, 1996. Print.

Cuddy-Keane, Melba. "The Politics of Comic Modes in Virginia Woolf's *Between the Acts*." *PMLA* 105.2 (Mar. 1990): 273–85. Print.

Cummings, Frederick J. Rev. of *The Diary of Benjamin Robert Haydon*, vol. 3. *Art Journal* 24.4 (Summer 1965): 396–97. Print.

Daugherty, Beth Rigel. "Taking Her Fences: The Equestrian Virginia Woolf." In *Virginia Woolf and the Natural World: Selected Papers from the Twentieth Annual International Conference on Virginia Woolf*. Ed. Kristin Czarnecki and Carrie Rohman. Clemson, S.C.: Clemson University Press, 2011. 61–71. Print.

Davidson-Pegan, Claire. Rev. of *Virginia Woolf and the Russian Point of View*, by Roberta Rubenstein. *Woolf Studies Annual* 18 (2012): 157. Print.

Davison, Sarah. "Catching Mrs. Brown: Max Beerbohm's Influence on Virginia Woolf's 'Mr. Bennett and Mrs. Brown.'" *Notes and Queries* 53.3 (Sept. 2006): 353–55. Print.

The Early Life and Education of John Evelyn. With a commentary by H. Maynard Smith. Volume 11, Oxford Historical and Literary Studies. Oxford: Clarendon Press, 1920. Print.

England, A. B. "Private and Public Rhetoric in the *Journal to Stella*." *Essays in Criticism* 22.2 (1972): 131–41. Print.

Fernald, Anne E. *Virginia Woolf: Feminism and the Reader*. New York: Palgrave Macmillan, 2006. Print.

———. "Woolf and Intertextuality." *Virginia Woolf in Context*. Ed. Bryony Randall and Jane Goldman. Cambridge: Cambridge University Press, 2012. 52–64. Print.

Gash, Norman. Rev. of *The Diary of Benjamin Robert Haydon*, vols. 1 and 2. *English Historical Review* 77.302 (Jan. 1962): 178–79. Print.

Glendinning, Victoria. *Leonard Woolf: A Biography*. New York: Free Press, 2006. Print.

Gordon, Ian A. "The Editing of Katherine Mansfield's Journal and Scrapbook." *Landfall* 49 (1959): 62–69. Print.

———. *Katherine Mansfield*. Rev. ed. London: Longmans, Green and Co., 1963. Print.

Gorky, Maxim. *Reminiscences of Tolstoy, Chekhov and Andreev*. Trans. Katherine Mansfield, S. S. Koteliansky, and Leonard Woolf. London: Hogarth Press, 1934. Print.

Gristwood, Sarah. *Recording Angels: The Secret World of Women's Diaries*. London: Harrap, 1988. Print.

Hamilton, G. *The English School: A Series of the Most Approved Productions in Painting and Sculpture Executed by British Artists from the Days of Hogarth to the Present Time*. Vol. 3. London: Charles Tilt, 1832. Web.

Handley, C. S. *An Annotated Bibliography of Diaries Printed in English*. 3rd ed. Aldeburgh, England: Hanover Press, 2002. Print.

Harris, Alexandra. *Virginia Woolf*. London: Thames and Hudson, 2011. Print.

Hemlow, Joyce. "Letters and Journals of Fanny Burney: Establishing the Text." *Editing Eighteenth-Century Texts*. Papers given at the Editorial Conference, University of Toronto, October 1967. Toronto: University of Toronto Press, 1968. 25–43. Print.

Holleyman, G. A. *Catalogue of Books from the Library of Leonard and Virginia Woolf*. Brighton: Holleyman and Treacher, 1975. Print.

Humm, Maggie, ed. *The Edinburgh Companion to Virginia Woolf and the Arts*. Edinburgh: Edinburgh University Press, 2010. Print.

Hynes, Samuel. "The Art of Beatrice Webb." *Edwardian Occasions: Essays on English Writing in the Early Twentieth Century*. New York: Oxford University Press, 1972. Print.

Jackson, Anna. *Diary Poetics: Form and Style in Writers' Diaries, 1915–1962*. New York: Routledge, 2010. Print.

———. "The *Notebooks, Journal,* and Papers of Katherine Mansfield: Is Any of This Her Diary?" *Journal of New Zealand Literature* 18–19 (2000–2001): 83–99.

Kagle, Steven E. *American Diary Literature, 1620–1799*. Boston: Twayne, 1979. Print.

Kenney, Susan M., and Edwin J. Kenney Jr. "Virginia Woolf and the Art of Madness." *Massachusetts Review: A Quarterly of Literature, the Arts and Public Affairs* 23.1 (Spring 1982): 161–85. Print.

Keynes, Geoffrey. *John Evelyn: A Study in Bibliophily with a Bibliography of His Writings*. Oxford: Clarendon Press, 1968. Print.

Klein, Lisa M. "Lady Anne Clifford as Mother and Matriarch: Domestic and Dynastic

Issues in her Life and Writings." *Journal of Family History* 26.1 (Jan. 2001): 18–38. Print.

Langford, Rachael, and Russell West, eds. *Marginal Voices, Marginal Forms: Diaries in European Literature and History.* Amsterdam: Rodopi, 1999. Print.

Leavis, F. R. "Introduction." *Mill on Bentham and Coleridge.* Cambridge: Cambridge University Press, 1950. 1–38. Print.

———. "Beatrice Webb in Partnership." Rev. of *Our Partnership. Scrutiny* 16.2 (June 1949): 173–76. Print.

Lee, Hermione. *Virginia Woolf.* New York: Knopf, 1997. Print.

Lejeune, Philippe. *On Diary.* Ed. Jeremy D. Popkin and Julie Rak. Trans. Katherine Durnin. Honolulu: University of Hawai'i Press, 2009. Print.

Levenson, Michael. *Modernism.* New Haven: Yale University Press, 2011. Print.

Lewis, Pericles. *The Cambridge Introduction to Modernism.* Cambridge: Cambridge University Press, 2007. Print.

Longford, Elizabeth. *A Pilgrimage of Passion: The Life of Wilfrid Scawen Blunt.* New York: Knopf, 1980. Print.

Lounsberry, Barbara. *Becoming Virginia Woolf: Her Early Diaries and the Diaries She Read.* Gainesville: University of Florida Press, 2014. Print.

Lowe, Peter. "Cultural Continuity in a Time of War: Virginia Woolf's *Between the Acts* and T. S. Eliot's 'East Coker.'" *Yeats Eliot Review* 25.1 (Spring 2008): 2–19. Print.

Mallon, Thomas. *A Book of One's Own: People and Their Diaries.* New York: Ticknor and Fields, 1984. Print.

Marburg, Clara. *Mr. Pepys and Mr. Evelyn.* Philadelphia: University of Pennsylvania Press, 1935. Print.

Martinson, Deborah. *In the Presence of Audience: The Self in Diaries and Fiction.* Columbus: Ohio State University Press, 2003. Print.

Nicolson, Nigel. *Portrait of a Marriage.* New York: Atheneum, 1973. Print.

Olney, Clarke. "John Keats and Benjamin Robert Haydon." *PMLA* 49.1 (Mar. 1934): 258–75. Print.

Patten, John A. *Sir Walter Scott: A Character Study.* London: James Clarke, 1932. Print.

Podnieks, Elizabeth. *Daily Modernism: The Literary Diaries of Virginia Woolf, Antonia White, Elizabeth Smart, and Anaïs Nin.* Montreal: McGill-Queen's University Press, 2000. Print.

Pollard, A. F. "An Essay in Historical Method: The Barbellion Diaries." *History* 6:21 (Apr. 1921): 23–31. Print.

Ponsonby, Arthur. *Samuel Pepys.* New York: Macmillan, 1928. Print.

Powell, Stephen D. "Cor Laceratum: Corresponding Till Death in Swift's *Journal to Stella.*" *Modern Language Review* 94.2 (Apr. 1999): 341–54. Print.

Quinones, Ricardo J. *Mapping Literary Modernism: Time and Development.* Princeton: Princeton University Press, 1985. Print.

Raitt, Suzanne. *Vita and Virginia: The Work and Friendship of V. Sackville-West and Virginia Woolf.* Oxford: Clarendon Press, 1993. Print.

Reid, Panthea. *Art and Affection: A Life of Virginia Woolf.* Oxford: Oxford University Press, 1996. Print.

Rubenstein, Roberta. *Virginia Woolf and the Russian Point of View.* New York: Palgrave Macmillan, 2009. Print.

Sackville-West, V. *Knole and the Sackvilles.* New York: George H. Doran, 1922. Print.

Schlaeger, Jürgen. "Self-Exploration in Early Modern Diaries." *Marginal Voices, Marginal Forms: Diaries in European Literature and History.* Ed. Rachael Langford and Russell West. Amsterdam: Rodopi, 1999. 22–36. Print.

Schmidt, Michael. *The Novel: A Biography.* Cambridge, Mass.: Belknap Press of Harvard University Press, 2014. Print.

Schoolcraft, Ralph. "For Whom the Beyle Toils: Stendhal and Pseudonymous Authorship." *PMLA* 119.2 (Mar. 2004): 247–64. Print.

Scott, Margaret. *Recollecting Mansfield.* Auckland, New Zealand: Godwit, 2001. Print.

Sellers, Susan. "Virginia Woolf's Diaries and Letters." *The Cambridge Companion to Virginia Woolf.* Ed. Sue Roe and Susan Sellers. Cambridge: Cambridge University Press, 2000. 109–26. Print.

Shannon, Drew Patrick. "The Deep Old Desk: The Diary of Virginia Woolf." Diss. University of Cincinnati, 2007. Online source.

Sherry, Vincent. *The Great War and the Language of Modernism.* Oxford: Oxford University Press, 2003. Print.

Simons, Judy. *Diaries and Journals of Literary Women from Fanny Burney to Virginia Woolf.* Iowa City: University of Iowa Press, 1990. Print.

Smith, H. Maynard. *The Early Life and Education of John Evelyn.* London: Oxford University Press, 1920. Print.

Spater, George. "The Monks House Library." *Virginia Woolf Quarterly* 1.3 (Spring 1973): 60–65. Print.

Spalding, P. A. *Self-Harvest: A Study of Diaries and the Diarist.* London: Independent Press, 1949. Print.

Sproles, Karyn Z. *Desiring Women: The Partnership of Virginia Woolf and Vita Sackville-West.* Toronto: University of Toronto Press, 2006. Print.

Stephen, Leslie. *Swift.* New York: Harper and Brothers, n.d. Print.

Tait, J. G. *The Missing Tenth of Sir Walter Scott's Journal.* Edinburgh: Oliver and Boyd, 1936. Print.

Tanner, J. R. *Mr. Pepys: An Introduction to the Diary together with a Sketch of His Later Life.* New York: Harcourt Brace, 1925. Print.

Tidwell, Joanne Campbell. *Politics and Aesthetics in The Diary of Virginia Woolf.* New York: Routledge, 2008. Print.

Truss, Lynne. Rev. of *A Genius for Failure: The Life of Benjamin Robert Haydon,* by Paul O'Keeffe. *The Sunday [London] Times,* Aug. 9, 2009.

Whitworth, Michael H. "Historicising Woolf: Context Studies." *Virginia Woolf in Context*. Ed. Bryony Randall and Jane Goldman. Cambridge: Cambridge University Press, 2012. 3–12. Print.

Williams, Harold, "Introduction." *Jonathan Swift: Journal to Stella*. Vol. 1. Oxford: Clarendon Press, 1948. ix–lix. Print.

Willison, Ian, Warwick Gould, and Warren Chernaik, eds. *Modernist Writers and the Marketplace*. Basingstoke: Macmillan, 1996. Print.

Willy, Margaret. *English Diarists: Evelyn and Pepys*. London: Longmans, Green, 1963. Print.

———. *Three Women Diarists* [Celia Fiennes, Dorothy Wordsworth, Katherine Mansfield]. London: Longmans, Green, 1964. Print.

Special thanks to

The Henry W. and Albert A. Berg Collection of English and American Literature
The New York Public Library
Astor, Lenox and Tilden Foundations

U.S. print rights

Excerpts from *The Diary of Virginia Woolf*, Volume I, *1915–1919*, edited by Anne Olivier Bell. Copyright © 1977 by Quentin Bell and Angelica Garnett. Reprinted by permission of Houghton Mifflin Harcourt Publishing Company. All rights reserved.

Excerpts from *The Diary of Virginia Woolf*, Volume II, *1920–1924*, edited by Anne Olivier Bell. Copyright © 1978 by Quentin Bell and Angelica Garnett. Reprinted by permission of Houghton Mifflin Harcourt Publishing Company. All rights reserved.

Excerpts from *The Diary of Virginia Woolf*, Volume III, 1925–1930, edited by Anne Olivier Bell. Copyright © 1980 by Quentin Bell and Angelica Garnett. Reprinted by permission of Houghton Mifflin Harcourt Publishing Company. All rights reserved.

Excerpts from *The Essays of Virginia Woolf*, Volume III, *1919–1924*, edited by Andrew McNeille. Text copyright © 1989 by Quentin Bell and Angelica Garnett. Reprinted by permission of Houghton Mifflin Harcourt Publishing Company. All rights reserved.

Excerpts from *The Essays of Virginia Woolf*, Volume IV, 1925–1928, edited by Andrew McNeille. Text copyright © 1994 by Quentin Bell and Angelica Garnett. Reprinted by permission of Houghton Mifflin Harcourt Publishing Company. All rights reserved.

Excerpts from *The Letters of Virginia Woolf*, Volume II, *1912–1922*. Copyright © 1976 by Quentin Bell and Angelica Garnett. Reprinted by permission of Houghton Mifflin Harcourt Publishing Company. All rights reserved.

Excerpts from *The Letters of Virginia Woolf*, Volume III, *1923–1928*. Copyright © 1977 by Quentin Bell and Angelica Garnett. Reprinted by permission of Houghton Mifflin Harcourt Publishing Company. All rights reserved.

World, excluding U.S., print rights

Excerpts from *The Diary of Virginia Woolf*, Volume I, *1915–1919*, edited by Anne Olivier Bell. Published by Hogarth Press. Reproduced by permission of The Random House Group Limited.

Excerpts from *The Diary of Virginia Woolf*, Volume II, *1920–1924*, edited by Anne Olivier Bell. Published by Hogarth Press. Reproduced by permission of The Random House Group Limited.

Excerpts from *The Diary of Virginia Woolf*, Volume III, *1925–1930*, edited by Anne Olivier Bell. Published by Hogarth Press. Reproduced by permission of The Random House Group Limited.

Electronic book rights

Index

Electra, 14

Elgin marbles, 176, 182, 183, 239n33

Eliot, George, 152, 239n27

Eliot, T. S.: 52; essays of, 37; intertextuality of, 221–22; poems of, 2, 24, 41, 71, 104, 224n15; praises Woolf, 56; shade cast by, 56, 226n2; Woolf diary play scene involving, 79; Woolf diary portraits of, 21, 41, 79–80, 92; Woolf writings for, 68, 122, 124

Eliot, Vivienne, 79

Elizabeth I, Queen, 107, 108, 109

Ellis, Havelock, 143

Elwin, Malcolm, 182

England, A. B., 134

Epicurus, 87

Erskine, Andrew, 84

Evelyn, John: diary of, 34, 47–50, 64, 76, 201, 227n12, 228n13; Pepys and, 47–48, 49; Stonehenge and, 48; wealth of, 48, 227n11; Christopher Wren and, 48

Fergussen, Dr. D. J., 67, 70

Fernald, Anne E., 136, 221–22

Fisher, Herbert, 14, 16, 18

Forster, E. M., 97, 127; diary of, 35, 36; portrait of, 23

Frank, Anne, 128

Froude, James Anthony, 152

Fry, Roger, 54, 121, 217, 234n7; model for Old Virginia, 19, 21, 38, 39, 54, 59, 210, 229n9; Omega Workshops and, 165; writings of, 31, 53

Fyfe, H. Hamilton, 55

Gaisford, Walter, 31

Galsworthy, John, 201

Garnett, Richard, 49

Garrick, David, 89, 176

Gash, Norman, 178, 239n34

General Strike (1919), 26

General Strike (1926), 26, 137, 138–40, 142, 147, 149, 237n19

George IV, King, 178, 184

Gertler, Mark, 58, 59, 70

Giffard, Lady Martha, 134. See also Swift, Jonathan

Gilbert, Mrs., 228n2

Godolphin, Lord Sidney, 128, 131. See also Swift, Jonathan

Godwin, William, 174

Goethe, Johann Wolfgang von, 167

Goldoni, Carlo, 103

Goldsmith, Dr. Oliver, 182

Goncourt brothers, 20–21, 29, 225n21

Gordon, Colonel Bill, 33

Gordon, General C. G., 33

Gordon, Ian A., 191, 241n6

Gorky, Maxim, 41, 51

Gosse, Sir Edmund, 26

Gosse, Ellen, 162

Gould, Warwick, 230n5

Grant, Duncan, 170; art of, 94; disparages William Arnold-Foster, 14; responses to Virginia's work, 118, 210; travels of, 206, 219; Woolf's diary and, 127; Woolf visits to and with, 39, 121

Gravé, Madame, 36

Gray, Thomas, 85, 89

Green, Minna, 58, 59, 68

Gregory, Lady Augusta, 30

Greville, Charles, 33

Greville, Fulke, 245n5

Guérin, Eugénie de, 43

Guilbert, Mélanie, 104. See also Stendhal

Hamilton, George, 240n37

Hamilton, Lord James, 132. See also Swift, Jonathan

Hammersmith Publishing Society, 163–64, 239n29. See also Cobden-Sanderson, Thomas

Hampstead: men and, 52, 58, 70; nature and, 9–10; women and, 9–10, 15, 17, 20, 24, 26, 37, 38, 54, 58, 185, 225n17, 226n3

Hannay, Alexander Howard, 36

Hardy, Florence, 141

Hardy, Thomas: funeral of, 135, 206, 208, 213; praise of Common Reader, 118; reputation of, 95, 142; Woolf visit to, 141, 143; Woolf's writing on, 60, 67, 206

Harley, Lord Robert, 131, 132, 133. See also Swift, Jonathan

Harris, Alexandra, 228n6

Harris, Lilian, 38, 58. See also Llewelyn Davies, Margaret; Women's Co-operative Guild

Harrison, Edward, dentist, 17, 139

Harrison, Jane, 213

Hawkesford, Mrs., 56–57

Haydon, Benjamin Robert, 239nn32,37, 240nn40,42,44,45; Fanny Burney and, 138; journals of, 138, 170–84, 221, 239nn31,33,34,35,

240nn38,39,41,43; Walter Scott and, 138, 172–74, 179; spontaneous invention and, 170, 171; suicide and, 170, 174, 178, 179, 181, 182, 184

Haydon, Frederic Wordsworth, 240n42

Haydon, Mary, 170, 179, 181

Hazlitt, William, 240nn38,45

Hemans, Felicia, 163

Herbert, Philip, Earl of Pembroke, 112

Hercules, 180–81

Hewlett, Maurice, 107

Hills, John ("Jack") Waller, 119, 234n5

Hobhouse, Emily, 74, 77, 78. *See also* Badenhorst, Alie

Hogarth Press, 121, 124, 140, 189, 215, 218, 239nn29,30, 242n25; aid to Woolf's art, 24, 54, 60, 61, 67, 70, 71, 72, 73, 74, 94, 98, 99, 119, 148, 230n5; distracts from diary-keeping, 51, 53, 55, 56, 59, 115, 117, 120, 121, 229n3; distracts from public art, 41, 55, 57, 71, 92, 229–30n3; Ralph Partridge partnership, 38, 70–72, 73, 75; Russian writers and, 41, 53, 61–65, 229n10

Homer, 40, 68, 87, 93, 177, 182

Hope, Lotty (or Lottie), 40, 72

Hudson, Dr. Bernard, 193–94, 221. *See also* Mansfield, Katherine

Hunt, Leigh, 59–60, 240n45

Hunter, Edward ("Ted"), 69

Hutchinson, Mary, 69, 95, 228n1

Huxley, Aldous: Haydon edition, 170, 182, 239n31; on Haydon's misplaced career, 174, 175; on Haydon's personality 178, 179, 181

Huxley, T. H., 152

Hynes, Samuel, 163, 239n27

Jackson, Anna, 1, 241n7, 243n30, 244nn32,37

James, Henry, 37, 60, 61, 142

James, William, 166

James I, King, 109, 110

Joad, Marjorie, 71–72, 124, 125, 232n4

Johnson, Esther ("Stella"), 126, 127–36, 141. *See also* Swift, Jonathan

Johnson, Dr. Samuel, 63, 84, 88, 89, 171, 177

Jolliffe, John, 182

Joyce, James, 56, 72, 222

Keats, John: Barbellion and, 43; Thomas Cobden-Sanderson and, 166; Benjamin Robert Haydon and, 179, 182, 183

Kenney, Edwin J., Jr., 234n6

Kenney, Susan M., 234n6

Keynes, John Maynard, 13, 39, 142, 145, 213; reputation of, 52, 95, 237n18; theatre and, 79, 82; on Woolf's works, 2, 118; writings of, 52, 55, 120

Kilvert, Francis, 178, 239n36

Klein, Lisa M., 114. *See also* Clifford, Lady Anne

Knight, Payne, 176, 239n33. *See also* Haydon, Benjamin Robert

Knowles, Sir James, 152. *See also* Webb, Beatrice Potter

Koteliansky, Samuel: Chekhov's notebooks and, 41, 55, 61, 62–63, 229n10; Hampstead and, 58, 70; Katherine Mansfield and, 61, 199, 200

Lamb, Charles, 173

Lamb, Walter, 22

Langford, Rachael, 5, 7, 223n2

Lawrence, D. H., 200

Lawrence, Thomas, 176. *See also* Haydon, Benjamin Robert

Leaf, Charles, 140, 146, 153

Leaf, Charlotte, 140, 146, 153

Leaf, Kitty, 140, 146, 153

Leaf, Walter, 140, 146, 153

League of Nations Union, 60

Leavis, F. R., 163, 238n26

Lee, Hermione, 223n5, 228n6, 236n4

Lejeune, Philippe, 1, 4, 5, 6, 7

Levenson, Michael, 64

Levy, Amy, 157. *See also* Webb, Beatrice Potter

Lewis, Pericles, 1

Llewelyn Davies, Margaret, 237n18, 238n21; criticism of Woolf's fiction, 26, 225n17, 226n3; Women's Co-operative Guild, 58, 225n17. *See also* Case, Janet; Harris, Lilian

Lloyd George, Prime Minister David, 78. *See also* Badenhorst, Alie

Longford, Elizabeth, 33, 226n26

Lopokova, Lydia, 79, 82, 118, 187, 213, 237n18

Lounsberry, Barbara, 223n1, 225n21, 228n6, 239n36

Lowe, Peter, 4

Löwenstein-Wertheim, Princess Anne, 187

Lucan, 87, 231n21

Lucas, F. L. ("Peter"), 93

Lynd, Robert, 37

Macaulay, Catharine, 89

Macaulay, Thomas, 100

MacCarthy, Desmond, 31, 142; on Barbellion's
Journal, 42; belittling of women, 208–9; war
and, 18; Woolf portraits of, 22, 123, 209; Woolf
writings for, 208; writings of, 29, 123
MacCarthy, Mary ("Molly"), 95, 246n11
MacClaren, Christabel, 209
MacKenzie, Jeanne, 149–50, 153, 238n24. *See also*
Webb, Beatrice Potter
MacKenzie, Norman, 149–50, 153, 238n24. *See
also* Webb, Beatrice Potter
Mallon, Thomas, 7
Manning, Cardinal Henry, 33
Mansfield, Katherine, 95, 229n2, 245n41;
journal of, 82, 185, 191–204, 212, 216, 221,
241nn5,6,8,10,11,12,13, 242nn15,16,17,18,1
9,20,21,22,23,24, 243nn26,27,28,29,30,31,
244nn32,33,34,35,36,37, 245n40; Samuel Ko-
teliansky and, 61; letters to and from Woolf,
231n17, 241n14, 243n25, 245n39; senses of,
244n36; suicide and, 195, 242nn19,21; visits to
and from Woolf, 10, 15, 20, 25, 36–37, 245n39;
on women, 70, 192, 193–94; Woolf's diary
portraits of, 22, 241n4; writings of, 55, 198, 199,
200–201, 242n25
Mante, Fortuné, 104. *See also* Stendhal
Margaret, Duchess of Newcastle, 48
Marsh, Edward ("Eddie"), 93
Marshall, Professor Alfred, 156, 164–65, 193, 221
Martineau, James, 152
Matthaei, Louise, 21, 224n12
Mayne, Ethel Colburn, 201
McAfee, Helen, 113
Melville, Herman, 212
Mencken, H. L., 34
Meredith, George, 96, 206
Meryon, Dr. Charles, 27, 31, 32
Mill, John Stuart, 164
Millais, Sir John Everett, 186
Milton, John, 14, 181
Mirrlees, Hope, 26
"Miss Jan" (Virginia Woolf's early nickname),
100
Mitford, Mary Russell, 183–84
Modernism, 13, 21, 24, 60, 73, 99, 192, 205, 212,
220, 230n5; Chekhov and British modernism,
64–65, 220, 230n14; formal experiment, 3–4, 5,
6, 10, 21, 34, 37, 53, 99, 210, 211, 212, 213, 216; Ho-
garth Press and, 230n5; interiority, 2–3, 19, 20,
29, 41, 81, 83, 90–91, 101–7, 137, 138, 142, 143–44,

146, 147, 149; 161, 185, 205, 210, 211, 213, 215, 218,
220, 230n14; nonlinear narration, 5, 21, 24, 37,
50, 98, 119; paradoxes in, 4, 5, 6, 65, 223n2; time
in, 6, 119, 145, 203, 212
Molière (Jean-Baptiste Poquelin), 102
Montaigne, Michel de, 92, 102, 112
Moore, George, 213
Morrell, Lady Ottoline, 23, 41, 80, 120
Morrell, Philip, 35, 120
Morris, Jane, 166
Morris, William, 166
Mounier, Claude-Edouard-Philippe, 104. *See also*
Stendhal
Mozart, Wolfgang Amadeus, 121
Munsil, Janet, 182–83
Murphy, Bernadette, 120, 124
Murry, John Middleton: 245n41; adultery and,
52; articles for, 27; dismisses Woolf's writing,
70; hostility to women, 58, 70; Mansfield's
journal and, 191–204, 241nn6,8,10,11,12,13,
242nn15,16,17,18,19,20,21,22,23,24,
243nn26,27,28,29,31, 244nn32,33,34,35,37,
245n40; poems of, 24, 25, 224n15; Sydney
Waterlow and, 52, 58; Woolf visits to and
from, 10, 25, 36–37; writings of, 57, 200,
229n9

Nero, 42, 231n21
Newnes, Sir George, 60
Nicolson, Nigel, 125, 235n15
Nin, Anaïs, 192
1917 Club, 12, 13, 41, 71, 224n12
Noel, Lady Annabella, 30
Noel-Baker, Irene, 121

Olney, Clarke, 182
Onasander, 51
Orage, A. R., 200
Ormerod, Eleanor, 27, 68
Ovid, 112

Pain, Barry, 201
Paoli, General Pascal, 84, 85, 86–88, 89,
231nn20,23. *See also* Boswell, James
Pargiter, Thomas, 26
Parry, Robert Lloyd, 182, 240n44
Partridge, Ralph, 39, 57; at Hogarth Press, 38, 53,
70–72, 73, 92, 229–30nn3,6; women and, 37, 38,
59, 70–72, 230n4

Penrose, Alexander P. D., 182

Pepys, Samuel: diary of, 13, 15, 36, 64, 76, 113, 126, 163, 172, 178, 239n36; John Evelyn and, 47–48, 49

Pilate, Pontius, 42

Pitt, William, 139

Plutarch, 87

Podnieks, Elizabeth, 220

Pollack, Sir Frederick, 165

Polydore, 49

Pope, William Bissell, 182, 240n43

Potter, Kate, 149, 236n5. *See also* Webb, Beatrice Potter

Potter, Laurencina, 149, 150, 152, 154–55, 237n14. *See also* Webb, Beatrice Potter

Potter, Richard, 155, 236n9, 237n11; diary of, 149; illness of, 153, 157; reading and, 150; wealth of, 151–52, 154, 236n11. *See also* Webb, Beatrice Potter

Powell, Stephen D., 133

Pratt, Grace, 100. *See also* Chalmers, Anne

Prior, Matthew, 129, 131. *See also* Swift, Jonathan

Prometheus, 57, 82

Proust, Marcel, 2, 81, 83, 212

Quinones, Ricardo J., 6, 223n2

Rainbow, Bishop Edward, 112

Raitt, Suzanne, 233n19

Raphael, 49

Raverat, Jacques, 123, 230n12, 232n4, 244n36

Rembrant, 180

Rétif de la Bretonne, Nicolas, 7

Reynolds, Joshua: Wilfrid Scawen Blunt and, 31; Fanny Burney and, 172; Benjamin Robert Haydon and, 172, 175, 176

Richmond, Bruce: objects to Woolf's writing, 61, 67, 70, 72, 73; visit from, 234n7; Woolf portrait of, 121–22; Woolf's Swift essay for, 126

Richmond, Elena, 72, 121–22, 125, 230n7, 234n7

Ricoeur, Paul, 24

Ritchie, Hon. Philip, 187, 232n5

Roberts, S. C., 84, 85, 89. *See also* Boswell, James

Robinson, Henry Crabb, 29, 89, 224n10

Romano, Julio, 49

Rossetti, Christina, 11, 24

Rousseau, Jean-Jacques, 84

Rowe, Nicholas, 131

Rubenstein, Roberta, 64

Ruskin, John, 166

Russell, Lady Arthur, 141

Russell, Bertrand, 53, 59, 167, 239n30

Russell, Frank, 167

Russell, John (Lord Amberley), 167, 239n30

Russell, Kate Stanley (Lady Amberley), 167, 239n30

Russell, Lady Margaret, Countess of Cumberland, 110, 111

Ryland, Frederick, 235n18

Rylands, George ("Dadie"), 92

Sackville, Lionel, 3rd Baron, 98, 206, 213

Sackville, Margaret, 109, 110. *See also* Clifford, Lady Anne

Sackville, Sir Richard, 108, 109, 110, 111, 112, 233nn13,16. *See also* Clifford, Lady Anne

Sackville-West, Edward ("Eddy"), 205, 211–12

Sackville-West, Vita, 206, 214; diary of, 114, 233n20; *Diary of Lady Anne Clifford* and, 90, 107–14, 232n11, 233nn12,13,14,16,17,18; first meeting with Woolf, 72–73, 74; *Knole and the Sackvilles*, 98, 233nn12,13; *Orlando* and, 90, 107, 109, 114, 115, 148–49, 187–88, 206, 233nn15,20, 246n10; rescues Woolf, 3, 115, 122, 124, 125, 127, 234nn8,11, 235n15; "Seducers in Ecuador," 96, 98; women and, 108, 114, 233nn15,19; Woolf's growing interest in, 90, 96, 98, 107, 122, 124, 186, 189; Woolf's letters to, 191, 200, 234n12, 235n3, 246n10

Sage, Robert, 102, 106. *See also* Stendhal

Salmon, Urbain-Pierre, 105. *See also* Stendhal

Sands, Ethel, 210, 234n12

Sappho, 106

Sassoon, Siegfried, 39

Schlaeger, Jürgen, 3

Schmidt, Michael, 8, 133, 224n10

Schoolcraft, Ralph, 104, 105, 106. *See also* Stendhal

Scott, Margaret, 191, 194–95, 241nn8,10,11,12,13, 242nn15,16,17,18,19,20,21,22,23,24, 243nn26,27,28,29,31, 244nn33,34,35,37, 245n40. *See also* Mansfield, Katherine

Scott, Sir Walter, 100, 236n7; diary of, 11–12, 113, 174, 223n3; Benjamin Robert Haydon and, 138, 172–74, 178, 179; Jonathan Swift and, 135, 235nn17,23

Seneca, Lucius Anneaus, 86, 231n21

Shakespeare, Judith, 135, 136, 203, 221

BARBARA LOUNSBERRY has devoted her life to the study and practice of artful nonfiction in its many forms. She has worked closely with literary journalism pioneer Gay Talese, with whom she edited *Writing Creative Nonfiction: The Literature of Reality*. Her own books include *Becoming Virginia Woolf: Her Early Diaries and the Diaries She Read, Virginia Woolf, the War Without, the War Within: Her Final Diaries and the Diaries She Read, The Art of Fact: Contemporary Artists of Nonfiction, The Writer in You*, and *The Tales We Tell: Perspectives on the Short Story* (coedited with Susan Lohafer).

From 2000 to 2003, Lounsberry served as the nonfiction editor for the *North American Review*, the oldest literary magazine in the United States, and was a contributing editor to *Keep It Real: Everything You Need to Know about Researching and Writing Creative Nonfiction*. She has served on the board of directors of the Norman Mailer Society and has published book chapters and essays on the nonfiction of Mailer, Talese, Ernest Hemingway, John McPhee, Joan Didion, Tom Wolfe, Patricia Hampl, Lewis Thomas, Virginia Woolf, and others.

Lounsberry regularly taught seminars on Virginia Woolf and on Literary Nonfiction at the University of Northern Iowa before retiring to write full time in 2006.